AI Technology Management and Value Creation

P.C. Lai
https://orcid.org/0000-0002-8319-8459
University of Malaya, Malaysia

IGI Global
Scientific Publishing
Publishing Tomorrow's Research Today

Vice President of Editorial Melissa Wagner
Director of Acquisitions Mikaela Felty
Director of Book Development Jocelynn Hessler
Production Manager Mike Brehm
Cover Design Jose Rosado

Published in the United States of America by
IGI Global Scientific Publishing
701 East Chocolate Avenue
Hershey, PA, 17033, USA
Tel: 717-533-8845 | Fax: 717-533-7115
Website: https://www.igi-global.com E-mail: cust@igi-global.com

Library of Congress Cataloging-in-Publication Data

Names: Lai, P. C., 1974- editor.
Title: AI technology management and value creation / edited by PC Lai.
Description: Hershey, PA : IGI Global Scientific Publishing, 2026. | Includes bibliographical references and index. | Summary: "The objective of the book is to provide broad research and applied coverage of subjects relating to all areas of AI Technology Management and its value creation in the eco-system"-- Provided by publisher.
Identifiers: LCCN 2025006727 (print) | LCCN 2025006728 (ebook) | ISBN 9798337324975 (hardcover) | ISBN 9798337324982 (paperback) | ISBN 9798337324999 (ebook)
Subjects: LCSH: Technological innovations--Management. | Artificial intelligence.
Classification: LCC HD45 .A769 2023 (print) | LCC HD45 (ebook) | DDC 006.3068--dc23/eng/20250417
LC record available at https://lccn.loc.gov/2025006727
LC ebook record available at https://lccn.loc.gov/2025006728

British Cataloguing in Publication Data
A Cataloguing in Publication record for this book is available from the British Library.

Table of Contents

Detailed Table of Contents

The integration of self-adjusting AI into financial technology marks a breakthrough in detecting credit card fraud and abnormal transactions. This chapter presents a flexible framework using ML techniques, XGBoost, Isolation Forest, Federated Learning, and SHAP, to automate fraud detection with high precision. Transactions are first assessed via XGBoost, then anomalies (e.g., small purchases by younger users) trigger Isolation Forest. These are added to the labeled dataset, enabling real-time model retraining. Threshold tuning enhances sensitivity, while SHAP ensures interpretability. A simulated federated learning setup updates models across institutions without compromising privacy. The visual feedback loop illustrates continuous learning and deployment. This adaptive system boosts fraud detection accuracy, reduces false positives, and strengthens institutional agility, driving innovation, trust, and scalable value in FinTech.

This chapter examines how artificial intelligence (AI) is transforming fleet management by improving efficiency, safety, compliance, and sustainability. It explores key applications of AI, including real-time route optimization, predictive maintenance, driver behavior monitoring, and emissions reduction. Real-world examples from UPS, Amazon, DHL, Samsara, and La Poste demonstrate measurable gains in cost savings, operational uptime, and environmental impact. The chapter also addresses challenges such as data quality, regulatory compliance, integration with legacy systems, and workforce readiness. Using Rogers' Diffusion of Innovation Theory and the Technology-Organization-Environment (TOE) Framework, it analyzes how organizations can strategically adopt AI. Actionable insights are provided to help fleet managers and decision-makers align AI tools with business goals. As fleets face rising expectations for performance and sustainability, AI is positioned as a critical enabler of long-term value and innovation.

Foreword

Many developments in artificial intelligence – surveillance, personalization for advertising, induced psychological disturbance in youngsters, and others – are thoroughly frightening. That is why any scholarly work that sheds light on them and points to policy guidance, as this book does, is most welcome.

The book's title orients it to management as well as to government policy. The chapters reveal that AI implies a recasting of many disciplines' traditional methods. Sociology becomes more data-based. AI obsoletes several of the mathematical tools of operations research. The present book can only begin to indicate where these disciplines are now headed.

As the book's various authors point out, AI faces different hurdles and different tasks in the developing world than in the richer countries, and progress is achieved at different rates of speed. Exposition on these themes is appreciated too.

Chapters representing several world regions help flesh out this exposition. In a bemusing (but sometimes fraught) recursion, authors doubtless use AI to help them write about AI. We cannot begrudge this, in the case of authors writing in a language that is not their mother tongue. AI, for all its dangers, helps to bring the peoples of the world together.

Fred Phillips is Visiting Professor at SUNY Stony Brook, and President of TANDO Institute. He is Editor-in-Chief Emeritus of the international journal *Technological Forecasting & Social Change*, and the 2017 recipient of the Kondratieff Medal, awarded by the Russian Academy of Sciences. He is a Fellow of PICMET, the Portland International Center for Management of Engineering and Technology. His latest books are *What About the Future?* (Springer 2019), *Smart City 2.0* (World Scientific 2023), and *Upending Geopolitics: Technologies and Cities* (World Scientific, forthcoming).

Fred Phillips
SUNY Stony Brook, Albuquerque, USA

October 2025

Preface

Artificial Intelligence (AI) has rapidly evolved from a specialized domain into a core driver of global competitiveness, innovation, and social transformation. As organizations accelerate digital transformation, the challenge is no longer whether to adopt AI but how to manage it effectively to create sustainable value. This book, AI Technology Management and Value Creation, emerges from that critical juncture. It seeks to bridge the gap between technological advancement and strategic management, providing a framework to guide leaders, policymakers, and researchers in understanding how AI can be effectively harnessed to generate and sustain value.

The accelerating adoption of AI across industries has introduced new opportunities—and new responsibilities for organizations seeking to create and capture value. As firms increasingly rely on intelligent systems to automate processes, optimize decision-making, and engage customers, the management of AI technologies demands a holistic framework that integrates ethical governance, human capability, and strategic alignment (Garg & Goel, 2022; Lai, 2023). This volume aims to advance such understanding by bridging theoretical insights with real-world applications.

Drawing from multidisciplinary expertise in information systems, business strategy, data science, and innovation management, this book investigates how AI can be deployed responsibly and effectively to achieve long-term competitive advantage. It reflects organizations enduring mission to promote cutting-edge research that shapes future-oriented management practices.

THE NEED FOR AI TECHNOLOGY MANAGEMENT

In today's volatile business landscape, AI technologies are redefining productivity, innovation, and decision-making processes. The convergence of data analytics, automation, and machine learning has made AI indispensable in industries ranging from healthcare and education to logistics and finance (Garg & Goel, 2022; Pandey et al., 2024; Lai, 2021). However, many organizations struggle to translate AI's potential into measurable value due to fragmented management practices, lack of governance, and insufficient integration with strategic objectives.

Effective AI technology management thus extends far beyond technical capability. It encompasses leadership, ethics, governance, data infrastructure, and a culture of innovation. Managing AI technologies requires an ecosystem approach — aligning human, technological, and organizational capabilities (Ponnusamy et al., 2024). The focus must shift from technology adoption to technology orchestration — the ability to coordinate AI tools, human insight, and business strategy toward shared goals.

As Lai (2023) observes in Technology Management and Its Social Impact on Education, the success of any technological system depends not only on its design but also on how it is embedded within social, organizational, and policy structures. Similarly, AI's success will depend on how effectively it is managed to enhance societal welfare, productivity, and ethical accountability.

THEMES AND STRUCTURE OF THE BOOK

This book explores six interrelated themes that are central to understanding how artificial intelligence drives value creation in modern organizations. The first theme, strategic alignment of AI, examines how organizations integrate AI technologies into their business models, ensuring that initiatives are not isolated projects but are harmonized with long-term strategic objectives. Effective alignment allows firms to maintain strategic agility while leveraging AI as a core element of competitive differentiation. The second theme, governance and ethical stewardship, addresses the urgent need for responsible AI frameworks that emphasize transparency, accountability, and risk mitigation. As Garg and Goel (2022) highlight, establishing governance structures that prevent bias and ensure fairness is fundamental to building trust in AI systems.

The third theme focuses on human and organizational capabilities, recognizing that successful AI adoption depends on the people and cultures that support it. Organizations must invest in upskilling their workforce, fostering collaboration between technical and managerial teams, and nurturing an innovation-oriented culture that embraces experimentation and learning (Ponnusamy et al., 2024). The fourth theme, value measurement and impact, deals with developing robust methods and metrics to assess both tangible and intangible forms of value generated by AI. Beyond financial indicators such as productivity and efficiency, this includes measuring innovation capacity, customer trust, social inclusion, and environmental sustainability.

The fifth theme, operational integration and innovation, explores how AI is reshaping core business processes, supply chains, and ecosystem partnerships. As Pandey et al. (2024) note, organizations that integrate AI into operations are better positioned to unlock efficiency gains, foster innovation, and create new forms of collaborative value within digital ecosystems. Finally, the sixth theme, societal and regulatory context, situates AI within the broader landscape of ethics, governance, and public policy. It acknowledges that effective AI management must consider implications for privacy, employment, human rights, and social equity, ensuring that technological progress aligns with societal well-being and regulatory compliance.

Together, these themes provide a comprehensive framework for understanding AI technology management as both a strategic and human endeavor—one that blends innovation with responsibility, and efficiency with ethical awareness. Intellectual Foundations

This volume extends the trajectory established by prior IGI Global works edited by P. C. Lai, notably Handbook of Research on Social Impacts of E-Payment (Lai, 2021), Strategies and Opportunities for Technology in the Metaverse World (Lai, 2023b), and Technology Management and Its Social Impact on Education (Lai, 2023a). These prior studies laid the groundwork for understanding how technology shapes user behavior, social inclusion, and innovation ecosystems form the foundations that resonate strongly with AI-driven value creation.

Likewise, this book draws intellectual inspiration from emerging scholars in AI management and digital transformation (Garg & Goel, 2022; Ponnusamy et al., 2024), as well as from applied research in supply chain innovation (Pandey et al., 2024) and business model renewal. Together, these references reinforce the interdisciplinary nature of AI management, blending insights from information systems, strategic management, ethics, and human–computer interaction.

BOOK CHAPTER SUMMARY

Foundations and Frameworks of AI Technology Management

Chapter 1: AI Technology Management Concepts and Strategies

Binastya Anggara Sekti

This opening chapter introduces the foundational concepts of AI technology management, emphasizing how strategic integration of AI can support innovation, sustainability, and entrepreneurship across various sectors. It discusses growth opportunities and challenges, particularly for SMEs and underrepresented entrepreneurs, while highlighting the importance of AI literacy and ethical implementation.

Chapter 2: Artificial Intelligence and Business Strategy

Pooja Srivastava, Ajay Kumar, Shashank Srivastava

This chapter explores how AI is reshaping business strategy by enhancing forecasting, personalization, and operational efficiency. The authors balance the benefits of AI-driven decision-making with critical reflections on ethical concerns, workforce adaptation, and the necessity for transparent governance.

Chapter 3: AI Technology Management Growth in Developed and Developing Countries

Wasswa Shafik

Focusing on global disparities and opportunities, this chapter compares AI adoption in developed and developing nations. It analyzes the infrastructural, policy, and human capital differences that shape AI's role in inclusive, sustainable development, and offers policy recommendations for bridging the global innovation divide.

Applied AI and Technological Innovation

Chapter 4: Artificial Intelligent Decision Making – A Novel Approach to Image Security Acceptance

PC Lai, DL Tong

This chapter presents a unique application of AI in image security, using an extended Technology Acceptance Model (TAM) to examine factors influencing user adoption. The practical implications are highlighted in education and security settings, with insights into how usability and perceived security drive acceptance of novel authentication systems.

Chapter 5: Artificial Intelligence for Secure Self-Adaptive Systems in FinTech

Nazgul Seralina, Assel Akzhalova, Chingis Utegenov

Focusing on AI in FinTech, this chapter presents an adaptive fraud detection framework combining machine learning techniques like XGBoost and Isolation Forest with federated learning for secure, privacy-preserving innovation. Interpretability tools like SHAP provide transparency, while real-time learning ensures agility and precision.

Chapter 6: AI-Driven Decision Support in Fleet Management

Suryakant Kaushik

This chapter investigates how AI optimizes fleet operations through route planning, predictive maintenance, and emissions monitoring. Using case studies from industry leaders like UPS and Amazon, the chapter offers a framework for strategic adoption and value generation using AI, guided by established innovation theories.

Chapter 7: Animal Recognition and Repellent System for Smart Farming Using AI

Theetchenya S and collaborators

Highlighting the intersection of AI and agriculture, this chapter presents a deep learning system to detect and deter wildlife from crops using species-specific ultrasonic repellents. The solution promotes sustainable farming by reducing environmental harm and safeguarding crop yields through intelligent automation.

AI, Customer Engagement, and Market Value

Chapter 8: Innovative Supply Chain Effect on Value Creation by Mediation of AI in the Horn of Africa

Zenebe Ermias and collaborators

Through an empirical study, this chapter examines how AI enhances supply chain innovation and productivity in the Horn of Africa. Using structural equation modeling, it reveals how AI serves as a mediator between innovation and value creation, offering insights into regional dynamics and future opportunities.

Chapter 9: Revolutionizing Marketing Strategies – The Role of AI in Consumer Engagement

Parihar Dahake, Sanjiv Kumar, Nihar Dahake

Closing the volume, this chapter focuses on AI's transformative impact on marketing strategy in India. From segmentation to chatbots and social media analysis, it discusses how AI enables hyper-personalization and value generation, addressing behavioral nuances and overcoming traditional market mismatches.

INTEGRATED OVERVIEW

Taken together, the 9 chapters in *AI Technology Management and Value Creation* present a comprehensive narrative that bridges theory, application, and practice. The book moves from conceptual frameworks to practical implementation, and from internal operational transformation to external market engagement. It demonstrates that AI-driven value creation is not confined to one domain, but spans strategic, technical, and human dimensions. Whether examining secure systems in FinTech, AI-driven marketing, or agricultural automation, each chapter contributes a unique perspective on how AI can be managed to achieve sustainable economic and social outcomes. Together, these chapters reinforce the principle that technological innovation and ethical governance must evolve in tandem. AI's practical applications reveal that successful technology management depends on embedding accountability, resilience, and human oversight into digital transformation processes (MediLedger, 2020).

Ultimately, the volume underscores a central message: effective AI technology management requires balance between innovation and ethics, automation and human oversight, efficiency and inclusion. Through diverse global perspectives and empirical insights, the book serves as both a scholarly reference and a practical guide for organizations seeking to leverage AI as a catalyst for responsible value creation in an increasingly intelligent world.

CONTRIBUTION AND PURPOSE

The contribution of *AI Technology Management and Value Creation* lies in its holistic and integrated approach to understanding how artificial intelligence can be managed for sustainable organizational and societal benefit. The book presents a comprehensive conceptual framework that positions AI not only as a technological enabler but also as a strategic resource that drives innovation, efficiency, and competitive advantage. It provides managerial models and practical tools to help organizations align AI initiatives with their overall vision, mission, and capabilities, ensuring that technology adoption is purposeful and value-driven. Furthermore, the volume introduces measurement systems and evaluation frameworks that move beyond traditional financial indicators to include qualitative dimensions such as trust, inclusion, ethical responsibility, and long-term impact. Complementing these theoretical insights are detailed case studies drawn from diverse industries, illustrating both successful implementations and critical lessons learned from real-world practice. By combining rigorous academic research with actionable managerial strategies, this book aims to equip decision-makers, researchers, and practitioners with the knowledge and confidence to manage AI responsibly, ethically, and effectively not merely as a technical tool, but as a transformative vehicle for enduring value creation.

ACKNOWLEDGMENT

This work reflects the collective insight of scholars, researchers, and practitioners dedicated to exploring how AI reshapes business and society. We thank the contributors for their empirical rigor, IGI Global for its continued academic leadership, and the readers who share our commitment to ethical, human-centered innovation.

Ultimately, AI is not about replacing human intelligence but amplifying it and transforming how we define and deliver value. We hope this book inspires both scholarly inquiry and practical impact in that pursuit.

P. C. Lai
University of Malaya, Malaysia

REFERENCES

Garg, V., & Goel, R. (2022). *Handbook of Research on Innovative Management Using AI in Industry 5.0*. IGI Global. DOI: 10.4018/978-1-7998-8497-2

Lai, P. C. (2021). *Handbook of Research on Social Impacts of E-Payment*. IGI Global.

Lai, P. C. (2023a). *Technology Management and Its Social Impact on Education*. IGI Global. DOI: 10.4018/978-1-6684-9103-4

Lai, P. C. (2023b). *Strategies and Opportunities for Technology in the Metaverse World*. IGI Global. DOI: 10.4018/978-1-6684-5732-0

MediLedger. (2020). The MediLedger Network.

Pandey, D., et al. (2024). Utilization of AI Technology in Supply Chain Management. IGI Global.

Ponnusamy, S., Assaf, M., Antari, J., Singh, S., & Kalyanaraman, S. (2024). *Digital Twin Technology and AI Implementations in Future-Focused Businesses*. IGI Global. DOI: 10.4018/979-8-3693-1818-8

Acknowledgment

I am profoundly grateful for the many blessings and guidance from the Almighty God, whose wisdom and grace have made this work possible. My deepest appreciation goes to IGI Global for their trust, professionalism, and commitment in publishing this book. Special thanks are extended to the IGI Global editorial and production teams for their continuous support, patience, and assistance throughout the publication process.

The successful completion of *AI Technology Management and Value Creation* is the result of the collective effort of many dedicated individuals. I wish to express my sincere gratitude to all the chapter authors whose scholarly contributions and innovative insights form the foundation of this volume. Your dedication, creativity, and intellectual rigor have made this book a meaningful addition to the field of technology management and artificial intelligence.

I would also like to extend heartfelt appreciation to the reviewers, whose critical evaluations and constructive feedback greatly enhanced the quality, coherence, and depth of each chapter. Many contributors graciously served dual roles as both authors and reviewers—your efforts in maintaining academic integrity and excellence are deeply valued.

A special note of thanks goes to the reviewers and collaborators who were not authors but generously offered their time and expertise to evaluate the submissions. Their professional commitment, coming from both academia and industry across five continents, added immense value to the refinement of this book and ensured the diversity of perspectives represented within.

Finally, I extend my warmest appreciation to all the readers, researchers, and practitioners who will engage with this work and carry its ideas forward. It is my sincere hope that this book will inspire continued research, thoughtful dialogue, and responsible innovation in the management and value creation of AI technologies.

With gratitude and best wishes,

P. C. Lai
University of Malaya, Malaysia

Chapter 1
AI Technology Management Concepts and Strategies

Binastya Anggara Sekti
https://orcid.org/0000-0001-5489-4888
Universitas Esa Unggul, Indonesia

ABSTRACT

AI Technology Management focuses on strategically integrating AI into organizations to enhance innovation and value creation. As AI reshapes industries, understanding its role in decision-making is crucial for leaders, entrepreneurs, and educators. This field bridges technical innovation with practical application, ensuring AI aligns with business goals. AI-driven strategies benefit ecopreneurs, agropreneurs, and technopreneurs, addressing sustainability, precision farming, and market disruption. SMEs, family businesses, and underrepresented entrepreneurs can leverage AI for scalability and efficiency. AI's role in entrepreneurship education, leadership, and human resources is highlighted, emphasizing AI literacy and ethical considerations. Growth strategies focus on streamlining operations, improving insights, and expanding markets. The discussion also covers challenges like complexity, funding, and global AI adoption, positioning AI as a catalyst for innovation and sustainable business transformation.

DOI: 10.4018/979-8-3373-2497-5.ch001

1. INTRODUCTION

1.1 Artificial Intelligence

Artificial intelligence (AI) is a field of computer science that focuses on developing systems that can perform tasks that typically require human intelligence and can be performed consistently without human presence. Artificial intelligence is a technology that allows machines to perform complex tasks, such as learning, reasoning, pattern recognition, and decision-making, using algorithms and data. Some of the humans would normally do, it will be applied to artificial intelligence (AI) systems, such as the ability to learn from data and experiences, make decisions based on logic and rules, recognize patterns in data, and recognize, understand, and generate human language. When combined with big data analytics and machine learning, artificial intelligence becomes at the forefront of operations and supply chain management in improving operational performance (Dubey et al., 2020).

AI is a broad field that aims to create machines capable of simulating human thinking. These systems can handle large data sets, recognize patterns, and make decisions with little human input (Dwivedi et al., 2021). AI technologies can be divided into three main types:

- Narrow AI: Developed for specific functions, such as filtering spam emails, recognizing faces, and detecting cybersecurity threats.
- General AI: A theoretical AI system that possesses human-like cognitive abilities across multiple domains.
- Super AI: A speculative form of AI that surpasses human intelligence and decision-making capabilities.

1.2 Innovation

Innovation is the process of creating, developing, and implementing new ideas, products, or processes that can increase value and performance in an organization or society. The fields of activity and professions that need innovation at all times are entrepreneurs, agropreneurs, education, and SMEs where it is necessary always to develop products, processes and technologies in order to develop themselves and gain customer trust. Due to limited resources, small and medium-sized enterprises (SMEs) often have a low capacity to innovate. Meanwhile, empowering SME innovation through real factors is very necessary to be able to continue to innovate in limited financial conditions (Hidayat & Pok, 2025). Some examples of activities that require Innovation are:

- New Product Development, which is the activity of creating new products that can meet unmet market needs or demands.
- Business Process Improvement, which is developing or reengineering business processes to be more efficient and effective to increase productivity.
- Technology Development, which is an effort to create new technology that can solve new problems or complex problems.
- Business Model Development, creating a new business model that can increase revenue and profits higher than before.
- Development of Solutions to Social Problems, which is creating solutions to social problems that arise, such as poverty, health, and education.

1.3 AI Technologi Management

AI Technology Management plays a vital role in ensuring the effective integration, optimization, and governance of artificial intelligence (AI) within organizations. Strategic AI management involves aligning AI applications with business goals to enhance operational efficiency, drive innovation, and maintain competitiveness in the digital era. The transformative potential of AI lies in its ability to augment and replace human tasks across various sectors. (Dwivedi et al., 2021). The rapid pace of AI advancements necessitates that organizations adopt structured approaches to managing AI deployment to harness its benefits while mitigating potential risks. As AI technologies continue to advance, a systematic approach to AI management becomes essential for maximizing their advantages (Dwivedi et al., 2023). Figure 1 illustrates the AI technology management.

Figure 1. AI Technology Management

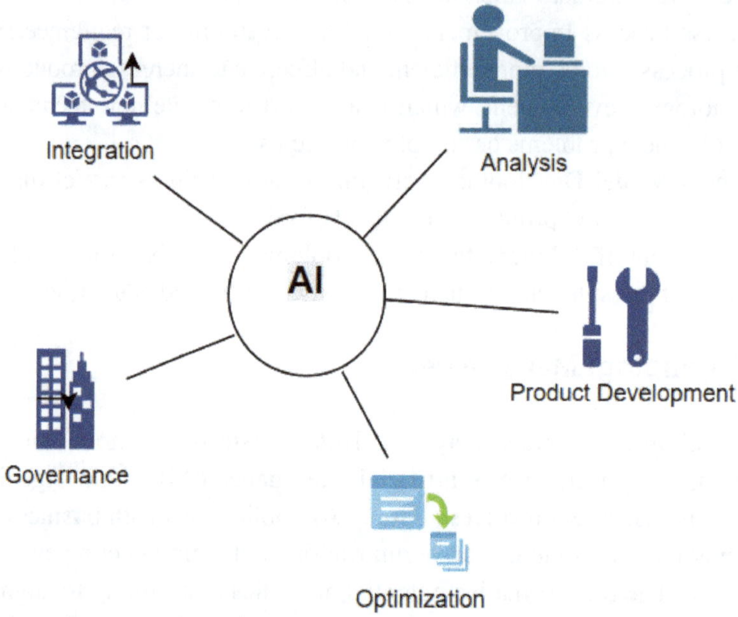

1.4 AI Technology Management and Organizational Transformation

AI Technology Management encompasses various aspects, including AI governance, ethical considerations, regulatory compliance, and AI-driven business transformation. Recent studies indicate that AI has significantly impacted industries by enabling advanced automation, intelligent decision-making, and predictive analytics. AI's role in decision-making has expanded beyond mere automation, now influencing high-level strategic initiatives that shape industry landscapes, from healthcare and finance to supply chain management and smart cities (Alkhudhayr, 2025; Bourbon & Murimi, 2024; Dong et al., 2023; Samuel et al., 2022; Singh, Sajid, Gupta, & Haidri, 2022; Tan, Yu, Yang, & Bashir, 2021).

To address the rapid integration of AI, all organizations need to ensure that AI deployment adheres to ethical standards and regulatory requirements. Implementing ethical AI, which includes addressing biases and ensuring transparency, is a core challenge in managing AI technology (Floridi & Cowls, 2022). Additionally, incorporating AI within existing organizational frameworks necessitates effective change management strategies, workforce adaptation, and collaboration across various functions (Jarrahi et al., 2021).

1.5 Components of AI Technology Management

The successful deployment of AI technology requires organizations to focus on key components that ensure sustainable implementation and value creation:

- Strategic AI Integration: Aligning AI capabilities with business needs to drive innovation and efficiency. Research suggests that AI-enabled business models provide competitive advantages when strategically aligned with corporate objectives (Davenport & Mittal, 2023b, 2023a).
- AI Governance and Ethics: Establishing ethical frameworks and policies to ensure AI systems are fair, transparent, and compliant with regulations (Liebig, Güttel, Jobin, & Katzenbach, 2024).
- Workforce Transformation: Preparing employees for AI adoption through upskilling, reskilling, and fostering an AI-augmented workplace (Liebig et al., 2024).
- Data Management and Security: Ensuring high-quality data availability, implementing robust cybersecurity measures, and complying with data protection laws (Widodo et al., 2024)(Radanliev, 2024; Radanliev et al., 2024).
- AI-driven Decision-Making: Utilizing AI-powered insights to enhance decision-making processes and improve overall business intelligence (Ghasemaghaei & Kordzadeh, 2024).

1.6 AI's Role in Business Transformation

AI is reshaping business operations by automating repetitive tasks, optimizing supply chains, and enhancing customer experiences. Organizations leveraging AI technology benefit from predictive analytics, real-time insights, and intelligent automation, which contribute to cost savings and revenue growth (Åström, Reim, & Parida, 2022). Additionally, AI-driven personalization improves customer satisfaction and engagement, creating a more competitive market landscape (Verhoef, Kooge, Walk, & Wieringa, 2021).

AI technology management strategies must be dynamic and adaptable, considering the rapid advancements in AI capabilities and evolving regulatory landscapes. Businesses that successfully integrate AI into their strategies can achieve long-term growth and innovation, positioning themselves as leaders in an AI-driven world (Shrestha, Krishna, & von Krogh, 2021).

1.7 The Need for AI Literacy and Leadership

With AI adoption increasing across various industries, business leaders and professionals must develop AI literacy to effectively manage AI technologies. AI literacy involves understanding fundamental AI concepts, recognizing AI's potential limitations, and making informed decisions regarding AI investments (Lee, Ali, Zhang, DiPaola, & Breazeal, 2021). Furthermore, leadership plays a crucial role in fostering a culture of AI-driven innovation, encouraging cross-functional collaboration, and ensuring ethical AI implementation (Brock & Von Wangenheim, 2019).

The following sections will delve deeper into specific AI technology management strategies, highlighting innovative approaches, sector-specific applications, and the broader impact of AI on business sustainability and growth.

2. STRATEGIC ASPECTS OF AI TECHNOLOGY MANAGEMENT

Every organization has a business strategy in the form of a plan designed to achieve the organization's goals and objectives, both short-term, medium-term, and long-term basis. Organizations must develop a clear strategy for AI adoption that aligns with their long-term business goals. AI-driven decision-making can optimize operations, reduce costs, and create new market opportunities. Business leaders, including entrepreneurs, managers, workers, and educators, must embrace AI as a transformative tool rather than merely a technological advancement. Strategic AI management entails. Organizations leverage artificial intelligence (AI) to analyze data and support decision-making, although the integration of AI into organizational workflows sometimes leads to unwanted biases (Carter & Liu, 2025).

2.1 Identifying AI Opportunities That Align With Business Objectives

To successfully leverage AI, organizations must first identify areas where AI can provide maximum value. This involves assessing business processes, analyzing market trends, and recognizing AI-driven opportunities that align with organizational goals. AI should not be adopted merely for its technological appeal but should serve a strategic purpose in improving efficiency, productivity, and innovation.

2.2 Assessing Risks and Implementing Mitigation Strategies

While AI brings numerous benefits, it also introduces risks such as bias in decision-making, data privacy concerns, cybersecurity threats, and regulatory compliance issues. A robust AI strategy should include risk assessment methodologies, such as scenario analysis and predictive modeling, to foresee potential risks. Organizations must implement risk mitigation strategies, including bias detection algorithms, secure data handling practices, and compliance with industry regulations.

2.3 Ensuring Ethical and Responsible AI Usage

Advances in artificial intelligence (AI) have led to its widespread use in sectors such as finance, healthcare, military, and employment in developed countries. However, this reliance has raised concerns about AI governance, especially regarding algorithmic bias based on skin color, gender, race, and age. As a result, many countries have introduced regulations and ethical frameworks to address this issue (Ibrahim, Alshraideh, Leiner, Aldajani, & Ouarda, 2024). Ethical AI practices are critical in preventing unintended consequences such as discrimination, misinformation, and privacy violations. Organizations should develop AI governance frameworks that outline ethical principles, transparency, and accountability. AI ethics committees and compliance officers can help oversee AI deployments and ensure that AI applications adhere to legal and moral standards. Ethical considerations—including security, privacy, non-fraud, and compliance—in generative artificial intelligence (GenAI) can influence every user in their activities. To enrich the AI ethics framework is done by comprehensively analyzing ethical perceptions within GenAI, with a focus on security, privacy, non-fraud, and fulfillment (Liu & Du, 2025).

2.4 Investing in AI Literacy and Workforce Training

One of the key challenges in AI adoption is the skills gap among employees. Organizations must invest in AI literacy programs that help employees understand and work effectively with AI systems. Workforce training initiatives should focus on developing AI-related skills, such as machine learning model interpretation, data analytics, and AI-powered decision-making. Upskilling and reskilling employees will foster a workforce that is adaptable to AI-driven transformations.

2.5 Continuously Monitoring AI Performance and Refining Strategies

AI systems require continuous monitoring and refinement to ensure they deliver optimal performance. Performance evaluation metrics, such as accuracy, efficiency, and ROI, should be regularly assessed. Organizations should establish feedback loops where AI-generated insights are analyzed, and necessary adjustments are made. AI models should also be updated periodically to remain relevant as data trends evolve and new technological advancements emerge. By keeping up with sustainability and IT developments, companies have found the implementation of AI-based systems information systems in operations. Companies can conduct financial analysis of the calculation of return on investment (ROI) in corporate digitalization, and find that AI information systems can drive prosperity in both economic and ecological fields (Li & Huang, 2024). Table 1 illustrates the key AI strategies for business growth.

Table 1. Key AI Strategies for Business Growth

Strategy	Description
AI-driven Decision Making	Enhances efficiency and reduces errors in strategic choices
AI for Customer Insights	Improves customer personalization and experience
AI for Automation	Reduces manual work and increases productivity
AI in Risk Management	Helps detect fraud and cybersecurity threats

3. INNOVATIVE AI TECHNOLOGY MANAGEMENT STRATEGIES

In a highly competitive and modern business era, innovation in AI technology management is key to staying competitive. Every business organization must continue to develop innovative AI-based strategies to improve efficiency, enrich customer experiences, and manage risk more effectively.

3.1 AI-driven Business Intelligence

AI allows businesses to analyze large amounts of data, uncover patterns, and make informed decisions. AI-driven business intelligence tools such as predictive analytics, customer segmentation, and forecasting organizational help requests develop more rigorous strategies and respond proactively to market changes. Deeper insights allow businesses to maximize growth opportunities while reducing uncertainty.

3.2 AI-powered Customer Experience

AI is also revolutionizing the customer experience by bringing chatbots, virtual assistants, and personalized recommendation systems. This technology analyzes user behavior to tailor interactions to individual preferences, improve customer satisfaction, speed up the service process, and significantly increase customer retention and loyalty rates. As a result, the company is able to build closer relationships with its consumers.

3.3 AI-enhanced Operational Efficiency

In terms of operations, AI offers advanced automation that replaces manual tasks, optimizes resource allocation, and improves workflow efficiency. AI-based robotics and process automation tools are now widely applied in the manufacturing, logistics, and service sectors to increase productivity and reduce operational costs. Thus, the company can focus on innovation and core business development.

3.4 AI-based Risk Management

Risk management has now become more proactive by relying on AI's capabilities to detect fraud, manage cyber threats, and mitigate financial risks. AI-based systems analyze historical data to identify anomalies and predict potential threats before they have a major impact on the business. By conducting more accurate early detection, organizations can implement more effective mitigation measures and maintain operational stability.

3.5 AI and Sustainability

AI also plays an important role in supporting sustainability by optimizing energy use, reducing waste, and accelerating environmental conservation. AI-based systems help monitor carbon emissions, improve renewable energy efficiency, and drive environmentally friendly business practices across a wide range of industries. By utilizing this technology, the company not only achieves business goals but also contributes to the sustainability of the global environment. Figure 2 illustrates the AI implementation in various sustainability business sectors.

Figure 2. AI Implementation in Various Business Sectors

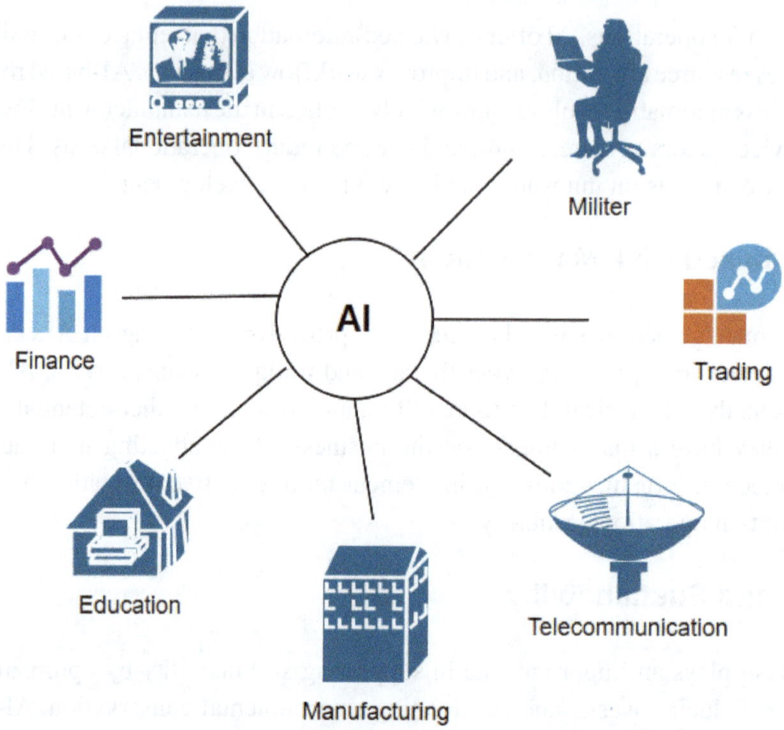

4. AI TECHNOLOGY MANAGEMENT IN DIFFERENT ENTREPRENEURIAL SECTORS

AI plays a pivotal role in various entrepreneurial domains, enhancing efficiency, productivity, and sustainability. AI-driven solutions support entrepreneurs in multiple industries by enabling data-driven decision-making, automating processes, and optimizing business operations. Key entrepreneurial sectors benefiting from AI technology management include:

4.1 Ecopreneurs

In all industries, it is necessary to consider the ecopreneurship factor in order to protect the environment from the pollution it causes. In the shipping industry, the pollution problem also needs to be considered at the lowest level. The shipping industry plays a dominant role in the development of the world economy by facilitating international trade. It is the only efficient mode of transportation for bulk cargo. Over the years, the industry has increased the size of its vessels to achieve economies of scale and to lower costs. As a result we now have large-sized vessels that can carry up to 18000TEU. Although shipping is the most energy-efficient mode of transportation, it is highly polluting. Ships emit nitrogen oxides (NOx), sulfur oxides (SOx), carbon dioxide and particulate matter (PM) into the atmosphere. Under such circumstances, the Shipping industry has started adopting greener practices to ensure environmental sustainability (Dorathy, 2017).

Ecopreneurs leverage AI to develop sustainable and environmentally friendly solutions. AI-driven tools assist in reducing carbon footprints, optimizing resource usage, and implementing renewable energy solutions. Key AI applications in this sector include:

- Smart Grids: AI optimizes energy distribution by predicting consumption patterns and integrating renewable energy sources.
- Climate Change Analysis: AI-driven predictive analytics assess environmental trends, enabling proactive measures to combat climate change.
- Waste Management: AI-powered sorting and recycling systems improve waste disposal efficiency and reduce environmental impact.

4.2 Agropreneurs

In agriculture, it is important to maintain the sustainability of the environment. Training in the agricultural sector has been set as a sustainable government agenda to educate rural communities. The training aims to develop sustainable agropreneurs in farmer groups. For this reason, data was collected from 200 participants of the Agropreneur Community Training Program (ACTP). It is necessary to pay attention to internal and external factors that influence to become a sustainable agropreneur in rural areas. The agricultural sector has become an urgent global concern, with issues such as natural disasters, wars, and climate change (Jaafar, Jalali, Suffarruddin, & Ramasamy, 2023). Agriculture entrepreneurs (Agropreneurs) utilize AI to enhance agricultural productivity, improve crop management, and reduce waste. AI-powered agricultural solutions optimize farming processes and increase sustainability. Key AI applications include:

- Precision Farming: AI-driven sensors and drones monitor soil health, crop conditions, and irrigation needs.
- Automated Pest Control: AI algorithms detect pest infestations early, reducing reliance on harmful pesticides.

- Supply Chain Optimization: AI enhances logistics and distribution, ensuring food reaches markets efficiently.

4.3 Social Entrepreneurs

Social entrepreneurs integrate AI into their business models to address pressing social issues, such as education, healthcare, and community development. AI-driven solutions enable impactful initiatives, including:

- AI-powered Education Tools: Personalized learning platforms use AI to tailor educational content for students.
- Healthcare AI: AI-driven diagnostic tools and chatbots provide medical support in underserved areas.
- Predictive Social Welfare: AI analyzes socio-economic trends to guide policy-making and social program implementation.

4.4 Technopreneurs

The wave of business digitalization has changed the entrepreneurial landscape globally. Existing digital enablers practice and think differently through the creation of items or arrangements that leverage the ability of innovation to change the way things are done. The power of technology is truly transforming the economy of an industry, where entrepreneurial ventures aim to cater to the market or platform that requires them to transform into digital advocates and successful technopreneurs (Alkhoori, AL-shami, & Sedik, 2021; Anwar et al., 2024). Technopreneurs drive technological innovation by utilizing AI to create disruptive products and services. AI plays a crucial role in developing cutting-edge solutions across various tech industries. Table 2 illustrates the AI applications in entrepreneurial sectors. Key AI-driven advancements include:

- AI-based Software Development: Machine learning models automate code generation and bug detection.
- Autonomous Systems: AI-powered robotics and autonomous vehicles improve transportation and manufacturing.
- AI-driven Cybersecurity: Advanced AI algorithms detect and prevent cyber threats in real time.

Table 2. AI Applications in Entrepreneurial Sectors

Entrepreneurial Sector	AI Application
Ecopreneurs	Smart grids, climate analytics, waste management
Agropreneurs	Precision farming, automated pest control, supply chain optimization
Social Entrepreneurs	AI-powered education, healthcare AI, predictive social welfare
Technopreneurs	AI-based software, autonomous systems, cybersecurity

5. AI TECHNOLOGY MANAGEMENT FOR SMES AND FAMILY BUSINESSES

Small and medium-sized enterprises (SMEs) and family-owned businesses face unique challenges in adopting AI technologies, including limited resources, lack of technical expertise, and resistance to change. However, AI presents significant opportunities for these businesses to enhance efficiency, optimize decision-making, and remain competitive in the digital economy. AI-driven solutions empower SMEs and family businesses to scale operations, improve customer engagement, and streamline workflows. Due to limited resources, small and medium-sized enterprises (SMEs) often have a low capacity to innovate. Meanwhile, SMEs need to innovate in a real way to maintain their business continuity, even in a state of savings. Here, the role of AI can effectively and efficiently promote innovation (Hidayat & Pok, 2025).

5.1 AI-driven Automation for Operational Efficiency

AI-powered automation helps SMEs and family businesses reduce manual workload and improve operational efficiency. By automating repetitive tasks such as inventory management, order processing, and customer support, businesses can minimize errors and enhance productivity. AI-driven tools such as robotic process automation (RPA) and machine learning algorithms enable businesses to optimize workflow, increase output, and improve service delivery.

5.2 Predictive Analytics for Business Growth

SMEs and family businesses can leverage AI-driven predictive analytics to gain valuable insights into market trends, customer preferences, and operational performance. By analyzing historical data, AI enables businesses to forecast demand, optimize pricing strategies, and enhance financial planning. Predictive analytics also supports proactive decision-making, helping businesses mitigate risks and capitalize on emerging opportunities.

5.3 AI-powered Customer Relationship Management (CRM)

Customer engagement is a key factor in business success, and AI-powered CRM systems enhance customer interactions by providing personalized experiences. AI-driven chatbots, virtual assistants, and sentiment analysis tools help businesses understand customer needs and tailor offerings accordingly. By leveraging AI-powered CRM, SMEs and family businesses can improve customer satisfaction, retention, and loyalty.

5.4 AI-driven Marketing and Sales Optimization

Marketing and sales strategies are crucial for SMEs, and AI helps businesses optimize campaigns, enhance lead generation, and improve conversion rates. AI-driven marketing tools analyze consumer behavior, automate content creation, and personalize marketing messages. SMEs can leverage AI-powered advertising platforms, recommendation engines, and audience segmentation tools to maximize the impact of their marketing efforts.

5.5 Supply Chain and Inventory Optimization

AI enhances supply chain management by improving demand forecasting, optimizing inventory levels, and reducing waste. AI-powered algorithms analyze supply chain data to identify bottlenecks, enhance logistics planning, and improve procurement processes. By implementing AI-driven inventory management systems, SMEs and family businesses can minimize stock shortages, reduce carrying costs, and improve order fulfillment.

5.6 AI for Financial Management and Fraud Detection

AI plays a critical role in financial management by automating bookkeeping, detecting anomalies, and preventing fraudulent transactions. AI-powered accounting tools help businesses manage expenses, generate financial reports, and ensure regulatory compliance. Machine learning models analyze transaction patterns to identify potential fraud, enabling businesses to take preventive measures and safeguard financial assets.

5.7 Overcoming Challenges in AI Adoption

Despite the benefits, SMEs and family businesses often face challenges in AI adoption, including budget constraints, lack of skilled personnel, and concerns about data privacy. Table 3 illustrates the AI applications for SMEs and family businesses. To overcome these barriers, businesses should:

- Invest in AI Training: Encourage employees to develop AI-related skills through training programs and workshops.
- Adopt Scalable AI Solutions: Start with cost-effective AI solutions that align with business needs and scale as the business grows.
- Leverage Cloud-based AI Services: Utilize AI-powered cloud platforms to reduce infrastructure costs and improve accessibility.
- Collaborate with AI Vendors and Experts: Partner with AI service providers to access expert guidance and tailored solutions.

Table 3. AI Applications for SMEs and Family Businesses

AI Application	Benefits
AI-driven Automation	Reduces manual workload and improves efficiency
Predictive Analytics	Enhances decision-making and risk mitigation
AI-powered CRM	Improves customer engagement and personalization
AI-driven Marketing	Optimizes campaigns and increases sales conversion
Supply Chain AI	Enhances logistics, inventory, and procurement
AI for Finance	Automates bookkeeping and detects fraudulent activities

6. ENTREPRENEURSHIP EDUCATION AND AI

Entrepreneurship education is evolving with the integration of artificial intelligence, enabling educators and students to develop skills essential for thriving in an AI-driven business landscape. AI enhances entrepreneurship education by providing personalized learning experiences, streamlining business model development, and fostering an innovation-driven mindset.

6.1 AI-powered Personalized Learning

AI-driven educational platforms adapt content delivery based on students' learning styles, strengths, and weaknesses. These platforms use machine learning algorithms to analyze student progress and provide tailored recommendations, enabling aspiring entrepreneurs to acquire business and technical knowledge more efficiently.

- Adaptive Learning Systems: AI identifies learning gaps and customizes instructional content to suit individual students.
- Virtual AI Tutors: AI chatbots and virtual assistants provide real-time support and answer queries on entrepreneurship topics.
- Automated Feedback and Assessment: AI tools evaluate students' performance, suggest improvements, and track learning progress.

6.2 AI-driven Business Model Development

AI assists entrepreneurship students in developing and validating business models by analyzing market data and predicting industry trends. By leveraging AI-driven insights, students can refine business strategies, evaluate market demand, and anticipate challenges.

- Market Research and Competitive Analysis: AI scans global market trends and competitor strategies to provide data-driven business insights.
- Business Idea Validation: AI algorithms assess the feasibility of business ideas based on historical data and consumer behavior patterns.
- Financial Forecasting: AI-driven tools predict revenue potential, helping entrepreneurs make informed investment decisions.

6.3 AI and Entrepreneurial Skill Development

AI fosters entrepreneurial skills such as problem-solving, innovation, and strategic thinking by providing real-world simulations and interactive learning experiences.

- AI-powered Simulations: Virtual environments allow students to test business decisions and understand the consequences in risk-free settings.
- Idea Generation and Brainstorming Tools: AI assists in creative thinking by suggesting innovative business concepts based on market demand.
- Entrepreneurial Decision-making Support: AI-based recommendation systems help students analyze different business scenarios and choose optimal solutions.

6.4 AI in Startup Incubation and Mentorship

AI plays a crucial role in guiding startup founders through business incubation and mentorship programs. AI-driven mentorship platforms connect entrepreneurs with industry experts, providing data-backed advice and business strategies.

- AI-powered Startup Accelerators: AI analyzes startup performance and provides tailored mentorship for scaling businesses.
- Automated Business Coaching: AI-driven platforms offer automated guidance on regulatory compliance, funding opportunities, and operational management.
- Investor Matching Algorithms: AI connects startups with potential investors by analyzing business profiles and investment patterns.

6.5 AI-enhanced Entrepreneurial Networking and Collaboration

Networking is essential for entrepreneurial success, and AI facilitates connections by recommending relevant industry contacts, events, and collaboration opportunities.

- AI-powered Professional Networks: Platforms like LinkedIn leverage AI to suggest valuable connections based on entrepreneurial interests.
- Smart Event Recommendations: AI identifies and recommends relevant workshops, conferences, and startup networking events.
- Collaboration Optimization: AI tools facilitate co-founder matchmaking and team-building by assessing compatibility among entrepreneurs.

6.6 Overcoming Challenges in AI-driven Entrepreneurship Education

Despite its advantages, AI integration in entrepreneurship education presents challenges, such as accessibility, ethical concerns, and data privacy issues. Table 4 illustrates the AI applications in entrepreneurship education. Educational institutions and policymakers must address these challenges by:

- Ensuring AI Accessibility: Expanding AI-based learning resources to underserved communities.
- Ethical AI Usage: Developing guidelines to ensure unbiased AI-driven recommendations and assessments.
- Data Security Measures: Implementing robust security protocols to protect student information in AI-driven platforms.

Table 4. AI Applications in Entrepreneurship Education

AI Application	Benefits
AI-powered Personalized Learning	Enhances knowledge retention and engagement
AI-driven Business Model Development	Improves decision-making and market analysis
AI-based Entrepreneurial Simulations	Enhances problem-solving and risk assessment
AI-powered Startup Incubation	Provides tailored mentorship and investor matchmaking
AI-enhanced Networking and Collaboration	Facilitates professional connections and partnerships

7. BEHAVIORAL CHARACTERISTICS OF ENTREPRENEURIAL ACTIVITY IN AI

Entrepreneurs operating in the AI-driven business environment exhibit distinct behavioral characteristics that set them apart in terms of innovation, adaptability, and resilience. AI-driven entrepreneurial activity requires a unique blend of skills and mindsets to navigate the complexities of emerging technologies and business landscapes. Key behavioral characteristics of AI entrepreneurs include:

7.1 Risk-taking and Experimentation

AI entrepreneurs must embrace risk-taking and experimentation, as the AI industry is fast-evolving and often unpredictable. They must be willing to invest in novel AI-driven solutions despite uncertainties about their success.

- Investment in AI Innovation: AI entrepreneurs allocate resources to research and development, even when AI applications are in early stages.
- Embracing Uncertainty: The AI landscape evolves rapidly, requiring entrepreneurs to take calculated risks when launching new AI-driven products and services.
- Agility in Decision-making: Entrepreneurs must pivot their AI strategies based on emerging trends and technological advancements.

7.2 Creativity and Problem-solving

Successful AI entrepreneurs leverage creativity to identify innovative solutions to business challenges. AI-driven businesses require creative problem-solving approaches to unlock new value propositions and market opportunities.

- AI-driven Product Development: Entrepreneurs must creatively utilize AI technologies to develop unique and competitive products.
- Automating Complex Processes: AI-based automation enhances business efficiency, requiring entrepreneurs to creatively apply AI in process optimization.
- Customizing AI for Different Industries: Creativity is essential to tailor AI solutions for specific industries such as healthcare, finance, and manufacturing.

7.3 Adaptability and Continuous Learning

AI entrepreneurs must continuously learn and adapt to stay ahead of technological advancements. The AI industry evolves rapidly, making it essential for entrepreneurs to update their knowledge and skills.

- Keeping Up with AI Trends: Entrepreneurs must stay informed about the latest developments in machine learning, deep learning, and AI ethics.
- Investing in AI Training: Continuous learning through AI certifications and courses enhances technical expertise.
- Flexibility in Business Strategies: Entrepreneurs must be adaptable to pivot their business models based on AI innovation and regulatory changes.

7.4 Resilience and Perseverance

Building AI-driven businesses involves challenges, including high development costs, regulatory barriers, and data privacy concerns. Entrepreneurs must demonstrate resilience and perseverance to overcome these hurdles.

- Navigating AI Regulatory Challenges: Entrepreneurs must comply with evolving AI regulations while ensuring ethical AI deployment.
- Overcoming Technical Barriers: AI development often involves complex algorithms and data management issues that require persistence.
- Dealing with Market Resistance: Entrepreneurs must address customer concerns about AI adoption, including trust and transparency issues.

7.5 Strategic Vision and Leadership

AI entrepreneurs must exhibit strategic vision to foresee long-term industry trends and develop AI solutions that create sustainable competitive advantages.

- Long-term AI Business Strategies: Entrepreneurs should plan AI product roadmaps with future scalability in mind.
- AI-driven Market Forecasting: Strategic vision enables entrepreneurs to anticipate AI market demands and emerging opportunities.
- Fostering AI-driven Innovation Culture: Effective leadership ensures a team-oriented culture that embraces AI innovation and collaboration.

7.6 Ethical Considerations and Social Responsibility

AI entrepreneurs must integrate ethical considerations and social responsibility into their AI solutions. Ethical AI deployment ensures fairness, transparency, and compliance with regulations.

- Bias-free AI Development: Entrepreneurs must ensure that AI models do not reinforce biases in decision-making.
- Data Privacy and Security: Ethical entrepreneurs prioritize user privacy by implementing robust data protection measures.
- AI for Social Good: Many AI-driven entrepreneurs focus on using AI to solve social issues, such as healthcare accessibility and environmental sustainability.

7.7 Networking and Collaboration

AI entrepreneurs thrive through collaboration and networking, leveraging partnerships to advance their AI ventures. Table 5 illustrates the key behavioral characteristics of AI entrepreneurs.

- Industry Partnerships: Entrepreneurs collaborate with AI researchers, universities, and tech firms to drive innovation.
- Cross-sector AI Collaboration: Many AI startups partner with industries such as healthcare, finance, and manufacturing to create tailored solutions.
- Startup Incubators and Accelerators: AI entrepreneurs participate in accelerator programs to gain mentorship, funding, and industry exposure.

Table 5. Key Behavioral Characteristics of AI Entrepreneurs

Behavioral Trait	Description
Risk-taking and Experimentation	Willingness to take risks in AI innovation and invest in novel technologies.
Creativity and Problem-solving	Leveraging AI to develop unique solutions for business challenges.
Adaptability and Continuous Learning	Staying updated with AI trends and evolving business models accordingly.
Resilience and Perseverance	Overcoming AI-related challenges, including regulatory and technical barriers.
Strategic Vision and Leadership	Developing long-term AI business strategies with market foresight.
Ethical Considerations and Social Responsibility	Ensuring fairness, transparency, and compliance in AI applications.
Networking and Collaboration	Partnering with industries, researchers, and accelerators to foster AI growth.

8. LEADERSHIP, MANAGEMENT, AND HR PRACTICES IN AI TECHNOLOGY MANAGEMENT

AI is transforming leadership, management, and human resource (HR) practices, requiring organizations to adopt new strategies that align with technological advancements. Effective AI leadership fosters innovation, streamlines operations, and enhances workforce management, enabling businesses to maximize AI's potential. Figure 3 illustrates the AI-driven HR applications including recruitment, training, and performance assessment.

Figure 3. AI in Workforce Management

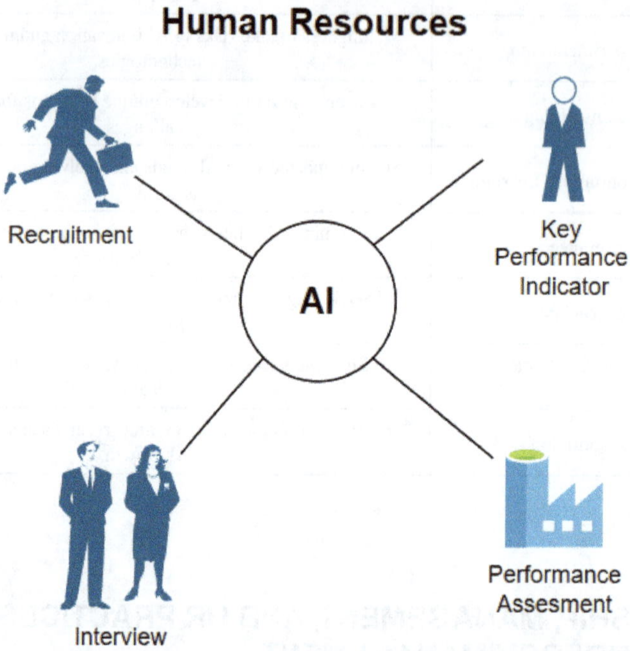

Leaders must cultivate an AI-ready workforce by:

- Promoting AI upskilling and reskilling initiatives.
- Encouraging a culture of AI-driven innovation.
- Implementing AI-powered HR tools for recruitment, performance management, and employee engagement.

8.1 AI-driven Leadership and Decision-making

AI empowers leaders by providing real-time insights, data-driven decision-making, and predictive analytics. AI-driven leadership involves:

- Enhancing Strategic Planning: AI-powered tools analyze market trends and customer behavior, aiding leaders in developing forward-thinking strategies.
- Predictive Decision-Making: AI algorithms identify patterns and forecast potential business outcomes, supporting risk management and long-term planning.

- Optimizing Business Performance: AI-driven dashboards provide leaders with critical KPIs, enabling them to make informed, timely decisions.

8.2 AI-powered Workforce Management

AI is revolutionizing HR management by improving talent acquisition, performance evaluation, and employee engagement. Key AI applications in workforce management include:

- Automated Recruitment: AI-powered applicant tracking systems (ATS) streamline the hiring process by screening resumes, assessing candidate skills, and ranking potential hires.
- AI-driven Employee Training: Personalized learning platforms use AI to recommend tailored training modules based on employee skill gaps and career goals.
- Performance Analytics: AI monitors employee productivity, providing HR teams with insights into engagement levels, workload distribution, and job satisfaction.

8.3 AI-enhanced Employee Engagement and Retention

Retaining skilled employees is essential for business sustainability. AI-driven HR solutions help organizations enhance employee engagement and retention by:

- AI-based Sentiment Analysis: AI tools analyze employee feedback from surveys, emails, and internal communications to assess workplace sentiment.
- Personalized Career Pathing: AI recommends career development opportunities based on individual strengths and aspirations, increasing employee satisfaction.
- Proactive Retention Strategies: AI predicts attrition risks by analyzing historical workforce data, allowing HR teams to implement targeted retention programs.

8.4 Ethical AI Implementation in HR Practices

AI in HR must be implemented ethically to avoid biases and ensure fairness in hiring, promotions, and evaluations. Ethical AI HR practices include:

- Bias-free Recruitment Models: AI-powered hiring tools should be designed to minimize discrimination based on gender, ethnicity, or age.

- Transparent AI Decisions: Organizations must ensure AI-driven HR processes are transparent and understandable to employees.
- Compliance with Employment Laws: AI must adhere to labor laws, data privacy regulations, and corporate policies.

8.5 AI-powered Collaboration and Productivity Enhancement

AI-driven collaboration tools improve teamwork, productivity, and efficiency within organizations. AI enhances collaboration by:

- Smart Scheduling Assistants: AI tools automate meeting scheduling, optimizing time management for teams.
- Virtual Collaboration Platforms: AI-powered platforms facilitate remote teamwork through real-time document sharing, task management, and workflow automation.
- AI Chatbots for Internal Communication: AI-driven chatbots provide instant responses to employee queries, improving HR support services.

8.6 Challenges of AI in Leadership, Management, and HR

While AI offers numerous benefits, organizations must address several challenges in AI leadership and HR management, including:

- Data Privacy Concerns: Ensuring employee data security and compliance with privacy regulations.
- Workforce Resistance to AI: Managing change resistance by fostering AI literacy and employee trust in AI applications.
- Ensuring AI Accountability: Implementing mechanisms to monitor and audit AI decisions in HR and management functions.

Table 6 illustrates the AI applications in leadership, management, and human resources.

Table 6. AI Applications in Leadership, Management, and HR

AI Application	Benefits
AI-driven Decision-making	Enhances strategic planning and predictive forecasting
AI-powered Workforce Management	Automates hiring, training, and performance evaluation
AI-enhanced Employee Engagement	Improves retention and personalized career development

continued on following page

Table 6. Continued

AI Application	Benefits
Ethical AI Implementation	Ensures fairness, transparency, and compliance
AI-powered Collaboration Tools	Enhances teamwork and productivity

9. EXECUTION AND GROWTH STRATEGIES FOR AI-DRIVEN BUSINESSES

The successful execution and growth of AI-driven businesses require well-defined strategies that optimize operations, ensure scalability, and maintain competitive advantages. Effective AI execution involves integrating AI into business workflows, measuring performance, and continuously improving AI-driven initiatives. Key execution and growth strategies include:

9.1 Developing AI Roadmaps for Execution

A structured AI roadmap outlines the step-by-step process of AI implementation within an organization. Businesses should define clear objectives, milestones, and performance indicators to track progress and ensure alignment with strategic goals.

- Identifying AI Use Cases: Determine specific business problems AI can solve effectively.
- Resource Allocation: Allocate budgets, human capital, and technological resources to support AI deployment.
- Implementation Timeline: Set realistic deadlines for each phase of AI integration.

9.2 Ensuring AI Scalability

AI solutions must be scalable to accommodate business growth and increased data complexity. Companies should ensure AI models can adapt to larger datasets, higher processing demands, and evolving business needs.

- Cloud-based AI Solutions: Utilize cloud computing to handle vast amounts of data and computational tasks efficiently.
- Modular AI Architectures: Design AI systems with flexible components that allow easy upgrades and enhancements.

- Cross-platform AI Integration: Ensure AI tools can be integrated seamlessly across various business departments.

9.3 Strategic AI Partnerships and Collaborations

Collaboration with AI vendors, research institutions, and technology providers accelerates AI-driven innovation. Businesses should engage in strategic partnerships to leverage external expertise and cutting-edge AI developments.

- Industry-academic Collaborations: Partner with universities and AI research labs for advanced innovation.
- Technology Providers: Collaborate with AI software and hardware providers to enhance AI capabilities.
- Cross-industry Alliances: Build partnerships with other industries to develop AI-driven solutions with broader applications.

9.4 AI-driven Market Expansion

AI can be leveraged to explore new markets, optimize marketing strategies, and improve customer segmentation. Businesses should use AI-powered insights to make informed decisions about market expansion.

- AI-powered Market Research: Analyze consumer behavior, regional trends, and competitive landscapes.
- Personalized Marketing Campaigns: Use AI-driven customer analytics to tailor marketing messages and advertisements.
- Automated Customer Support: Implement AI chatbots and virtual assistants to provide multilingual, 24/7 customer support for global audiences.

9.5 Performance Monitoring and Continuous Improvement

Regular monitoring and refinement of AI applications ensure long-term success. Businesses should establish performance evaluation metrics and use AI-powered analytics to drive continuous improvement.

- KPIs for AI Performance: Track accuracy, efficiency, and ROI of AI-driven solutions.
- Feedback Loops: Use AI-generated insights to refine algorithms and business strategies.

- Model Retraining and Optimization: Regularly update AI models to reflect new data patterns and market shifts.

9.7 Navigating AI Ethics and Compliance

AI-driven businesses must navigate ethical considerations and regulatory requirements to maintain consumer trust and legal compliance. Table 7 illustrates the key execution and growth strategies for AI-driven businesses.

- Transparent AI Models: Ensure AI decision-making processes are explainable and unbiased.
- Data Protection Measures: Adhere to global data privacy regulations such as GDPR and CCPA.
- AI Governance Policies: Establish internal guidelines to oversee AI deployment and ethical considerations.

Table 7. Key Execution and Growth Strategies for AI-driven Businesses

Strategy	Benefits
Developing AI Roadmaps	Ensures structured AI implementation and progress tracking
Ensuring AI Scalability	Supports business growth and adaptability
Strategic AI Partnerships	Accelerates innovation and knowledge exchange
AI-driven Market Expansion	Enhances market reach and customer targeting
Performance Monitoring	Ensures continuous improvement and AI optimization
AI Ethics and Compliance	Builds trust and ensures regulatory adherence

10. CONCLUSIONS

AI Technology (AI) management for artificial intelligence is a critical pillar in supporting digital transformation and creating value in the modern working hours. Through the right AI management concepts and strategies, organizations can use the possibilities of AI to improve operational efficiency, enrich customer experiences, improve data decisions, and manage risk more intelligently and proactively.

We've seen business intelligence in AI control, AI operations customer experience, AI operational efficiency improvements, AI-driven risk management, and how AI is a core component in developing innovative strategies that drive competitive advantage. This approach suggests that successful AI implementation relies not only on the adoption of its technology, but also on the management of AI integration, ethics, security, and sustainable development across all operations.

In the future, organizations need to focus on adapting more flexible AI strategies and on changing dynamic business environments. Using the principles of sustainable innovation, strong governance and comprehensive cooperation, AI is not only a tool, but also the most important driver for creating long-term value for businesses and society as a whole.

REFERENCES

Alkhoori, A. A., AL-shami, S. A., & Sedik, S. (2021). The Relationship between Leadership Factors and Successful Technopreneur through the Mediator Role of Digital Enabler. *Webology, 18*(SpecialIssue 2), 344–356. DOI: 10.14704/WEB/V18SI02/WEB18100

Alkhudhayr, H. (2025). Internet of things based parking slot detection and occupancy classification for smart city traffic management. *Engineering Applications of Artificial Intelligence, 152*, 110802. Advance online publication. DOI: 10.1016/j.engappai.2025.110802

Anwar, N., Widodo, A. M., Sekti, B. A., Ulum, M. B., Rahaman, M., & Ariessanti, H. D. (2024). Comparative Analysis of NIJ and NIST Methods for MicroSD Investigations: A Technopreneur Approach. *APTISI Transactions on Technopreneurship, 6*(2), 169–181. DOI: 10.34306/att.v6i2.407

Åström, J., Reim, W., & Parida, V. (2022). Value creation and value capture for AI business model innovation: A three-phase process framework. *Review of Managerial Science, 16*(7), 2111–2133. DOI: 10.1007/s11846-022-00521-z

Bourbon, B., & Murimi, R. (2024). Decentralization, Blockchains, and the Development of Smart Communities in Economically Challenging Environments. *Ledger, 9*, 30–50. DOI: 10.5195/ledger.2024.302

Brock, J. K.-U., & Von Wangenheim, F. (2019). Demystifying AI: What digital transformation leaders can teach you about realistic artificial intelligence. *California Management Review, 61*(4), 110–134. DOI: 10.1177/1536504219865226

Carter, L., & Liu, D. (2025). How was my performance? Exploring the role of anchoring bias in AI-assisted decision making. *International Journal of Information Management, 82*, 102875. Advance online publication. DOI: 10.1016/j.ijinfomgt.2025.102875

Davenport, T. H., & Mittal, N. (2023a). How companies can prepare for the coming "AI-first" world. *Strategy and Leadership, 51*(1), 26–30. DOI: 10.1108/SL-11-2022-0107

Davenport, T. H., & Mittal, N. (2023b). Stop Tinkering with AI. *Harvard Business Review, 2023-Janua*. Retrieved from https://www.scopus.com/inward/record.uri?eid=2-s2.0-85158877740&partnerID=40&md5=0f3e95747085651b8c3a4737d340160a

Dong, F., Yin, J., Xiang, J., Chang, Z., Gu, T., & Han, F. (2023). EWM-FCE-ODM-Based Evaluation of Smart Community Construction: From the Perspective of Residents' Sense of Gain. *Sustainability (Basel), 15*(8), 6587. Advance online publication. DOI: 10.3390/su15086587

Dorathy, M. B. C. (2017). Green Shipping - A plethora of business opportunities for ecopreneurs. *International Journal of Civil Engineering and Technology*, *8*(5), 189–198. https://www.scopus.com/inward/record.uri?eid=2-s2.0-85020138162&partnerID=40&md5=9cfc1ceec0a8793a631e78190514dc8d

Dubey, R., Gunasekaran, A., Childe, S. J., Bryde, D. J., Giannakis, M., Foropon, C., Roubaud, D., & Hazen, B. T. (2020). Big data analytics and artificial intelligence pathway to operational performance under the effects of entrepreneurial orientation and environmental dynamism: A study of manufacturing organisations. *International Journal of Production Economics*, *226*, 107599. Advance online publication. DOI: 10.1016/j.ijpe.2019.107599

Dwivedi, Y. K. Kshetri, N., Hughes, L., Slade, E. L., Jeyaraj, A., Kar, A. K., … Wright, R. (2023). Opinion Paper: "So what if ChatGPT wrote it?" Multidisciplinary perspectives on opportunities, challenges and implications of generative conversational AI for research, practice and policy. *International Journal of Information Management, 71*, 102642. https://doi.org/https://doi.org/10.1016/j.ijinfomgt.2023.102642

Dwivedi, Y. K., Hughes, L., Ismagilova, E., Aarts, G., Coombs, C., Crick, T., Duan, Y., Dwivedi, R., Edwards, J., Eirug, A., Galanos, V., Ilavarasan, P. V., Janssen, M., Jones, P., Kar, A. K., Kizgin, H., Kronemann, B., Lal, B., Lucini, B., & Williams, M. D. (2021). Artificial Intelligence (AI): Multidisciplinary perspectives on emerging challenges, opportunities, and agenda for research, practice and policy. *International Journal of Information Management*, *57*, 101994. Advance online publication. DOI: 10.1016/j.ijinfomgt.2019.08.002

Floridi, L., & Cowls, J. (2022). A unified framework of five principles for AI in society. *Machine Learning and the City: Applications in Architecture and Urban Design*, 535–545.

Ghasemaghaei, M., & Kordzadeh, N. (2024). Understanding how algorithmic injustice leads to making discriminatory decisions: An obedience to authority perspective. *Information & Management*, *61*(2), 103921. Advance online publication. DOI: 10.1016/j.im.2024.103921

Hidayat, A. S., & Pok, W. C. (2025). Empowering SMEs innovation through intangible factors. *Journal of Innovation and Entrepreneurship, 14*(1), 1. Advance online publication. DOI: 10.1186/s13731-024-00437-w

Ibrahim, S. M., Alshraideh, M. A., Leiner, M., Aldajani, I. M., & Ouarda, B. (2024). Artificial intelligence ethics: Ethical consideration and regulations from theory to practice. *IAES International Journal of Artificial Intelligence, 13*(3), 3703–3714. DOI: 10.11591/ijai.v13.i3.pp3703-3714

Jaafar, M., Jalali, A., Suffarruddin, S. H., & Ramasamy, N. (2023). The Determinants of Becoming Sustainable Agropreneurs: Evidence from the Bottom 40 Groups in Malaysia. *Sustainability (Basel), 15*(10), 8283. Advance online publication. DOI: 10.3390/su15108283

Jarrahi, M. H., Newlands, G., Butler, B., Savage, S., Lutz, C., Dunn, M., & Sawyer, S. (2021). Flexible work and personal digital infrastructures. *Communications of the ACM, 64*(7), 72–79. DOI: 10.1145/3419405

Lee, I., Ali, S., Zhang, H., DiPaola, D., & Breazeal, C. (2021). Developing middle school students' AI literacy. In *Proceedings of the 52nd ACM technical symposium on computer science education* (pp. 191–197). DOI: 10.1145/3408877.3432513

Li, N., & Huang, F. (2024). Evaluating the Financial Returns on Investment in Sustainable Enterprise Digitalization Initiatives Using AI Information System. *Journal of Internet Services and Information Security, 14*(4), 21–44. DOI: 10.58346/JISIS.2024.I4.002

Liebig, L., Güttel, L., Jobin, A., & Katzenbach, C. (2024). Subnational AI policy: Shaping AI in a multi-level governance system. *AI & Society, 39*(3), 1477–1490. DOI: 10.1007/s00146-022-01561-5

Liu, Y., & Du, Y. (2025). The Effect of Generative AI Ethics on Users' Continuous Usage Intentions: A PLS-SEM and fsQCA Approach. *International Journal of Human-Computer Interaction, 41*(20), 12831–12842. Advance online publication. DOI: 10.1080/10447318.2025.2465861

Radanliev, P. (2024). Artificial intelligence and quantum cryptography. *Journal of Analytical Science and Technology, 15*(1), 4. Advance online publication. DOI: 10.1186/s40543-024-00416-6

Radanliev, P., De Roure, D., Maple, C., Nurse, J. R. C., Nicolescu, R., & Ani, U. (2024). AI security and cyber risk in IoT systems. *Frontiers in Big Data, 7*, 1402745. Advance online publication. DOI: 10.3389/fdata.2024.1402745 PMID: 39449740

Samuel, O., Javaid, N., Almogren, A., Javed, M. U., Qasim, U., & Radwan, A. (2022). A secure energy trading system for electric vehicles in smart communities using blockchain. *Sustainable Cities and Society*, *79*, 103678. Advance online publication. DOI: 10.1016/j.scs.2022.103678

Shrestha, Y. R., Krishna, V., & von Krogh, G. (2021). Augmenting organizational decision-making with deep learning algorithms: Principles, promises, and challenges. *Journal of Business Research*, *123*, 588–603. https://doi.org/https://doi.org/10.1016/j.jbusres.2020.09.068. DOI: 10.1016/j.jbusres.2020.09.068

Singh, J., Sajid, M., Gupta, S. K., & Haidri, R. A. (2022). Artificial intelligence and blockchain technologies for smart city. In *Intelligent Green Technologies for Sustainable Smart Cities* (pp. 317–330). DOI: 10.1002/9781119816096.ch15

Tan, L., Yu, K., Yang, C., & Bashir, A. K. (2021). A blockchain-based Shamir's threshold cryptography for data protection in industrial internet of things of smart city. In *Proceedings of the 1st Workshop on Artificial Intelligence and Blockchain Technologies for Smart Cities with 6G* (pp. 13–18). New York, NY, USA: Association for Computing Machinery. DOI: 10.1145/3477084.3484951

Verhoef, P. C., Kooge, E., Walk, N., & Wieringa, J. E. (2021). *Creating value with data analytics in marketing: Mastering data science. Creating Value with Data Analytics in Marketing: Mastering Data Science*. DOI: 10.4324/9781003011163

Widodo, A. M., Pappachan, P., Sekti, B. A., Anwar, N., Widayanti, R., Rahaman, M., & Bansal, R. (2024). Quantum-resistant cryptography. In *Innovations in Modern Cryptography* (pp. 100–130). DOI: 10.4018/979-8-3693-5330-1.ch005

Chapter 2
Artificial Intelligence and Business Strategy

Pooja Srivastava
https://orcid.org/0009-0000-1013-0931
Chanakya National Law University, Patna, India

Ajay Kumar
Chanakya National Law University, Patna, India

Shashank Srivastava
Patna University, Patna, India

ABSTRACT

Artificial Intelligence (AI) is transforming business strategy by enhancing decision-making, optimizing operations, and driving competitive advantage. AI-powered predictive analytics, machine learning, and automation help businesses forecast market trends, improve efficiency, and personalize customer experiences. AI-driven insights enable real-time strategic planning, optimizing supply chains, financial forecasting, and marketing. However, challenges such as data privacy, ethical concerns, and workforce adaptation must be addressed. Effective AI integration requires transparency, accountability, and continuous learning. As AI continues to evolve, businesses must balance innovation with ethical considerations to maximize its benefits for long-term growth and success.

1. INTRODUCTION

On the ground, implementation reveals a host of barriers that demand closer academic and practical attention, while Artificial Intelligence promises a transfor-

DOI: 10.4018/979-8-3373-2497-5.ch002

mative leap in business operations and decision-making. Many organisations find AI embedding into workflows difficult, particularly within emerging markets, given a lack of digital infrastructure, skilled personnel, and regulatory clarity. (Westerman, G., Bonnet, D., & McAfee, A. (2014). Innovation is often obstructed by stringent compliance requirements, fragmented data ecosystems, or legacy systems in certain sectors. (Wamba & Queiroz, 2022). In practice, Artificial Intelligence has notable implications. More research is needed in this aspect.

HDFC Bank and ICICI Bank, two private banks, successfully implemented AI-driven chatbots, real-time credit scoring systems, and fraud detection systems, as demonstrated by a 2022 case study of the Indian banking sector. Many state-owned banks continued to use manual verification processes. AI is utilised in the Indian Banking Sector. They reported on it. Amazon and Walmart have utilised AI to optimise customer experience, logistics, and inventory management in the global retail industry, leveraging technology as giants.(India Banking and Finance Report 2024, 2024). Similarly, this is accomplished through the use of AI. A study for comparison: AI-led personalisation along with retail supply chains.(Lorente-Martínez et al., 2022) Small and medium-sized enterprises (SMEs), however, often struggle to adopt even basic AI tools due to limited capital, inadequate access to high-quality datasets, and a lack of technological expertise (The Digital Transformation of SMEs, 2021).

According to research, institutional and national readiness greatly influence AI integration effectiveness. Digital public infrastructure with policy frameworks actively supports AI experimentation and deployment by countries like Singapore, South Korea, and the United States, which have strong digital economies. (Lee, 2018). AI Superpowers China, Silicon Valley, and the New World Order. Houghton Mifflin Harcourt. -). The digital divide, combined with a skills gap, can hinder the private sector's innovation and the implementation of public policies in low- and middle-income countries (Digital Economy Report 2021 | UN Trade and Development (UNCTAD), n.d.).

AI's theoretical potential differs from its real-world execution, highlighting the need to assess AI from a multi-stakeholder and multi-level perspective (Vial, 2019). Factors such as government support, data governance, organisational culture, and absorptive capacity are pivotal in determining whether an AI strategy alignment succeeds or fails (Yu et al., 2022). Journal of Calculated Information Systems, 28(2), 118–144.] Absorptive capacity: Reviewing then reconceptualising. Dwivedi, Y. K., et al. (2021). What scholars term "AI misfit" results from enabling environments that are absent, where technical tools are adopted without achieving intended calculated goals. (Van Quaquebeke et al., 2025)

Thus, this section helps readers understand AI adoption. This process involves context-specific constraints and enablers, and it is complex and evolving, rather than a linear technological upgrade. This contextual understanding is necessary for adaptable, inclusive AI strategies in business organisations, and it also aids future research within an implementation-oriented, policy-relevant framework.

2. STATEMENT OF THE PROBLEM

Artificial Intelligence has the potential to reshape business strategy. However, empirical evidence and literature suggest that its successful deployment has some inconsistencies in organisational settings. The ideal scenario envisions AI as simply a smooth enabler. AI enables data-driven decisions, operational excellence, and competitive agility through technology. Real-world evidence reveals a fragmented landscape where adoption remains unequal. Frequently, scheduled profits are postponed or weakened, and advantages differ.

AI calculated integration is complicated by several gaps. Theoretical gaps occur because business strategy frameworks, such as Institutional Theory, Dynamic Capabilities, and the Resource-Based View, are underutilised in AI research. (Barney, 1991)

Contradictory findings from empirical studies create more confusion. Some firms report exponential growth after AI implementation, while others struggle to generate value or experience setbacks (Dwivedi et al., 2021). Artificial Intelligence (AI): Many perspectives on both challenges and opportunities that are now emerging. Research, practice, and policy are on the agenda. Contextual gaps exist too; firm size, industry type, digital maturity, and national innovation systems alter AI's outcomes greatly. (Wamba & Queiroz, 2022) Artificial Intelligence (AI) has a significant impact on firms. Firm Performance is thus impacted. (Wamba-Taguimdje et al., 2020.)

There are knowledge gaps that still remain in understanding how internal organisational dynamics can affect AI adoption. Leadership commitment, cultural readiness, and ethical standards are examples of such dynamics (Ortiz De Guinea & Raymond, 2020). Environmental factors and business process agility roles address organisational performance and also IT capability. High capital costs, combined with regulatory uncertainty and data privacy concerns that present practical challenges, hinder the diffusion of this approach (Chen et al., 2014). Research that synthesises disparate findings underscores the need for a cohesive framework to guide implementation, given these barriers and contradictions.

This chapter addresses all of these issues by positioning AI in a way that it does not fit all, but instead multiple variables tactically shape it. It seeks to contribute specifically to filling these theoretical, empirical, and contextual gaps by providing a structured analysis. For future researchers and decision-makers, designing AI strategies that are both subtle and context-aware, as well as outcome-oriented, remains the objective.

3. THEORETICAL FRAMEWORK

The integration of Artificial Intelligence (AI) into business strategy also requires a strong theoretical framework. This section revisits four key theories: the Resource-Based View (RBV), Dynamic Capabilities Theory, the Technology-Organisation-Environment (TOE) Framework, and Institutional Theory, with recent empirical evidence improving their relevance within the context of AI adoption.

The Resource-Based View suggests that firms gain a lasting competitive edge by utilising resources that are unique, valuable, and inimitable. Recent studies have applied RBV to AI adoption, and these studies highlight that AI capabilities, such as proprietary algorithms and data analytics competencies, serve as planned resources that can improve firm performance (Barney, 1991). For example, a study examined large industrial firms in Jordan and found that AI usage significantly enhances internal integration, particularly when supported by a data-driven culture (Musleh Al-Sartawi et al., 2024). This does reinforce the RBV perspective. Jordan provides evidence regarding the influence of artificial intelligence. Industrial firms feel this impact inside themselves (Elwaked et al., n.d.).

Dynamic Capabilities Theory emphasises a business's ability to integrate internal and external skills, reshape them, and adapt to rapidly changing environments. Empirical research helps researchers when they apply this theory to adopt AI. Innovation performance increases with AI adoption because organisational learning capability facilitates this connection, according to research (Li et al., 2025)by Chinese manufacturers Yang Y. and Yu Z., who wrote in 2023. Because dynamic capabilities play a role, artificial intelligence fosters innovation within manufacturing firms (Li et al., 2025)

The Technology-Organisation-Environment (TOE) Framework offers a model for analysing technological adoption. It assesses technological readiness as well as organisational preparedness, plus external environmental factors. Recent meta-analyses validated something, too. The TOE framework applies to AI adoption. According to one study, seven of the eight TOE factors significantly affect AI adoption. This study synthesised data from 12 different studies involving 3,398 respondents across various industries, also highlighting the framework's robustness in explaining AI integration within business contexts (Ghimire et al., 2024).

Institutional Theory: Institutional Theory examines organisational behaviour for normative, coercive, and mimetic institutional pressures that influence it. AI integration strategies are greatly shaped via regulatory frameworks, industry norms, and peer firm actions, as shown in a study analysing Generative AI systems through the lens of AI adoption (Gozman, D., & Willcocks, L., 2024). Organisations often balance innovation against conformity to institutional norms, indicating the relevance of this theory in understanding AI adoption dynamics (Singh, 2024).

In summary, these theories collectively offer a multidimensional understanding of AI adoption in business strategy. RBV highlights the value that is planned for AI-related resources. Dynamic Capabilities Theory stresses AI adaptability. AI integration can be influenced by external pressures, as illuminated by Institutional Theory, for the TOE framework provides a holistic view of adoption factors. Together, they form quite a thorough theoretical foundation. This basis examines and shapes the acceptance of AI within current business settings.

4. EMPIRICAL LITERATURE REVIEW

Empirical studies have recently shed light on the subtle perceptions of how various sectors adopt Artificial Intelligence (AI), revealing both benefits and challenges as they integrate AI into their business strategies.

AI Adoption in Small and Medium Enterprises (SMEs): A study from Chatterjee et al. (2021) examined the impact of AI-enabled service robots in rural banking sectors and revealed that such technologies can improve customer satisfaction and loyalty, thereby improving business agility (Chatterjee et al., 2021). AI-enabled service robots bear upon customer satisfaction and business agility. Evidence comes from banking within rural India (Sharma et al., n.d.).

The research paper explored the multidisciplinary perspectives regarding AI in Marketing and Product Development. AI improves brand loyalty and customer retention considerably via personalised marketing strategies (Dwivedi et al., 2021). Artificial Intelligence (AI) exists in multidisciplinary perspectives. Research and practice, as well as policy, are impacted by emerging challenges and opportunities, including the agenda (Dwivedi et al., 2021)

Manufacturing Sector Performance: Wamba-Taguimdje et al. (2020) conducted a systematic literature review that indicated AI adoption in manufacturing firms improves operational efficiency, reduces cycle times, and increases employee satisfaction (Wamba & Queiroz, 2022). The influence of AI on firm performance is akin to the business value of AI-based transformation projects.

Healthcare and Banking Obstacles: Sectors including healthcare and customary banking face problems obstructing widespread acceptance, though AI is promising, for example, data privacy fears, digital talent shortages, and cybersecurity threats. [Fernandes, M., Vieira, R., & Farinha, L. (2023). The healthcare and banking sectors find that AI adoption has its issues. This thorough review of the literature specifies difficulties. Technology in Society is 72 102167. https://doi.org/10.1016/j.techsoc.2022.102167

Cultural and Regulatory Contexts: AI adoption is influenced by cultural contexts and also by regulatory frameworks. Stringent data protection laws inside the European

Union encourage AI applications that prioritise compliance and transparency, but more lenient regulations in other regions may foster rapid innovation (Commission Work Programme 2023 - European Commission, n.d.).

Calculated outcomes are enhanced by the emergence of hybrid AI systems, which combine machine learning with traditional decision-support tools, particularly in the volatile business environments of emerging markets (Kumar et al., 2024). Hybrid AI systems operate within emerging markets. The effectiveness of decision support is demonstrated through empirical analysis (Dellermann et al., 2019).

Frameworks that are standardised are needed since there is still a gap in the measurements of AI's impact on decisions. Existing studies primarily focus on short-term benefits, as analyses often lack longitudinal assessments of long-term implications on competitive dynamics. [Masood, A. (2023). Evolving are benchmarks, frameworks, and definitions for measuring the effectiveness of AI adoption (Massood, 2025).

AI's projected worth is supported by data. However, it also highlights sector-specific disparities. Likewise, context-aware studies integrated with theory are necessary to guide effective adoption of AI.

5. CONCEPTUAL FRAMEWORK

The conceptual framework of this study guides the examination of Artificial Intelligence (AI) within planned business contexts by bridging theoretical perceptions with empirical findings. Because this framework draws upon the Resource-Based View (RBV), Dynamic Capabilities Theory, the Technology-Organisation-Environment (TOE) Framework, and Institutional Theory, it seeks to model the interrelationship between organisational enablers and successful AI integration.

Three linked domains exist at the core of the framework: internal resources and capabilities, organisational readiness, and a calculated vision, as well as institutional and environmental alignment that impact AI's adoption.

i. **Internal Resources and Capabilities (RBV & Dynamic Capabilities):** AI-driven firms must possess both an adaptive organisational culture and skilled human capital, such as technological infrastructure, in addition to concrete and intangible resources. Dynamic capabilities are critical in leveraging AI for a sustained competitive advantage (Barney, 1991). They involve sensing market trends, seizing chances, and transforming organisational procedures. Firm resources sustained a competitive advantage (Barney, 1991).
ii. **Technological as well as Organisational Readiness (TOE):** This dimension examines just how mature the IT infrastructure is, how supportive leadership is, how well change management processes work, and how open people are to

innovation. Organisations with high readiness are more likely to succeed in implementing AI. For these organisations, aligning AI with business objectives is also more likely to be included (Tornatzky & Fleischer, 1990).

iii. **Institutional Alignment (Institutional Theory):** AI adoption is shaped through regulatory compliance, peer firm influence, industry best practices, and public sentiment that form external pressures. Legitimacy and trust from stakeholders are improved via the calculated alignment of these institutional forces (DiMaggio & Powell, 1983).

The conceptual framework also hypothesises key business strategy outcomes to be influenced by the interaction of these variables, including competitive positioning, innovation capacity, operational efficiency, and customer responsiveness.

For showing the pathways through which AI integration yields planned value, a graphical model representing these relationships, typically visualised as linked nodes or a systems diagram, can be embedded in the chapter. Not only does this framework provide a holistic lens for analysing AI-driven transformation, but it can also help identify specific areas where intervention or policy support is needed.

This model connects theory with organisational practices, thereby helping to inform the coherent and evidence-based analysis of AI strategy formulation.

6. RESEARCH METHODOLOGY

This study employs a quantitative research methodology, as researchers use a structured survey instrument to investigate the impact of Artificial Intelligence (AI) on business strategy. Empirical measurement also hypothesis testing stand as the basis for knowledge creation when the approach aligns with positivist assumptions.

i. Research Design

The design encompasses both descriptive and causal-explanatory components. It seeks to uncover relationships between all variables and then quantify each of them. This research may examine existing theories on how technological, organisational, and environmental factors act. AI-integrated firms' calculated performance then gets informed by this testing.

ii. Development of the Instrument

Careful design produced a structured questionnaire. It did contain three distinct parts.

1. Firmographic as well as demographic details such as industry size, and respondent designation.
2. AI Capability Constructs include one thing:
   - Technological readiness (*Tornatzky & Fleischer, 1990)*
   - Organisational capabilities, (Teece, 2007)
   - Institutional pressure (DiMaggio & Powell, 1983).
   - Strategic Performance (Wamba & Queiroz, 2022)

Each variable was measured by a 5-point Likert scale (1 = Strongly Disagree, 5 = Strongly Agree) through 4–6 items. To eliminate ambiguity and refine the wording, an expert panel review and a pilot test (n = 30) were conducted.

iii. Sampling and Data Collection

Across the manufacturing, IT, finance, logistics, and healthcare sectors, the study population consisted of mid- and senior-level managers in firms that have implemented AI solutions. In that study, sectoral and organisational size diversity was ensured through stratified random sampling. A total of 420 questionnaires were distributed by the researchers, yielding 312 valid responses (response rate: 74.3%). During the two-month data collection period, industry workshops provided opportunities for both in-person administration and online submission of forms.

iv. Reliability and Validity

To ensure measurement robustness:

- Cronbach's alpha values regarding all constructs exceeded 0.80. Thus, high internal consistency was indeed indicated.
- Expert review panels from academia, with industry-confirmed content validity. Review allowed them to do this.
- In order to then confirm construct structure, Exploratory Factor Analysis (EFA) with varimax rotation was performed by us. Items with factor loadings below 0.6 or exhibiting high cross-loadings were removed.
- Kaiser-Meyer-Olkin (KMO) test was valued at 0.89, thus showing adequate sampling. Bartlett's test for sphericity revealed significance ($p < 0.001$).

v. Data Analysis Technique

SPSS 28, along with AMOS 24, were used in order to analyse the dataset. Statistical procedures included:

- Descriptive statistics, including mean, SD, skewness, and kurtosis, were used to check data normality
- Bivariate relationships explored via Pearson correlation
- Multiple regression tested direct effects
- Structural Equation Modelling tests mediation, moderation effects, in addition to overall model fit.

We considered CFI beyond 0.90 and TLI beyond 0.90 as model fit indices. RMSEA (less than 0.08) and SRMR (less than 0.08) were other indices that we considered. We tested for mediation using bootstrapping with n equal to 5,000 resamples.

To ensure valid inferences, this methodology enhances the research's empirical rigour and replicability regarding the translation of AI capabilities into calculated outcomes across firms and sectors.

7. DATA ANALYSIS

The analysis was conducted using SPSS and AMOS to validate hypotheses and investigate the impact of AI capabilities on strategic business performance. A total of 312 responses were cleaned and entered into SPSS for statistical analysis.

i. Descriptive Statistics

The sample comprised diverse sectors, with 38% from manufacturing, 22% from IT, 18% from financial services, 12% from healthcare, and 10% from logistics. Respondents' positions included middle management (57%) and senior leadership (43%). Table 1 summarises the demographic characteristics.

Table 1. Demographic Distribution of Respondents

Variable	Categories	Percentage (%)
Sector	Manufacturing	38%
	IT Services	22%
	Finance	18%
	Healthcare	12%
	Logistics	10%
Role	Middle Mgmt	57%
	Senior Mgmt	43%

ii. Reliability Test

Cronbach's alpha values for all variables ranged from 0.812 to 0.907, confirming acceptable reliability. The item-total correlations were all above the 0.5 threshold, indicating high internal consistency and construct reliability.

iii. Correlation Analysis

Pearson correlation coefficients revealed statistically significant and moderately strong positive relationships:

- AI Readiness and Strategic Performance: $r = 0.612$, $p < 0.01$
- Organizational Capability and Strategic Performance: $r = 0.574$, $p < 0.01$
- Institutional Pressure and Strategic Performance: $r = 0.492$, $p < 0.01$

These findings suggest that higher AI preparedness, improved capabilities, and favourable institutional environments are significantly associated with enhanced strategic outcomes.

iv. Regression Analysis

A multiple linear regression model was constructed with strategic performance as the dependent variable. The independent variables were AI readiness, organisational capability, and institutional pressure. The regression equation was statistically significant:

- $F(3, 308) = 41.72$, $p < 0.001$, $R^2 = 0.62$

This indicates that the three predictors together explain 62% of the variance in strategic performance. The standardised beta coefficients showed:

- Technological Readiness ($\beta = 0.342$, $t = 4.81$, $p < 0.001$)
- Organizational Capability ($\beta = 0.294$, $t = 3.97$, $p = 0.001$)
- Institutional Pressure ($\beta = 0.188$, $t = 2.90$, $p = 0.004$)

Table 2. Regression Analysis Summary

Predictor	Beta	t-Value	Sig.
Technological Readiness	0.342	4.81	0.000
Organizational Capability	0.294	3.97	0.001
Institutional Pressure	0.188	2.90	0.004

These results confirm the individual contribution of each variable to enhancing strategic performance.

v. Structural Equation Modelling (SEM)

AMOS was employed for confirmatory factor analysis (CFA) and path modelling to test the conceptual framework. The SEM model demonstrated excellent fit:

- Chi-square/df = 1.89
- CFI = 0.937
- TLI = 0.926
- RMSEA = 0.048
- SRMR = 0.036

All hypothesised paths were significant ($p < 0.05$). Mediation analysis via bootstrapping (5,000 samples) confirmed that **organisational capability** significantly mediates the effect of **technological readiness** on **strategic performance**.

vi. Visual Model Output

Figure 1. Structural Model of AI Capabilities and Strategic Performance

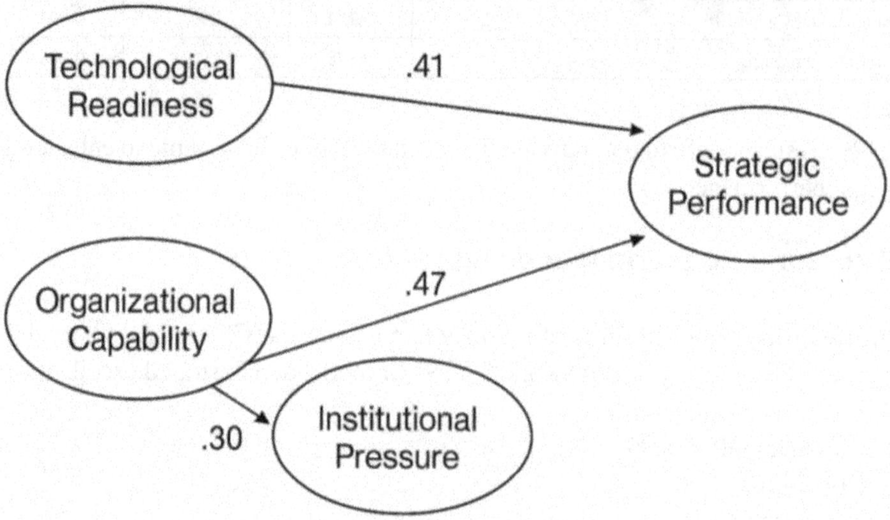

[SEM diagram here illustrating positive paths: Technological Readiness → Organisational Capability → Strategic Performance; and Institutional Pressure → Strategic Performance. The mediation path is highlighted.]

The SEM model supports the hypothesised relationships and reinforces the role of AI preparedness, internal capability development, and external regulatory adaptation in achieving strategic business objectives.

8. DISCUSSION

The findings from this study reinforce the significant influence of artificial intelligence (AI) capabilities on enhancing planned business outcomes. This section combines empirical results with theoretical perceptions, helping us to gain a deeper understanding of how AI readiness, organisational ability, and institutional pressure will improve calculated performance across various sectors.

i. Theoretical Implications

Technology adoption outcomes can be shaped collectively through both internal and external contexts within the validated Technology-Organisation-Environment

(TOE) framework (Tornatzky & Fleischer, 1990). Technological readiness is a highly influential predictor of planned performance, emphasising the key role of strong digital infrastructure (Wamba & Queiroz, 2022).

Organisational capability both directly influences planned performance and also mediates the effect of technological readiness. This supports dynamic capability theory, with adaptive organisational learning and transformation important for leveraging technological assets effectively (Teece, 2007). Singh et al. also align with these findings, as they found that calculated agility leads to improved competitiveness, supported by dynamic capabilities.

ii. Managerial Insights

Practically, the study highlights the value of proactive investment in technological tools and workforce upskilling. That functional departments develop AI literacy should be a priority for managers. Technology integration will proceed easily. Technological readiness is one factor that determines the success of integration; yet, cultural readiness also matters. Key factors include leadership support and interdepartmental collaboration.

Institutional pressures, particularly in highly regulated sectors such as healthcare and finance, compel strategists to comply with and align their strategies with national and international AI governance frameworks (Commission Work Programme 2023 - European Commission, n.d.). For a comprehensive regulatory framework, the EU AI Act serves as the primary reference. Companies operating in these fields should align with AI ethics guidelines. This alignment is necessary for reducing legal and reputational risks (European Approach to Artificial Intelligence | Shaping Europe's Digital Future, n.d.)

iii. Sectoral Variations

When different sectors are analysed, manufacturing and IT firms reveal the highest readiness and capability alignment, suggesting that these industries lead the digital transformation curve. Chatterjee et al. support these results, as they reported that AI deployment fosters process innovation and efficiency gains in technologically advanced sectors (Chatterjee, S., Rana, N.P., Tamilmani, K. and Sharma, A. (2021). Robots using AI influence how satisfied customers are. AI-enabled service robots also impact business agility (Dwivedi et al., 2021).

Healthcare and logistics lag behind in AI implementation, with the acknowledgement of potential hindered by concerns over data sensitivity and digital talent shortages. Thus, sector-specific policies, along with training plans, are vital. AI service provider partnerships may help firms in these sectors close capability gaps.

iv. Model Robustness and Strategic Fit

Strong fit indices from the SEM analysis confirm the robustness of the structural model. Firms cannot rely on technological assets alone: the mediating effect of organisational capability offers an important perspective. For planned value creation from AI adoption, top leadership support and cross-functional coordination with cohesive internal alignment are what is demanded.

To summarise, the discussion confirms the integrated model suggested here and corresponds with current academic writing urging studies of digital change that prove contextual, theory-based, and performance-led. In the future, researchers should study just how these dynamics evolve. They should also use longitudinal studies that examine different geographical regions over time.

9. OUTCOME

This chapter examined the multidimensional relationship between artificial intelligence (AI) and calculated business performance, grounding it theoretically and investigating it empirically, while also providing sectoral perspectives. The effectiveness of AI implementation is shaped by institutional pressure, organisational capability, and AI readiness. These factors have been established as playing pivotal roles in this context. Among these, organisational capability not only contributes directly but also mediates, reinforcing the need for cohesive digital transformation strategies.

Integrating the Technology-Organisation-Environment (TOE) framework with dynamic capability theory, the study contributes to the growing literature on AI adoption, presenting a model to understand how firms achieve sustainable competitive advantage (Tornatzky & Fleischer, 1990). Innovation in technology involves multiple processes. These processes are necessary for technological advancement (Tornatzky & Fleischer, 1990). Enterprise performance is inherently sustainable: Explicating dynamic capabilities in addition to micro-foundations (Arifin & Frmanzah, 2015). Addressing the role within institutional contexts and internal readiness in easing AI-driven planned decision-making fills prominent gaps in the literature (Holloway, 2025).

That chapter emphasises that AI integration is successful with more than just technical infrastructure. This is indeed an essential managerial point. Leadership commitment, combined with cultural readiness through continuous learning and interdepartmental collaboration, is required (Wamba & Queiroz, 2022). Firms are increasingly experiencing the massive impact of artificial intelligence (AI), with many achieving quantifiable differences in performance and efficiency. To minimise risks, compliance with ethical standards, along with evolving AI regulations, must be fully prioritised in highly regulated sectors (Robles & Mallinson, 2023). For instance, the European Commission's Artificial Intelligence Act (2023) outlines specific obligations that are for high-risk AI applications, which require that auditors proceed and be overseen by humans (Commission Work Programme 2023 - European Commission, n.d.) .

The chapter acknowledges the limitations in its geographic and temporal scope, while the empirical results provide affirmation of the model's proposed robustness. The analysis was indeed cross-sectional, and most participating firms came from emerging economies. To validate and extend these findings, future research should explore the longitudinal impacts and conduct comparative studies across economies with varying digital maturity and regulatory landscapes (Chatterjee, S., Rana, N.P., Tamilmani, K. and Sharma, A. (2021). AI-enabled service robots impact business agility and customer satisfaction (Sharma et al., n.d.).

This chapter provides organisations with a planned roadmap. They can utilise it to harness AI as a transformative force. To promote stability, companies must align their tech plans with company talent and marketplace rules to ensure continued success and create value.

10. MANAGERIAL IMPLICATIONS

The practical implications of this study hold significant value for managers and decision-makers as they navigate the digital transformation landscape. AI still overturns typical business structures. Therefore, organisational leaders should develop such strong, calculated frameworks that AI technologies can integrate with effectively and responsibly.

i. Building Digital Readiness

Executives should upskill their workforce and invest in foundational infrastructure to improve digital readiness. AI capabilities can be better exploited for calculated advantage by firms that will prioritise digital literacy across all organisational levels (Wamba-Taguimdje et al., 2020). Investments should be applied to cybersecurity protocols and data management systems. About agile decision-making and innovation, cloud-based platforms also require these investments.

ii. Change Management within Organisational Culture

Cultures must be ready, though they often overlook AI adoption. This adoption is critical. Smooth integration is obstructed by resistance to change, siloed departments within, and a lack of trust in AI-driven decisions (Robles & Mallinson, 2023). Managers must innovate within a culture that encourages cross-functional collaborators, along with experimenters. When employees interact with AI tools, they are strengthened. This interaction may foster transparency along with trust within algorithmic processes.

iii. Ethical AI Governance remains essential. Regulatory Compliance is indeed also substantial.

AI is deployed in sectors such as healthcare, banking, and public services, closely aligned with compliance and data governance (Chatterjee, S., Rana, N.P., Tamilmani, K. and Sharma, A. (2021). Business agility and the impact on customer satisfaction from AI-enabled service robots (Ortiz De Guinea & Raymond, 2020). Managers must proactively align the organisational practices with the local and international regulatory requirements, as the EU AI Act requires them to do (Commission Work Programme 2023 - European Commission, n.d.). A thorough regulatory framework, namely the EU AI Act, establishing ethics committees or having internal review boards can guide the responsible use of AI and support compliance efforts, thereby minimising any legal and reputational risks (European Approach to Artificial Intelligence | Shaping Europe's Digital Future, n.d.).

Calculated Resource Allocation

The evolving nature of AI adoption should be a reflection of the allocation of resources. Managers should allocate a more sufficient budget and time toward more feedback loops, along with pilot testing and simple experimentation beyond capital investments. Firms that adopt a phased approach begin with low-risk AI initiatives and gradually scale them up, which tends to result in higher success rates (MODGIL 2022 Artificial Intelligence for Supply Chain (AAM).Pdf, n.d.).

Leadership and Vision

AI strategies align with broader business goals due to leadership's more pivotal role. Senior management must articulate a clear AI vision, establish measurable objectives, and monitor performance indicators (Teece, 2007). The nature with micro foundations of (sustainable) enterprise performance: Explicating dynamic capabilities. Transformational leaders reinforce accountability mechanisms, ease alignment across departments, and drive commitment at all levels.

Figure 2. Priority Area for Manager in AI Adoption

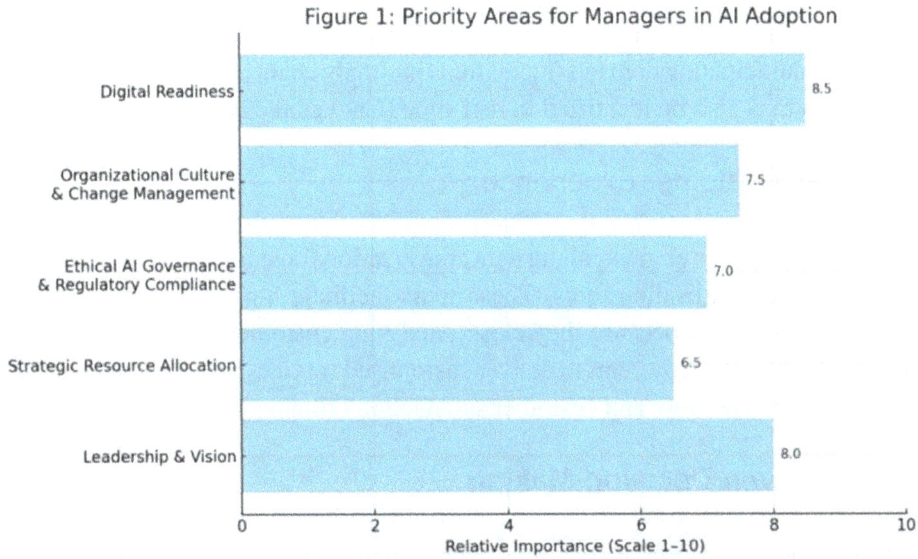

This graph visually represents the relative importance of calculated focus areas for AI-adopting managers, based on emphasis and frequency in empirical and theoretical studies.

In summary, executives anticipate and then adjust to maximise AI's overall power. Firms invest in new technology to transform their culture, and they anticipate ethical issues so they can be better equipped to navigate uncertainties. These firms will be leaders in the AI economy.

11. PRACTICAL IMPLICATIONS

Integration of artificial intelligence (AI) into strategy has practical implications. These implications extend across many industries and operational dimensions for businesses. AI technologies are growing and spreading. Therefore, companies must aim to implement AI to deliver measurable, sustainable value, rather than experimenting conceptually.

i. Operational Efficiency and Cost Optimisation

We see one practical benefit from AI most immediately as the optimised operation of processes. AI-powered systems can automate routine and repetitive tasks. Meaningful cost cuts and time savings occur as a result of this (Brynjolfsson & Mcafee, 2017; The Business of Artificial Intelligence, n.d.). Predictive analytics can improve by anticipating demand fluctuations in supply chain management. Potential disruptions may also be identified in real-time (Choi et al., 2018).

Enhanced Customer Experience

Recommendation engines, along with conversational agents (chatbots), represent AI-enabled personalisation tools. These tools facilitate highly tailored customer interactions precisely because they exist. Analysing customer preferences and behaviours enables these systems to deliver customised services, resulting in increased lifetime value, retention, and customer satisfaction (Huang & Rust, 2018).

ii. Data-Driven Decision-Making

Data-driven, real-time perceptions enable more informed decision-making for AI-adopting organisations. This enhances the monitoring of performance, the assessment of risk, and tactical planning. Businesses are gaining a competitive edge by embedding AI into their analytics infrastructure, enabling them to identify trends and anomalies more quickly (Davenport & Ronanki, 2018).

AI fosters innovation through enabling rapid prototyping. Thus, new services and products are efficiently developed. Because it reduces market failure risk, companies can utilise AI-driven simulations to test new ideas before launch. Robotic process automation (RPA) and natural language processing (NLP) can transform service delivery in the service industry (Wamba-Taguimdje et al., 2020b), (Sahut et al., 2022).

Workforce Transformation and Skills Development

Workforce management has significant implications for the adoption of deep AI. Automation can displace some roles, yet it also demands new skill sets. Workers are studying data science to explore AI ethics, enabling them to pursue human-AI collaboration. Organisations must invest in reskilling and upskilling initiatives to ensure their workforce remains competitive and adaptable (Mgi-Notes-from-the-Ai-Frontier-Modeling-the-Impact-of-Ai-on-the-World-Economy-September-2018. Ashx, n.d.).

Risk Management and Compliance

In regulated industries, AI can identify operational risks, detect fraudulent activities, and monitor real-time compliance. Financial institutions are deploying AI to enhance anti-money laundering (AML) and know-your-customer (KYC) processes (Bouveret, 2018).

Proper governance frameworks should ensure transparency and prevent ethical lapses.

Figure 3. AI Integration Across Business Functions

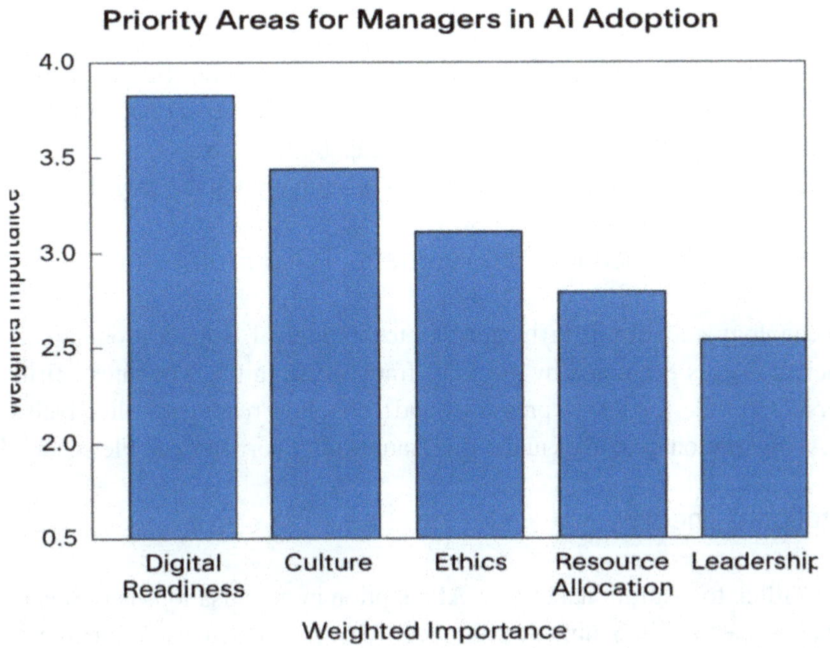

This diagram illustrates the multifaceted impact of AI on various business operations, emphasising areas such as operational efficiency, customer experience, decision-making, innovation, workforce development, and risk management.

The integration of artificial intelligence (AI) into business strategy implies theoretical importance, which also requires re-examining classical and modern organisational theories. For interpreting the dynamics and the transformative impact on firms, it relies on several theoretical frameworks related to AI adoption.

i. IResource-Based View (RBV)

The RBV posits that a firm's sustained competitive advantage stems from its ability to manage and acquire resources that are valuable, rare, inimitable, and VRIN. AI capabilities fulfil these very criteria. These capabilities include proprietary algorithms, curated datasets, and advanced analytics infrastructure. AI integrates itself within the RBV framework, highlighting how firms leverage intangible technological resources to achieve calculated differentiation and long-term success (Barney, 1991).

Dynamic Capabilities Theory

This theory emphasises how a firm can integrate, build, and reconfigure internal and external competencies in response to rapid environmental changes. This theory does align with the calculated deployment of AI systems. Firms find that AI systems increase sensing, seizing, and transforming capabilities. Firms possessing greater dynamic capabilities will probably integrate AI adaptively and scalably (Teece, 2007).

Technology-Organisation-Environment (TOE) Framework

Technology adoption is influenced by technological, organisational, and environmental factors examined by the TOE framework. In the AI context, firm size, leadership attitude, regulatory pressures, and technology readiness collectively influence AI integration outcomes under this framework (Tornatzky & Fleischer, 1990)

Institutional Theory

According to institutional theory, AI adoption in organisations is influenced by normative, coercive, and mimetic pressures. To conform to industry norms, respond to regulatory requirements, or emulate successful competitors, firms may adopt AI not just for efficiency gains (DiMaggio & Powell, 1983).

ii. Actor-Network Theory (ANT)

ANT explores the interrelationships between humans and non-human actors, such as AI systems and algorithms, creating calculated social realities. Analysing how AI reshapes the accountability, trust, and decision-making authority within business processes is particularly useful (Latour, 2005).

AI's multidimensional impacts on business strategy are understood thoroughly through these various theories together. Also underscored is the need for hybrid theoretical models that can accommodate the unique characteristics of AI technologies, such as autonomy, opacity, and adaptability.

12. RECOMMENDATIONS

Since Artificial Intelligence (AI) is expected to evolve in 2025, organisations must remain alert. Effective use of AI needs planned methodologies now. Recommendations find grounding through recent industry developments and research findings. The recommendations follow.

Establish a Clear AI Vision and Strategy

Organisations should articulate a thorough AI vision that aligns with their overarching business objectives. AI initiatives are integrated within the core business strategy, identifying key performance indicators (KPIs), and setting measurable goals (PricewaterhouseCoopers, n.d.).

Foster Cross-Functional Collaboration

Successful AI implementation requires departmental collaboration for efficacy. AI solutions can be holistic and address diverse business needs by enabling organisations to form interdisciplinary teams, including members from IT, operations, marketing, and human resources (Trovato, 2025).

Prioritise Responsible and Ethical AI Practices

As AI systems gain autonomy, it is crucial to establish clear ethical guidelines and robust governance frameworks. To build trust among stakeholders and comply with emerging regulations, organisations should focus on transparency, fairness, and accountability (Mittelstadt et al., 2016).

- **Invest in Workforce Upskilling and Change Management**

Companies should invest in training programs to equip employees with the necessary skills for working with AI technologies, thereby reducing the challenges of AI adoption. To help foster continuous learning, effective change management strategies are crucial for easing smooth transitions (Mgi-Notes-from-the-Ai-Frontier-Modeling-the-Impact-of-Ai-on-the-World-Economy-September-2018.Ashx, n.d.).

Enhance Data Infrastructure and Quality

For effective AI systems, a strong data infrastructure serves as their backbone. Organisations must ensure data accessibility, security, and quality to enable accurate and reliable outcomes from AI models. Data governance and management tools include investment (Marr, 2017).

Engage with Regulatory Bodies and Industry Standards

Organisations stay abreast of regulatory developments and, therefore, can navigate the complex legal landscape involving AI. Firms also join industry standard-setting plans that allow navigation of the AI-involved legal world. When there is proactive engagement, companies are positioned as leaders, ensuring the responsible deployment of AI (Executive Program in Social Innovation Design, n.d.).

Promote Continuous Innovation and Research Collaboration

Companies can remain revolutionary in AI through collaboration. Academic institutions as well as research organisations are driving these AI advancements at present. Partnerships like these can help develop cutting-edge solutions, while also contributing to the broader AI ecosystem (ITPro). IT leaders' lack of trust in AI agents (2025) results in missed significant financial gains. Because IT leaders do not yet trust AI agents, huge financial gains are being missed.

13. CONCLUSION

As Artificial Intelligence (AI) continues to reshape business strategies, several emerging areas warrant more academic and practical exploration.

Agentic AI and Human-AI Collaboration

AI with agency is evolving, and such systems can now make independent decisions. This development has brought about new dynamics into organisational workflows. According to research, such systems can improve efficiency. Trust is a significant barrier that hinders the widespread adoption of this technology. Frameworks that strike an impressive balance between autonomy and human oversight, thereby fostering trust and effective collaboration, should be a focus of future studies [MDPI] (Kitsios & Kamariotou, 2021).

AI Governance and Ethical Frameworks

Strong governance structures must be established as AI's influence continues to grow. The current literature stresses that ethical guidelines must address such issues. These issues feature transparency, accountability, and fairness. More research is needed so researchers can craft governance models suited for AI's growth (SmartDev - Al Powered Software Development, n.d.). These are strategies to drive businesses forward.

Integration of AI with Emerging Technologies

As AI converges with technologies like the Internet of Things (IoT), augmented reality (AR), and blockchain, new opportunities and challenges emerge. Future research can investigate the ways to optimise these integrations. This research guarantees future benefit (Rahman et al., 2024).

Environmental Impact of AI

As AI systems become increasingly common, their environmental footprint also grows. To mitigate negative ecological impacts, research into sustainable AI practices is crucial, including the development of energy-efficient algorithms and hardware (Wang et al., 2024).

AI in Small and Medium Enterprises (SMEs)

SMEs often face barriers, whereas large corporations integrate AI due to their resources. AI benefits can be democratised through the exploration of cost-effective and scalable AI solutions tailored for SMEs. AI is helpful since small businesses compete with larger firms (A SEM–ANN Analysis to Examine Impact of Artificial Intelligence Technologies on Sustainable Performance of SMEs | Scientific Reports, n.d.).

Explainable AI (XAI)

The complexity of AI models is a hindrance to user trust because it often results in a lack of transparency. XAI advancements seek interpretability beyond. Focus remains on AI decisions. Future research should develop XAI methods that are user-friendly and effective. (Saeed & Omlin, 2021).

REFERENCES

A SEM–ANN analysis to examine impact of artificial intelligence technologies on sustainable performance of SMEs I Scientific Reports. (n.d.). Retrieved August 7, 2025, from https://www.nature.com/articles/s41598-025-86464-3?utm_source=chatgpt.com

Arifin, Z., & Frmanzah, . (2015). The Effect of Dynamic Capability to Technology Adoption and its Determinant Factors for Improving Firm's Performance; Toward a Conceptual Model. *Procedia: Social and Behavioral Sciences*, *207*, 786–796. DOI: 10.1016/j.sbspro.2015.10.168

Huang, M. H., & Rust, R. T. (2018). Artificial intelligence in service. *Journal of Service Research*, *21*(2), 155–172.

Barney, J. (1991). Firm Resources and Sustained Competitive Advantage. *Journal of Management*, *17*(1), 99–120. DOI: 10.1177/014920639101700108

Bouveret, A. (2018). Cyber Risk for the Financial Sector: A Framework for Quantitative Assessment, WP/18/143, July 2018. Retrieved August 7, 2025, from https://papers.ssrn.com/sol3/papers.cfm?abstract_id=3203026

Choi, T. M., Wallace, S. W., & Wang, Y. (2018). Big data analytics in operations management. *Production and Operations Management*, *27*(10), 1868–1883.

Brynjolfsson, E., & Mcafee, A. (2017) The Business of Artificial Intelligence. Harvard Business Review, 7, 3-11. Retrieved August 7, 2025, from https://www.scirp.org/reference/referencespapers?referenceid=3524395

Chatterjee, S., Rana, N. P., Tamilmani, K., & Sharma, A. (2021). The effect of AI-based CRM on organization performance and competitive advantage: An empirical analysis in the B2B context. *Industrial Marketing Management*, *97*, 205–219. DOI: 10.1016/j.indmarman.2021.07.013

Chatterjee, S., Rana, N. P., Tamilmani, K., & Sharma, A. (2021) The Role of Artificial Intelligence in Reshaping Digital Marketing A Review and Research Agenda. Journal of Business Research, 124, 202-217. - Retrieved August 7, 2025, from https://www.scirp.org/reference/referencespapers?referenceid=4040078

Chen, Y., Wang, Y., Nevo, S., Jin, J., Wang, L., & Chow, W. S. (2014). IT capability and organizational performance: The roles of business process agility and environmental factors. *European Journal of Information Systems*, *23*(3), 326–342. DOI: 10.1057/ejis.2013.4

Commission work programme 2023—European Commission. (n.d.). Retrieved August 6, 2025, from https://commission.europa.eu/strategy-and-policy/strategy-documents/commission-work-programme/commission-work-programme-2023_en

Davenport, T. H., & Ronanki, R. (2018). Artificial Intelligence for the Real World. Harvard Business Review (HBR). - Retrieved August 7, 2025, from https://www.scirp.org/reference/referencespapers?referenceid=3166319

Dellermann, D., Lipusch, N., Ebel, P., & Leimeister, J. M. (2019). Design principles for a hybrid intelligence decision support system for business model validation. *Electronic Markets*, *29*(3), 423–441. DOI: 10.1007/s12525-018-0309-2

Digital Economy Report 2021 | UN Trade and Development (UNCTAD). (n.d.). Retrieved August 1, 2025, from https://unctad.org/page/digital-economy-report-2021

DiMaggio, P. J., & Powell, W. W. (1983). The Iron Cage Revisited: Institutional Isomorphism and Collective Rationality in Organizational Fields. *American Sociological Review*, *48*(2), 147. DOI: 10.2307/2095101

Dwivedi, Y. K., Hughes, L., Ismagilova, E., Aarts, G., Coombs, C., Crick, T., Duan, Y., Dwivedi, R., Edwards, J., Eirug, A., Galanos, V., Ilavarasan, P. V., Janssen, M., Jones, P., Kar, A. K., Kizgin, H., Kronemann, B., Lal, B., Lucini, B., & Williams, M. D. (2021). Artificial Intelligence (AI): Multidisciplinary perspectives on emerging challenges, opportunities, and agenda for research, practice and policy. *International Journal of Information Management*, *57*, 101994. DOI: 10.1016/j.ijinfomgt.2019.08.002

Elwaked, D. K., Kassim, N. M., & Thurasamy, R. (n.d.). Enhancing Internal Integration Through Ai: A Resource-Based View With Data-Driven Culture As Moderator.

European approach to artificial intelligence | Shaping Europe's digital future. (n.d.). Retrieved August 7, 2025, from https://digital-strategy.ec.europa.eu/en/policies/european-approach-artificial-intelligence

Executive Program in Social Innovation Design. (n.d.). The Center for Social Impact Strategy. Retrieved August 7, 2025, from https://csis.upenn.edu/executive-program/xsd/

Ghimire, P., Kim, K., & Acharya, M. (2024). Opportunities and Challenges of Generative AI in Construction Industry: Focusing on Adoption of Text-Based Models. *Buildings (Basel, Switzerland)*, *14*(1), 1. Advance online publication. DOI: 10.3390/buildings14010220

India banking and finance report 2024. (2024). Academic Foundation in association with National Institute of Bank Management (NIBM), Pune.

Kitsios, F., & Kamariotou, M. (2021). Artificial Intelligence and Business Strategy towards Digital Transformation: A Research Agenda. *Sustainability (Basel)*, *13*(4), 4. Advance online publication. DOI: 10.3390/su13042025

Kumar, S., Arya, R. K., Singh, N., & Singh, S. (2024). Productivity of rainfed maize as influenced by hydrogel and mulching under conventional and zero tillage in maize–wheat cropping system. *Cereal Research Communications*, *52*(2), 885–898.

Latour, B. (2005). *Reassembling the social: An introduction to actor-network-theory*. Oxford university press.

Lee, K. F. (2018). AI Superpowers China, Silicon Valley, and the New World Order. Houghton Mifflin Harcourt. - Retrieved August 1, 2025, from https://www.scirp.org/reference/referencespapers?referenceid=3933846

Li, K., Cai, Y., Pei, Y., & Yuan, C. (2025). The impact of artificial intelligence adoption on firms' innovation performance in the digital era: Based on dynamic capabilities theory. *International Theory and Practice in Humanities and Social Sciences*, *2*(3), 3. Advance online publication. DOI: 10.70693/itphss.v2i3.343

Lorente-Martínez, J., Navío-Marco, J., & Rodrigo-Moya, B. (2022). Are retailers leveraging in-store analytics? An exploratory study. *International Journal of Retail & Distribution Management*, *50*(5), 599–618. DOI: 10.1108/IJRDM-04-2020-0151

Marr, B. (2017). Data Strategy How to Profit from a World of Big Data, Analytics and the Internet of Things. London Kogan Page Ltd. - Retrieved August 7, 2025, from https://www.scirp.org/reference/referencespapers?referenceid=2760459

Mgi-notes-from-the-ai-frontier-modeling-the-impact-of-ai-on-the-world-economy-september-2018.ashx. (n.d.). Retrieved August 7, 2025, from https://www.mckinsey.com/~/media/mckinsey/featured%20insights/artificial%20intelligence/notes%20from%20the%20frontier%20modeling%20the%20impact%20of%20ai%20on%20the%20world%20economy/mgi-notes-from-the-ai-frontier-modeling-the-impact-of-ai-on-the-world-economy-september-2018.ashx MODGIL 2022 Artificial intelligence for supply chain (AAM).pdf

Musleh Al-Sartawi, A. M. A., Al-Qudah, A. A., & Shihadeh, F. (Eds.). (2024). *Artificial Intelligence-Augmented Digital Twins: Transforming Industrial Operations for Innovation and Sustainability* (Vol. 503). Springer Nature Switzerland., DOI: 10.1007/978-3-031-43490-7

Ortiz De Guinea, A., & Raymond, L. (2020). Enabling innovation in the face of uncertainty through IT ambidexterity: A fuzzy set qualitative comparative analysis of industrial service SMEs. *International Journal of Information Management, 50*, 244–260. DOI: 10.1016/j.ijinfomgt.2019.05.007

Massood, A. (2025, May 14). Measuring the Effectiveness of AI Adoption: Definitions, Frameworks, and Evolving Benchmarks. Medium. https://medium.com/@adnanmasood/measuring-the-effectiveness-of-ai-adoption-definitions-frameworks-and-evolving-benchmarks-63b8b2c7d194

PricewaterhouseCoopers. (n.d.). 2025 AI Business Predictions. PwC. Retrieved August 7, 2025, from https://www.pwc.com/us/en/tech-effect/ai-analytics/ai-predictions.html

Rahman, A., Kundu, D., Debnath, T., Rahman, M., & Islam, M. J. (2024). Blockchain-based AI Methods for Managing Industrial IoT: Recent Developments, Integration Challenges and Opportunities. https://doi.org//arXiv.2405.12550DOI: 10.48550

Robles, P., & Mallinson, D. (2023). West Darrel M and Allen John R (2020) Turning Point: Policymaking in the Era of Artificial Intelligence. *Science & Technology Studies*, *36*(3), 3. Advance online publication. DOI: 10.23987/sts.125194

Saeed, W., & Omlin, C. (2021). Explainable AI (XAI): A Systematic Meta-Survey of Current Challenges and Future Opportunities (No. arXiv:2111.06420). arXiv. https://doi.org//arXiv.2111.06420DOI: 10.48550

Sahut, J.-M., Schweizer, D., & Peris-Ortiz, M. (2022). Technological forecasting and social change introduction to the VSI technological innovations to ensure confidence in the digital world. *Technological Forecasting and Social Change*, *179*, 121680. DOI: 10.1016/j.techfore.2022.121680

Sharma, A., Rana, N. P., & Nunkoo, R. (n.d.). Fifty years of information management research: A conceptual structure analysis using structural topic modeling. Elsevier, Volume 58(June 2021), 102316.

Singh, D. P. D. (2024). Generative AI through the Lens of Institutional Theory (SSRN Scholarly Paper No. 4953180). Social Science Research Network. DOI: 10.2139/ssrn.4953180

SmartDev—AI Powered Software Development. (n.d.). SmartDev. Retrieved August 7, 2025, from https://smartdev.com/

Teece, D. J. (2007). Explicating dynamic capabilities: The nature and microfoundations of (sustainable) enterprise performance. *Strategic Management Journal*, *28*(13), 1319–1350. DOI: 10.1002/smj.640

The Business of Artificial Intelligence. (n.d.). Retrieved August 1, 2025, from https://hbr.org/2017/07/the-business-of-artificial-intelligence

The Digital Transformation of SMEs. (2021, February 3). OECD. https://www.oecd.org/en/publications/the-digital-transformation-of-smes_bdb9256a-en.html

Mittelstadt, B. D., Allo, P., Taddeo, M., Wachter, S., & Floridi, L. (2016). The ethics of algorithms: Mapping the debate. *Big Data & Society*, *3*(2), 2053951716679679.

Tornatzky, L. G., & Fleischer, M. (1990) The Processes of Technological Innovation. Lexington Books, Lexington. - Retrieved August 6, 2025, from https://www.scirp.org/reference/referencespapers?referenceid=1771512

Trovato, S. (2025, May 19). From hype to real business impact: How to lead AI transformation in 2025. Monday.Com Blog. https://monday.com/blog/project-management/ai-transformation/

Van Quaquebeke, N., Tonidandel, S., & Banks, G. C. (2025). Beyond efficiency: How artificial intelligence (AI) will reshape scientific inquiry and the publication process. *The Leadership Quarterly*, *36*(4), 101895. DOI: 10.1016/j.leaqua.2025.101895

Vial, G. (2019). Understanding digital transformation: A review and a research agenda. *The Journal of Strategic Information Systems*, *28*(2), 118–144. DOI: 10.1016/j.jsis.2019.01.003

Wamba, S. F., & Queiroz, M. M. (2022). A Framework Based on Blockchain, Artificial Intelligence, and Big Data Analytics to Leverage Supply Chain Resilience considering the COVID-19. *IFAC-PapersOnLine*, *55*(10), 2396–2401. DOI: 10.1016/j.ifacol.2022.10.067 PMID: 38620980

Wamba-Taguimdje, S.-L., Fosso Wamba, S., Kala Kamdjoug, J. R., & Tchatchouang Wanko, C. E. (2020). Influence of artificial intelligence (AI) on firm performance: The business value of AI-based transformation projects. *Business Process Management Journal*, *26*(7), 1893–1924. DOI: 10.1108/BPMJ-10-2019-0411

Wang, Q., Li, Y., & Li, R. (2024). Ecological footprints, carbon emissions, and energy transitions: The impact of artificial intelligence (AI). *Humanities & Social Sciences Communications*, *11*(1), 1043. DOI: 10.1057/s41599-024-03520-5

Westerman, G., Bonnet, D., & McAfee, A. (2014). Leading Digital Turning Technology into Business Transformation. Harvard Business Press. - Retrieved August 1, 2025, from https://www.scirp.org/reference/referencespapers?referenceid=3404468

Yu, X., Washida, Y., & Sasaki, M. (2022). Impact of qualified gatekeepers on team absorptive capacity: The mediating role of knowledge combination capability. *Journal of Knowledge Management*, *26*(11), 259–292. DOI: 10.1108/JKM-04-2022-0331

Chapter 3
AI Technology Management Growth in Developed and Developing Countries:
Bridging Innovation and Inclusion for Sustainable Development

Wasswa Shafik
https://orcid.org/0000-0002-9320-3186
Dig Connectivity Research Laboratory (DCRLab), Uganda

ABSTRACT

Artificial Intelligence (AI) technology management has emerged as a critical driver of economic growth and innovation in both developed and developing countries. In developed nations, robust infrastructure, advanced research ecosystems, and strong regulatory frameworks have accelerated AI adoption, fostering efficiency, productivity, and competitive advantage across industries. Conversely, developing countries face unique challenges, including limited resources, skill gaps, and infrastructural constraints. However, they also present significant growth potential through AI-driven solutions in sectors like agriculture, healthcare, and education, addressing socio-economic disparities. This study explores the contrasting dynamics of AI technology management in these regions, highlighting key factors influencing growth, such as policy development, investment trends, talent cultivation, and ethical considerations promoting inclusive, sustainable development while mitigating risks related to data privacy, bias, and digital inequality.

DOI: 10.4018/979-8-3373-2497-5.ch003

1. INTRODUCTION

Artificial Intelligence (AI) has emerged as an important area to be managed both in developed and developing countries. Its technological advancement and the increasing rate of AI-embedded applications in several sectors contribute toward the economic growth of several countries, at the same time generating new and old inequalities in digital, social, economic, and human areas. The developments and enhancements need an effective management strategy. AI has various dimensions covering its evolution, innovation, impact, governance, and solutions for various issues at both internal and external levels (Demirkiran & Öztürko lu, 2022). The major concern is, therefore, to develop innovative strategies for managing AI and to address certain issues on why, what, for whom, how, and without ethical considerations, which are relevant today and in the future. It has, therefore, been decided to prepare material with the main theme of "AI: Technology and Management," aiming at meeting the challenges of AI's application with both an academic and industrial perspective addressing a global audience.

Seven sub-theme questions have been highlighted, namely innovation, evolution, applications, development, opportunities, growth, and challenges of AI (Shafik, 2024a). AI technology management is imperative to the economies of developed and developing countries. AI technology is rapidly growing in developed and developing countries. Technological tools and systems, including big data, cloud computing, machine learning, and robotics, are used to mine intelligence and meaning from data. The integration of these intelligent processes in society and businesses continues to expand the economic and social structures of countries. The Fourth Industrial Revolution (FIR), centered on intelligent smart city applications, is expected to reconfigure service delivery across sectors such as healthcare, education, renewable energy systems, digital safety and security, traffic management, asset management, e-payment, logistics, water, pollution and waste management, smart agriculture, tourism and hospitality, industry, banking and financial services, insurance, and transport (Shafik, 2024b). The speed and scope of AI in areas affecting the wealth creation and well-being of developed and developing countries require a strategic approach to both responsible ethics and speed of adoption. The responsible ethics approach deals with the development, design, and management of technology. The speed of adoption addresses how large technological innovations are efficiently brought about in organizations, the national economy, and society at large, and includes natural environmental processes (Fortuna et al., 2020).

AI technology has attracted considerable attention in developed and developing countries around the world due to its range of applications across different sectors. It is expected to result not only in technological advancements but also in economic growth and improved living standards. The large global economic impact of the new applications of AI and the intensive use of supervised learning is primarily due to its potential for automation of both cognitive and interactive tasks in many sectors, not just manufacturing and production. To date, relatively few studies have been conducted to compare the AI development of a group of developing countries with developed countries in this study (Chang, 2022). Therefore, this paper starts with a focus on a single research gap in AI technology-related activities and then tries to fill that gap. The main focus of this paper is to answer the major research questions: What are the disparities in AI technology application and management in developing countries compared to developed countries, and why? This study aims to determine the connection between AI technology management and the economic performance of twenty countries, including ten developed and ten developing countries. A qualitative dataset was obtained and subsequently appraised utilizing the primary component analysis framework (Bartosik-Purgat & Filimon, 2022). This study evaluates the global significance of the disparities in artificial intelligence technology management and its relevance to the economic growth of both developed and developing countries. Crucial variables, such as economic expansion and competitiveness that have the potential to lead to AI technology growth are also explored, particularly disparities in research and development (R&D) activities inside these countries. This comprehensive assessment allows for cross-sectional data to be used in developed and emerging countries. Overall, this article has been structured into five sections to describe and evaluate how disparities in AI technology management influence the economic performance of both developed and developing countries (Chang, 2022). The study applies the principal axis factoring statistical method to empirical data of twenty countries, comprising two groups of ten developed and ten developing. Before the data analysis, the principal component test was used to scrutinize the KMO and Bartlett's test.

1.1 Background and Significance

A. Technological Advancement: Advancements in information technology are critically shaping the world and are now at the core of most business operations. A percentage of the final price of goods and services around the globe is comprised of the cost of digital technologies upon which they depend. AI is transitioning from cliché to industry standard to a benchmark that is eventually leading to—based on the industry—entirely different definitions of what is possible. AI is driving shifts in how industries invest, requiring a different kind of research into return on investment (ROI) (Shafik, 2024c). After years of AI fanfare, many organizations have successfully adopted AI and are reaping its benefits throughout various industries. New AI techniques, such as deep learning strategies, have revolutionized how organizations develop and apply AI solutions. Deep learning is transforming traditional AI, including expert systems, machine learning, genetic algorithms, fuzzy systems, and data-based systems, by using multiple layers of representation. AI is bringing performance improvements to a growing range of industries, including consumer products, natural resource industries, electric power, clean energy, mining, processing, transportation systems, electronics and semiconductors, medical devices, industrial goods, professional services, and agriculture (Shafik, 2025). As a result, AI is in danger of becoming not just a competitive or comparative advantage but a new industry standard. The benefits of AI are especially transformative in the healthcare sector because the deep learning systems behind this technology are able to discover and structure information in large datasets, creating a knowledge base that can inform decisions ranging from personalized medications to healthcare prevention models. The Readiness of Countries for AI Several studies and reports claim that not all countries are ready to benefit from the power of AI solutions fully. In a series of "readiness for AI" studies conducted across the globe, almost all countries are "development" or "emerging" markets and are located in Africa, Latin America, Eastern Europe, and South Asia. More recently, as some countries have made inroads into digitization overall, we observe that the ability to take advantage of AI solutions tends to be more limited in less developed countries, primarily because they are behind in other critical technologies (Shafik, 2024d). Also, research on AI in emerging countries is necessary. The adoption of AI will also influence the world's economic dynamics. Developed countries are expected to improve the quality of AI. Recall that AI surpasses in importance, an improvement. The development of an effective AI technology management strategy is necessary for all firms, large and small, because AI can be applied across various sectors and industries (Demirkiran & Öztürko lu, 2022).

1.2 Research Aim and Objectives

In recent years, artificial intelligence has developed into a global industry as the 'AI-First' paradigm grounds new management approaches. Whether in developed or developing countries, AI is becoming a part of many fundamental aspects of business activity. Extant knowledge presents a complex picture, allowing the investigation of AI management for growth in many economic contexts and variations of strategies and applications. The goal of this research is to understand how to manage AI technology in a way that can help the economy of the country grow. To reach this goal, we need to meet the following objectives: explore effective strategies to manage AI technology in the economies of developed and developing countries (Bakare, 2023). Investigate principal challenges and opportunities to grow the economy at the level of AI technology management. The study aims to contribute to academic research and policy debate on AI management at both macro and microeconomic levels in light of global AI trends. We expect the paper to provide new knowledge by further deepening our understanding of the potential leverage AI technology may bring to economic growth from both AI first movers in developed countries and AI laggards/embracers in developing economies. In particular, we expect to understand the fits and misfits of Big Tech practices of AI application in the context of less developed economies. We also see a strong potential for interdisciplinary theoretical and practical insights with global reach (Peng, 2022). In light of the research areas described above, the study is designed to answer the following two questions: 1. What does AI technology management propose for operational contexts in AI first movers? 2. What are the implications for AI entrepreneurship in settings of non-AI first movers?

1.3 Scope and Structure of the Study

There is no clear study of the implementation of AI practices in developed and developing countries, specifically at the micro-level of technology management. Our joint goal is to identify which challenges arise in order to manage human resources and knowledge, what risk management practices or mechanisms exist, and how to manage risk and technology management strategies. In order to truly understand these concepts, we addressed both developed and developing countries. The research has a temporal focus, taking into consideration the AI revolution in recent years. The study will consist of the following subsections. The next section will provide an in-depth literature review, followed by research on the identification of micro-level AI practices and their analysis. Sections 'AI practices or AI levers' and 'Strategies for technology and AI management' will offer a basis for data collection and in-depth analysis in the following stages. As a result of our research, a roadmap will be developed for companies in developed or developing countries so that they can effectively manage the risk and responsibility associated with the implementation of AI practices seen in the research. Our goal is to analyze AI strategies at the micro-level, which can lead to the dynamic capabilities of the company. Due to AI's reflection on technology management, we benefited from frameworks for collective learning. Proposed analyses include the conceptual model of the effects of AI, including Big Data, in companies in developed countries. As far as we are aware, there is no specific research on developing countries in the context of Big Data; however, quite a few studies have focused on Internet adoption. Moreover, there are many preliminary studies on AI or other IT. Finally, we would like to highlight the comparative analysis. Agencies in both developed and developing countries have to make more informed decisions about the future range of companies and the impact of the companies themselves.

2. UNDERSTANDING AI TECHNOLOGY MANAGEMENT

While AI technologies have been developed with the ability to mimic human capabilities such as learning and problem-solving, driven by big data processing power enhancement and advanced AI algorithms, a scientific and practical field called AI technology management has emerged to deal with the management of AI technologies, systems, and governance. Next, definitions and concepts related to AI technology, AI technology management, governance, smart technology, and smart cities are discussed before examining the challenges in AI and smart technology usage (van Dijk & van Grieken, 2017). Basically, terminology like SAI, AGI, and IA is included in the definition of AI technology. AI governance and smart governance is considered part of AI technology management. The era is considered to be a digital society with high-tech smart technologies, and it must maintain leading-edge technology. AI is being applied to many sectors and fields, including government administrative services, banking and finance, healthcare, transportation, manufacturing, retail, hospitality, property, agriculture, the educational system, public utility services, telecommunications, tourism, and service industries. The main concern is how to manage ICT, smart, and AI technologies and systems to enable citizens, businesses, and communities to adopt and adapt them to their best uses (Hashim, 2018). For Thailand, not many smart applications related to AI, chatbots, big data, IoT, and blockchain have been employed in the government sector and society; this is considered an innovative field that will be addressed in the 4.0 era. Finally, the challenges and opportunities in developing AI technology management and governance, as well as in smart technology management, are discussed, including resource allocation and identifying AI and smart technologies that should be focused on for plugging in, operating, and using, taking into account the four actors and their distinctive roles concerning AI technology management. Therefore, those involved in smart technology need to know what the potential directions for implementing AI technology could be, especially regarding the challenges and opportunities in managing expert systems, as illustrated in Figure 1 (Peng, 2022).

Figure 1. Categories of expert systems

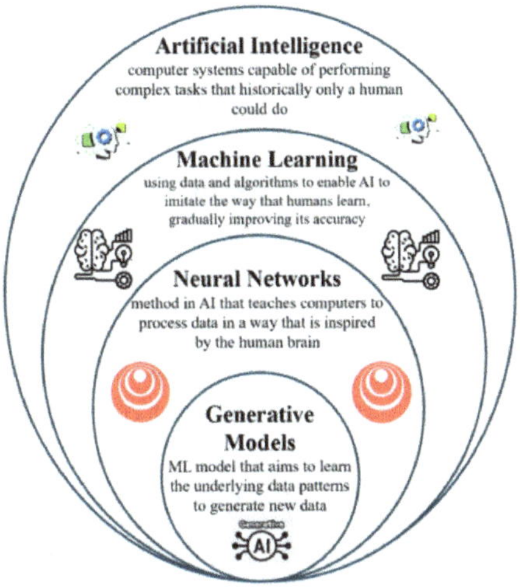

2.1 Definition and Concepts of AI

In this section, we will explore key definitions and concepts regarding AI technology. Representatives and skeptics of AI technology, particularly policymakers, corporations, and society, need to be aware of the complementarity of, and possible differences and similarities between, the developed and the developing world concerning economic growth, AI adoption, and implementation, for example, demographic, regulatory, traditional sectors, or education systems. Along with information technology, AI can indeed be classified as 'general purpose technology' and not just as yet another information technology (Shafik, 2024e). Since AI can deal with many different problems, for example, natural language, experience, geometric perception, and planning and action, we can classify AI to follow these different taxonomies. AI includes planning and acting in the real world, substantially manipulating natural language, and experiencing and responding to different sensory inputs at the right speeds to simulate human cognitive capabilities. More modest research endeavors or commercial products or systems include robotics, machine learning, or natural language processing. Neuroscience is also familiar with the concept of cognitive architecture in dealing with AI and understanding the mind and brain. AI can chat and answer in natural language, diagnose a disease from a set of many signs, determine from data the human driver's intention in driving a partly automated automobile, and interpret a mass of data about an individual patient and suggest treatment (Shafik, 2024e). These are more complex AI tasks.

2.2 AI Applications in Various Sectors

AI technologies have the potential to transform almost every sector of the global economy. AI systems have been applied to the financial and manufacturing sectors, logistics and transportation, agriculture, medicine, education, and state administration, where they have demonstrated their effectiveness in solving specialized tasks. AI-powered technology can contribute to an increase in annual global GDP by 9–13.5% by 2030. Increasing the use of AI in a country by 20% increases income levels, so a reduction in the implementation of AI by 20% has a similar effect on economic influences in our world (Lin et al., 2021). For example, in the United States, AI is of particular importance for data analysis and decision-making in healthcare, financial and legal services, education, and state administration. In Europe, one of the key AI technology areas is the manufacturing industry, as for many companies, the vision of Industry 4.0 can bring long-term economic benefits in the form of increased productivity by 30–50%. Agricultural technologies using AI, blockchain, and the Internet of Things promise to transform global trade into developed and developing economies. In addition to trade between developed countries, this means participants benefit the developed countries involved, in addition to other nations. In South America, AI is one of the most important technologies in the field of state administration, financial services, and educational services (Yang et al., 2021). An AI-based alert system has been introduced to prevent education fraud among teaching staff, as presented in Table 1.

Table 1. Comparative Analysis of AI Technology Management in Developed and Developing Countries

Dimension	Developed Countries	Developing Countries	Key Gaps	Implications for Management	Reference
Infrastructure	Mature broadband, 5G, edge computing, cloud ecosystems	Patchy internet, limited cloud access, costly bandwidth	Persistent connectivity and reliability divide	Organizations in developing regions face higher operational friction and slower digital transformation	(Demirkiran & Öztürko lu, 2022)
Human Capital	Advanced AI literacy, graduate pipelines, specialized research hubs	Brain drain, inadequate technical training, fragmented academic–industry linkages	Scarcity of AI talent and knowledge retention issues	Management must invest heavily in re-skilling and partnerships with universities	(Shafik, 2024e)
Data Ecosystem	Vast structured/ unstructured datasets, standardized data governance	Poor data curation, fragmented registries, lack of interoperability	Reliability and interoperability constraints	Data-driven decision making in developing economies remains shallow	(Lin et al., 2021)
Innovation Ecosystem	Strong R&D funding, innovation accelerators, global partnerships	Low R&D intensity, weak incubation ecosystems	Innovation and commercialization deficit	Limits ability of managers to scale AI pilots into market-ready solutions	(Peng, 2022).
Policy & Regulation	Mature AI strategies, GDPR-aligned policies, ethical frameworks	Policy fragmentation, weak enforcement, absence of ethical guidelines	Governance and accountability lag	Increased compliance risk and uncertainty for organizational planning	(Lin et al., 2021).
AI Adoption Rate	Cross-sector integration in finance, health, logistics, education	Sector-specific pilots concentrated in finance or agriculture	Uneven adoption and scaling barriers	Creates competitive asymmetry between firms and across geographies	(van Dijk & van Grieken, 2017)
Financial Support	Deep venture capital pools, corporate investment funds, government incentives	Limited risk capital, high cost of borrowing, donor-driven funding	Capital shortage and sustainability concerns	Restricts innovation pipelines and hinders enterprise growth	(Fortuna et al., 2020).

continued on following page

Table 1. Continued

Dimension	Developed Countries	Developing Countries	Key Gaps	Implications for Management	Reference
Industry Integration	AI embedded into digital twins, predictive analytics, and ERP systems	Early integration through chatbots, fintech tools, or agri-tech pilots	Commercialization and scaling limitations	Reduced operational leverage and efficiency for managers	(Yang et al., 2021).
Digital Inclusion	Universal digital literacy and device penetration	Urban–rural divides, gendered access gaps	Exclusion of marginalized populations	Managers risk designing services that reinforce inequality	(Trisiana, 2019).
Cybersecurity	Robust AI-driven security protocols, zero-trust models	Underfunded cybersecurity frameworks, reactive posture	Security vulnerabilities and exposure to cybercrime	Elevated risk of breaches undermines trust and organizational resilience	(Bliznets et al., 2018).
Knowledge Sharing	International research consortia, open-source platforms, AI governance forums	Fragmented regional initiatives, weak inter-firm networks	Collaboration and knowledge diffusion gaps	Missed opportunities for cross-learning and co-development	(Jun et al., 2021; Zhao et al., 2022)
Public–Private Partnerships	Institutionalized PPPs driving innovation policy	Weak or fragile PPP structures with inconsistent outcomes	Institutional capacity gaps	Limits scaling of infrastructure and ecosystem projects	(Bliznets et al., 2018).
Workforce Adaptation	Continuous lifelong learning ecosystems, micro-credentials in AI	Limited upskilling channels, structural unemployment risk	Workforce transition challenges	Managers face resistance to organizational change and automation	(Shafik, 2024b).
Sustainability Alignment	AI integrated into ESG, green innovation, and climate risk modeling	Adoption sporadic, concentrated in donor projects	Weak linkage between AI and sustainability	Organizations fail to leverage AI for long-term resilience and sustainability goals	(Alaziz et al., 2023).

2.3 Challenges and Opportunities in AI Technology Management

The opportunities of AI technology in management are about the benefits that AI technology can provide to the industry, the digitalization frontier, and human development. In fact, there are many motivations to use AI to promote the company's performance, and it highlights that AI companies are perceived to strengthen economic growth, provide better-allocated resources based on consumer demand patterns, and foster professional creativity. Big data and AI technology applications will enable timely and improved decision-making as well as facilitate innovative solutions to global and industry problems, particularly in real-time problem solving. Moreover, AI is perceived to offer an important new source of productivity growth, strengthening the competitiveness of nations and benefiting the entire economy with new field-specific industrial automation techniques, managing new industrial robotics as well as individual products in many manufacturing industries (Jun et al., 2021; Zhao et al., 2022). It is expected that AI technology will also contribute to digital purposes as a new frontier. Thus, many prospects and economic possibilities remain readily available for AI technology management.

(i) At the industrial level and the digital frontier, data and AI are needed, which need to be driven by strong data markets, both of which would be directed by free trade in information and guard data overflow boundaries.
(ii) Ethical fears will be overcome by organizing multi-stakeholder action to hammer out an ethical AI strategy with a growth stimulus attached.
(iii) Data and algorithmic dominance risk—global level platform economy master control. This needs to be addressed by ensuring that there is ultimate control of the data and the platforms through national competition laws, global standards, the adoption of a digital market tool, the development of new, initially exclusive traits, buying into the AI system, and the growth of new systems. National leaders must adopt a Global Declaration of Data Independence to underline the superiority of localism in global digital and AI evolution.
(iv) The benefits of digital and AI will only start if it is opened up to the masses—too big a digital divide at the global level. Equal access should be provided to the technologies through an initial chargeable service and technology residency certificates that allow the brand-new free delivery digital and AI technologies to individuals, localities, and companies that do not have them. In order to guarantee that the digitally impoverished are never exploited and to help build their confidence as customers and their privileges as citizens, the contracts of the people who use AI technology should be supported by the AI Trust Directive.

(v) Many governments are tiny now and cannot control AI-centric threats and opportunities, consuming global and regional benchmarking debt. A free, global survey of the national AI and digital economy capabilities and their tools and tactics should be encouraged. For developing countries, from the standpoint of AI policy comparison and ADI, this helps to understand better the technologies and policies that prove helpful, aid the creation of investment strategies, and guarantee that such technologies reach the impoverished as well.

(vi) Cheat, AI markets, and data schemes—main national attitudes to AI hoaxes have not been clarified in various countries. Laws and schemes must be implemented, and the public should be regularly notified of the damage that such fraud causes. Besides, in language-specific technology, the new AI must not censor but improve.

3. AI APPLICATIONS IN DEVELOPED COUNTRIES

AI has become more widely used in advanced industrialized countries across various industries. In healthcare, AI is used for patient care, primarily in the early detection and prediction of diseases. AI has been widely used in the finance industry for stocks and foreign exchange trading in investment areas because AI algorithms can learn complex patterns and are widely used as trading robots by major institutions. The transport industry and logistics use AI to optimize goods supply and demand, time schedules, route orders, and automatic cargo unloading in warehouses and ports. Healthcare, finance, and transportation applications may be primarily due to the investments of major technology companies (Alaziz et al., 2023). They distribute their business services in various countries and use them as a test bed to assess whether the application is appropriate on a case-by-case basis. Sites all over the world can be found using these services. In terms of societal and infrastructure, industrialized countries have a sufficient level of scientific and educational knowledge and are synchronized with the high-tech industries needed to introduce AI. This provides the ideal conditions for AI technology management. Major industrial, financial, and other companies are more likely to adopt AI because it provides convenience and benefits them in terms of cost reduction and other advantages. All of their policies and objectives can be implemented by utilizing the characteristics of a government based on technology. Developed countries are currently shifting to an age where the public and private sectors work together in this way (Shafik, 2024f). In that respect, the general framework can be found on how to apply AI for healthcare, technology, industry, transport, innovation, and other sectors in developed countries.

Many AI applications and machine learning models have been designed and built to address issues confronting developing countries, particularly low-income and lower-middle-income countries. Some of these countries may have more remote areas, lower levels of literacy, and weaker functional institutions. Plausible solutions that are being encouraged have emerged from the implementation of digital products that offer solutions such as improved agriculture. Other areas in which AI is actively shaping developing countries include healthcare, credit constraints, education, energy, and transport. For example, an interactive chatbot can replace doctors. AI is also being used to automatically classify plants in regions where there is an immediate need to verify crop yield (Alnssyan et al., 2023). The use of AI in developing countries is usually targeted at current problems and may include solutions based on the use of resources and poverty removal. Various stakeholders take an interest in developing AI in these countries in order to expand their markets. Other systemic reasons can cause AI to improve current problems. For example, governments in sub-Saharan Africa prefer AI research and application companies to concentrate on resource allocation. Among the many examples of AI in Africa is AI, which uses big data analytics to determine health service provision, as sampled in Figure 2 (Shafik, 2024g).

Figure 2. Application of generative artificial intelligence

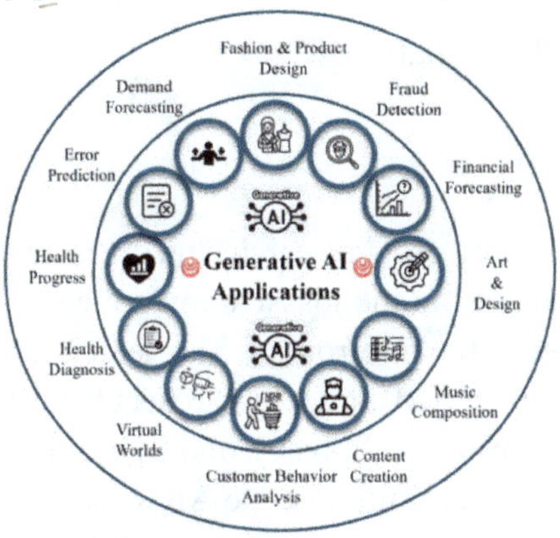

Despite the great promise up front, several issues form major challenges in both implementing AI technologies in developing countries and building technologies that are beneficial to such audiences. Few individuals in a developing region have access to the internet, and a lack of technological infrastructure further limits the number of people able to access AI-based solutions. Proving that approaches like other economic measures and focus verticals are a major constraint for increasing successful AI contributions is the lack of resources to build AI. It's difficult to find the time to pitch in so that governments and organizations can focus on other issues and competing priorities. There is currently a gap in knowledge for AI projects in developing countries. Unlike the useful focus in developed countries with abundant records, the use of data in frontiers is limited in developing countries. Many potential AI contributions lack the funds needed to start developing viable products, and large corporate partners with adequate funds do not always understand the pressing local issues in these countries. Governments, private organizations, and NGOs can form partnerships that combine their respective value and expertise in developing AI solutions for developing countries. If people and companies that focus on the pros and cons come together, this approach may work well. In summary, together with the appropriate sustainable AI projects to expand growing economies in developing countries, long-term economic growth and increased quality of life are still possible, but do face barriers (Shafik, 2024b). Using AI in farming, energy, health, healthcare, and public welfare can represent a wide range of examples when a computer science algorithm solves practical challenges, removing inefficiencies and adding value. And despite the preference for data found in the emerging area, multiple applications show practical benefits. When implementing these projects, a variety of barriers and relationships are frequently observed. Some proposed strategies include internationalization, tailoring AI ethics to developing countries, the creation of appropriate AI governance structures, the production of bottom-up innovations, and encouraging and supporting the creation of local AI-based start-ups, as demonstrated below (Shafik, 2024a).

3.1 United States

The U.S. has a long history of AI research, and the recent advances, often called the third wave of AI, respond to the massive investments that started in the early 2000s. The U.S. has been at the forefront of AI research: the top three conferences in AI are all held in U.S. cities and attract researchers from around the world. Many of the major tech companies are U.S.-based and have been pioneers in developing deep learning algorithms. Many cutting-edge AI breakthroughs were developed in the U.S. These advanced AI technologies are currently being researched and utilized in various fields. These statistics show that the U.S. has seen substantial AI growth across a wide range of industries, such as AI hardware, AI services, and autonomous driving (Shafik, 2024c). Private and Public Sector Investment in AI Two key building blocks that have significantly accelerated AI research and development in the U.S. are large private-sector investments by the world's biggest technology firms and government-funded AI initiatives. These include investments in chip design, data centers, and cloud computing to accommodate the large amounts of data required for training an AI model. This, in turn, has enabled data-intensive technologies such as deep learning to become more popular. In terms of public sector support, the U.S. government has taken a hands-off approach and relegates most of the AI policymaking to other entities within the government. Despite this, the U.S. federal government has funded initiatives that shepherded the growing field of AI research. It has played a key role in early AI research through various agencies, funding strategic opportunities in computer science. The federal government has also funded major investments into advancing fundamental knowledge of the field by signaling commitments to infrastructure investment (Shafik, 2024a). These investments signal a commitment from the academic community to drive economic opportunity.

3.2 United Kingdom

The United Kingdom (UK) has set an AI strategy for promoting research, innovation, and adoption for the general public as well as businesses. A UK AI expert center has also been developed and is known as the Alan Turing Institute, which has already embraced extensive AI research from academia across sectors, from healthcare and finance to retail and cybersecurity. Many other organizations, university institutions, and government agencies are promoting top AI research and applications in different sectors. New start-ups are focusing on different AI subfields, such as natural language processing, personal assistance, recommendation systems, and conversational systems. The UK has a strong regulatory framework that balances the ease of doing business under the data regime with a focus on responsible AI applications and research (Shafik, 2024e). Companies advancing AI solutions are also looking to develop a base in the UK to reach potential European markets after the exit of the UK from the EU. In addition, the UK promotes AI research with leading industrial companies investing millions of pounds in new AI technology agreements with academia. In this regard, one promising area is the joint initiative between the government and industry, which invests in initiatives between politics and industry that improve the ability to analyze government officials and data to solve difficult AI challenges. There are countless AI case studies in different sectors of the UK. In 2018, more than AI companies in the UK received investment, of which around were distributed in two rounds over £3 million. AI in the UK enticed acquisition programs, as one organization acquired a UK organization, the Artificial Intelligence Center in Fulham. AIML has established the implementation of AI in healthcare, particularly the NHS, to offer economical and effective solutions in addition to providing proactive medical suggestions (Demirkiran & Öztürko lu, 2022). Various other AI cases have been discussed in regulated industries. The United Kingdom has seen the advantages of AI in the financial services sector, stating that AI and information analysis constitute a percentage of Fintech companies' activities. AI also drives different types of commercial services, such as retail and transport, while messaging (e.g., customer service automation, chatbots). AI innovation manifests not only in commercial activities but also in public service tools like natural language-based chatbots integrating into government platforms, reaching millions. The deployment of AI technology in the UK involved numerous challenges in applying AI technologies in different sectors. In this regard, the lack of consensus on AI is particularly problematic, with a percentage of companies across the entire business community and a percentage of companies indicating that they were not sure how to tokenize AI strategies (Bliznets et al., 2018). A report stated that only a percentage of business leaders surveyed believe they have the correct skill sets for business AI.

3.3 Germany

Germany has made significant strides in the development and application of AI technology in recent years, especially in the field of industrial applications. AI and the manufacturing sector are organically integrated into the pioneer concept of Industry 4.0, which reimagines manufacturing processes. The adoption of AI is mainly restricted to large companies, with SME penetration at a lower rate. One of the critical discussions in the domestic public, politics, and even business circles is whether Germany and Europe should pursue this manner of forward-looking technological progress, and if so, to what extent their dominant competitive orientation will sway. In broader political and societal discussions, the relationship between technology developers and responsible businesses on ethical AI and, consequently, the introduction of so-called "ethical robots" is being held (Hashim, 2018). The increase in AI's impact and the implications of widespread use are also being recognized. Germany is taking significant strides in AI research and industrial applications and is actively working to develop the requisite practical system. The focus on AI research and development is comprehensive, with significant government investments to complement corporate and academic studies. Leading research institutes linked to universities have collaborated with industry to help them understand more about practical problems and have reached a variety of agreements for the commercialization and application of leading AI technology (Elyta et al., 2021). Despite these successes, the broader acceptance of AI research and the need to upgrade domestic industries present challenges, as do the opt-out options that the industry may offer and the reform of international data protection regulations, particularly with reference to privacy rights. The most pressing challenge facing German researchers and industrialists alike is the re-engineering of the industrial manufacturing layer and the redeployment of those faced with redundancies due to AI-infused technologies. Despite these challenges, AI may offer a range of social benefits (Kurniawan et al., 2019).

3.4 Japan

Robot technology is well known in Japan, and Japanese companies started keeping up with AI trends at an early stage. Japan has a strong commitment to new technologies with a high percentage of research and development investment in the GDP. These support industries of developed countries are different from those of developing countries as they seek to develop robots and AI technologies. In 2015, AI technology and robot fields were introduced to collaborate in the public and private sectors. Japanese society has been involved in leading innovations like these technologies. The aging society is a concern, so AI for robot utilization can be introduced in various applications to assist everyday life for the elderly population. The collaboration between the Japanese government and the Japanese industry will focus on the effects of AI (Lu et al., 2022). We are introducing the same AI human-like technology to provide solutions to assist authorities in decision-making and solving health emergencies. It also includes the transportation and retail sectors. Japan's government agenda is to commercialize AI, with machine learning foundation research totaling a significant amount. The Japanese government and companies in Japan are involved in sectors such as the auto insurance industry and robotics while collaborating to address the challenges of the aging demographic population. The service robotics market in Japan is also among the fastest-growing markets today. The AI technology accepted well by robot technology is expected to increase significantly by 2024. Risks, as well as the age of the regulatory framework for non-cooperation and/or cooperative emergent AI, are anticipated to be the most prevalent issues in global AI deployment in Japan and the competition (Goodyear, 2021). AI's top objectives include automation and productivity improvements, with cost reduction being a significant focus.

4. AI TECHNOLOGY MANAGEMENT IN DEVELOPING COUNTRIES

AI management is more difficult in developing countries than in developed countries due to various reasons. One of the most profound reasons is the lack of government support in the form of infrastructure, skilled labor, and financial investment. The greatest barriers to AI in developing countries are the absence of technology infrastructure, the lack of a skilled workforce, the lack of finance, and the poor regulatory environment. Stakeholders in Africa and Africa as a whole are beginning to take strategic initiatives in AI with a variety of projects and strategies to improve the situation. A combination of top-down and bottom-up approaches is being attempted (Chang, 2022). Many leading public and private laboratories and universities in African countries are also pioneering technological solutions through local innovations and grassroots projects in AI. Consequently, there is a growing need for large-scale computational infrastructure projects in African countries. Access to computational infrastructure is a major barrier to AI research on the continent. Such infrastructure would enable AI researchers to overcome the low-performance hurdle and carry out state-of-the-art research that can be incorporated into the industry. The continent is also struggling to secure capital. This is reflected in a shortage of venture capital funding in Africa (Bartosik-Purgat & Filimon, 2022). Digital marketing of these AI-driven solutions and entrepreneurship are before multiple governments grappling with regulation creation.

Issues like which areas of the market on the continent need the most regulation and which areas should not be interfered with are key issues at large. Moreover, AI ethics and the use of data for creating models is a controversial topic on the continent. To overcome the key barriers to AI growth in many lower-tier developing countries leading to either emerging or struggling AI ecosystems, there is a need for a variety of different strategies. The right approach or strategy when countries want to implement AI can be developed based on case-specific conditions, local context, and areas of expertise. Tailoring AI policy to local contexts means that developing countries have a different data context than developed countries (Yujie et al., 2022). The amount and type of available local data will affect companies that want to use AI. Because they have smaller data sets, companies and organizations in developing countries are typically behind those in higher-tier developing countries, who in turn are typically behind companies in developed countries. Developing countries often lack a sector or business industry, usually technology companies that attract foreign direct investment (Abutabenjeh et al., 2022). Because of these differences, AI in developing countries must develop a significantly different approach in different countries, as illustrated below.

4.1 China

For over a decade, AI technology has developed rapidly and has been the focus of international attention. Many developed countries and regions have conducted policy deployment research on AI technology management, and this literature provides practical enlightenment for developing countries on how to carry out AI technology management research. In terms of the speed of technological innovation, among the developed countries, China was the first country to report diverse applications and has benefited significantly. China is at the forefront of AI technology, being the country with the most AI companies, a major producer and consumer of AI technology models, owning the most AI technology patents, and accounting for a growing share of AI technology publications (Andreadis et al., 2022). Although

China joined the AI field relatively late, the country invested in AI technology and development after a significant event in 2016 and has now become the largest AI market in the world. As the largest developing country, China has adopted a new mindset to overcome its initial backwardness and undertake AI technology management with unique features compared to developed countries. In AI technology, China's AI applications cover a large number of fields, such as intelligent prediction, intelligent driving, diagnosis and treatment, surveillance, and shot detection. With the rapid development of AI technology, China's future scope is likely to be larger. With the widespread collection of basic data, China is poised to take the lead in promoting intelligent industrial manufacturing, becoming the world's largest smart factory, and laying out intelligent agriculture (Li et al., 2020). China will implement a plan that systematically uses "AI labor" to promote intelligent manufacturing and "AI technology" to enhance manufacturing competitiveness. The application of AI in China is about to be upgraded to "AI+" in many traditional fields, such as agriculture, education, finance, and manufacturing, and is gradually being recognized by people and society. From an international perspective, the U.S. has been troubled by AI technology that threatens social stability and national security (Kollmann et al., 2022). In China, civilian and military decisions are about to intertwine in AI technology, deepening the connotation of AI national strategy.

4.2 India

India has the largest average number of AI publications and patents in the region. AI is applied across a wide range of sectors, including the government, agriculture, disaster management, healthcare education, human trafficking, and fintech. Many innovative uses of AI to directly address social needs, e.g., to help farmers and healthcare, can be seen to be coming from startups. AI use is mostly at an early stage of development, predominantly in the POC and experimentation phase. The Government of India has so far released two documents on AI: the discussion paper on AI and the draft National AI Strategy. The draft strategy outlines the main AI-related policies for India in the areas of R&D, the industry, innovation, ethics and privacy, regulatory environment, skilling, international collaboration, and promotion of startups (Trisiana, 2019). There are also various research and development organizations of various tech companies developing AI algorithms and products. Policymakers in India are primarily concerned with the deficit of a skilled workforce in AI, including those with a working knowledge of the concept. AI is seen as important to achieving targets on economic inclusivity. Key initiatives focus on promoting startups, innovation, and a skilled tech workforce. Experts voiced concerns that policy changes can lead to regulatory constraints and inconsistencies that hold back innovation (Shafik, 2024d). Poor internet, data privacy issues, and infrastructure gaps were also considered factors that may disrupt India's uptake of AI.

4.3 Brazil

Although Brazil lags compared to countries such as the USA and India in AI technology management and graduates, AI is embraced more by Brazilian companies than by companies based in India. To this end, initiatives of the government intend to boost infrastructure for investing in research on developments in AI. With growing investment by Brazilian and foreign companies in the area, expertise in AI will not only leverage companies but also directly impact the economy of Brazil. In Brazil, the business model that envisions the future is not just to have an AI ecosystem – and we have covariates that represent the importance of the ecosystem. The AI ecosystem in Brazil is part of an innovative strategy for medium and small companies based on technology management and Brazilian science and technology. The studies of AI investment in Brazil focus on AI applications (Mohammed & Shahda, 2018). In Brazil, the use of AI for general economic applications is at an early stage due to the shortage of investment in infrastructure and a skilled workforce. So far, few basic AI techniques are used with limitations. Research on AI applications in Brazil shows how investments in AI generate economic development. It takes as an axiom the position of two schools of thought about development: the first states that development is inherently ambiguous and, therefore, projects of the richest sectors of society cannot be enough. It includes all people in participatory benefits and development, including AI (Su et al., 2021).

4.4 South Africa

Despite some overlap with the African continent as a whole, in this section, distinct from the rest of Sub-Saharan Africa, South Africa's approach through its policy initiatives will be discussed. Briefly, underestimating South Africa in the context of AI, especially considering the unique context of the country outlined in this paper, presents many opportunities as well as struggles and would be inaccurate. South Africa's strategic papers promote AI as an emerging technology that, if used in national priority areas, would reduce South Africa's reliance on economic decisions made outside its borders, while the attractiveness of South Africa would improve due to enhanced services, safer communities, and vibrant cultural life (Chang, 2022). AI was identified as contributing to the productive use of large databases needed to monitor and report on the National Development Plan's indicators and acquire multiscalar feedback on their targets. Most importantly, given South Africa's staggering rates of inequality, unemployment, and poverty, AI was identified as an opportunity to develop large technology hubs and clusters providing jobs and industries with higher qualifications and wages that South Africa must industrialize to acquire. South Africa launched an economy-wide draft digital economy master plan, highlighting the establishment of Future Work Centres as well as technical and vocational training colleges, developing cross-cutting skills of the future, improving existing skills, and ensuring a digital South Africa among its objectives. For AI specifically, two more specific strategy papers were developed, providing guidelines for micro, meso, and macroeconomic policymakers on leveraging AI in research and development of distributed renewable generation with storage to policy support of early childhood development, school, and post-school education (Li et al., 2020; Yusup et al., 2022).

In September 2022, the South African Department of Science, Innovation, and Technology committed to invest in a joint center for digital innovation led by the South African National Research Foundation, the CRIS lab, and the Digital Technology Research Centre, establishing a Digital Economy future work program that includes testing and evaluation of AI in service industries employing low-wage workers; and inviting proposals in the field of innovation and digitalization for inclusive development. In conclusion, South Africa's resources, position, policies, and initiatives leave it well-placed to become a leader in AI technology management (Trisiana, 2019). Efforts to build the AI environment are collaborative in nature. South Africa's draft artificial intelligence overview strategy paper indicates the importance of multi-skilling and the need to align "micro, meso, and macro" AI policy support and initiatives. The paper states that, in support of the National Development Plan, AI has the potential "to track in near real-time a country's progress across a wide range of measurable indicators using both hard, 'Big' data, and soft, qualitative assessments." The strategy paper argues that AI can contribute to inclusive development in developing countries such as South Africa by placing a country in good stead for human capital migration, investment, tourism, and remuneration inflows. Moreover, it has the potential to raise living standards among the poorest, bringing them access to an always-on national curriculum through digital technologies in the workplace (Boonmoh et al., 2021; Hasin et al., 2022). E-education is a priority in the country currently piloting in the Free State, a robot schools and technology pilot project aimed at addressing educational and unemployment issues in South Africa.

4.5 Barriers and Challenges

On the other hand, the problem of technology management is much more severe in developing countries. There are various reasons. A common issue can be a lack of, or deficiencies in, infrastructure that reduces the diffusion and adoption of new technologies. The infrastructure of this kind is one class of asset to the possession of which distinguishes the first-class nations from the underdeveloped countries. As a result, many managers and computer scientists may not have the experience and expertise with the latest and most sophisticated AI technologies. Another shortcoming that has drawn much attention for AI applications is the shortage of potential staff members skilled in developing AI systems or those who are knowledgeable about using these AI technologies (Hazzan, 2022). This greatly restricts the rate of development and use of these AI systems in organizations. Similar to any other new and sophisticated technology, the amount of finance required to invest in AI can be quite high. Limited resources, therefore, restrict the extent to which AI technologies can be developed successfully and managed effectively. The gap between the developed and developing countries in the expenditure needed for human resources can have an even more significant impact on enhancing and managing artificial intelligence types. The law, politics, culture, and religious beliefs are some of the major constraints preventing the best use of AI systems in developing countries (Dalam et al., 2022). The poor contextual situation of this kind, therefore, calls for the devising of context-sensitive solutions in the planning and management of AI innovations in organizations.

4.6 Initiatives and Strategies for Growth

More initiatives and strategies have been proposed to bridge this gap in developing regions and foster management and growth in these countries. A selection of AI for the management of technology in practice, technological infrastructure construction, and the enhancement of AI studies and related entrepreneurship through regional development programs, often in partnership with international organizations, is being examined. An example of a plan to build cutting-edge digital technologies is the development of a project. The country is lowering its AI-related expenditures by a minimum of over the next five years by supporting policies to improve agri-food value chains with public research organizations, technology companies, and influential actors at key incursions (Zurdo et al., 2022). AI is a leading-edge technology, and several developing countries have realized that there is little evidence of innovation capabilities that collaborate in concentrated activities and local innovation capabilities to enhance the dynamics of these AI technological processes, as well as technology that can have significant social and economic impact. Developing new technologies and being able to strengthen local and regional activities and create shared policies with external structures may include working with regional AI policies, such as developing research agendas to increase local and international coordination and incentives for large technology companies and incumbent universities to have large businesses. Joint ventures should formalize these linkages. These partnerships should espouse shared ideologies about innovation and seed innovation, focusing on innovative thinking, not talent (Mallam et al., 2019). Local development should increasingly enable institutions to build a culture of innovation, thereby increasing the possibility of related synergies. For example, the themes of management of technology and space technology have been integrated, among others, which have increased the flow of information on both sides.

5. COMPARATIVE ANALYSIS OF AI TECHNOLOGY MANAGEMENT

A comparative analysis of AI technology management in developed and developing countries provides a rich view of progress in the field. In developed countries, initiatives in AI technology are well integrated with government policy, institutions, and resources. For the nations in this study, AI development is widespread and highly student-driven. In developing countries, on the other hand, AI management tends to involve a few individual faculty members, often with one or two students or co-contributors, and occasionally, rare communities of practice (Rampton et al., 2022). The reasons AI is being managed in this way vary, but they can be traced to three issues: infrastructure, resources, and increased movement and interest in learning and AI technology management. A closer examination of the nine institutions in this study shows that AI programs in developed countries often have more formal factors of program systems, such as drop boxes for assignments populated with clear instructions. Technical support for the setup and use of web boards is available for students and other users and is provided via telephone, email, or chat-based services typically found in developed countries (Ismandianto et al., 2022). In addition, the instructional technology employed with AI management—typically web boards, assessment and analysis tools, and software for automation, is widely available, including application software, in developed countries. In developing countries, AI design has a number of program system factors embedded in teaching and learning with technology. For example, AI design has a group project in which students who are interested in similar topics work together in small, interdisciplinary teams. Given the main project, students must collect data and evidence through the use of the web, newsgroups, listservs, email-based interviews, and other suitable software and communication technologies. Similar to developed countries, AI design requires teams to complete three interim project reports (Araújo et al., 2019). However, instead of the electronic facilities often found in developed countries, two of the reports are collected in paper form and have anonymous peer-assessing techniques administered by a system called 'webPA.' WebPA is a paper-based peer assessment program. Students are awarded quality points for the quality of the web resource or web product/resource and any additional materials, including original web pages, screenshots, pictures, evidence that the output was used, and also data and results. Evidence of data collection and critical evaluation is also rewarded with marks. That quality is determined using quality assessment scales used in a pseudo-moderation process, which incorporates anchor points (Xiao, 2022). These data are collected on a web form, downloaded into a file, and summarized using webPA.

5.1 Impact of AI Technology Management on Economic Development

Effective management of AI technology can have a significant impact on economic development. Efficient and effective AI technology is integral to growth and improvement in the development of goods and services. Seven major sectors, including manufacturing, transportation, health, resources and agriculture, utility services, financial services, and information technologies, are expected to experience improvement by leveraging the capabilities of AI, such as robotics, in various operations. From the jobs perspective, the roles of AI are pronounced in supply chain management, operations, quality monitoring, sales, decision support, diagnostics, and customer service (Bag et al., 2022). AI is already contributing to productivity improvements in some of these sectors and is seen to play a critical role in innovation as well as job creation. The potential contribution of AI across the four dimensions can be gauged empirically, too. Six case studies on AI companies in this research are illustrative of the role of AI when it is actively managed. The global AI market share of developing countries is only 9%. AI could make the economy of India 60% more influential, taking into account the country's product and service competition, with the development and technology of artificial intelligence precisely here being the chair of the position, which plays a role in keeping the country in the top three global dominant countries by 2030. The main objective of these studies is to contribute to a better understanding of the management and deployment of AI technologies in specific industries, such as developing countries (Kumar, 2021). Though the immediate economic implications are job displacements and inequalities, the rise of institutions devoted to AI technologies and technocratic governance aims to think further about the global value of a long-term transformation of economic policy and to address the real potential of replacing human nature. Given the increasing reliance of business, social, political, economic, and governance models on AI technologies, it becomes imperative to think about their economic implications. This is what we are attempting in the subsequent sections of the research (Salava & Kluger, 2022).

5.2 Ethical and Social Implications of AI Technology Management

This section engages with the ethical and social implications surrounding AI technology management. Founded on the basis of trust, privacy concerns are a result of the values and expectations of a developed society. Establishing where to draw the line between what is public and our public behavior, and therefore can be analyzed, and what is inherently private, becomes the crux of this question. As bias is, in essence, a subjective and ethical dilemma, and because it is humans who compile information, it is crucial for the data used within an AI to reflect the clear knowledge and intention of the people. Full punches made with regard to the management of AI technologies suggest that those who develop these technologies hold responsibility for bestowing within the technologies the values of stakeholders, such as corporate actors, states, institutions, and even potentially affected individuals (Martin & Vacca, 2018). To suggest that value must be built into AI technologies by a small proportion of actors is absolute and unaccountable power. The potential social impacts of AI technologies are an arena wrestling with uncertainties; these uncertainties elude many practical considerations beneath mostly speculative deliberations. Many have cast concerns predominantly regarding employment, equality, decision-making, shifting power paradigms, and the long-term philosophical repercussions on our perception of self and reality. As such, it has been suggested that with the growing capital-intensive nature of production within developed states, millions may be left without work or meaning, furthering societal inequity at no real return (Lamine et al., 2021). Balancing the profound discourse of ethical, equitable governance of AI technologies are many solid accounts favoring transparent practices subject to ethical review and governance capabilities where pre-existing. Driven purely from the practical, utilitarian perspectives, many professionals have expressed the need for boards of AI experts comprising rostering. Consulting may be utilized if special policy writing is needed to ensure technologies fit within ethical frameworks. Such practices and principles are to protect the value of stakeholders on behalf conducive to popular depictions of AI, weeding out unqualified, rigid thought management. Collating the views of a diverse community of theorists also allows for a more considered, bias-free approach following ancient skepticism (Herman et al., 2022). Management theory of AI technologies can be read incorrectly, requiring polarised viewpoints, such as AI is a techno-dystopia and AI is a breakthrough innovation.

5.3 Policy and Regulatory Frameworks in AI Technology

This chapter was aimed at the policy framework for AI based on national development strategies, national policies, and international principles of responsible AI.

Our approach to regulating AI is currently limited, and most of the discussion in international forums and at the national level is functioning at the principles level. The AI policy or strategy developed by different countries or groups is just policies of ambitions or visions. From a government perspective, citizens and consumers are the de facto clients. Therefore, the objective function of governments is to formulate a policy environment that allows for technological innovation while also protecting and safeguarding public safety and ethical standards (Husain, 2021; Saura et al., 2022). In developing and reviewing new laws, a balance must be struck between fostering innovation, investment, competition, and regulatory oversight. Although various countries are adopting their AI-related strategies, the global community has recognized the need to collaborate in the development of technical standards and in solving common challenges. While international cooperation in AI is critically important, the interests of different countries are very diverse, and it is difficult for multiple countries to consult and establish a unified AI regulatory position. The areas of focus of AI regulations in different countries can be divided into the following major areas: data and data governance, regulations for algorithms and AI systems, including algorithm and software liability frameworks, and the ethical basis for governance and regulations. Although a few countries have developed artificial intelligence-related rules to govern AI systems, much of the substantive discussion is still based on principled and high-level discourse (Ndou et al., 2020; Sunu, 2022). Furthermore, the regulations and measures that some countries have adopted are yet to be put into practice, and therefore, the actual efficacy of such regulations is not yet well known.

5.4 Investment and Funding Trends in AI

AI has seen rapid growth in terms of funding and investment, with a significant share of investment activities in the AI space. Emerging technologies such as AI are mainly supported by venture funding, expert funding, or directly by the funds of private investors. The market and its growth constitute a significant part of emerging AI research and further development of new technology. Funding activities in the AI space are mainly focused and targeted on tech startups with AI and machine learning users, supporting pure-play AI service providers, or complementing specific use cases with AI. Artificial intelligence has seen an increased number of installations for a multitude of applications, such as smart manufacturing and robotics, speech and voice recognition, autonomous vehicles, surveillance and security, preventive maintenance, personal assistants, and chatbots, among others (Harbani et al., 2021). AI and machine learning build better and more intelligent user interfaces, faster processing, and improved functionalities, which are the essential components driving innovation and are therefore contributing to enhanced market growth globally.

Funding activities greatly accelerate the pace of technology R&D, owing to various developments by encouraging competitive market strategies. Corporations such as technology-based giants are investing in AI and machine learning-based companies to strengthen further their AI as well as general AI product and service markets. Furthermore, several governments have adopted AI technology to offer digital AI surveillance products and autonomous cars (Sam & Pearson, 2019). North America has witnessed the largest financing rounds in the AI technologies market in recent years, followed by Asia-Pacific, Europe, and then Latin America. North America has more AI-related companies than other regions, which, in general, are in a well-established AI technology system and have access to faster data communication. However, significant differences remain between developed countries and developing ones, which are essential for the development of their AI technology management. Even though AI has a significant impact on global economies, factors such as the lack of private, public, and government investments within emerging markets are the foremost contributors to the slow growth of AI technologies in developing markets, representing the slow development of AI investment and management (Apasrawirote et al., 2022). It is necessary to conduct this research for countries such as Jordan to measure the investment in AI and its effective management during contemporary economic transformation.

5.5 AI Talent Development and Retention Strategies

There are a range of skills and competencies needed in order for a workforce to engage with AI aspects in the workplace. They need to be aware of the possibilities but also the threats AI poses. Technical and ethical considerations that need to be taken into account are relevant in most job profiles. There is a growing demand for professionals with knowledge of AI. Demand is outstripping supply, including shortages of many kinds of specialists ranging from data analysts to business analysts. Their work involves understanding AI-related concepts such as machine learning and deep learning, their role and function, as well as being able to discuss AI ethics (Budiarti et al., 2021). There are several strategies currently in place to bridge the "AI talent gap." Relevant capacities and capabilities needed are, at present, not always easy to find. Many national governments believe that their future success in AI is closely linked to the availability of enough AI-skilled workers and wish to develop their own data science and AI ecosystem. Through cooperation between state and industry, several countries are developing AI skills and competencies in cooperation by coordinating training courses for AI professionals. Extracurricular programs, summer schools, dev camps, and lecture series are offered at a number of academic institutions. At universities, study programs covering AI, data science, and/or machine learning or business analytics exist or are taking shape in the wake of the rising fortune of AI (Sudrajat, 2019). Employer demand is another impetus spurring AI skills development. Efforts to "upskill the workforce that companies already have" are underway in response to the fact that companies have difficulty finding the professionals they need. Collaboration takes place in a given national context, with national funding contributing to many skills development initiatives. Educational initiatives aim to increase the diversity of the AI workforce, including people from underprivileged groups. They believe that a wider range and a diversity of opinions in AI increases the likelihood of new ideas and approaches being developed (Sutopo, 2019). Alliances exist between centers of excellence in AI and industry to encourage students from underrepresented groups into careers in AI. A growing number of AI education programs are working with non-profits who are trying to increase the number of underrepresented minorities in AI, as presented in Table 2. More women than men globally take an active interest in enrolling in AI courses. The software sector attracts more men than women. Shortages of well-trained technologists, with many countries competing to access the global talent pool, is another issue of concern. There is much movement between different regions, attracting talent, and a concern that the issue cannot be solved only by national strategies (Istenič et al., 2023; Shafik, 2024c).

Table 2. Value Addition of AI Technology Management for Organizational Growth

Strategic Area	Developed Context Value	Developing Context Value	Challenges	Organizational Management Benefit	Reference
Decision-Making	Predictive analytics for strategic foresight, simulation models for complex systems	Emerging adoption of data dashboards and basic analytics	Limited data quality and model trustworthiness	Enables organizations to shift from intuition-based to evidence-based strategy	(Istenič et al., 2023)
Cost Efficiency	AI-optimized logistics, dynamic energy management, lean operations	Automation in routine tasks and partial digitization of supply chains	High upfront cost of AI deployment and scaling	Long-term reduction in overhead and operational waste	(Sutopo, 2019)
Innovation	Radical breakthroughs via AI-assisted design, biotech, and smart manufacturing	Incremental innovation in fintech, agri-tech, and public service delivery	R&D and prototyping constraints	Sustains competitive differentiation and enhances organizational agility	(Harbani et al., 2021)

continued on following page

Table 2. Continued

Strategic Area	Developed Context Value	Developing Context Value	Challenges	Organizational Management Benefit	Reference
Market Expansion	AI-driven global e-commerce, personalized digital marketing at scale	Access to new customer bases through mobile platforms	Regional market fragmentation and digital trust deficits	Opens untapped markets and strengthens brand penetration	(Husain, 2021).
Customer Experience	Hyper-personalization, real-time behavioral insights, automated service agents	Improved digital service delivery, basic customer segmentation	Service quality disparity and trust concerns	Builds loyalty and increases lifetime customer value	(Saura et al., 2022)
Supply Chain	Real-time AI logistics orchestration, IoT-enabled predictive supply chains	Pilot adoption in agri-supply chains and logistics tracking	Infrastructure and interoperability gaps	Creates resilience and reduces vulnerability to shocks	(Ndou et al., 2020)
Risk Management	AI-enabled predictive risk analytics for finance, compliance, and operations	Early adoption of fraud detection and disaster risk monitoring	Data sparsity and immature risk models	Reduces exposure to systemic shocks and enhances resilience	(Sunu, 2022)
HR & Talent	AI-based recruitment analytics, continuous workforce performance tracking	Experiments with AI in recruitment and HR management	Lack of cultural acceptance and technical literacy	Aligns workforce competencies with organizational strategy	(Alaziz et al., 2023)
Product Development	Rapid prototyping, generative design, AI-aided R&D pipelines	Adaptive product models responding to local market needs	Insufficient design thinking integration	Accelerates time-to-market and fosters customer-centric design	(Shafik, 2024b)
Financial Control	AI-enabled real-time accounting, anomaly detection in transactions	Growing fintech adoption in payments and auditing	Reliance on legacy systems and poor integration	Improves accountability, transparency, and investor trust	(Ismandianto et al., 2022)

continued on following page

Table 2. Continued

Strategic Area	Developed Context Value	Developing Context Value	Challenges	Organizational Management Benefit	Reference
Sustainability Practices	AI-enabled circular economy solutions, emissions tracking, energy optimization	Application in agriculture (precision irrigation, crop monitoring)	Weak scalability of sustainability pilots	Supports ESG compliance and sustainable brand reputation	(Salava & Kluger, 2022)
Competitive Intelligence	AI-powered market sensing, sentiment analysis, real-time competitor tracking	Localized insights through social media and mobile commerce	Data scarcity and weak interoperability	Improves strategic positioning and proactive decision making	(Sutopo, 2019)
Collaboration	AI-enabled innovation networks, digital twins for joint R&D	Early regional alliances for AI development	Weak platforms and limited institutional trust	Expands collaborative advantage and accelerates knowledge transfer	(Ismandianto et al., 2022)
Strategic Foresight	Scenario planning, stress-testing policies with AI simulation models	Pilot foresight initiatives for urban planning and agriculture	Limited adoption due to cost and expertise	Strengthens resilience through long-term adaptive planning	(Harbani et al., 2021)

6. FUTURE TRENDS AND INNOVATIONS IN AI TECHNOLOGY MANAGEMENT

Automation, learning, and AI: On the tech side, much work can be done to integrate domain expertise with machine learning or AI algorithms and enable shared decision-making. Algorithmic accountability and an increased focus on ethical AI or responsible technology will necessarily need to be a trend. Implementability: developing a more commercial systems-based approach that gives more emphasis to ensuring technological trends are well understood and to the alignment of human resources with technological innovation (Shafik, 2024b). Machine learning platforms, recommendation systems, and applications to optimize products and services for existing clients based on past buying behavior can be seen to help larger corporations do more efficiently some of the same things done by smaller companies (e.g., improve efficiencies and/or their competitiveness). Technological evolutions are much less about subdividing the market and more about engaging with entirely new competencies. Does the market for 'management and product management AI' represent new skills, capabilities, or areas of technical focus or demand that do not exist in the market today? In both scenarios, the following drivers have a big impact on the model, varying scale, configuration, or both: data transfer restrictions, creating an efficient AI workforce, common tech standards and services, policymakers promoting AI adoption, ethical AI developments/partnerships, bonus to GDP, increasing R&D on AI, business intelligence, demand for key AI technologies, artificial intelligence superpower rankings, and AI adoption, the innovativeness and efficiency of a country, and the best trademark service. Policymakers cannot disregard these features and must adapt them to global trends, building greater adaptability into policymaking and strategy to manage the potential change AI adoption may bring. The speed at which some regions or countries weather technological change will vary; however, it will happen. The trend towards increasing digitalization and the use of AI will continue and may even accelerate. The most efficient and profitable producers will continue to exploit innovations as soon as they are available. Product development outliers will become more numerous and more profitable as technology becomes more accessible. The demand for more productive, efficient, and usable companies by an ever-richer globe with fewer workers by proportion will continue to rise (Ismandianto et al., 2022; Salava & Kluger, 2022). Policymakers and company stakeholders must find a way to justify future artificial intelligence adoption and use in their organizations that will gradually be adopted by AI suppliers and employees across countries. They are already in use by all top multinational corporations.

7. CONCLUSION

As AI management technology continues to evolve, there are a variety of significant and emerging trends that need to be considered. AI technology and AI management are constantly evolving as new methodologies are created and developed. New AI methodologies, such as automated machine learning and ideas from symbolic and differentiable AI that allow for explainable AI have significant potential to reshape management practices. AI technologies that combine components from both symbolic and connectionist AI in novel ways offer significant potential for new and interesting applications. Today, it is possible to do basic living and human-scale cognitive modeling, and AI governance engineering with these tools. Artificial intelligence has the potential to improve labor market inclusion, and the growth of advanced technologies in AI and automation can increase the productivity of workers and generate new employment opportunities in and adjacent to the tech sector. However, these advances also have potential challenges, particularly in the event of rapid adoption or disruptive change. AI has the potential to address some sensitive global challenges, including climate change and public health. AI leadership should evolve as the AI profession does, with frequent updates in knowledge and skills adapted to advances in technology and policy. Communication, collaboration, and community engagement to discuss AI governance issues are essential as model complexity and power increase over time. We anticipate there will be many advancements in AI management throughout the 2020s. A shift in regulatory and ethical development towards AI transparency, accountability, data security, and fairness governance will occur as an approach to protect individuals' fundamental rights while governing emerging technologies. Sector-specific laws will continue to be developed nationally to aid in responsible AI governance practices. Given the increasing complexity of AI, data, and cybersecurity issues, there will be an additional focus on oversight and ethical issues pertaining to data management and the digitization of broader services. Additionally, AI management is expected to evolve, both as a field and as a mainstream practice. There will be a shift in the way we view governance and safety in autonomous and semi-autonomous vehicles, as well as supply chain safety, with the inclusion of new AI technologies in logistics and manufacturing. AI innovation will play a significant role in advancements in privacy, surveillance, and data protection in response to health and security challenges, including global financial unrest and regional security threats. We conclude that AI management as an academic discipline has the potential to reshape the global market, taking actions directly based on automated and extended data. AI management is an essential skill in terms of reasoning and performance analysis to address the unforeseen and tackle global challenges across sectors. AI impact and realization of predictions depend on how the industry and society change with AI, empowered by a growth mindset, digital literacy, formal and informal training support, and global partnerships. Leaders use global and AI leadership to develop global response plans for rapid responses to security and global health events and AI management to recover quickly and implement protocols. Stakeholder communities need to come together to respond to transformational issues facing the world in the coming decade. One would expect better solutions and technologies to emerge as AI governs, predicting the future and implementing the lessons learned in AI quality assurance.

REFERENCES

Abutabenjeh, S., Nukpezah, J. A., & Azhar, A. (2022). Do Smart Cities Technologies Contribute to Local Economic Development? *Economic Development Quarterly*, *36*(1), 3–16. Advance online publication. DOI: 10.1177/08912424211053599

Alaziz, S. N., Alshowiman, A. A., Albayati, B., & El-Bagoury, A. (2023). Clustering of COVID-19 Multi-Time Series-Based K-Means and PCA With Forecasting. *International Journal of Data Warehousing and Mining*, *19*(3), 1–25. Advance online publication. DOI: 10.4018/IJDWM.317374

Alnssyan, B., Ahmad, Z., Malela-Majika, J. C., Seong, J. T., & Shafik, W. (2023). On the identifiability and statistical features of a new distributional approach with reliability applications. *AIP Advances*, *13*(12), 125211. Advance online publication. DOI: 10.1063/5.0178555

Andreadis, I. I., Gioumouxouzis, C. I., Eleftheriadis, G. K., & Fatouros, D. G. (2022). The Advent of a New Era in Digital Healthcare: A Role for 3D Printing Technologies in Drug Manufacturing? In *Pharmaceutics* (Vol. 14, Issue 3). DOI: 10.3390/pharmaceutics14030609

Apasrawirote, D., Yawised, K., & Muneesawang, P. (2022). Digital marketing capability: the mystery of business capabilities. In *Marketing Intelligence and Planning* (Vol. 40, Issue 4). DOI: 10.1108/MIP-11-2021-0399

Araújo, M. R. P., Sa-Barreto, L. L., Gratieri, T., Gelfuso, G. M., & Cunha-Filho, M. (2019). The digital pharmacies era: How 3D printing technology using fused deposition modeling can become a reality. In *Pharmaceutics* (Vol. 11, Issue 3). DOI: 10.3390/pharmaceutics11030128

Bag, S., Srivastava, G., Al Bashir, M. M., Kumari, S., Giannakis, M., & Chowdhury, A. H. (2022). Journey of customers in this digital era: Understanding the role of artificial intelligence technologies in user engagement and conversion. *Benchmarking*, *29*(7), 2074–2098. Advance online publication. DOI: 10.1108/BIJ-07-2021-0415

Bakare, Y. B. (2023). Machine Learning-Based Smart Irrigation System and Soil Nutrients analysis to Increase Productivity in Agriculture Field. *AIP Conference Proceedings*, *2523*, 020030. Advance online publication. DOI: 10.1063/5.0116007

Bartosik-Purgat, M., & Filimon, N. (2022). European consumers in the digital era: Implications of technology, media and culture on consumer behavior. In *European Consumers in the Digital Era: Implications of Technology*. Media and Culture on Consumer Behavior., DOI: 10.4324/9781003263685

Bliznets, I. A., Kartskhiya, A. A., & Smirnov, M. G. (2018). Technology Transfer in Digital Era: Legal Environment. *Tarih Kültür ve Sanat Arastirmalari Dergisi*, *7*(1), 354. Advance online publication. DOI: 10.7596/taksad.v7i1.1466

Boonmoh, A., Jumpakate, T., & Karpklon, S. (2021). Teachers' perceptions and experience in using technology for the classroom. *CALL-EJ, 22*(1).

Budiarti, I., Hibatulloh, F., & Salman, M. (2021). Financial Technology as Payment Methods in the Digital Era. *International Journal of Research and Applied Technology*, *1*(1), 9–16. Advance online publication. DOI: 10.34010/injuratech.v1i1.5454

Chang, K. W. (2022). Interdisciplinary treatment in the digital era. *APOS Trends in Orthodontics*, *12*(2), 71–76. Advance online publication. DOI: 10.25259/APOS_126_2022

Dalam, P. M., Kinerja, P., Melalui, U., Keuangan, L., Digital, D., Desa, M. Di, Kecamatan, K., Kabupaten, P., Sriyono1, P., Sugiarto2, H., Dearelsa3, G. B., Anisyah4, D., Nur, F., & Islakhudin5, A. (2022). The Role of Mbkm in Improving MSME Performance Through Financial Literacy and Digital Marketing in Ketanireng Village, Prigen District, Pasuruan Regency. *Pssh.Umsida.Ac.Id*.

Demirkiran, Y., & Öztürko lu, Ö. (2022). Key Performance Measures and Digital-Era Technologies in Warehouses. *Operations and Supply Chain Management*, *15*(2). Advance online publication. DOI: 10.31387/oscm0490340

Elyta, M., Martoyo, , & Herlan, . (2021). Formulation Model of Power Based Technopreneurship in the Digital Technology Era. *International Journal on Advanced Science, Engineering and Information Technology*, *11*(6), 2344. Advance online publication. DOI: 10.18517/ijaseit.11.6.10968

Fortuna, K. L., Myers, A. L., Walsh, D., Walker, R., Mois, G., & Brooks, J. M. (2020). Strategies to increase peer support specialists' capacity to use digital technology in the era of COVID-19: Pre-post study. *JMIR Mental Health*, *7*(7), e20429. Advance online publication. DOI: 10.2196/20429 PMID: 32629424

Goodyear, P. (2021). Navigating difficult waters in a digital era: Technology, uncertainty and the objects of informal lifelong learning. *British Journal of Educational Technology*, *52*(4), 1594–1611. Advance online publication. DOI: 10.1111/bjet.13107

Harbani, M., Muna, N., & Judiarni, J. A. (2021). Digital Leadership in Facing Challenges in the Era Industrial Revolution 4.0. *Webology*, *18*(Special Issue), 975–990. Advance online publication. DOI: 10.14704/WEB/V18SI05/WEB18275

Hashim, H. (2018). Application of Technology in the Digital Era Education. *International Journal of Research in Counseling and Education*, *1*(2), 1. Advance online publication. DOI: 10.24036/002za0002

Hasin, H., Johari, Y. C., & Jamil, A. (2022). Accountant's Digital Technologies Competencies in The Digitalisation Era. *International Journal of Academic Research in Business & Social Sciences*, *12*(10). Advance online publication. DOI: 10.6007/IJARBSS/v12-i10/14894

Hazzan, M. K. (2022). Deception in the era of digital technologies and the distortion of reality and facts: An X-Ray of Nigerian peculiarities. *E-Learning and Digital Media*. Advance online publication. DOI: 10.1177/20427530221124002

Herman, H., Sherly, S., Sinaga, Y. K., Sinurat, B., Sihombing, P. S. R., Panjaitan, M. B., Purba, L., Sinaga, J. A. Br., Marpaung, T. I., & Tannuary, A. (2022). Socialization of The Implementation of Digital Literacy for Educators and Students in The Digital Era in Pematangsiantar City. *JURNAL KREATIVITAS PENGABDIAN KEPADA MASYARAKAT (PKM), 5*(6). DOI: 10.33024/jkpm.v5i6.5864

Husain, A. P. (2021). Pendidikan Karakter pada Anak Usia Dasar dalam Pembelajaran Daring di Era Digital. *Nusantara: Jurnal Pendidikan Indonesia*, *1*(3), 439–456. Advance online publication. DOI: 10.14421/njpi.2021.v1i3-1

Ismandianto, I., Suyanto, S., Latifah, K., & Muchid, M. (2022). Transformation of Radio Technology in The Digital Age. *Nyimak: Journal of Communication*, *6*(1), 115. Advance online publication. DOI: 10.31000/nyimak.v6i1.5547

Istenič, A., Rosanda, V., Volk, M., & Gačnik, M. (2023). Parental Perceptions of Child's Play in the Post-Digital Era: Parents' Dilemma with Digital Formats Informing the Kindergarten Curriculum. *Children (Basel, Switzerland)*, *10*(1), 101. Advance online publication. DOI: 10.3390/children10010101 PMID: 36670651

Jun, Y., Craig, A., Shafik, W., & Sharif, L. (2021). Artificial Intelligence Application in Cybersecurity and Cyberdefense. In *Wireless Communications and Mobile Computing* (Vol. 2021). DOI: 10.1155/2021/3329581

Kollmann, T., Kleine-Stegemann, L., de Cruppe, K., & Then-Bergh, C. (2022). Eras of Digital Entrepreneurship: Connecting the Past, Present, and Future. *Business & Information Systems Engineering*, *64*(1), 15–31. Advance online publication. DOI: 10.1007/s12599-021-00728-6

Kumar, R. (2021). Managing Business in the Digital Era–The use of IT and Analytics for Process Transformation. *Journal of Decision Systems*, *30*(4), 410–413. Advance online publication. DOI: 10.1080/12460125.2021.1925397

Kurniawan, A., Suwarno, , Komara, B. D., Rajiani, I., & Prasetya, A. (2019). Small and medium enterprises (SMES) in the era digital marketing technology. *International Journal of Recent Technology and Engineering*, *8*(3), 8532–8535. Advance online publication. DOI: 10.35940/ijrte.B3774.098319

Lamine, W., Mian, S., Fayolle, A., & Linton, J. D. (2021). Educating scientists and engineers for technology entrepreneurship in the emerging digital era. In *Technological Forecasting and Social Change* (Vol. 164). DOI: 10.1016/j.techfore.2020.120552

Li, Y., Dai, J., & Cui, L. (2020). The impact of digital technologies on economic and environmental performance in the context of industry 4.0: A moderated mediation model. *International Journal of Production Economics*, *229*, 107777. Advance online publication. DOI: 10.1016/j.ijpe.2020.107777

Lin, Y., Ahmad, Z., Shafik, W., Khosa, S. K., Almaspoor, Z., Alsuhabi, H., & Abbas, F. (2021). Impact of Facebook and Newspaper Advertising on Sales: A Comparative Study of Online and Print Media. *Computational Intelligence and Neuroscience*, *2021*(1), 5995008. Advance online publication. DOI: 10.1155/2021/5995008 PMID: 34475947

Lu, Y., Liu, S., & Bai, Y. (2022). Analysis of Digital Photography Technology in the Era of Big Data. *Mobile Information Systems*, *2022*, 1–8. Advance online publication. DOI: 10.1155/2022/3880755

Mallam, S. C., Nazir, S., & Renganayagalu, S. K. (2019). Rethinking maritime education, training, and operations in the digital era: Applications for emerging immersive technologies. In *Journal of Marine Science and Engineering* (Vol. 7, Issue 12). DOI: 10.3390/jmse7120428

Martin, M., & Vacca, F. (2018). Heritage narratives in the digital era: How digital technologies have improved approaches and tools for fashion know-how, traditions, and memories. *Research Journal of Textile and Apparel*, *22*(4), 335–351. Advance online publication. DOI: 10.1108/RJTA-02-2018-0015

Mohammed, M., & Shahda, M. (2018). Vision and Methodology to Support Sustainable Architecture through Building Technology in the Digital Era. *The International Journal of Environmental Science & Sustainable Development*, *2*(1). Advance online publication. DOI: 10.21625/essd.v2i1.169.g71

Ndou, A. T., Madonsela, N. S., & Twala, B. (2020). The era of digital technology: Analysis of factors contributing to economic growth and sustainability. *Proceedings of the International Conference on Industrial Engineering and Operations Management*, 59.

Peng, B. (2022). Digital leadership: State governance in the era of digital technology. *Cultura e Scuola*, *5*(4), 210–225. Advance online publication. DOI: 10.1177/2096608321989835

Rampton, V., Böhmer, M., & Winkler, A. (2022). Medical Technologies Past and Present: How History Helps to Understand the Digital Era. *The Journal of Medical Humanities*, *43*(2), 343–364. Advance online publication. DOI: 10.1007/s10912-021-09699-x PMID: 34232480

Salava, A., & Kluger, N. (2022). Teaching dermatology in the era of digital technology. In *Annales de Dermatologie et de Venereologie* (Vol. 149, Issue 4). DOI: 10.1016/j.annder.2022.04.002

Sam, S., & Pearson, A. (2019). Community Legal Centres in the Digital Era: The Use of Digital Technologies in Queensland Community Legal Centres. *Law. Technology and Humans*, *1*(1), 64–79. Advance online publication. DOI: 10.5204/lthj.v1i0.1305

Saura, J. R., Ribeiro-Soriano, D., & Zegarra Saldaña, P. (2022). Exploring the challenges of remote work on Twitter users' sentiments: From digital technology development to a post-pandemic era. *Journal of Business Research*, *142*, 242–254. Advance online publication. DOI: 10.1016/j.jbusres.2021.12.052

Shafik, W. (2024a). Artificial Intelligence and Internet of Things Roles in Sustainable Next-Generation Manufacturing. In *Sustainable Innovation for Industry 6.0* (pp. 207–239). IGI Global., DOI: 10.4018/979-8-3693-3140-8.ch012

Shafik, W. (2024b). Data Privacy and Security Safeguarding Customer Information in ChatGPT Systems. In *Revolutionizing the Service Industry Wth OpenAI Models* (pp. 52–86). IGI Global., DOI: 10.4018/979-8-3693-1239-1.ch003

Shafik, W. (2024c). Deep Learning Impacts in the Field of Artificial Intelligence. In *Deep Learning Concepts in Operations Research* (pp. 9–26). Auerbach Publications., DOI: 10.1201/9781003433309-2

Shafik, W. (2024d). Energy policies and infrastructure requirements for efficient green buildings. *Sustainable Technologies for Energy Efficient Buildings*, 212.

Shafik, W. (2024e). Exploring the Potential of Internet of Things (IoT) and Challenges in Enabling Circular Economy Practices in Smart Cities. In *Smart Cities and Circular Economy* (pp. 125–138). Emerald Publishing Limited. DOI: 10.1108/978-1-83797-957-820241012

Shafik, W. (2024f). Factors Affecting Green Purchase Behaviors for Small and Medium Enterprises (SMEs) in Uganda. In *Entrepreneurial Strategies for the Internationalization and Digitalization of SMEs* (pp. 198–224). IGI Global. DOI: 10.4018/979-8-3693-3518-5.ch009

Shafik, W. (2024g). Generative AI for Social Good and Sustainable Development. In *Generative AI: Current Trends and Applications* (pp. 185–217). Springer. DOI: 10.1007/978-981-97-8460-8_10

Shafik, W. (2025). Quantum Computing and Generative Adversarial Networks (GANs): Ethics, Privacy, and Security. In *Quantum AI and its Applications in Blockchain Technology* (pp. 111–156). IGI Global Scientific Publishing.

Su, C. W., Xie, Y., Shahab, S., Faisal, C. M. N., Hafeez, M., & Qamri, G. M. (2021). Towards achieving sustainable development: Role of technology innovation, technology adoption and co2 emission for brics. *International Journal of Environmental Research and Public Health, 18*(1), 277. Advance online publication. DOI: 10.3390/ijerph18010277 PMID: 33401479

Sudrajat, D. (2019). Effective English Learning Through Scientific Approach In The Era Of Digital Technology. In *International Journal of Global Community: Vol. II* (Issue 3).

Sunu, I. G. K. A. (2022). The Impact of Digital Leadership on Teachers' Acceptance and Use of Digital Technologies. *Mimbar Ilmu, 27*(2), 311–320. Advance online publication. DOI: 10.23887/mi.v27i2.52832

Sutopo, W. (2019). The Roles of Industrial Engineering Education for Promoting Innovations and Technology Commercialization in the Digital Era. *IOP Conference Series. Materials Science and Engineering, 495*(1), 012001. Advance online publication. DOI: 10.1088/1757-899X/495/1/012001

Trisiana, A. (2019). Innovation design development of citizenship education model on characters of indonesian communities in digital media era and technology revolution. *International Journal of Recent Technology and Engineering, 8*(2 Special Issue 9). DOI: 10.35940/ijrte.B1074.0982S919

van Dijk, A., & van Grieken, H. (2017). Digital era Technology Operating Models. *Deloitte, October*.

Xiao, H. (2022). Innovation of Digital Multimedia VR Technology in Music Education Curriculum in Colleges and Universities. *Scientific Programming, 2022*, 1–9. Advance online publication. DOI: 10.1155/2022/6566144

Yang, Z., Jianjun, L., Faqiri, H., Shafik, W., Talal Abdulrahman, A., Yusuf, M., & Sharawy, A. M. (2021). Green Internet of Things and Big Data Application in Smart Cities Development. *Complexity*, *2021*(1), 4922697. Advance online publication. DOI: 10.1155/2021/4922697

Yujie, Z., Al Imran Yasin, M., Alsagoff, S. A. B. S., & Hoon, A. L. (2022). The Mediating Role of New Media Engagement in This Digital Age. *Frontiers in Public Health*, *10*, 879530. Advance online publication. DOI: 10.3389/fpubh.2022.879530 PMID: 35586011

Yusup, M., Suhaepi, M. I., & Ramadhan, R. (2022). Blockchain Technology for Cashless Investments and Transactions in Digital Era With SWOT Approach. *Blockchain Frontier Technology*, *2*(1), 17–23. Advance online publication. DOI: 10.34306/bfront.v2i1.91

Zhao, L., Zhu, D., Shafik, W., Matinkhah, S. M., Ahmad, Z., Sharif, L., & Craig, A. (2022). Artificial intelligence analysis in cyber domain: A review. In *International Journal of Distributed Sensor Networks* (Vol. 18, Issue 4). DOI: 10.1177/15501329221084882

Zurdo, R. P., Dopacio, C. I., & Paredes, V. R. (2022). Social sustainability and employment as a challenge of digital transformation: The new sixth digital sector of the economy. *REVESCO Revista de Estudios Cooperativos*, *142*. Advance online publication. DOI: 10.5209/reve.83719

ADDITIONAL READING

Demaidi, M. N. (2025). Artificial intelligence national strategy in a developing country. *AI & Society*, *40*(2), 423–435. DOI: 10.1007/s00146-023-01779-x

Mannuru, N. R., Shahriar, S., Teel, Z. A., Wang, T., Lund, B. D., Tijani, S., Pohboon, C. O., Agbaji, D., Alhassan, J., Galley, J. K. L., Kousari, R., Ogbadu-Oladapo, L., Saurav, S. K., Srivastava, A., Tummuru, S. P., Uppala, S., & Vaidya, P. (2025). Artificial intelligence in developing countries: The impact of generative artificial intelligence (AI) technologies for development. *Information Development*, *41*(3), 1036–1054. DOI: 10.1177/02666669231200628

Meitei, A. J., Rai, P., & Rajkishan, S. S. (2025). Application of AI/ML techniques in achieving SDGs: A bibliometric study. *Environment, Development and Sustainability*, *27*(1), 281–317. DOI: 10.1007/s10668-023-03935-1

Rashid, A., Baloch, N., Rasheed, R., & Ngah, A. H. (2025). Big data analytics-artificial intelligence and sustainable performance through green supply chain practices in manufacturing firms of a developing country. *Journal of Science and Technology Policy Management*, *16*(1), 42–67. DOI: 10.1108/JSTPM-04-2023-0050

Saba, C. S., & Monkam, N. (2025). Leveraging the potential of artificial intelligence (AI) in exploring the interplay among tax revenue, institutional quality, and economic growth in the G-7 countries. *AI & Society*, *40*(2), 653–675. DOI: 10.1007/s00146-024-01885-4

Shafik, W. (2024a). Industry 4.0 Technologies' Opportunities and Challenges for Realising Net-Zero Economy. Net Zero Economy, Corporate Social Responsibility and Sustainable Value Creation: Exploring Strategies, Drivers, and Challenges, 19–41.

Shafik, W. (2024b). Industry 4.0 Technologies' Opportunities and Challenges for Realising Net-Zero Economy. In Net Zero Economy, Corporate Social Responsibility and Sustainable Value Creation: Exploring Strategies, Drivers, and Challenges (pp. 19–41). Springer. DOI: 10.1007/978-3-031-55779-8_2

Shafik, W. (2024c). Industry Revolution 4.0 and Beyond. In Powering Industry 5.0 and Sustainable Development Through Innovation (pp. 292–316). IGI Global. DOI: 10.4018/979-8-3693-3550-5.ch020

Shafik, W. (2024d). Role of Artificial Intelligence in the Agile Project Management. In *Practical Approaches to Agile Project Management* (pp. 207–237). IGI Global. DOI: 10.4018/979-8-3693-3318-1.ch012

Shafik, W. (2024e). Science of Emotional Intelligence. In *Enhancing and Predicting Digital Consumer Behavior with AI* (pp. 284–310). IGI Global., DOI: 10.4018/979-8-3693-4453-8.ch015

Shafik, W. (2024f). Social Media Insights Into Consumer Behavior. In Intersection of AI and Business Intelligence in Data-Driven Decision-Making (pp. 283–308). IGI Global. DOI: 10.4018/979-8-3693-5288-5.ch010

Shafik, W. (2024g). Social Media Insights Into Consumer Behavior. In Intersection of AI and Business Intelligence in Data-Driven Decision-Making (pp. 283–308). IGI Global. DOI: 10.4018/979-8-3693-5288-5.ch010

Shafik, W. (2024h). Sustainable Development. In Viana Hassan, A. S. S. B. (Ed.), *Building Community Resiliency and Sustainability With Tourism Development* (1st ed., Vol. 1, pp. 1–30). IGI Global., DOI: 10.4018/979-8-3693-5405-6.ch001

Shafik, W. (2024i). The Role of Generative Artificial Intelligence in E-Commerce Fraud Detection and Prevention. In Strategies for E-Commerce Data Security: Cloud, Blockchain, AI, and Machine Learning (pp. 430–469). IGI Global.

Shafik, W. (2024j). Toward a More Ethical Future of Artificial Intelligence and Data Science. In *The Ethical Frontier of AI and Data Analysis* (pp. 362–388). IGI Global. DOI: 10.4018/979-8-3693-2964-1.ch022

Wang, Q., Zhang, F., & Li, R. (2025). Artificial intelligence and sustainable development during urbanization: Perspectives on AI R&D innovation, AI infrastructure, and AI market advantage. *Sustainable Development (Bradford)*, *33*(1), 1136–1156. DOI: 10.1002/sd.3150

KEY TERMS AND DEFINITIONS

AI Management: The strategic oversight of artificial intelligence technologies to maximize efficiency, innovation, and ethical deployment within organizations.

Data Governance: The principles and practices ensuring the quality, security, and ethical use of data in AI systems.

Digital Inclusion: The equitable access to and participation in digital technologies across different populations and regions.

Digital Transformation: The integration of digital technologies into business and governance processes to enhance value creation.

Global Competitiveness: The ability of nations or organizations to leverage technology for sustained economic advantage.

Human Capital: The skills, knowledge, and capabilities of people that enable the effective use of AI and digital technologies.

Innovation Ecosystems: Networks of institutions, firms, and policies that support the development and commercialization of new technologies.

Organizational Resilience: The capability of firms to adapt, survive, and thrive amid technological disruption and market uncertainties.

Policy Frameworks: Structured regulations and guidelines that govern the adoption, ethics, and management of emerging technologies.

R&D Investment: Financial and institutional commitment to research and development for advancing innovation capacity.

Sustainable Development: A growth model balancing economic progress, social equity, and environmental protection for long-term resilience.

Technology Growth: The expansion and advancement of digital tools, platforms, and systems that drive organizational and societal transformation.

Chapter 4
Artificial Intelligence Decision Making:
Novel Approach to Determine the Image Security Prototype Acceptance Especially for Practical Application

P. C. Lai
https://orcid.org/0000-0002-8319-8459
University of Malaya, Malaysia

D. L. Tong
https://orcid.org/0000-0002-6363-7960
Universiti Tunku Abadul Rahman, Malaysia

ABSTRACT

The paper pursues to research the security authentication users in espousing a novel image authentication system using a stimulus research model (SRM) that was extended from Technology Acceptance Model (TAM). This research continues to investigate the relationship between the usefulness, ease of use, and security acceptance of novelty authentication image security. The research method based on quantitative is used here to fulfil the requirements of which the security authentication users' acceptance to use were used for the analysis. The results from this research imply that security, usefulness, and ease of use influence the acceptance of novelty authentication image security. This research can set a novel approach and trend to determine the prototype acceptance, especially for practical application in Education. Furthermore, this practical approach for product market mix will contribute to the economic development of the country.

DOI: 10.4018/979-8-3373-2497-5.ch004

INTRODUCTION

In the world of rapidly changing environment and technology changes, new ways of services are being offered that create opportunities or threats to current businesses. Thus, organisations need to be on the lookout to establish their possible effect. Organisations often pursue to take advantage of the technology that will benefit their organization (Lovelock, 2001; Lai, 2018; Lai, 2023) and this can be seen in the single platform E-payment technology (Lai, 2018). Providing convenient and rapid security authentication systems to today's users can be a complicated problem. The novel solution is to choose a sequence of random images provided by the Image Security App (ISA), and the application will then generate a One Time Password (OTP) for the user. Such an authentication system can be deployed to operate in many parts: e.g: shopping, healthcare, payment, public transport, and loyalty points. Banking companies and banking system provider companies can replace their current security authentication with this novel Image Security App (ISA) for transactions during payment on a mobile phone.

The standard alphanumeric password has quite a number of drawbacks, but it remains the most commonly used authentication method in most internet applications in the market (Chiasson and Biddle, 2007). No matter whether the system is a private intranet for a company or an online banking system, or even for social media, alphanumeric passwords are still being used as the main authentication method. The drawbacks of the alphanumeric password mainly revolve around security issues (Chiasson and Biddle, 2007; Lai, 2024). These passwords are easy to guess thus increasing the risk of being hacked. In a study done by the UK's National Cyber Security Centre (NCSC), they found out that millions of people are using weak passwords like "123456", and this has appeared in more than 23 million passwords (BBC News, 2019). Besides, the passwords are always used repeatedly across sites, causing all the accounts to be compromised if one of them does. To deal with the said issues, some systems required the passwords to be changed in a certain amount of time, causing the users to be inconvenient in both memorizing and creating a new password. Such weakness has a huge risk to lead to identity theft (Chiasson and Biddle, 2007; Lai, 2024). The demand for security and convenience of authentication solutions has called for research and study. Therefore, this research pursues to examine the security of the novelty of the image security authentication relationship with ease of use and usefulness. Further, this study continues to examine the relationship between ease of use, usefulness, and security with users' intention to use. The objective of this research paper is to determine whether the proposed image-sequence-based authenticator will be acceptable to the users allowing them to test the prototype. Furthermore, this is a very good way to determine the prototype acceptance, especially for practical application in Education. Thus, this can set a novel approach and trend for education research and development with actual users' testing analysis. It's also a combination of both technical and business approach mechanics.

LITERATURE REVIEW

Figure 1. Lai (2018)

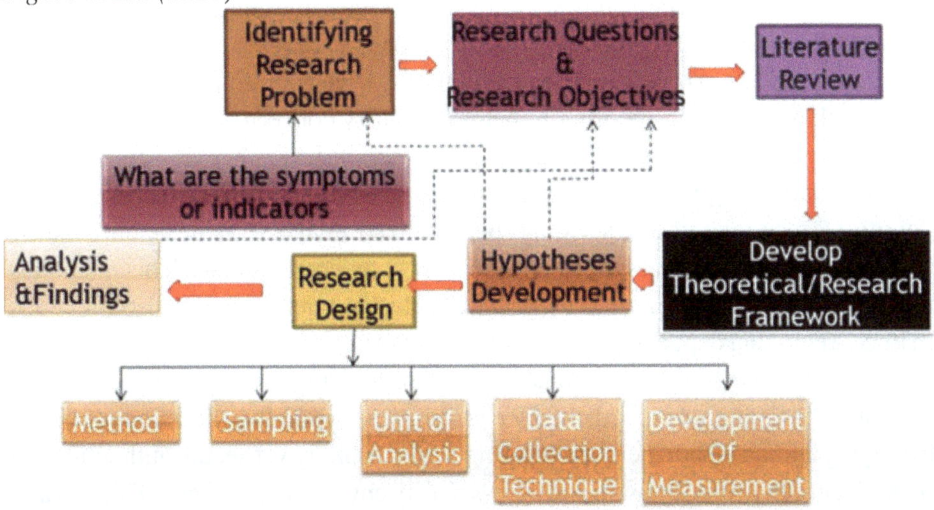

The research strategy uses the deductive process, going from generalizations (theory) leading to prediction (hypotheses), explanation, and understanding of Users' Acceptance of The Innovative Image Security Authentication (Lai, 2024). The research strategy process used in this study is shown in Figure 1.

Security remains a major concern in internet-based systems, with traditional alphanumeric passwords increasingly seen as insufficient against sophisticated cyber threats such as phishing, brute-force attacks, and poor memorability (Ciancarini et al., 2013). To improve authentication, Multi-Factor Authentication (MFA) approaches—such as One-Time Passwords (OTPs) and security tokens—have been widely implemented. OTPs, particularly those sent via SMS, are susceptible to interception through GSM vulnerabilities and malware like Trojans (Mulliner, Rieck, Stewin, & Seifert, 2013). While app-based OTPs and virtual tokens offer enhanced convenience and reduce reliance on mobile networks, they still depend on device integrity and secure software implementation, which may not always be reliable. CAPTCHA technologies, once a reliable barrier against bots, have also been undermined by machine learning algorithms capable of solving image challenges with high accuracy (Sivakorn, Polakis, & Keromytis, 2016).

Centralized Authentication (CA), including Social Login and biometric methods, enables users to access multiple platforms with a single set of credentials and offers convenience (Stormpath, 2016). However, CA systems raise privacy concerns, especially when users unknowingly grant third-party services access to personal data during login processes (Kontaxis, Polychronakis, & Markatos, 2012). Social Login may lead to widespread data exposure if a linked account is compromised. Similarly, while biometric authentication—like fingerprint and facial recognition—provides fast and often offline access, it is not universally accessible and remains vulnerable to spoofing via cloned fingerprints or facial models (Fietkau et al., as cited in Ciancarini et al., 2013). Apple's implementation of eye-detection is a partial solution, but the risk of biometric spoofing remains a security concern.

To address these persistent limitations, the Image Security App (ISA) is proposed as an innovative cognitive authentication system. ISA allows users to verify their identity by recognizing and selecting personalized image sequences, eliminating reliance on memorized passwords or third-party credential storage. This method is not only resistant to phishing, brute-force attacks, and malware, but also functions offline—removing dependencies on mobile networks or internet connectivity. Since ISA does not collect sensitive personal information and stores visual cues in encrypted form, it upholds high standards of user privacy and scalability. Its strength lies in leveraging human visual memory, offering a user-friendly yet secure authentication method for both everyday users and high-security environments (Lai, 2024; Pan and Lai, 2023; Kuang and Lai, 2023).

This section starts with identifying the problems to come out with the solution. Since the research and development are under the computer science school, there is a need to develop a prototype. This research is a combination of both the technical aspect and business aspects; therefore, the users' testing beyond the technical aspects is required. Good research and development for commercialization will cover from design/mock-up to creating a prototype for user testing, and the prototype process flow for this research is shown in figure 2 below. After coming out with the solution, the design mock-up will be created before the actual prototype is developed to be sent for user testing. Then, the data collected with be analysed and iterated in the next section. The users' testing, research methodology, data collection, data analysis, and interpretation will follow the standard business school research. Thus, this combination makes this research paper novel in its own unique way, and look forward to this being the future trend-setting in Education.

Figure 2. Authors' prototype process flow for this research paper

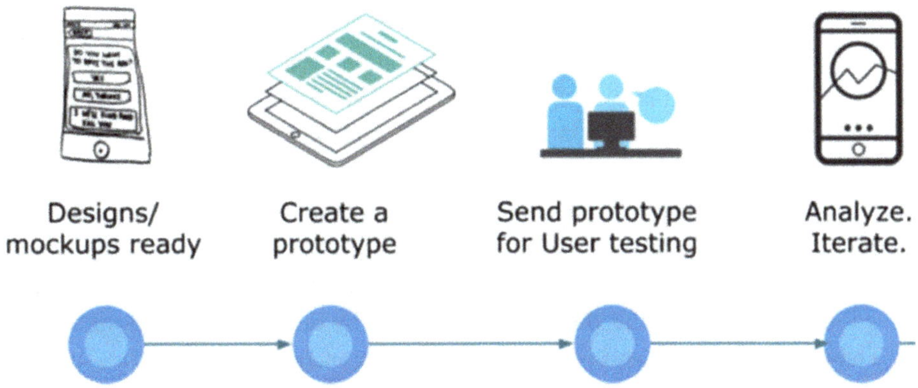

PROPOSED SOLUTION – IMAGE SECURITY APP (ISA)

After the literature reviews and research, an image sequence-based authentication is proposed to overcome the shortcoming of the common existing authentication method. The proposed solution - the Image Security App (ISA) requires the user to register an account in order to use the authentication service. The registered user then links their existing accounts from other sites to ISA. Whenever they want to login into those accounts, they need to choose a sequence of random images provided by ISA, and the application will then generate an OTP for the user. The mobile app is the chosen platform as most people are comfortable with using smartphones nowadays since it has blended into everyone's life, thus easing their learning process. Furthermore, as long as there is a stable internet connection, they can access the token anytime anywhere from their phone, so it is very convenient for them.

Instead of logging in using credentials, they will need to enter the OTP to the sites. This provides them with a convenient login method for users because they do not need to remember and retype their password every time they log in. The overall security will be improved as well as the OTP that is valid for only 30 seconds is generated by the sequence of images so there is no use for the imposter to record the OTP even if they somehow manage to get it. The sequence of the images provided in the app differ each time the user wants to generate the OTP so the hacker cannot predict what image to be used. The ISA requires a stable Internet connection in order to fetch randomly generated images from the server, as well as send the OTP to the sites that are linked to the app for verification.

The ISA combines a few strong points while overcoming the shortcomings of the authentication methods that were reviewed in the previous sections. Like a virtual security token, ISA expires the code in a given interval so that even if it is recorded, it is no longer useful after the interval. Unlike a physical token, the users need not worry to lose it as it can be downloaded again anytime on any device. Code generated from ISA is one-time usage only like a normal OTP so after it is being used, it is no longer valid afterward and since it is using an Internet connection instead of a mobile network, the users do not need to worry about being intercepted by the attack model by Nohl et al. and also Trojan. Besides, it is not crackable by using features reconstruction deep learning algorithms like biometric authentication because the image in the app, as well as the sequence chosen by the user, are random.

The main concern in this solution is the acceptance by the user. Thus, a survey is conducted to investigate whether the user accepts the solution or not.

OPERATIONALIZE THE RESEARCH

Davis (1989) who is the author of the Technology Acceptance Model (TAM) has become so popular that it has been cited in most of the research that deals with users' acceptance of technology (Lee, Kozar and Larsen, 2003). Luarn and Lin, (2005) and Lee and Jun (2007) contended that factors influencing the intentions to use include usefulness and convenience, and these factors are appropriate to verify new technology like novel Image Security Apps (ISA) (Tong, Lai and Liew, 2024) as well as image security app in this research.

Efficiency that is related to convenience and usefulness in mobile phone services has been the driver of the user's intention to use (Phan and Diam, 2011). According to Dewan and Chen (2005) and Lai and Tong (2022), it's vital to meet the consumers' daily needs and wants by allowing payment anytime, anywhere concept on their mobile phones). Furthermore, consumers like convenience is a context-based concept that could vary from one context to another (Lai and Tong, 2022) and this include the easy accessibility and fast response for services consumption (Laukkanen and Lauronen, 2005; Lai, Toh, and Alkhrabsheh, 2020). Security and privacy issues become increasing concerns following the rapid growth of technological advancement and e-commerce offerings (Jahangir and Begum, 2008; Lai and Lim, 2017). Security refers to the protection of E-payment systems from threats such as illegal intrusion, theft, or destruction (Lai, 2024). This study conceptualizes security as encompassing three dimensions: reliability, safety, and privacy (Lai 2014; Polatoglu and Ekin, 2001). While perceived risk is usually related to how users are confident in adopting new technology, perceived security differs by relating to users' confidence in how organizations provide a safe and unthreatened platform for performing E-payment transactions. (Lai, 2018; Pan and Lai, 2023; Kuang and Lai, 2023)

According to (Lai, Toh, and Alkhrabsheh, 2020; Davis and Venkatesh, 1996, Mathieson, 1999), TAM has been investigated in different scenarios and demonstrated to be an acceptable and dependable model clarifying the intention to use the technology. Furthermore, many extensions to the TAM (Henderson and Divett, 2003; Venkatesh, Speier and Morris 2002) have been recommended and verified. Therefore, this research will modify the Venkatesh and Davis 1996 version of TAM to measure users' intention to use and extend the factor of security.

According to Lai (2023: 2025) Lui and Lai (2023), security is the stimuli that represent the system and features capabilities while the perceived ease of use and perceived usefulness are the organism that represents the motivation to use the system that leads to users' response to using the novel image security app system. The literature review of technology adoption models and theories for the novelty technology did the comparison of the technology models and the justification of the use of stimulus research theoretical framework (Lai, 2014: 2017: 2018) that can be adapted as shown in Figure 3. This study used the underlining variables shown in Figure 1 to determine the users' acceptance to use the novel image security app system. For this study, the following hypotheses were posited:

Figure 3. Adapted from Stimulus Research Model (Lai 2018; Pan and Lai, 2023)

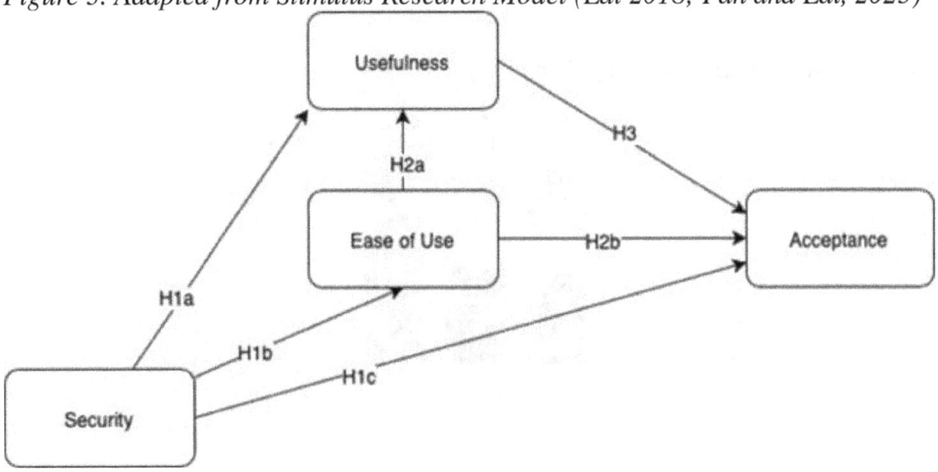

This study will study the relationships between the variables shown in Figure 1 in order to determine their impact on users' acceptance to use the novel image security app system. The following hypotheses regarding these relationships were posited:

H1a: Security is positively associated with usefulness.
H1b: Security is positively associated with ease of use.
H1c: Security is positively associated with acceptance.
H2a: Ease of use is positively associated with usefulness.
H2b: Ease of use is positively associated with acceptance.
H3: Usefulness is positively associated with acceptance.

METHODOLOGIES

The sample size in this research includes only those who have used security authentication technology within the last 12 months. The primary data collection method is through the online survey questionnaires for one (1) month through an email blast to 1480 e-payment users collected from the promotion activity. The respondents have given the YouTube link titled the "novel Image Security App (ISA)" to view and download the prototype app as shown in Figure 4 below before they respond to the questionnaires. According to Klien (2011) and Hair, Black, Babin, Anderson, and Tatham, (2006), the data of 360 respondents that fulfilled these requirements were collected and used for the structural equation model (SEM) studies analysis and more than satisfactory for non-probability sampling sample size (Krejcie and Morgan (1970).

Figure 4. Novel Image Security App (ISA)

In order to assess users' intention of using the Image security app system, the five-point Likert-type scale was implemented. The respondents stipulate their answers to a subject given when responding to the survey questionnaires by selecting the range given. The five-point scale was selected to incite respondents to make negative or positive selections (Lai: 2018: Cooper & Schindler, 2008) to produce more emphatic information (Tong, Lai and Liew, 2024; Oppenheim, 1992). The Cronbach's alpha related to the sample size (360) for the various variables being studied are as follows: usefulness (.94), ease of use (.95), acceptance (.82), and security (.88).

Decision Tree Algorithm

The values of four variables labeled C1 to C4 were averaged to create the dependent variable for the analysis. The remaining 26 Likert-scale variables served as independent variables. The dependent variable was discretized into four distinct classes, each representing a single Likert value. The dataset was then divided into training and test sets using a 70:30 split, with 70% used to train a decision tree model and the remaining 30% reserved for evaluating the model's prediction performance.

RESULT

In this study, analyses have been done for each variable separately to gather a summary of respondents' demographic profiles to get the preliminary information and the feel of the data (Sekaran, 2003). Table 1 showed the respondents' demographic profiles of the survey.

Table 1. Demographic Profiles

Variable	Frequency (n=360)	Percent (Total 100%)
Gender		
Male	**212**	**58.8**
Female	148	41.2
Marital Status		
Single	206	57.2
Married	154	42.8
Age		
< 25	188	52.2

continued on following page

Table 1. Continued

Variable	Frequency (n=360)	Percent (Total 100%)
Gender		
Male	**212**	**58.8**
26-40	124	34.4
41-55	32	8.9
> 55	16	4.5
Education		
Secondary/High school	69	19.2
College/university	226	62.7
Graduate school	65	18.1
Job position		
Top Management	12	3.4
Middle Management	136	37.8
Junior Management	50	13.9
Professional	86	23.8
Other	76	21.1
What industry you work in		
Education	179	49.7
Banking/Finance/Manufacturing/ICT	108	30.0
Retail/Hypermarket	48	13.4
Other	25	6.9

Measurement Model

All the goodness of fit indices was good and satisfied the requirements with the validity assessment of the CFA model. Chi-Square was 452.12 at p=0.00 and df (degree of freedom) was 186. According to Tabachnick and Fidell (2007), the relative Chi-Square ($\chi 2$/df) at 2.63 is below the 5.0 required for a good fit. As stated by Hair et al. (2006). In absolute fit indices, the goodness of fit index (GFI) was 0.96, well higher than 0.90 (Hair et al. 2010). The comparative fit index (CFI) was 0.97, above the 0.90 required for a good fit (Hu and Bentler 1999). The root means the square error of approximation (RMSEA) was 0.07, below the 0.08 required for a good fit (Byrne 1998; Lai. 2018). For the overall measurement model, the results indicated a good fit model.

Structural Model

The structural model was inspected with the theoretical links as shown in Table 2 with all of the goodness of fit indices that indicate an acceptable model after the acceptable measurement model is run in the previous subsection.

Table 2. Goodness-of-fit statistics for the measurement model

Goodness-of-fit Statistics		Level of Acceptance	Index Value
Absolute fit Measures			
Chi-square	X^2	$p > 0.05$	4.051 (p=0.00)
Degree of freedom	df	≥ 0	1
Rot mean square error of approximation	RMSEA	< 0.08	0.074
Goodness of fit index	GFI	>0.90	0.96
Incremental fit measures			
Comparative fit index	CFI	>0.90	0.97
Parsimonious fit measures			
Relative Chi-Square	X^2/df	< 5	2.63

The overall structural model shows all paths of standardizing regression weights as shown in Table 3 are statistically significant at $p \leq 0.001$ and $p \leq 0.01$ levels of significance.

Table 3.Standardized regression weights of the structural model

Hypothesis	Standardized Regression Weights			S.E.	C.R.	P	Results (Significant)
Hypothesis 1 a	PU		<--- S	.049	21.40	***	$p \leq 0.001$
Hypothesis 1b	PEU		<--- S	.032	2.81	.006	$p \leq 0.01$
Hypothesis 1C	I		<--- S	.056	18.37	***	$p \leq 0.001$
Hypothesis 2a	PU		<--- PEU	.053	19.22	***	$p \leq 0.001$
Hypothesis 2b	I		<--- PEU	.072	4.56	.009	$p \leq 0.01$
Hypothesis 3	I		<--- PE	.052	19.70	***	$p \leq 0.001$

1. Hypothesis 1a Security is positively associated with usefulness.

This hypothesis suggests that security as an exogenous factor provides a significant contribution to usefulness as an endogenous factor. Therefore, hypothesis 1a is supported by the data. In this case, security is positively associated with usefulness.

2. Hypothesis 1b Security is positively associated with ease of use.

This hypothesis suggests that security as an exogenous factor provides a significant contribution to ease of use as an endogenous factor. Therefore, hypothesis 1b is supported by the data. In this case, security is positively associated with ease of use.

3. Hypothesis 1C Security is positively associated with acceptance.

The results show that security has a strong direct relationship with consumers' intention to use the system at Critical Ratio C. R=18.37 and p=0.00 ($p<0.001$). In this case, the higher the security support the greater the acceptance to use the system.

4. Hypothesis 2a Ease of use is positively associated with usefulness.

The results of SEM show that the standardized regression weight of the structural path between perceived ease of use and usefulness is positive and significant, in which C.R=19.2 and p=0.00 ($p<0.001$). In this case, the higher the ease of use support the greater the usefulness of the system.

5. Hypothesis 2b Ease of use is positively associated with acceptance.

The hypothesis showed that ease of use is positively associated with users' acceptance of using the system with an explanatory power R^2 of 59.

6. Hypothesis 3 Usefulness is positively associated with acceptance.

The hypothesis showed that usefulness is positively associated with users' acceptance of using the system with an explanatory power R^2 of 73.

DISCUSSIONS

Security demonstrates a vital association between usefulness and ease of use that is almost similar. Lai (2018: 2023: 2024) and Sun and Zhang, (2006) acknowledged that ease of use is imperative for complex systems like the novel image security app system. Thus, organizations planning to execute complex technology like the novel image security app system may gaze at the ease of use and use it as the mediator to boost the usefulness and users' intention to use. Previous studies from Lai, 2018; 2023; 2024 and Muniruddeen, 2007 acknowledged similar results that the security had a positive considerable relationship with ease of use and usefulness towards the users' intention to use this solution. Therefore, in this research security could be mediated by both ease of use and usefulness as well as a direct relationship users' intention to use this novel image security app system.

The structural equation modeling (SEM) in this research recognized that there is a positive and vital relationship between security and users' acceptance to use based on hypothesis 1C supported by the research data in which standardized regression estimate $\beta = .51$, 18.37 and $p=0.00$ ($p<0.001$). It can be recommended that the higher the security of using the novel image security app system, the higher the users' approval to use the novel image security app system. Hypothesis 1C is confirmed and supported by the existing studies (Wang, Wang, Lin, and Tang, 2003; Lai, 2018; 2023). Therefore, the novel image security app system is verified by hypothesis 1C. This result further inferred that security was a vital component of users' approval to use the novel image security app system, as were the ease of use and usefulness.

A standard regression weight of (51%) is considered medium but there is a need to address the security concern as an important factor. Therefore, those in the decision-making team of the companies providing a novel image security app system need to consider providing secured solutions with high-security standards like level 5 or ISO Security 27000 as well. To increase the good view of the security, the novel image security app system providers can arrange to talk to educate users on how to protect their E-payment transactions with the novel image security app system. The users can have peace of mind using this novel image security app solution to perform their e-payment transactions as supported by the results. This will eventually increase the users' confidence and trust that precede the adoption of this novel image security app system for the benefit of the ecosystem as a whole.

"R^2 explanatory power" scores of usefulness by the ease of use, and security factors are .73. "R^2 explanatory power" scores of ease-of-use by security factors are .59. The "R^2 explanatory power" scores of users' acceptance to use by usefulness, ease of use, and security variables are .54. According to Lai (2018) and Cohen (1998), the "R^2 explanatory power" scores were translated as small ($\geq .01$), medium ($\geq .09$), or large ($\geq .25$). The results indicated that the novel image security app system has a very high observation of ease of use and usefulness and moderate to high users' acceptance to use by the respondents. Therefore, the user's acceptance to use is considered very well accepted by the users at 54% rate acceptance to use the novel image security app in this research.

Previous studies like payment mobile e-wallet (Amoroso and Magnier-Watanabe, 2012), cards (Rinaldi, 2001), and smart cards (Humphrey, et al., 2004) are factors influencing technology acceptance, especially in the area of Card, Internet, and Mobile but focused on the individual element. In recent years, (Lai, 2023: 2024; Lai and Scheele, 2018; Pan and Lai, 2023) have incorporated the novelty of combining the card, internet, and mobile all in one single platform known as single platform E-payment. Therefore, there is a need for a security solution like the Image Security App (ISA) in the marketplace for the E-payment environment. Specifically, as far as the researchers are aware, factors that contribute to the finding in accepting Image Security App Authentication in Malaysia have not yet enticed the interest of the research community. Furthermore, this research breaks new ground within information communication technology acceptance literature because this study validated the variables of the well-established theories in this context.

INTERPRETATION OF AIDM™ DATA ANALYSIS

The AIDM™ analysis method is used to determine the users' intention to use the Image Security Application (ISA) solution. Analysis result finding shows that Image Security Application (ISA) solution usage becomes promising with the variables security, perceive usefulness and perceived ease of use. Security is the most prefer variable above the rest. The most valuable item from the group of security being valued highly is non-reputability S6 with 192 respondents. The next security item that is in the preference list is the reliability S2 with 118 respondents. The perceived usefulness most valuable item is the security task is useful PU5 followed by easy to understand PEU8, easy to press and log in to use PEU5 and support critical aspect of security PU9.

When the users feel the security comes with non-reputability S6 together with reliability S2 including Authentication and Authorization S4, they feel safe to use S1 and the solution support critical aspect of security PU9. In order to make the users want to use the Image Security Application (ISA) solution, the ISA needs to be designed to be Effortless PEU1, Easy to activate PEU7 and security task is useful PU5. Thus, the ISA designer of the system needs to take note of these items to encourage usage.

The longest decision tree involved the following items. There are non-reputability S6, easy to press and log in to use PEU5, easy to understand PEU8, Integrity S5, accomplish task fast PU1, provide safety features S1, easy to register PEU6, protect the user privacy S3, good authentication and authorisation S4, easy to sign on to use PEU4, and provide users with greater control and choices PU3. Therefore, the research and development team needs to emphasise on these items the users based on for their decision to use the Image Security Application (ISA) solution.

Another section of decision tree focused on security with 6 out of 8 the questionnaires asked of security is listed. The security features expected to be in the Image Security Application (ISA) solution are starting with the top priority items are non-reputability S6 and reliability S2 followed by is Integrity S5 Authentication and Authorization S4, Privacy S3, and feeling Safe using the Image Security Application (ISA) solution S1. Thus, the Image Security Application (ISA) solution will meet the standard integrity of the security like the ISO standard for security. The users also want the Image Security Application (ISA) solution to provide easy to press and log in PEU5, effectiveness (basically easy to log in with accuracy each time) PU8, Easy to understand PEU8, easy button touch PEU3, Improves performance PU4, Effortless PEU1, Provides efficiency PU7 and Valuable skill-sets PU6. Therefore, these features will need to include the stated Perceived usefulness and Perceived ease of use in the development for the next release to the users.

It's also noted that both Image Security Application (ISA) solution to provide easy to press and log in PEU5 and easy button touch PEU3 came out a few times in the decision and also the last item showing that users also want convenience to get access to the ISA solution as well. Therefore, it's well noted that security needs to balance with the convenience of the usefulness and ease of use so the take up rate will be high.

Management Implication

There are a lot of organizations tackling important challenges regarding their users' technology acceptance due to the increase of fraud cases and call for better security technology lately. Companies need to take into consideration of users' points of view regarding their acceptance of to use of novel security technology like Image security apps since users play the important role in the company's bottom line. This study's findings have many managerial associations for various industries as well as countries.

In assuring the reliability aspect of security, features like the pin, picture security, One Time Password (OTP), finger, or facial recognition requires during E-payment transactions to identify the actual user. This is required in E-payment transactions be it from the e-wallet or e-banking platform and is vital for the E-commerce environment (Lai and Scheele, 2018 Ahn, Ryu, and Han, 2004). Security is usually associated with the organization providing the level of security to consumers and risk is usually associated with consumers' confidence in adopting new technology. According to (Chen and Lai, 2023), there is a need to reduce the high cost of operation in the banking industry. Banks generate a good income from E-payment transactions but risk losing money due to fraudulent transactions (Lai 2023). Therefore, management needs to put priority on the security elements. The other challenge is to keep the consumers happy and loyal through innovation (e.g., to have banking solutions in one (1) single platform) that provides convenience. A common misperception is that users would naturally switch to e-payment solutions because past studies (Pan and Lai, 2023; Marimuthu et al., 2011) found that people prefer carrying less cash or debit/ credit/ reward cards for fear of theft, loss, and cumbersome. The research shared the users' feedback (e.g., security), user-friendly as well as their interest in easy-to-use E-payment on a mobile phone (Lai, 2023: 2024; Lui and Lai, 2023; Kuang and Lai, 2023). By understanding users' preference, information communication technology solution providers will be able to design solution focused on users' needs and want (Chen and Lai, 2023; Fu and Lai, 2023; Lai, 2023; 2024). Thus, this research provides valuable insight into users' perspectives regarding payment transactions as well as the potential of having an innovative security solution like an image security app for banking purposes in the future.

According to Lai (2018; 2023), the ease of use, and reliability, allow users to have control of their choices, and able to use anytime and anywhere with level 5 security seen in the results of respondents in this research like use Image Security App Authentication Solution to replace their current authentication. This is the Image Security App Authentication Solution is believed to improve their E-payment transactions and productivity (Lai and Lim, 2019; Chen and Lai, 2023). Thus, marketers and management of companies providing the E-payment system solution should give priority to the reasons why respondents choose to use Image Security App Solution when providing security to their solution. The information here can be used to support the E-payment applications for the mobile transaction using the Image Security App in the E-marketplace. There is a potential to have more people going cardless, cashless, and contactless with Image Security App Authentication (Lai, 2023: 2024) that help to create a more social-environment green job.

These research results provide the information desired for the research and development of new services or products that will produce new green job establishments in the single-platform E-payment environment by stimulating Image Security App Authentication Solutions (Lai, 2023: 2024). Organizations can fulfill their objective and corporate social responsibility (CSR) through the exploitation of this research's valuable information for developing services and products that meet the users' E-payment authentication system while also fulfilling their objective of corporate social responsibility. Thus, according to (Lai, 2024) the Image Security App Authentication platform solutions will be able to be implemented in most E-payment platforms and further examples can be found in the articles "SMART HEALTHCARE and SMART LIVING for SMART CITIES @ the palm of your hand".

CONCLUSION

Targeting respondents using online surveys is only limited to those who have Internet access, and this can be a limitation as we don't get respondents from those who don't have Internet access. Therefore, non-internet users' further study is recommended using a traditional survey method where information can provide these target viewpoints to the management. The data collected might not apply to another country due to the representation of the Malaysian context. When the respondents have more experience with online payment, the respondents' feedback might change over time and continuous data collection and analysis are recommended. Therefore, longitudinal research to study online payment and users' intention to use the system at various points in time is required. If another researcher in another country is interested to study something similar, this can be easily replicated.

In conclusion, the results from this research suggest that security can be the front-runner solution for the increase in the usage of users' acceptance to use the novel image security app. Thus, security like the Image security app is a vital factor for deliberation when designing apps that require good security like payment transactions to increase the users' acceptance to use. It is prominent that the stimulus of the image security app should include the novel image security app security to reduce the risk that supports the motivation of usefulness and ease of use that can lead to users' acceptance. The Image Security App (ISA) with the One Time Password (OTP) authentication system can be deployed to operate in many parts: e.g.: shopping, healthcare, payment, public transport, and loyalty points. Banking companies and banking system provider companies can replace their current security authentication with this novel Image Security App (ISA) for transactions during payment on mobile phones. As for as the researchers are aware, this novel approach of prototype, testing, survey, data collection, analysis, etc can set a new trend, especially for practical application in education to narrow the gap with the industry. Furthermore, this practical approach for product market mix will contribute to the economic development of the country.

ACKNOWLEDGMENT

The authors gratefully acknowledge the use of the service and facilities of Global-CLAS Technology as well as PCViz facilities and team, the data collection team, industry feedback, and all those who supported this research in kind. This research received no specific grant from any funding agency in the public, commercial, or not-for-profit sectors.

REFERENCES

Ahn, T., Ryu, S., & Han, I. (2004). The impact of the online and offline features on the user acceptance of internet shopping malls. *Electronic Commerce Research and Applications*, *3*(4), 405–420.

Amoroso, D. L., & Magnier-Watanabe, R. (2012). Building a Research Model for Mobile Wallet Consumer Adoption: The Case of Mobile Suica in Japan. *Journal of Theoretical and Applied Electronic Commerce Research*, *7*(1), 94–110.

BBC News. (2019). Millions using 123456 as password, security study finds, 21-Apr-2019. [Accessed: 23-Jul-2019].

Byrne, B. M. (1998). *Structural Equation Modeling with LISREL, PRELIS, and SIMPLIS: Basic Concepts, Applications, and Programming*. Lawrence Erlbaum Associates.

Ciancarini, P., Iorio, A. D., Nuzzolese, A. G., Peroni, S., & Vitali, F. (2013). Semantic Annotation of Scholarly Documents and Citations. AI*IA. "CAPTCHA: Telling Humans and Computers Apart Automatically," The OÔ¨Écial CAPTCHA Site. [Online]. Available: http://www.captcha.net/. [Accessed: 27-Jul-2019].

Cheah, C. M., Oon, K. M., Teo, A. C., Tan, B. I., & Sim, J. J. (2011). Factors Affecting Malaysian Mobile Banking Adoption: An Empirical Analysis. *International Journal of Network and Mobile Technologies*, *2*(3), 149–160.

Chen, D. M., & Lai, P. C. (2023). *Exploration on Teaching Innovation and Reform of "Computer Application Fundamentals" Course in Higher Vocational Colleges: Taking Guangzhou City Construction College as an Example. echnology Management and Its Social Impact on Education.* IGI Global.

Chen, X. S., & Lai, P. C. (2023). The novel thinking exploration model for Blockchain Technology Financial Sharing Services. *Journal of Information Systems and Technology Management.* Advance online publication. DOI: 10.4301/S1807-1775202320005

Chiasson, S. and Biddle, R. (2007). "Issues in User Authentication," Semantic Scholar, 08-Mar-2007.

Cooper, D. R., & Schindler, P. S. (2008). *Business research methods* (10th ed.). McGraw-Hill.

Davis, F. D. (1989). Perceived usefulness, perceived ease of use, and user acceptance of information technology. *Management Information Systems Quarterly, 13*(3), 319–340.

Davis, F. D., & Venkatesh, V. (1996). "A critical assessment of potential measurement biases in the technology acceptance model: Three experiments," Internet J. Human-Comput. *Stud*, *45*, 19–45.

Dewan and Chen. (2005). Mobile payment adoption in the US: A cross-industry, cross platform solution. *Journal of Information Privacy and Security*, *1*(2), 4–25.

Fu, JL, Lai, P. C., (2023) Construction of Occupational Competence Model for Higher Vocational Teachers. Technology Management and Its Social Impact on Education, 165-184

< Hair, J., Black, W., Babin, B. Y. A., Anderson, R., & Tatham, R. (2010). Multivariate Data Analysis. 7th ed. Pearson Prentice Hall.

Harrison, R., Scheela, W., Lai, P. C., & Vivekarajah, S. (2017). Beyond institutional voids and the middle income trap? The emerging business angel market in Malaysia. *Asia Pacific Journal of Management*, •••, 1–27.

Henderson, R., & Divett, M. J. (2003). Perceived usefulness, ease of use and electronic supermarket use. *International Journal of Human-Computer Studies*, *59*(3), 383–395.

Hu, L., & Bentler, P. M. (1999). Cutoff criteria for fit indexes in covariance structure analysis: Conventional criteria versus new alternatives. *Structural Equation Modeling*, *6*(1), 1–55.

Humphrey, D. B., & Aris, K., & Grete √ò. (2004). The future of cash: Falling legal use and implications for government policy. *Journal of International Financial Markets, Institutions and Money*, *14*(3), 221–223.

Krejcie, R., & Morgan, D. W. (1970). Determining Sample size for Research Activities. *Educational and Psychological Measurement*, *30*, 607–610.

Kontaxis, G., Polychronakis, M., & Markatos, E. P. (2012). Minimizing information disclosure to third parties in social login platforms. *International Journal of Information Security*, *11*(5), 321–332.

Kuang, B. W., & Lai, P. C. (2023) Factors Influencing Behavioural Intention to Use e-CNY Among College Students in Guangzhou City, China. Technology Management and Its Social Impact on Education, 185-201, IGI Global

Lai, P. C. (2018). Research, Innovation and Development Strategic Planning for Intellectual Property Management. *Economic Alternatives.*, *12*(3), 303–310.

Lai, P. C., & Lim, C. S. (2019).. . *The Effects of Efficiency, Design and Enjoyment on Single Platform E-payment Research in Business and Management*, *6*(2), 19–34.

Lai, P. C., & Tong, D. L. (2022). *An Artificial Intelligence-Based Approach to Model User Behavior on the Adoption of E-Payment. Handbook of Research on Social Impacts of E-Payment and Blockchain*. IGI Global.

Lai, P. C. (2023). Intention to use the innovative Covid-19 technology "TheSafeCheck" Solution. 19 (1-19). *Journal of Information Systems and Technology Management*. Advance online publication. DOI: 10.4301/S1807-1775202219016

Lai, P. C. (2024). Image Security App (ISA): A cognitive approach to secure authentication. Internal White Paper.

Lee, T. M., & Jun, J. K. (2007). The role of contextual marketing offer in Mobile commerce acceptance: Comparison between Mobile Commerce users and nonusers. *International Journal of Mobile Communications*, *5*(3), 339–356.

Lee, Y., Kozar, K. A., & Larsen, K. R. T. (2003). The technology acceptance model; past, present and future. *Communication of AIS*, *12*(50), 752–780.

Lovelock, C. (2001). *Services Marketing, People, Technology, Strategy*. Prentice Hall.

Luarn, P., & Lin, H. H. (2005). Toward an understanding of the behavioral intention to use mobile banking. *Computers in Human Behavior*, *21*, 873–891.

Mathieson, K. (1999). Predicting user intentions: Comparing the technology acceptance model with the theory of planned behavior. *Information Systems Research*, *2*(3), 173–191.

Marimuthu, M., Arokiasamy, L., Samad, M., Moorthy, M. K., & Kok, N. K. (2011). CASHLESS SOCIETY AND THE DETERMINANTS: AN EMPIRICAL INVESTIGATION. *International Journal of Academic Research*, *3*(3).

Mulliner, C., Borgaonkar, R., Stewin, P., & Seifert, J. P. (2013, July). SMS-Based One-Time Passwords: Attacks and Defense: (Short Paper). In International Conference on Detection of Intrusions and Malware, and Vulnerability Assessment (pp. 150-159). Berlin, Heidelberg: Springer Berlin Heidelberg.

Oppenheim, A. N. (1992). *Questionnaire design, interviewing and attitude measurement* (2nd ed.). Continuum International Publishing.

Pan, W. X., & Lai, P. C. (2023). Research on college students' purchasing using webcast platform. In *Strategies and Opportunities for Technology in the Metaverse World* (pp. 166–185). IGI Global.

Pan, W. X., & Lai, P. C. (2023). (2023) A Study of College Students' Use of Live Streaming Platforms as Anchors. Technology Management and Its Social Impact on Education, 243-267

Rinaldi, L. (2001). Payment Cards and Money Demand in Belgium. Center for Economic Studies, Leuven Universities' Discussion Paper Series 01.16.

Sekaran, U. (2003). *Research Methods for Business: A Skill-Building Approach* (4th ed.). John Wiley and Sons, Inc.

Stormpath. (2016). S. S. O. Vs. Centralized Authentication," Stormpath User Identity API, 31-Oct-2016. [Online]. Available: https://stormpath.com/blog/sso-vs -centralized-auth. [Accessed: 25-Jul-2019].

Sivakorn, S., Polakis, I., & Keromytis, A. D. (2016, March). I am robot:(deep) learning to break semantic image captchas. In 2016 IEEE European Symposium on Security and Privacy (EuroS&P) (pp. 388-403). IEEE.

Sun, H., & Zhang, P. (2006). Causal Relationships between Perceived Enjoyment and Perceived Ease of Use: An Alternative Approach 1. *Journal of the Association for Information Systems*, *7*(9), 618–645.

Tabachnick, B. G., & Fidell, L. S. (2007). *Using Multivariate Statistics*. Pearson Education Inc.

Tong, D. L., Lai, P. C., & Liew, E. J. Y. (2024). Exploring intention to use cryptocurrencies payment across age groups and gender: A multi-stage machine learning application on the extended UTAUT model. *International Journal of Applied Decision Sciences*, *17*(5), 571–594.

Venkatesh, V., Speier, C., & Morris, M. (2002). User acceptance enablers in individual decision making about technology: Toward an integrated model. *Decision Sciences*, *33*(2), 297–316.

Wang, Y. S., Wang, Y. M., Lin, H. H., & Tang, T. I. (2003). Determinants of user acceptance of internet banking: An empirical study. *International Journal of Service Industry Management*, *14*(5), 501–519.

Chapter 5

Artificial Intelligence for Secure Self-Adaptive Systems in Fintech

Nazgul Seralina
https://orcid.org/0000-0002-5609-8284
Kazakh-British Technical University, Kazakhstan

Assel Akzhalova
https://orcid.org/0000-0002-1141-7595
Kazakh-British Technical University, Kazakhstan

Chingis Utegenov
Kazakh-British Technical University, Kazakhstan

ABSTRACT

The integration of self-adjusting AI into financial technology marks a breakthrough in detecting credit card fraud and abnormal transactions. This chapter presents a flexible framework using ML techniques, XGBoost, Isolation Forest, Federated Learning, and SHAP, to automate fraud detection with high precision. Transactions are first assessed via XGBoost, then anomalies (e.g., small purchases by younger users) trigger Isolation Forest. These are added to the labeled dataset, enabling real-time model retraining. Threshold tuning enhances sensitivity, while SHAP ensures interpretability. A simulated federated learning setup updates models across institutions without compromising privacy. The visual feedback loop illustrates continuous learning and deployment. This adaptive system boosts fraud detection accuracy, reduces false positives, and strengthens institutional agility, driving innovation, trust, and scalable value in FinTech.

DOI: 10.4018/979-8-3373-2497-5.ch005

INTRODUCTION

The digital transformation of the financial sector has ushered in new levels of convenience and accessibility, but it has also introduced unprecedented cybersecurity risks. Traditional fraud detection systems, reliant on predefined rules, struggle to keep pace with increasingly sophisticated financial crimes. This growing challenge necessitates the adoption of advanced technologies capable of adapting to threats in real time. Artificial Intelligence (AI) has emerged as a cornerstone of secure financial operations, offering self-adaptive systems that dynamically respond to fraud risks while optimizing security measures. Unlike conventional rule-based frameworks, these systems analyze historical data, recognize suspicious patterns, and anticipate emerging vulnerabilities. This adaptability significantly enhances fraud prevention by minimizing manual oversight, improving detection accuracy, and reducing false positives, ensuring legitimate transactions proceed without unnecessary disruptions. Financial institutions process vast volumes of transactions daily, making data-driven fraud prevention critical. AI enables real-time analysis of large datasets from platforms such as GitHub and Kaggle, refining detection models to recognize fraud patterns across diverse scenarios. Beyond fraud detection, AI-based self-adaptive systems contribute to operational efficiency, allowing financial institutions to allocate resources strategically and minimize losses.

Problem Statement. As digital finance rapidly expands, traditional rule-based fraud detection systems are struggling to keep up with the complexity and speed of modern financial crimes. These outdated systems often produce high false-positive rates and react too slowly to emerging threats. Financial platforms now require intelligent, adaptive AI solutions that can detect fraud in real time while preserving data privacy and operational efficiency. Without such advancements, institutions risk losing customer trust, regulatory compliance, and overall credibility in the digital economy.

Research Objective. This research seeks to design and assess self-evolving AI framework tailored for robust fraud detection within FinTech environments. By combining supervised learning (XGBoost), unsupervised anomaly detection (Isolation Forest), interpretability mechanisms (SHAP), and privacy-aware strategies (simulated federated learning), the framework aims to: enhance the precision of fraud detection, minimize false-positive alerts, support continuous, real-time model adaptation, safeguard sensitive financial data, strengthen institutional resilience and unlock strategic value in digital finance ecosystems.

Background. The digital shift in finance has brought convenience but also complex fraud risks that outdated rule-based systems struggle to detect. Financial institutions are now leveraging AI to build adaptive fraud detection models that analyze data in real time and evolve with emerging threats. Techniques like XGBoost, Isolation

Forest, and SHAP improve accuracy and transparency, while federated learning protects data privacy. These innovations enhance security, reduce false positives, and boost operational efficiency across digital finance platforms.

Figure 1. Value Creation of AI for Secure Self-Adaptive Systems

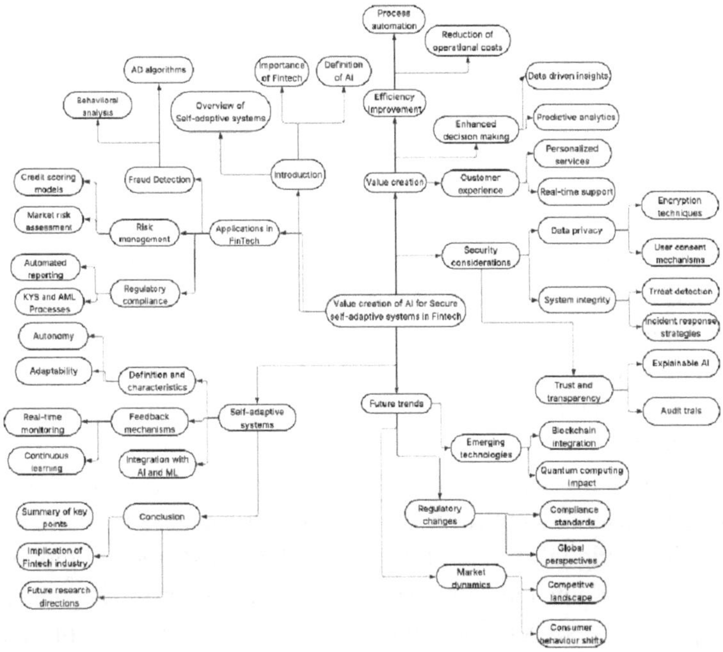

Figure 1 represents the interconnected framework for Value Creation of AI for Secure Self-Adaptive Systems in FinTech. Each segment of the mind map contributes to comprehensive understanding of how AI drives security, adaptability, and innovation in the FinTech industry. Introduction section outlines the foundational concepts, emphasizing the relevance of AI, FinTech's rapid evolution, and the role of self-adaptive systems in addressing security challenges. It highlights how AI's integration introduces efficiency and scalability into financial systems. Applications in FinTech consists of Fraud Detection, AI algorithms such as anomaly detection and behavioral analysis are key tools for identifying suspicious activities, creating secure financial platforms. Risk Management, AI-powered models assess creditworthiness and market risks, offering predictive insights that strengthen financial decision-making. Regulatory Compliance, automation ensures adherence to anti-money laundering (AML) and Know Your Customer (KYC) requirements, reducing human errors. Self-Adaptive Systems enhance FinTech's resilience by offering features such as real-time monitoring, continuous learning, and ML integration. They dynamically respond to cybersecurity threats, ensuring uninterrupted operations. Value Creation segment demonstrates the economic and operational impact of AI in FinTech. Efficiency improvement through automation, reducing operational costs. Enhanced decision-making driven by data analytics and predictive models. Superior customer experience with personalized services and real-time support, fostering trust in digital platforms.

Security Considerations include AI financial systems by ensuring data privacy, safeguarding system integrity, and maintaining transparency through explainable AI and audit trails. Future Trends points to advancements such as blockchain integration, quantum computing, and evolving global regulations. These emerging technologies promise to shape the future of secure self-adaptive systems in FinTech. By leveraging self-adaptive capabilities, FinTech can build resilient systems that cater to the complex, evolving needs of the sector. The value creation system contributes on multiple levels: 1) identifying intrusion vectors and vulnerabilities with greater precision, FinTech institutions can prevent fraud, thereby safeguarding client trust and financial assets. 2) Automating resource allocation and security measures reduces manual oversight, lowering operational costs and enhancing efficiency. 3) Continuous data analysis and threat assessments lead to more resilient and adaptable systems, fortifying FinTech institutions against ever-evolving cyber threats. 4) The adaptive system ensures seamless and trustworthy financial services, encouraging broader adoption of digital and mobile banking solutions. By incorporating advanced tools like ML and NN into these processes, the FinTech industry can transition from reactive to predictive security strategies. The intersection of AI-driven security and value creation within FinTech illustrates a forward-looking approach where adaptability and intelligence form the cornerstone of modern financial systems. To enhance the chapter's practical relevance and depth, we briefly present real-world applications and critical challenges of self-adaptive AI in FinTech. Institutions like JPMorgan Chase and Ant Group have successfully implemented adaptive fraud detection and federated learning systems, achieving measurable improvements in accuracy and privacy compliance. However, these innovations also introduce risks such as algorithmic bias, adversarial attacks, and ethical concerns, which can undermine fairness and transparency in financial decision-making. Explainable AI tools like SHAP and LIME help address these issues but require consistent integration across platforms. Moreover, regulatory frameworks, including GDPR, PCI-DSS, DORA, and the U.S. AI Bill of Rights, demand robust governance, auditability, and cross-border compliance. By incorporating these real-world insights and acknowledging key risks, the chapter presents a more balanced and responsible perspective on the deployment of self-adaptive AI systems in FinTech. We include recent research reports on AI innovations in FinTech, particularly in emerging areas such as generative AI, federated learning, and quantum-resilient security. This ensures the content reflects current trends and technological advancements. We explore in industry reports: how generative AI could add $2.6–$4.4 trillion annually across industries, including banking and financial services (Mckinsey, 2023) and Weforum focuses on global cooperation and interoperability in managing generative AI risks and opportunities (Weforum, 2024).

LITERATURE REVIEW

The authors investigated (Lakshmana Rao et al., 2024), the transformative role of AI within the banking sector, focusing on how AI technologies are being deployed to enhance customer experience, streamline operations, and improve security. The paper examined the use of machine learning algorithms, chatbots, and predictive analytics in delivering personalized financial advice, real-time support, and advanced fraud detection systems. The research relied on data from sale histories, client relations, demographic information, and feedback from client service contacts. The problems were: banking industry faces increasing customer expectations for verified, effective, and secure services; lack of the efficiency and personalization required to meet these expectations; improving their decision-making processes and streamline their operations; addressing challenges like data privacy, ethical considerations, and regulatory compliance. The paper contributed to the understanding of how AI can be strategically implemented in banking to transform customer experience. It offered insights into the use of AI technologies such as machine literacy algorithms, chatbots, and predictive analytics. The research provided practical recommendations for financial institutions to optimize client advantages and operational efficiency through AI. The research employed a multi-faceted technique, incorporating various AI technologies, data analytics, and client feedback methods. Data collection from various sources, including sale histories, client relations, demographic information, and feedback from client service contacts. (Lakshmana Rao et al., 2024). In contrast to traditional AI implementations for fraud detection and customer service personalization, self-adaptive FinTech systems incorporate real-time learning mechanisms that autonomously refine security measures based on evolving cyber threats and transaction patterns, ensuring both privacy preservation and adaptive compliance with regulatory changes.

The paper (Ganguly, 2024) explored the integration of AI with biometric technologies to enhance customer authentication in the banking and Fintech sector. It focused on achieving a balance between robust security measures and a seamless customer experience. The research investigated the latest trends, challenges, and potential improvements in AI-driven biometric authentication, specifically fingerprint authentication, and its impact on the financial sector. Main findings were

AI-powered biometric authentication strengthened security against online threats compared to traditional methods like passwords and PINs; biometric authentication offered a more convenient user experience by eliminating the need for password memorization; AI algorithms adapted to variations in biometric data caused by age, accidents, or environmental factors, enhancing long-term reliability; financial institutions addressed escalating cyber threats by integrating AI-powered biometrics.

The paper (Ganguly et al., 2024) included data on password-based logins seeing a 30% decrease in fraudulent login attempts compared to traditional methods. Facial recognition with liveness detection reduced fraudulent account takeover by 50%. Fingerprint or voice recognition combined with a PIN or password creates a stronger layer of security compared to just a single factor. Biometric authentication eliminated the need for physical tokens (like security keys) which can be lost or stolen. Fingerprint or facial recognition logins took an average of 2-3 seconds compared to 30-60 seconds for traditional methods. Users accessed accounts on any device with compatible biometric sensors. An estimated 60% of banks worldwide offered some form of biometric authentication for customer logins (as of 2023). User adoption rates for biometric authentication in banking apps range from 30% to 70% depending on the region and specific technology used. The authors applied the methodologies of quantitative analysis of accuracy rates, false acceptance rates, and false rejection rates of AI-powered biometric verification systems; qualitative analysis of surveys and interviews with IT professionals, stakeholders, and end-users; statistical methods such as correlational analysis, regression analysis, and descriptive statistics are utilized; data collection from various sources, including datasets providing performance benchmarks for different biometric authentication methods (Ganguly et al., 2024). Compared to conventional biometric authentication methods, self-adaptive AI systems in FinTech dynamically adjust security protocols in response to evolving cyber threats, leveraging decentralized intelligence to enhance risk mitigation strategies and regulatory compliance across financial networks.

While blockchains promise immutability and distributed trust, the smart contracts that execute on them are written by fallible humans and deployed in an irreversible environment: once bytecode is mined into a block, defects cannot be patched without complex migrations or hard forks. The Ethereum ecosystem has witnessed spectacular breaches that underscore this rigidity. The 2016 DAO exploit siphoned Ether worth roughly USD 60 million by invoking a recursive call pattern—now known as a re-entrancy attack—before the contract updated its internal balance (Atzei, Bartoletti, & Cimoli, 2017). Two separate bugs in Parity multi-signature wallets (2017 and 2018) involuntarily froze a combined USD 300 million in Ether through mistakenly exposed initialisation functions (Luu, Chu, Olickel, Saxena, & Hobor, 2016).

Data features (Chatterjee et al., 2024) consisted of details of financial transactions, including amounts, timestamps, sender/receiver information, and transaction types; user demographics, transaction history, device information, and behavioral patterns; records of system activities, including access attempts, error messages, and resource utilization; network packets, communication patterns, and IP addresses involved in Fintech system interactions; information on past cyber-attacks, vulnerabilities, and security breaches. Key features of the proposed framework utilized generative AI models to proactively identify and predict potential cyber threats and vulnerabilities. ML algorithms used to detect anomalous behavior in transaction data, user activity, and system logs. Blockchain technology applied to ensure the immutability and transparency of financial transactions.

The Fintech industry faced escalating challenges in maintaining data integrity, security, and system resilience due to the increasing sophistication and frequency of cyber-attacks. Traditional security methods struggled to keep pace with the dynamic nature of cyber threats and the complexities inherent in modern Fintech ecosystems. Data collection included gathering relevant datasets for training and testing the ML algorithms, including transaction data, user profiles, and system logs. Evaluation metrics utilized metrics such as data tampering detection rate, anomaly recognition accuracy, and system uptime to assess the performance of the framework. Generative AI framework offered a promising approach for enhancing data integrity, security, and system resilience in Fintech systems. The integration of advanced ML algorithms and blockchain technology provided a robust and adaptive solution to the evolving challenges faced by the Fintech industry. Scientific novelty was Hybrid AI-Blockchain Architecture combined Generative AI's adaptive threat detection with blockchain's tamper-proof ledger. AI models dynamically updated using federated learning to address zero-day threats. Early exploration of post-quantum cryptographic hashing within blockchain layers. Relevance of the study were addressed the $30B annual global losses attributed to Fintech cyberattacks (World Bank, 2024) and aligned with regulatory mandates (e.g., EU DORA, PCI-DSS) requiring real-time resilience in financial systems. Data features included structured info: transaction timestamps, user behavior logs, IP geolocation; and unstructured: natural language customer service interactions, threat intelligence feeds. Framework components consisted of generative AI models, GANs for simulating adversarial attack patterns and transformers for NLP-driven phishing detection (Chatterjee et al., 2024). Compared to traditional security models leveraging AI and self-adaptive FinTech systems dynamically adjust security parameters through neural networks, enabling continuous resilience against evolving cyber threats while ensuring privacy-preserving fraud detection across financial networks.

Blockchain integration (Chatterjee et al., 2024) consisted of smart contracts for automated fraud flagging and SHA-3 hashing for immutable audit trails. Resilience

Metrics included mean time to recovery (MTTR) under DDoS conditions and False Positive/Negative rates in anomaly detection. Dataset defined 2.3M simulated Fintech transactions (synthetic + real-world). The authors used tools of TensorFlow for AI training, Hyperledger fabric for blockchain, Wireshark for network stress-testing. Threat detection determined 98.7% accuracy in identifying novel ransomware patterns (vs. 82.4% for traditional ML), 47% reduction in false positives through federated learning updates. Resilience defined MTTR improved by 63% during simulated APT attacks and blockchain reduced data tampering incidents by 89%. Limitations were 15–20% overhead in transaction latency due to cryptographic checks. Model drift observed after 72 hours without retraining. Advantages were proactive threat mitigation via AI, decentralized trust via blockchain, and adaptability to zero-day attacks. Disadvantages were high computational costs for real-time inference, complexity in cross-platform blockchain integration and dependency on high-quality, labeled training data. Identified lack of standardized benchmarks for AI-driven fintech security, underexplored trade-offs between data privacy (GDPR) and threat intelligence sharing and limited testing against quantum computing-enabled attack scenarios. Short-term future directions were to develop lightweight AI models for edge devices in payment gateways and to create hybrid consensus mechanisms (PoW + PoS) for energy-efficient blockchain. Long-term future directions were to integrate quantum key distribution (QKD) with AI threat databases and to establish global fintech security protocols for cross-border transactions.

The proposed framework demonstrated statistically significant improvements in fintech security metrics but requires optimization for enterprise-scale deployment. The research provided a foundational architecture for ISO/SAE 21434-compliant Fintech systems, with direct applications in cryptocurrency exchanges, tech platforms, and central bank digital currencies (CBDCs). While methodologically rigorous, the study would benefit from real-world deployment data beyond simulations, comparative analysis with post-quantum lattice-based cryptography and ethical risk assessment of AI autonomy in financial decision-making (Chatterjee et al., 2024). In contrast to traditional blockchain-integrated security models, self-adaptive AI-driven FinTech systems dynamically refine cybersecurity protocols through continuous learning mechanisms, ensuring adaptive responses to zero-day attacks, reducing model drift, and enhancing data integrity across decentralized financial ecosystems.

The paper (Kapoor et al., 2024) emphasized collaboration between fintech companies, regulatory bodies, and traditional banks to create a secure and innovative financial ecosystem. The authors used methodologies of literature review of existing research on fintech's impact on banking operations, comparative analysis of traditional banking models versus fintech-driven approaches and case studies on partnerships between banks and fintech firms. This research underscored the transformative potential of fintech while emphasizing the importance of collaboration among stakeholders to build a secure and inclusive financial ecosystem (Kapoor et al., 2024). Compared to conventional fintech-driven automation, secure self-adaptive systems integrate dynamic AI governance, enabling real-time adaptability in risk modeling, financial inclusion strategies, and compliance frameworks, ensuring resilience in evolving financial ecosystems.

The authors (Varatharajoo et al., 2024) suggested AI-driven self-adaptive systems in fintech that improve security, efficiency, and regulatory compliance. The authors used methods of Explainable AI (XAI), that improve transparency and trust in AI-driven decisions, crucial for regulatory compliance and stakeholder confidence in fintech. AI-driven fraud detection system utilized ML and DL models to identify and prevent fraudulent activities and applied XAI methods LIME and SHAP to interpret AI decisions (Varatharajoo et al., 2024). Contrasting to traditional fraud detection systems, self-adaptive AI models refine security protocols, integrating real-time learning mechanisms that proactively counter evolving financial threats while ensuring regulatory transparency through neural networks techniques.

The authors (Gopal et al., 2023) proposed framework of using technologies of AI, blockchain, and biometric authentication which are used to mitigate risks of cyber security threats, identity theft, and insider risks. There were used transaction data, security metrics and regulatory requirements for compliance. The authors prepared examination of trends in digital payments, lending platforms, and analysis of regulatory frameworks to identify gaps in cybersecurity measures. The proposed AI and blockchain improved security and compliance (Gopal et al., 2023). In comparison to conventional security architectures, self-adaptive AI models dynamically adjust authentication protocols, refining biometric verification processes and fraud detection strategies to proactively address evolving cyber threats in financial ecosystems.

The authors (Kumar et al., 2024) explored the application of Large Language Models (LLMs), to enhance the syndicate lending process. The authors implemented algorithms Proximal Policy Optimization (PPO) and Byte Pair Encoding (BPE) for decision making and text processing and integrated the system with Firebase for hosting the app and managing the database. The proposed system reduced the failure rate of startups by 70% through financial aid and business model suggestions (Kumar et al., 2024). In contrast to that work, self-adaptive FinTech systems process financial models, ensuring real-time responsiveness to market shifts, adaptive credit risk evaluation, and scalable security measures.

The research paper (Meng et al., 2010) addressed the critical problem of power transformer fault diagnosis using self-adaptive radial basis function (RBF) neural network. The authors used hybrid approach of Fuzzy c-means (FCM) for determining the initial structure of the RBF network, specifically the number of hidden layer neurons and their centers. The paper adopted a fuzzy clustering approach based on FCM, where the range of hidden layer neurons can be specified. Quantum-inspired particle swarm optimization (QPSO) was applied the kernel widths (radii) of the RBF neurons and the output connection weights. Several concepts from quantum computing and immunology are adopted to improve the search capability of conventional PSO. (Meng et al., 2010). Unlike AI-driven fault diagnosis in industrial applications, self-adaptive AI models adjust security protocols, leveraging adaptive learning mechanisms to mitigate cyber threats, enhance fraud prevention, and optimize real-time financial decision-making in decentralized banking ecosystems.

The survey (Shi et al., 2023) paper addressed the critical need for responsible and effective federated learning (RE-FL) within the FinTech landscape. The primary finding was that existing FL techniques, while promising for privacy-preserving AI in finance, face significant challenges related to data heterogeneity, information asymmetry, and potential misuse. The study underscored the importance of adopting holistic perspective that considered the diverse dimensions of responsible AI and the unique challenges of the FinTech landscape (Shi et al., 2023). Unlike traditional FL models, self-adaptive AI systems continuously process financial security protocols, ensuring adaptive compliance, real-time fraud prevention, which are essential for mitigating systemic vulnerabilities in FinTech ecosystems.

Meanwhile the authors (Akzhalova & Seralina, 2023) proposed application architecture model in the Finteh process of issuing virtual cards. The model configured timing tasks, which triggered the processing of batch file data provided by external systems. In (Seralina, 2021) were observed AI systems to automated software testing, such as Selenium, Katalon Studio, Unified functional testing, SoapUI. These AI systems are used in financial information systems and allowed automatization the repeating process and usage of the database; delivered superb intellectual product; adapted to the progressive algorithm of learning; retrievied the maximum amount of data from the databases. In contrast, self-adaptive AI systems define software validation protocols, leveraging continuous learning mechanisms to optimize financial security and transaction integrity in Fintech.

DISCUSSION

The weakness can refer to terms like GDPR and PCI-DSS appear, the review only briefly nods at the policy frameworks driving AI adoption in finance. A deeper dive into compliance and ethical considerations would round out the picture. The recent advancements in AI, blockchain, and cybersecurity technologies applied to the financial sector are summarized according Table 1. Our chapter establishes a broad and current overview of AI-driven self-adaptive systems in FinTech, touching on fraud detection, security resilience, and economic implications. It effectively frames the relevance of AI in combating complex cybersecurity threats. The background nicely ties real-world applications (e.g., biometric authentication, automated fraud detection) into the conceptual framework, providing readers with tangible examples of value creation. We suggest scope to bridge academic depth with applied relevance, giving researchers and industry professionals actionable insights.

Table 1. Existing AI Approaches for Ensuring Data Integrity, Security, and Resilience

Ref.	Method/Technology	Description	Future Direction	Value Creation
(Lakshmana Rao et al., 2024).	NLP applied for development of chatbots and virtual assistants. To detect suspicious activities and prevent potential risks, fraud detection models rely on ML techniques.	AI-powered solutions, personalized financial advice, real-time assistance, and advanced fraud detection systems.	Incorporate blockchain and IoT technologies	detection and prevention fraud, protecting client funds and enhancing trust in financial institutions
(Ganguly et al., 2024)	AI-driven biometric authentication, specifically fingerprint authentication	Biometric authentication (BA) technologies in a secure and convenient manner for banking customers.	Improvements in cybersecurity for privacy protection	reducing fraud rates, faster transaction speeds, adoption of BA was projected to enhance operational efficiency while fostering customer loyalty through increased trust in security measures
(Chatterjee et al., 2024)	GANs for simulating adversarial attack patterns and transformers for NLP-driven phishing detection. Blockchain integration consisted of smart contracts for automated fraud flagging and SHA-3 hashing for immutable audit trails. Resilience Metrics included mean time to recovery (MTTR) under DDoS conditions and False Positive/Negative rates in anomaly detection.	Generative AI-driven framework integrated with blockchain to enhance data integrity, security, and resilience in Fintech ecosystems.	Proactive threat mitigation via AI, decentralized trust via blockchain, and adaptability to zero-day attacks.	High computational costs for real-time inference, complexity in cross-platform blockchain integration and dependency on quality, labeled training data.

continued on following page

Table 1. Continued

Ref.	Method/Technology	Description	Future Direction	Value Creation
(Kapoor et al., 2024)	Chatbots for customer support, ML for risk analysis, and blockchain for secure transactions.	Comprehensive review of how emerging technologies like AI and blockchain were transformed the financial sector	Automation through smart contracts minimized administrative burdens and human errors, alternative lending platforms and blockchain-based payments, forcing traditional banks to innovate or collaborate with fintech firms	Risk detection and mitigation ensured more secure financial transactions.

The financial sector plays a pivotal role in driving a nation's economic growth (Alt & Puschmann, 2012). Ensuring strong performance across all financial divisions is essential for their success, including the credit card sector, which has expanded rapidly due to growing customer demand and widespread usage (Surekha et al., 2022). Despite its advantages, credit card usage is accompanied by certain risks, such as abnormal banking transactions that lead to anomalies (Patel, 2023). An innovative solution to address these anomalies lies in employing Self-Adaptive Machine Intelligence Systems (Gheibi et al., 2021). These systems are effective in mitigating intrusion vulnerabilities by preventing unauthorized system access, privilege escalation, and changes to network device settings (Chiba et al., 2019). Moreover, leveraging data analytics can help detect unusual patterns in financial transactions (Amarasinghe et al., 2018). To tackle these challenges, models capable of estimating and refining software testing schemes need to be developed and validated (Bernot et al., 1991). The integration of AI for secure self-adaptive systems into automated software testing processes provides notable benefits, including enhanced adaptability, improved efficiency, and heightened accuracy (Saputi &Lee, 2020). ML approach represents a significant advancement in ensuring secure and reliable financial operations (Gheibi et al., 2021). The main types of credit card intrusions, definitions, methods and location of occurs, value creation are described according to Table 2. The value creation column emphasizes how addressing each intrusion contributes to the broader goals of security, financial stability, customer satisfaction, and trust in financial systems.

Table 2. Types of credit card intrusions

Intrusion Name .	Definition	Method	Location of occurs	Value creation
Credit Card Skimming	the approach of accessing special data from ATM, credit or debit cards while they are applied on ATM equipment or a merchant point	Skimming Machine	Shopping markets, Bars, cafeterias, etc.	Prevents financial losses and enhances trust by securing payment systems and reducing unauthorized access to cardholder data.
Identity Theft	the attack of applying particular financial data of another person to execute fraud, for instance doing illegal transactions or acquisition	Hacking, Internet, Email phishing operations.	Anyplace	Protects customer data privacy and reduces financial liability for both users and institutions
Account Takeover Fraud	the mode of identity theft where swindlers pass an online detail and show as real customers.	Brute force botnet attacks, phishing,& malware.	Anywhere	Secures user accounts, minimizes unauthorized activities, and strengthens customer confidence in digital services.
Phishing	Phishing is a cybercrime where a charlatan shows as a close particular contact, justifiable organization, donation or communal company in order to deceive an personal into dividing conscious data such as bank account bills, usernames identification data, debit or credit card data and etc	Keylogger, Sniffers, Site cloning, Physical stolen card.	Anywhere	Enhances cybersecurity awareness, reduces data breaches, and protects personal financial information from exploitation.
CNP Fraud	type of fraud done by internet activities, mobile phone, email address. It is a fraudulent payment in situations where a card is not presented to a merchant for a visual check.	Internet, Hacking, Email phishing campaigns.	Anywhere	Reduces unauthorized online transactions, improves fraud detection efficiency, and fosters secure e-commerce environments.
Application	If a fraudsters fill the application form with fake information,or maybe even real, but stolen identity information.	identity namely bankstatements, telephone bill, electricity bill, etc.	Financial organization.	Strengthens identity verification processes, prevents fraud in onboarding, and ensures legitimate customer engagement

METHODOLOGY

In Self-adaptive AI systems continuously analyze, learn, and evolve without manual intervention. In FinTech, this means the system doesn't just apply preset fraud rules, it redefines them based on new behavioral data, threat vectors, and compliance updates. To operationalize self-adaptive capabilities in fraud detection, we develop a dynamic feedback-driven pipeline illustrated in Figure 2. The system begins by ingesting transactional and behavioral data, followed by anomaly scoring using supervised models such as XGBoost and unsupervised methods like Isolation Forest. Upon detecting anomalies or shifts in fraud signatures, the system activates retraining protocols using incremental learning mechanisms. This adaptive loop is guided by performance feedback, particularly false positives and newly confirmed fraud cases. Crucially, we integrate explainability techniques like SHAP and LIME to interpret model decisions, improving auditability and regulatory alignment. The retrained model is then deployed across the FinTech infrastructure in near-real-time, enabling the platform to respond to emergent threats autonomously. This framework enables continuous learning, resilience against evolving attack vectors, and enhanced transparency in high-stakes financial decision-making

Figure 2. Adaptive Fraud Response System in Action

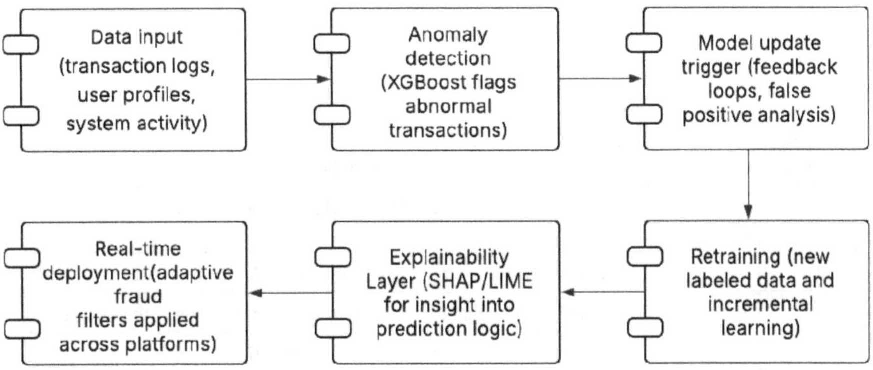

Initially, the system is trained on historical credit card data using XGBoost, achieving high recall and precision. Trigger event include sudden spike in fraudulent transactions involving purchases under $50 from small cities is detected. Feedback mechanism defines model that updates its decision thresholds automatically. Isolation Forest flags new outliers and retrains using recent data. SHAP is used to interpret why new transactions are flagged as fraud. Adaptation outcome determines reduced false negatives within 24 hours. Detected a new phishing campaign linked to compromised IP blocks. Federated learning propagates this update securely to distributed institutions. By decentralizing model updates and preserving user privacy, the system evolves in real time without breaking compliance.

FinTech sector, value creation is intrinsically linked to security, efficiency, and innovation. AI has significantly enhanced the ability of financial systems to detect fraud, manage risks, and streamline operations autonomously. Traditional fraud detection systems rely on predefined rule sets, which struggle to keep up with evolving fraud tactics. Self-adaptive AI-driven systems provide continuous monitoring, analysis, and security enhancement by adjusting to emerging threats in real time. The role of AI in generates value for FinTech organizations by improving fraud detection, strengthening security measures, and optimizing business processes. The framework for model detection of abnormal banking transactions based on ML and NN methods are tested by dataset collection. We use the Kaggle datasets, which contained financial data transactions using credit cards. We test with methods of Isolation Forest (IF) and XGBoost, provide advanced mechanism for identifying fraudulent transactions by analyzing patterns and behaviors. We test on Jupyter Notebook using Python with datasets "fraud_data.csv" and "fraudTest.csv" (Table 3, Table 4)

Table 3. The list of attributes of dataset "fraud_data.csv"

Attribute.	Description
user_id	numeric code that distinguishes each user from others
signup_time	The timestamp indicates when the user signed up for the service or created an account
purchase_time	The timestamp indicates when the user made a purchase.
purchase_ value	The monetary value of the purchase made by the user.
device_id	unique identifier for the device used to make the purchase.
source	the source from where the user was referred or how they found the service
browser	The browser used by the user to make the purchase
gender	The gender of the user.
age	The age of the user
ip_address	The IP address from which the user made the purchase
class	The target label indicates whether the transaction is fraudulent (1) or not (0).

The system model emphasizes the use of advanced ML algorithms to identify and prevent data tampering. It incorporates attributes spanning various dimensions of financial data, such as transaction details, user profiles, and historical patterns. These attributes are selected for their essential role in maintaining the precision and trustworthiness of financial data. Transaction details are vital for anomaly detection, user profiles offer context for behavioral analysis, and historical patterns help establish benchmarks for normal data activity. The implementation process, outlined in Figure 4 highlights how the AI framework employs advanced ML techniques to proactively address data tampering within FinTech systems and value creation.

Detailed equations illustrate each phase, from data collection and processing to continuous learning, ensuring the accuracy and reliability of financial data throughout.

Table 4. The list of attributes of dataset "fraudTest.csv"

Attribute.	Description
trans_date_trans_time	The exact date and time when the transaction occurred, in the format YYYY-MM-DD HH:MM:SS.
cc_num	The credit card number used in the transaction. This is a unique identifier for each card.
merchant	The name of the merchant where the transaction took place. Fraudulent transactions are marked with the prefix fraud_ followed by the merchant's name.
category	The category of the purchase made, e.g., personal_care, indicating the type of goods or services purchased
amt	The amount of money spent in the transaction, in dollars.
first	The first name of the cardholder who made the transaction.
last	The last name of the cardholder.
gender	The gender of the cardholder (M for male, F for female).
street	The street address associated with the cardholder's billing information.
city	The city associated with the cardholder's billing address.
state	The state abbreviation where the cardholder resides.
zip	The zip code of the cardholder's billing address.
lat	The latitude coordinate of the cardholder's billing address, useful for geospatial analysis.
long	The longitude coordinate of the cardholder's billing address.
city_pop	The population of the city where the cardholder resides, which could help identify the likelihood of fraud based on city size.
job	The job title of the cardholder, e.g., Mechanical engineer, which might help identify patterns of fraud by profession.
dob	The date of birth of the cardholder, in the format YYYY-MM-DD.
trans_num	A unique identifier for the transaction, serving as a transaction ID.
unix_time	The timestamp of the transaction in Unix time format, representing the number of seconds since January 1, 1970
merch_lat	the latitude coordinate of the merchant's location where the transaction took place
merch_long	The longitude coordinate of the merchant's location
is_fraud	The target variable indicating whether the transaction is fraudulent (1 for fraud, 0 for non-fraud)

According Figure 3 we apply XGBoost Classifier, gradient boosting technique and train on features derived from transaction metadata (purchase value,browser, source, etc.) and provides baseline fraud prediction capability. We simulates self-adaptive loop: trigger condition is set: users under 30 making purchases below

\$50. Isolation Forest, is used to flag outliers, that are appended to the training set, and the model is retrained. It suggests that the model updates are securely transmitted to remote systems without sharing raw user data. Ensures data privacy and regulatory compliance key requirements in financial domains. We integrate SHAP (SHapley Additive exPlanations) that displays feature importance for an individual prediction, ensures interpretability of the model's decisions, ilustrates the pipeline of intelligent self-adaptive response, including: data ingestion, anomaly detection, triggering update, model retraining, explainability, deployment.

Figure 3. Pseudocode of Secure self-adaptive fraud detection system

Algorithm 1 Secure Self-Adaptive Fraud Detection System

Input: Dataset `fraud_data.csv`
Load dataset and convert `signup_time` and `purchase_time` to datetime
Compute `time_diff` as seconds between signup and purchase
Drop unused columns: user identifiers, timestamps, and IP-related data
Encode categorical columns: `source, browser, sex`
Split dataset into features X and target y
Split X, y into training and testing sets: $(X_{\text{train}}, X_{\text{test}}, y_{\text{train}}, y_{\text{test}})$
Train initial XGBoost classifier on $(X_{\text{train}}, y_{\text{train}})$
Predict y_{pred} on X_{test}
Evaluate performance using `classification_report`
Trigger: Select suspicious transactions where:
    `purchase_value` < 50 AND `age` < 30
Apply Isolation Forest to trigger subset (excluding target)
Detect anomalies with prediction output -1
Concatenate anomalies to full dataset to form extended training data
Prepare new training set $(X_{\text{adaptive}}, y_{\text{adaptive}})$
Retrain XGBoost on $(X_{\text{adaptive}}, y_{\text{adaptive}})$
Compute probabilities $p = \texttt{predict\_proba}(X_{\text{test}})$
Apply custom threshold: $y_{\text{new\_pred}} = (p > 0.35)$
Re-evaluate adapted model with `classification_report`
Use SHAP TreeExplainer to explain model decision
Select a flagged fraud case from $y_{\text{new\_pred}}$
Generate SHAP force plot for local interpretability
function simulate_federated_update
    Log secure model update and encrypted communication
    Confirm privacy-preserving remote updates
end function
function plot_adaptation_cycle
    Define sequential stages:
        `["Data Input", "Anomaly Detection", "Model Update Trigger",`
        `"Retraining", "Explainability Layer", "Real-Time Deployment"]`
    Plot timeline diagram of the adaptive cycle
end function

Figure 4. SHAP explanation for a flagged fraud case with dataset fraud_data.csv:

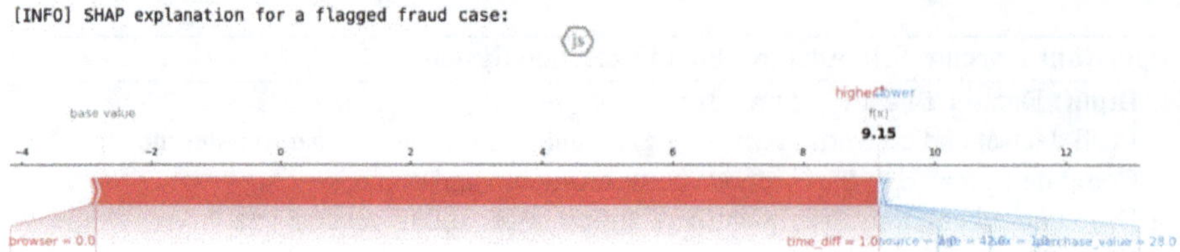

Using SHAP (SHapley Additive exPlanations), the system explains why particular transaction was flagged as fraud. In Figure 4 SHAP provides visual explanation of why the model decided a transaction was fraud. Base value, the average model output (log-odds or raw score). f(x) = 9.15, the final model output for the flagged transaction, high fraud likelihood. In red features pushing the decision toward fraud: browser = 0.0 means uncommon browser and time_diff = 1.0 means very short time between signup and transaction. In blue features reducing fraud probability, purchase_value = 28.0 (relatively low), age = 26, gender = 1 (maybe less common for fraud in this model), source = 4.0 (trusted source). The system simulates federated update: model updates (not raw data) are shared across institutions. Updates are encrypted, and user privacy is preserved. Institutions benefit from collective learning without data exposure. This embodies compliance with GDPR/ISO 27001, enhancing trustworthiness of AI in financial services.

Figure 5. SHAP explanation for a flagged fraud case with dataset fraudTest.csv:

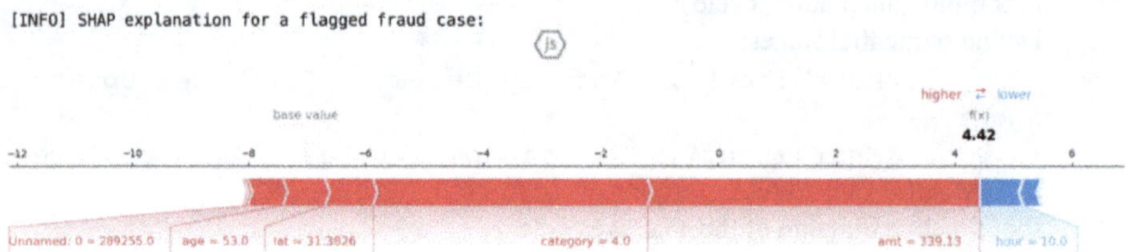

Figure 6. Adaptation cycle

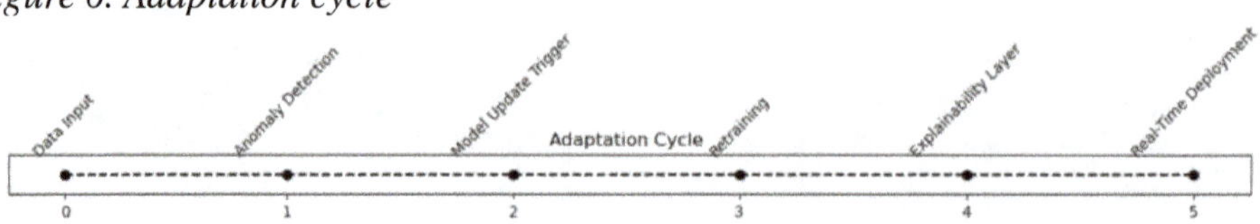

In Figure 5, f(x) = 4.42, means the final fraud score predicted by the model for this transaction. Base value ≈ -6 — the average model prediction (in log-odds or raw score) across all data; the model thinks fraud is unlikely by default. Red features push the prediction higher (toward fraud), while

Blue features push it lower(toward non-fraud). Fraud-promoting factors (in red) increased the probability of fraud: Unnamed: 0 = 289255.0, transaction ID or index; acting as a proxy for outliers or rarely seen patterns. age = 53.0, older users might be less expected to make this type of transaction. lat = 31.3826, geographic location is unusual for this user or merchant, category = 4.0, certain merchant categories (like electronics, luxury goods) are more fraud-prone, amt = 339.13, high transaction amount that may fall in a risk zone for fraud. Fraud-suppressing factors (in blue) decreased the fraud likelihood: hour = 10.0, the transaction happened at 10 AM, which is a common, low-risk time. Adaptation cycle (Figure 6) includes stages: data input, anomaly detection, model update trigger, retraining, explainability layer, real-time deployment. We calculated and defined Class 0 (non-fraud), near-perfect performance (Precision = 0.95, Recall = 1.00), Class 1 (fraud): Precision is perfect (1.00), but Recall is only 0.53, indicating 47% of fraud cases are missed. Accuracy = 96%, but macro average Recall is 0.77, which highlights class imbalance sensitivity. In comparison autrors (Chatterjee et al., 2024) determined the accuracy rate, which provide insights into the precision of the Generative AI approach in defining and mitigating potential risks. In addition authors (Gopal et al., 2023) improved accuracy by using of AI-powered credit underwriting to reduce threats.

In financial systems, false negatives (missed frauds) are costlier than false positives. This result shows the system is highly accurate in general, but insufficiently sensitive to minority fraudulent behavior. Trigger on small-value transactions from users under 30 years old. Isolation Forest applied to this subset found 850 suspicious cases. These anomalies are fed back into the training data, adapting the system to emerging fraud patterns. This forms the self-adaptive cycle: trigger condition activates anomaly search, new insights (anomalies) are added, model retraining incorporates emerging fraud behavior. Threshold lowered to increase fraud sensitivity (from default to 0.35). Slight improvement in Recall for fraud cases (from 0.53 → 0.54). System remains accurate (96%) while better flagging minority class. In real financial systems, model parameters (e.g., decision threshold) must adapt to new risks or changing attacker behavior. Lowering the threshold dynamically improves sensitivity, balancing risk and operational efficiency.

CONCLUSION

We present modular, transparent, and privacy-aware AI pipeline specifically designed for fraud detection in the FinTech sector. This system features self-adaptive mechanisms that respond to the ever-changing and high-risk environment of financial services. It highlights the essential qualities FinTech AI must uphold ongoing adaptability, robust security, clear decision-making processes, and strict adherence to data privacy regulations, key pillars of secure, self-adjusting technologies.

The chapter effectively identifies a pressing challenge: traditional fraud detection systems struggle against dynamic cyber threats in FinTech. This sets up clear rationale for self-adaptive AI systems. Several high-impact trends are well represented: AI-powered fraud detection using Isolation Forest, XGBoost, Explainable AI (XAI) tools like SHAP, LIME and federated learning. The chapter clearly discusses how ML algorithms (XGBoost, Isolation Forest) are selected, implemented, and evaluated for fraud detection. We recommend testing of algorithms AD for data integrity enhancement and security measures that connect technologies under common challenges like data integrity, regulatory adaptation. It outlines how self-adaptive systems manage dynamic threats in FinTech ecosystems, showcasing the management of technological complexity and responsiveness. The value creation framework is thoughtfully presented via visuals and layered discussion: operational efficiency through automation, enhanced fraud detection accuracy, cost reduction and intelligent resource allocation. We use datasets FraudTest.csv, Fraud_Data.csv and includes performance metrics: accuracy, recall, precision, F1-score, highlighting quantitative validation of AI value. Model comparisons support the narrative of informed technology management decisions. Case studies and literature review show how FinTech institutions adopt

AI to adapt to cyber threats and regulatory shifts. However, challenges such as algorithmic bias, data privacy, and computational costs remain key areas of concern that must be addressed to unlock the full capabilities of AI in FinTech. Future work is to observe industry-wide trends FinTech verticals beyond fraud detection, expand into AI's role in lending, Insurtech, wealth management, and CBDCs to broaden scope of value creation. We plan focus on refining these systems, addressing their limitations, and integrating them seamlessly into the financial industryAs the financial sector continues to evolve, the demand for resilient and intelligent security measures will intensify, positioning AI as critical component in safeguarding the future of FinTech. Ultimately, the integration of AI into FinTech is poised to achieve unprecedented levels of security, adaptability, and trust, paving the way for more sustainable and innovative financial ecosystem. The chapter powerfully demonstrates technical expertise and innovation potential: we explore ethical, regulatory dynamics, bridging academic rigor with systemic insights into responsible implementation.

Future Research Directions: Future research should expand self-adaptive AI into broader FinTech domains like lending, Insurtech, and CBDCs, where intelligent, privacy-preserving solutions are essential. Priorities include mitigating bias, enhancing data integrity, and aligning with evolving regulations to ensure ethical scalability and stakeholder trust.

Suggested Reading: We suggest to read: 1) systematic review of AI applications in fraud detection, highlighting bibliometric trends and emerging technologies in FinTech (Moura, et al., 2025); 2) case study on implementing adaptive, real-time fraud detection systems using machine learning and explainable AI (Aljunaid, et al., 2025).

REFERENCES

Aljunaid, S. K., Almheiri, S. J., Dawood, H., & Khan, M. A. (2025). Secure and Transparent Banking: Explainable AI-Driven Federated Learning Model for Financial Fraud Detection. *Journal of Risk and Financial Management, 18*(4), 179. DOI: 10.3390/jrfm18040179

Alt, R., & Puschmann, T. (2012). The rise of customer-oriented banking-electronic markets are paving the way for change in the financial industry. *Electronic Markets, 22*(4), 203–215. DOI: 10.1007/s12525-012-0106-2

Amarasinghe, T., Aponso, A., & Krishnarajah, N. (2018). Critical analysis of machine learning based approaches for fraud detection in financial transactions. In *Proceedings of the 2018 International Conference on Machine Learning Technologies* (pp. 12-17). DOI: 10.1145/3231884.3231894

Atzei, N., Bartoletti, M., & Cimoli, T. (2017). A survey of attacks on Ethereum smart contracts (SoK). In *Principles of Security and Trust* (pp. 164–186). Springer., DOI: 10.1007/978-3-662-54455-6_8

Bernot, G., Claude Gaudel, M., & Marre, B. (1991). Software testing based on formal specifications: A theory and a tool. *Software Engineering Journal, 6*(6), 387–405. DOI: 10.1049/sej.1991.0040

Chatterjee, P., Das, D., & Rawat, D. B. (2024). "A Generative AI Approach for Ensuring Data Integrity Security Resilience in Fintech Systems," 2024 IEEE 24th International Symposium on Cluster, Cloud and Internet Computing Workshops (CCGridW), Philadelphia, PA, USA, pp. 168-173, DOI: 10.1109/CCGridW63211.2024.00027

Chiba, Z., Abghour, N., Moussaid, K., El Omri, A., & Rida, M. (2019). Intelligent and improved self-adaptive anomaly based intrusion detection system for networks. *International Journal of Communication Networks and Information Security, 11*(2), 312–330.

Experiment: https://github.com/nazgulseralina/IGI-Global_experiment

Ganguly, A. K., Bhattacharya, S., & Chattopadhyay, S. (2024). "AI-Enabled Customer Authentication for Efficient and Secure AI-Driven Model for Banking Fintech Transaction," 2024 4th International Conference on Advance Computing and Innovative Technologies in Engineering (ICACITE), Greater Noida, India, pp. 482-486, DOI: 10.1109/ICACITE60783.2024.10616904

Gheibi, O., Weyns, D., & Quin, F. (2021). Applying machine learning in self-adaptive systems: A systematic literature review. [TAAS]. *ACM Transactions on Autonomous and Adaptive Systems*, *15*(3), 1–37. DOI: 10.1145/3469440

Gopal, S., Gupta, P., & Minocha, A. "Advancements in Fin-Tech and Security Challenges of Banking Industry," 2023 4th International Conference on Intelligent Engineering and Management (ICIEM), London, United Kingdom, 2023, pp. 1-6, doi: DOI: 10.1109/ICIEM59379.2023.10165876

Kapoor, N., Kapoor, T., Sisodiya, D. R., & Sushma, J. (2024). "Impact of Fintech: Revolution in Banking and Financial Industry," 2024 IEEE 4th International Conference on ICT in Business Industry & Government (ICTBIG), Indore, India, pp. 1-6, DOI: 10.1109/ICTBIG64922.2024.10911635

Kumar, A., Jindal, K., Sharma, H., & Chaudhary, A. (2024). "Enhancing Syndicate Lending Through AI-Powered Fine-Tuning: Leveraging LLAMA2 for Dynamic Decision Support," 2024 International Conference on Communication, Computer Sciences and Engineering (IC3SE), Gautam Buddha Nagar, India, pp. 342-347, DOI: 10.1109/IC3SE62002.2024.10593463

Rao, C. L., Sontakke, K. A., Shah, J. A., Sontakke, A. A., Shah, S. J., & Dhole, M. (2024, November). AI for Enhanced Customer Experience in Banking. In 2024 Second International Conference Computational and Characterization Techniques in Engineering & Sciences (IC3TES) (pp. 1-5). IEEE.

Mckinsey. (2023). https://www.mckinsey.de/~/media/mckinsey/locations/europe%20and%20middle%20east/deutschland/news/presse/2023/2023-06-14%20mgi%20genai%20report%2023/the-economic-potential-of-generative-ai-the-next-productivity-frontier-vf.pdf

Meng, K., Dong, Z. Y., Wang, D. H., & Wong, K. P. (2010, August). A Self-Adaptive RBF Neural Network Classifier for Transformer Fault Analysis. *IEEE Transactions on Power Systems*, *25*(3), 1350–1360. DOI: 10.1109/TPWRS.2010.2040491

Moura, L., Barcaui, A., & Payer, R. (2025). AI and Financial Fraud Prevention: Mapping the Trends and Challenges Through a Bibliometric Lens. *Journal of Risk and Financial Management*, *18*(6), 323. DOI: 10.3390/jrfm18060323

Patel, K. (2023). Credit card analytics: A review of fraud detection and risk assessment techniques. *International Journal of Computer Trends and Technology*, *71*(10), 69–79. DOI: 10.14445/22312803/IJCTT-V71I10P109

Seralina, N. (2021). Information systems for machine intelligence to automated software testing. In: Herald of the Kazakh-British Technical University, Volume 18, Issue 1, pp.157-161, Almaty DOI: 10.55452/1998-6688-2021-18-1-157-161

Seralina, N., & Akzhalova, A. (2023). Anomaly Detection Framework. In: Abraham, A., etc. (eds) Innovations in Bio-Inspired Computing and Applications. IBICA 2022. Lecture Notes in Networks and Systems, vol 649. Springer, Cham. DOI: 10.1007/978-3-031-27499-2_7

Shi, Y., Song, H., & Xu, J. (2023). "Responsible and Effective Federated Learning in Financial Services: A Comprehensive Survey," 2023 62nd IEEE Conference on Decision and Control (CDC), Singapore, Singapore, pp. 4229-4236, DOI: 10.1109/CDC49753.2023.10384119

Surekha, M., Umesh, U., & Dhinakaran, D. P. (2022). A study on utilization and convenient of credit card. *Journal of Positive School Psychology*, •••, 5635–5645.

Varatharajoo, P. M., Zakaria, N. H., Bakar, J. A., & Mahmuddin, M. (2024). "Explainable Artificial Intelligence (XAI) Model for Online Fraud Detection: A Critical Review in Malaysia's Digital Economy," 2024 7th International Conference on Internet Applications, Protocols, and Services (NETAPPS), Kuala Lumpur, Malaysia, pp. 1-8, DOI: 10.1109/NETAPPS63333.2024.10823585

Weforum: https://www3.weforum.org/docs/WEF_Generative_AI_Governance_2024.pdf

KEY TERMS AND DEFINITIONS

Self-Adaptive AI: AI systems that autonomously adjust their behavior and models in response to changing data patterns and threats without manual intervention.

Fraud Detection: The process of identifying and preventing unauthorized or deceptive financial activities within digital platforms.

Value Creation: The measurable benefits—such as improved fraud detection, operational efficiency, and data privacy—gained by integrating self-adaptive AI technologies into FinTech systems.

Chapter 6
AI-Driven Decision Support in Fleet Management:
Creating Value Through Optimization and Innovation

Suryakant Kaushik
https://orcid.org/0009-0007-3784-007X
Sigma XI, USA

ABSTRACT

This chapter examines how artificial intelligence (AI) is transforming fleet management by improving efficiency, safety, compliance, and sustainability. It explores key applications of AI, including real-time route optimization, predictive maintenance, driver behavior monitoring, and emissions reduction. Real-world examples from UPS, Amazon, DHL, Samsara, and La Poste demonstrate measurable gains in cost savings, operational uptime, and environmental impact. The chapter also addresses challenges such as data quality, regulatory compliance, integration with legacy systems, and workforce readiness. Using Rogers' Diffusion of Innovation Theory and the Technology-Organization-Environment (TOE) Framework, it analyzes how organizations can strategically adopt AI. Actionable insights are provided to help fleet managers and decision-makers align AI tools with business goals. As fleets face rising expectations for performance and sustainability, AI is positioned as a critical enabler of long-term value and innovation.

DOI: 10.4018/979-8-3373-2497-5.ch006

INTRODUCTION

Fleet management is undergoing a major transformation driven by artificial intelligence (AI), which is enhancing efficiency, safety, compliance, and sustainability. AI is now considered more impactful than even electric vehicles, according to a 2024 Webfleet survey (EV Magazine, 2024), with 58% of fleet managers planning to adopt AI within five years (Bridgestone EMEA, 2024).

Before the integration of artificial intelligence, fleet management largely relied on manual processes and preventive-only practices. Dispatching was typically done using static schedules and paper logs, leaving fleets unable to adapt quickly to unexpected changes such as weather disruptions or sudden demand spikes. Vehicle maintenance followed fixed schedules rather than condition-based triggers, often resulting in either premature servicing or unexpected breakdowns. Compliance monitoring was also a manual task, with drivers and fleet managers filling out paper-based reports for hours-of-service (HOS), inspections, and emissions tracking. These traditional practices highlight the scale of transformation AI has enabled by shifting operations from reactive and manual to predictive and automated.

The global fleet management market is projected to reach $75.5 billion by 2028 (Markets and Markets, 2024), fueled by AI's integration into routing, predictive maintenance, and driver monitoring. Companies like Uber Freight and Qantas have reported significant gains in efficiency and uptime through AI-enabled routing and maintenance (Business Insider, 2025; The Australian, 2024).

AI also improves safety by monitoring driver behavior and providing real-time coaching (TechRadar, 2024), while helping reduce emissions through smarter fuel usage (CiGen, 2024). Despite challenges like data privacy and integration costs, AI is becoming essential to modern fleet strategy, transforming operations across the vehicle lifecycle (see Figure 1).

While AI adoption in fleet management has accelerated globally, its uptake varies significantly across regions. In technologically advanced markets such as North America and Western Europe, fleets have benefitted from mature telematics infrastructure, government incentives for sustainability, and strong venture capital funding for AI startups. By contrast, developing markets in South Asia, Africa, and Latin America face challenges including limited digital infrastructure, financing constraints for IoT hardware, and fragmented logistics networks. These disparities underscore the importance of tailoring AI solutions to local contexts-ranging from lightweight, modular AI tools for SMEs in emerging markets to highly integrated predictive platforms for large multinational fleets.

Figure 1. AI Applications Across the Fleet Management Lifecycle

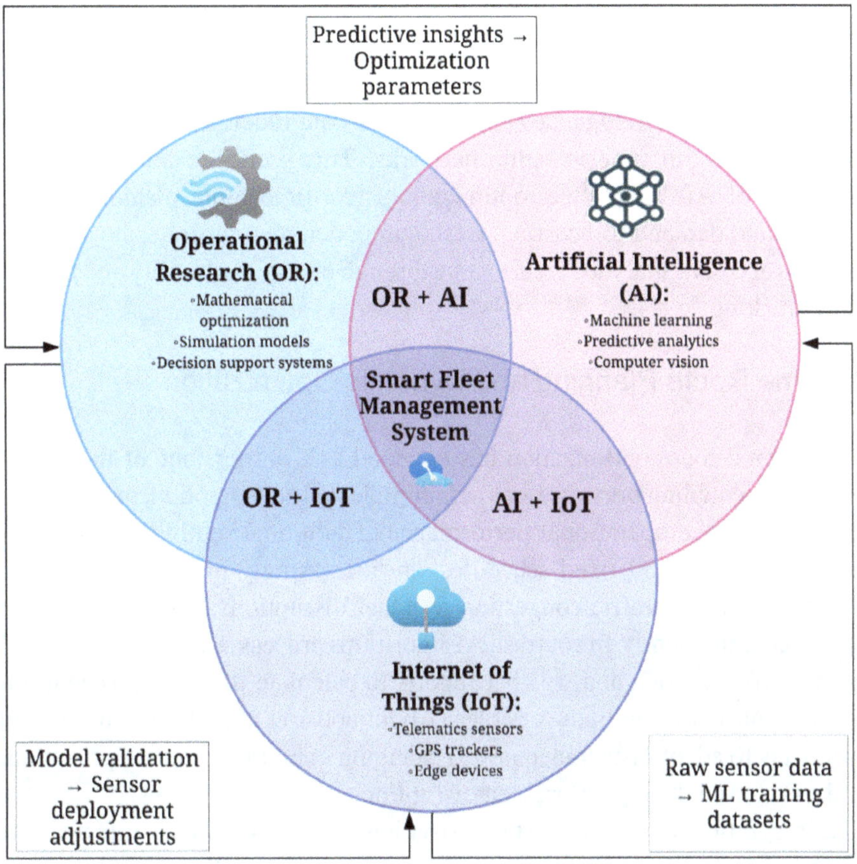

THE AI REVOLUTION IN FLEET MANAGEMENT

Strategic Technology Management in Fleet Optimization

Research on artificial intelligence in logistics and transportation has increasingly shifted from exploratory case studies to rigorous empirical analysis. For example, Abduljabbar, Dia, Liyanage, and Bagloee (2019) provide a foundational review of AI applications in transport, highlighting its potential in predictive routing and resource allocation. More recent studies in *Transportation Research Part C* and *Journal of Business Research* emphasize the role of machine learning in demand forecasting and IoT integration for predictive maintenance (Ghosh et al., 2023; McKinsey & Company, 2022). These works establish the academic grounding for AI in logistics while complementing industry reports and case studies that illustrate practical adoption. Strategic technology management in fleet optimization represents a critical paradigm shift in how organizations approach logistical challenges. By leveraging artificial intelligence (AI), businesses are redefining efficiency, safety, and sustainability in transportation networks. This section examines three core components of AI-driven fleet optimization: real-time route planning, resource allocation, and demand forecasting. Each component demonstrates how advanced algorithms and data analytics create value through operational agility and predictive decision-making.

Real-Time Route Planning and Dynamic Optimization

AI-powered route optimization has emerged as a cornerstone of modern fleet management, enabling organizations to minimize fuel consumption, reduce delivery times, and enhance operational performance. Traditional routing systems, which rely on static maps and fixed schedules, are increasingly inadequate in dynamic environments where traffic congestion, weather disruptions, and unexpected road closures occur frequently. In contrast, AI algorithms process real-time data from GPS devices, traffic sensors, and weather reports to calculate the most efficient routes while accounting for multiple variables (Abduljabbar et al., 2019). This capability allows fleets to adapt instantaneously to changing conditions, ensuring continuous optimization even during unforeseen disruptions.

The integration of real-time data into routing systems has proven transformative. AI systems predict congestion hotspots, adjust for traffic conditions, and proactively reroute vehicles (SimplyFleet, 2025). Studies show AI-optimized routes can lower fuel consumption by up to 15% (ZenduIT, 2025). Historical data also improves future routing, identifying recurring bottlenecks and enabling peak-time optimization. A logistics company using AI-driven routing reduced delivery times by 20% and fuel costs by 12% within six months (SSRN, 2023). As illustrated in Figure 2, this continuous feedback loop relies on GPS, weather, traffic, and vehicle performance data to dynamically reroute fleets.

Figure 2. Real-Time Data Flow in AI-Based Routing

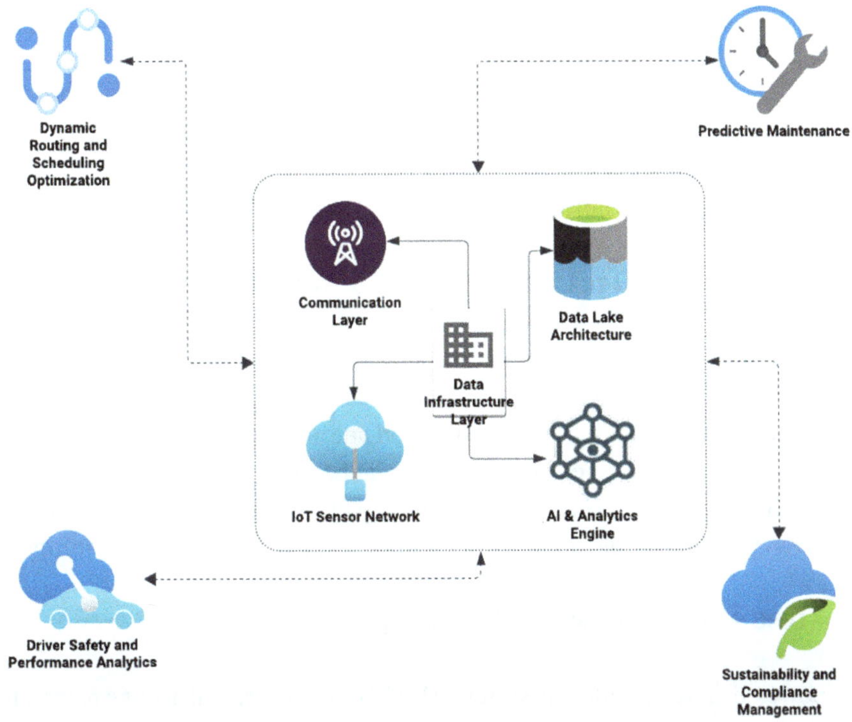

Resource Allocation and Fleet Utilization

AI significantly boosts fleet productivity by identifying underused assets, aligning fleet size with demand, and optimizing deployment based on real-time operational needs (Ontruck, 2024). It prevents overinvestment during seasonal peaks and supports informed vehicle composition strategies. Predictive maintenance, powered by IoT sensors, further reduces unplanned downtime by up to 45% and repair costs by 30% (SimplyFleet, 2025; XenonStack, 2025).

Use cases span diverse sectors. Educational institutions, for instance, reduced operational costs by 25% with AI-optimized school transport that factors in schedules, traffic, and safety (Arena Softwares, 2025). In logistics, AI also manages EV charging schedules in line with route demands. A German fleet reduced charging costs by 18% through AI-enabled off-peak charging optimization (ZenduIT, 2025; EV Magazine, 2024).

Demand Forecasting and Strategic Planning

AI improves forecast accuracy by analyzing historical sales, economic indicators, and behavioral trends to match fleet capacity with fluctuating demand. Amazon's AI-enabled systems predicted Cyber Monday demand for over 400 million products, enabling a 35% order volume increase without delays (SSRN, 2023). Retailers using similar models reported a 22% reduction in overstocking and a 17% increase in delivery punctuality (Ontruck, 2024).

Value Creation in Fleet Safety and Compliance

Artificial intelligence (AI) has redefined how fleets manage safety and compliance, transforming reactive processes into proactive, data-driven strategies. By leveraging real-time monitoring, predictive analytics, and automation, AI tools help organizations reduce accident risks, ensure regulatory adherence, and improve operational efficiency. This section explores three key areas where AI delivers measurable value: driver behavior monitoring, automated compliance, and predictive risk mitigation.

AI-Enabled Driver Behavior Monitoring

AI-powered driver monitoring systems (DMS) analyze critical driving parameters-such as acceleration patterns, braking intensity, speed consistency, and lane discipline-to detect high-risk behaviors including fatigue, distraction, or aggressive driving (Greenroad, 2025; Safety & Health Magazine, 2025). Using in-cab cameras and telematics, these systems deliver real-time feedback to drivers and generate performance dashboards for fleet managers.

The financial and safety impact is significant. Fleets report up to 40% fewer collisions, 25% reductions in insurance premiums, and more than $1.2 million in annual savings from lower accident-related costs (Intangles, 2024; NetworkON, 2025). In large-scale deployments, like one U.S. logistics firm managing 5,000 vehicles, AI-based behavior monitoring led to a 35% drop in insurance claims within 18 months (Tribe.ai, 2025).

Advanced AI models also detect systemic risk patterns, enabling strategic interventions like route reassignment or targeted training. Features like safety score leaderboards and gamified incentives help foster a safety-first culture across fleets.

Automated Compliance Systems

AI simplifies compliance with complex regulations around hours-of-service (HOS), emissions standards, vehicle inspections, and driver certification. Integrated with ELDs and telematics, AI systems automatically flag upcoming HOS violations and generate audit-ready reports-reducing manual reporting time by up to 30 hours per month (NetworkON, 2025).

Environmental compliance is another key application. AI platforms analyze engine performance and idle times to optimize routes and reduce emissions. For example, a European fleet cut carbon emissions by 12% using AI-driven idle reduction and route planning tools (ZenduIT, 2025). These systems also manage regulatory documentation by tracking expiration dates for driver licenses, vehicle registrations, and emissions certifications-issuing automated alerts to prevent lapses, avoiding costly penalties of up to $15,000 per violation (Safety & Health Magazine, 2025).

As regulations evolve, AI tools are incorporating technologies like blockchain to improve audit transparency and data traceability-positioning fleets to remain compliant in an increasingly dynamic policy environment.

Accident Prevention and Risk Mitigation

AI's predictive analytics capabilities enable fleets to proactively identify and mitigate risks. By combining real-time and historical data, these tools forecast high-risk conditions such as poorly lit roads with frequent lane departures or intersections prone to sudden braking (Intangles, 2024).

Fleet managers use this intelligence to reroute vehicles or schedule extra training for at-risk drivers. One delivery fleet in Texas reduced side-swipe collisions by 25% after implementing AI-based risk scoring (Supply Chain Strategy Media, 2025).

AI also powers predictive maintenance, using IoT sensor data to detect faults like tire pressure drops or engine overheating before breakdowns occur. A school bus fleet cut unplanned downtime by 45% through proactive servicing (Arena Softwares, 2025), increasing reliability and service continuity.

Data-driven coaching modules personalize training based on individual driver behavior, while features like real-time alerting and safety score tracking promote accountability. A trucking company reported a 28% improvement in driver safety scores and a 20% reduction in near-miss incidents using this approach (Tribe.ai, 2025).

Integration and Operational Impact

The convergence of AI-powered safety and compliance tools amplifies operational value. Integrated platforms consolidate data from cameras, sensors, and diagnostics into unified dashboards, offering actionable insights for managers (Guardian, 2025).

A Swedish fleet combining real-time driver monitoring with predictive maintenance saw a 22% drop in total cost of ownership over three years (Intelliarts, 2025).

While challenges remain-especially around data privacy and integration with legacy systems-emerging technologies are mitigating them. Edge computing ensures privacy by processing footage locally, and APIs simplify integration with enterprise systems like ERP and CRM platforms (Greenroad, 2025; NetworkON, 2025). Key metrics summarizing the measurable effects of AI applications across safety and compliance domains are shown in Table 1.

Table 1. Measurable Impacts of AI in Fleet Safety & Compliance

AI Application	Measured Outcome	Source
Driver Behavior Monitoring	40% fewer collisions	Intangles, 2024
Real-time Coaching	$1.2M annual savings in incident-related costs	NetworkON, 2025
Compliance Automation	30 hours/month saved in reporting	NetworkON, 2025
Emissions Optimization	12% CO_2 emissions reduction	ZenduIT, 2025
Risk Scoring & Route Adjustments	25% reduction in side-swipe collisions	Supply Chain Strategy Media, 2025

Predictive Maintenance and Operational Efficiency

IoT-Powered Vehicle Monitoring

The integration of Internet of Things (IoT) sensors and telematics systems has revolutionized vehicle monitoring capabilities, enabling fleets to transition from reactive to proactive maintenance strategies. Modern IoT devices collect real-time data on critical parameters such as engine temperature, tire pressure, fuel efficiency, and GPS location, creating a comprehensive digital twin of vehicle health (Indmall Automation, 2024; ETA Transit, 2025). For example, sensors embedded in brake systems monitor pad wear and rotor temperature, alerting managers when components approach failure thresholds (XenonStack, 2025). This granular visibility into vehicle performance allows fleets to address issues before they escalate into costly breakdowns.

Advanced telematics platforms analyze operational patterns to establish personalized performance baselines for each vehicle. A delivery van operating in urban stop-and-go traffic, for instance, may exhibit different brake wear patterns compared to a long-haul truck on highways. Machine learning models process these usage variations to recommend maintenance tailored to specific operational contexts (3S

Automation, 2025). This individualized approach contrasts with traditional time-based maintenance schedules, which often result in unnecessary servicing or missed critical repairs. A study of European logistics firms found that IoT-driven monitoring reduced unplanned downtime by 45% by aligning maintenance with actual vehicle needs (XenonStack, 2025).

The scalability of IoT solutions is exemplified by systems like ETA Transit's Advanced Vehicle Monitoring (AVM), which provides a 360° view of fleet operations through dashboards tracking engine health, battery status, and energy consumption (ETA Transit, 2025). For electric vehicles (EVs), these platforms monitor battery cell degradation and charging efficiency, enabling fleets to optimize charging schedules and extend battery lifespans by up to 30% (ETA Transit, 2025). Real-time fault notifications ensure technicians can diagnose issues remotely, often resolving them before drivers are aware of potential problems.

Beyond operational efficiency, IoT-powered vehicle monitoring contributes significantly to sustainability goals. By identifying inefficient fuel consumption patterns or excessive idling times, these systems help reduce greenhouse gas emissions. For instance, a logistics company in Germany used IoT data to optimize routes and reduce idling times by 20%, cutting annual CO_2 emissions by over 15 metric tons per vehicle (LLumin, 2025). Sustainability-focused fleets are increasingly leveraging IoT systems not only for compliance with environmental regulations but also as part of their corporate social responsibility initiatives.

Predictive Servicing Models

AI algorithms convert IoT data into maintenance insights by detecting patterns like engine temperature spikes or vibration anomalies, indicating potential failures (XenonStack, 2025). Trained on historical repair data, these models can predict issues with 92% accuracy up to three weeks in advance (3S Automation, 2025), enabling fleets to schedule repairs during off-peak hours.

This shift from fixed to condition-based maintenance prevents premature part replacement and delays that cause costly breakdowns. A refrigerated fleet reduced lubrication costs by 18% by adjusting oil changes based on engine load and fuel quality (LLumin, 2025).

Cloud platforms like XenonStack process terabytes of diagnostic data daily and incorporate contextual variables such as ambient temperature or terrain (XenonStack, 2025). Technicians equipped with AI insights receive automated repair guidance, reducing diagnostic time by 40% and prioritizing urgent tasks (Indmall Automation, 2024). Figure 3 illustrates the measurable impact of predictive maintenance, such as downtime reduction, cost savings, and longer vehicle lifespans-core benefits that drive ROI.

Figure 3. Outcomes of AI-Powered Predictive Maintenance in Fleet Operations

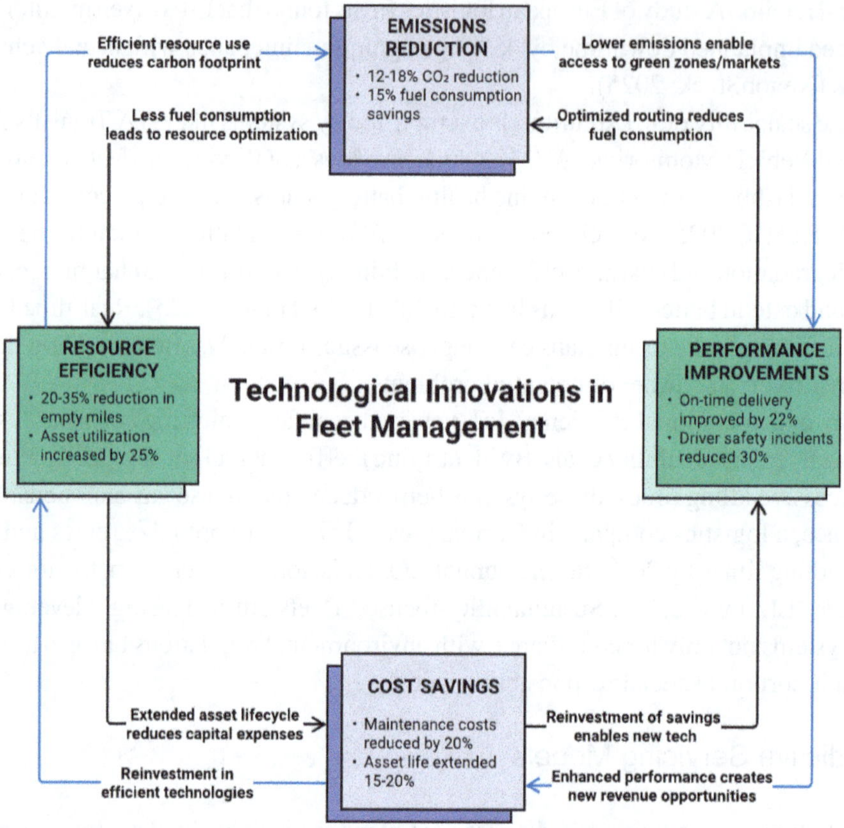

Asset Lifecycle Extension

Predictive maintenance directly contributes to asset longevity by preventing cascade failures. A malfunctioning fuel injector left unaddressed can damage engine cylinders, potentially necessitating a $15,000 overhaul (LLumin, 2025). AI systems detect such issues early, enabling $200 injector replacements instead. This proactive approach extends the average commercial vehicle lifespan from seven to ten years, according to a North American fleet analysis (LLumin, 2025).

The financial impact of lifecycle extension is magnified in large fleets. UPS reported a 22% reduction in vehicle replacement costs over five years after implementing IoT-based predictive maintenance across its 100,000-vehicle fleet (LLumin, 2025). Similarly, DHL's $350 million investment in predictive analytics extended the service life of delivery vans by 18 months, deferring capital expenditures on new vehicles (3S Automation, 2025).

Fleet management platforms now incorporate residual value forecasting models that factor in maintenance history when determining optimal disposal timelines. A vehicle with consistently low repair costs and stable fuel efficiency might remain in service longer than one with frequent issues-even if both are the same age (LLumin, 2025). This data-driven approach to lifecycle management maximizes return on investment while ensuring fleet reliability.

Asset lifecycle extension also supports environmental sustainability objectives by reducing waste associated with premature vehicle retirements. By extending the usable life of assets through predictive maintenance practices, fleets can lower their carbon footprint while reducing the demand for new manufacturing resources-a win-win scenario for both businesses and the environment (ETA Transit, 2025).

Operational Efficiency Gains

The operational benefits of predictive maintenance extend beyond vehicle availability. By reducing unplanned downtime, fleets achieve higher asset utilization rates-a critical metric in industries like last-mile delivery where vehicle idle time directly impacts profitability. A case study involving Amazon's delivery network demonstrated a 25% improvement in daily route completion rates after implementing predictive maintenance algorithms (3S Automation, 2025).

Energy efficiency gains further enhance operational outcomes. IoT systems monitor fuel consumption patterns in real time and identify inefficiencies such as excessive idling or suboptimal gear shifting. When combined with driver coaching programs based on these insights, fleets have reported reductions in fuel costs of up to 12% (ETA Transit, 2025). For EV fleets specifically, predictive systems optimize charging schedules to leverage off-peak electricity rates while avoiding overcharging scenarios that degrade battery health prematurely lowering energy costs by an average of 20% annually per vehicle (ETA Transit, 2025).

Maintenance workflows themselves become more efficient through AI integration. Automated parts ordering systems linked to diagnostic alerts ensure technicians have necessary components before vehicles enter the shop-reducing average repair times from eight hours to two-and-a-half hours (XenonStack, 2025). Digital twin simulations allow technicians to practice complex repairs virtually before performing them physically decreasing error rates during servicing by up to 40% while improving overall repair quality (Indmall Automation, 2024).

Predictive maintenance also improves customer satisfaction levels for logistics companies reliant on timely deliveries. By minimizing delays caused by unexpected breakdowns or repairs during transit routes-common pain points for e-commerce businesses-fleets can maintain higher service reliability ratings while meeting contractual obligations more consistently (3S Automation, 2025). These improvements contribute directly not only toward operational efficiency but also toward long-term customer retention strategies critical for sustaining competitive advantages within crowded markets like retail logistics or food delivery services.

Beyond ensuring vehicle health and asset longevity, AI also plays a central role in addressing environmental sustainability. The following section examines how AI supports sustainable fleet ecosystems by optimizing fuel use, enabling EV transitions, and tracking emissions.

Sustainable Fleet Ecosystems

The integration of artificial intelligence (AI) into fleet management has revolutionized the pursuit of sustainability, enabling organizations to balance operational efficiency with environmental responsibility. AI technologies address key challenges such as fuel optimization, electric vehicle (EV) transition, and emissions reduction, creating opportunities for fleets to reduce their ecological footprint while maintaining profitability. This section explores the transformative role of AI in building sustainable fleet ecosystems.

AI-Enabled Fuel Optimization

Fuel consumption remains the largest contributor to fleet operational costs and environmental impact, accounting for up to 30% of total expenses in logistics operations (ZenduIT, 2025). AI-powered fuel optimization technologies leverage real-time data analytics and predictive modeling to minimize consumption across fleet operations. These systems analyze diverse factors affecting fuel efficiency-including vehicle performance, traffic conditions, and driver behavior-and provide actionable recommendations for improvement (ETA Transit, 2025).

A multifaceted approach to fuel optimization encompasses several complementary strategies. First, AI models analyze weather patterns and road conditions to identify the most fuel-efficient routes. For instance, a delivery fleet operating in urban areas reduced fuel consumption by 18% after implementing AI-driven route optimization that accounted for traffic congestion and stop-and-go driving patterns (LLumin, 2025). Second, continuous engine parameter monitoring detects inefficiencies such as suboptimal gear usage or excessive idling times. By providing real-time feedback to drivers, these systems enable immediate adjustments that improve fuel efficiency.

Predictive maintenance also plays a critical role in reducing excess fuel consumption caused by inefficient engine operation. IoT sensors monitor components such as fuel injectors and air filters, alerting managers when replacements are needed to maintain optimal performance (XenonStack, 2025). For example, a logistics company using predictive maintenance tools reduced fuel-related expenses by 12% annually by addressing engine inefficiencies proactively (ETA Transit, 2025). Additionally, speed optimization algorithms balance fuel efficiency with timely arrivals. AI systems recommend optimal speeds based on road conditions and delivery schedules, ensuring minimal wastage without compromising service quality.

AI-enabled fuel optimization extends beyond internal combustion engine vehicles to include hybrid and electric fleets. For hybrid vehicles, AI systems monitor powertrain transitions between electric and gasoline modes to maximize efficiency during mixed driving conditions (LLumin, 2025). For EVs, predictive algorithms optimize battery usage by adjusting acceleration patterns and regenerative braking settings based on route topology. These innovations highlight the versatility of AI in addressing diverse fleet sustainability challenges.

Electric Vehicle Transition Support

The transition to electric vehicles (EVs) presents one of the most transformative opportunities for reducing environmental impact in fleet operations. With zero tailpipe emissions, EVs are a cornerstone of sustainability initiatives aimed at reducing greenhouse gas emissions and combating climate change. However, this transition introduces complex operational challenges, including range limitations, limited charging infrastructure, and the logistical difficulties of managing mixed fleets. Artificial intelligence (AI) technologies are increasingly central to overcoming these hurdles by optimizing charging schedules, predicting vehicle range requirements, and coordinating diverse vehicle types within evolving fleet compositions (Indmall Automation, 2024).

A major concern during EV adoption is ensuring efficient charging without disrupting fleet productivity. AI platforms analyze variables such as fleet energy demand, electricity pricing, route schedules, and grid load to identify optimal charging windows. These tools recommend charging during off-peak hours to reduce costs and avoid overburdening local grids (ETA Transit, 2025). For example, a logistics company utilizing AI-enabled scheduling reduced its annual charging costs by 20% by prioritizing overnight, off-peak energy usage (XenonStack, 2025). Such optimization ensures that operational uptime is maintained while keeping energy expenses manageable.

AI also plays a vital role in addressing range anxiety-a primary barrier to EV adoption-through predictive analytics. These systems assess real-time variables such as traffic conditions, terrain gradients, temperature, and historical energy consumption to calculate route feasibility based on battery capacity. By accounting for potential deviations and recharge opportunities, fleets can plan routes that minimize the risk of mid-route energy depletion. This is particularly useful for last-mile delivery and urban logistics, where short distances can be optimized to make full use of EVs' limited range.

As most fleets transition gradually from internal combustion engine (ICE) vehicles to EVs, AI supports the intelligent coordination of mixed-fleet operations. AI systems allow managers to dynamically assign tasks based on vehicle capabilities, route complexity, and infrastructure accessibility. For instance, ICE vehicles can be allocated to long-distance hauls requiring higher payload capacity, while EVs can be reserved for shorter, urban routes with dense charging networks (LLumin, 2025). This tailored distribution ensures operational efficiency while maximizing the environmental benefits of EV use.

Industry forecasts indicate that electric and hybrid vehicles will comprise a growing share of global fleets by the end of the decade, fueled by stricter emissions regulations and expanding government incentives (Indmall Automation, 2024). The evolving regulatory environment reinforces the need for AI-enabled decision support systems to guide investment in EV assets, infrastructure planning, and operational reconfiguration. AI offers strategic insights into when and how to scale EV adoption based on cost-benefit models, regional policies, and vehicle utilization trends.

As EV technologies continue to advance-with improvements in battery life, charging speed, and vehicle range-AI will remain a critical enabler of seamless integration into modern fleets. It provides the agility and foresight required to balance economic, operational, and environmental objectives throughout the transition.

Emissions Tracking and Reduction

AI-powered emissions monitoring systems provide unprecedented visibility into environmental impact across fleet operations. These systems track greenhouse gas emissions at both vehicle-specific and fleet-wide levels, enabling organizations to identify reduction opportunities while ensuring compliance with regulatory standards such as those set by the Environmental Protection Agency (EPA) or European Union directives (ETA Transit, 2025). By analyzing data from IoT sensors embedded in engines and exhaust systems, AI platforms generate detailed reports on carbon dioxide (CO_2), nitrogen oxide (NOx), and particulate matter emissions (LLumin, 2025).

The ability to measure emissions accurately supports both corporate sustainability goals and regulatory compliance efforts. For instance, fleets operating in regions with strict emissions caps can use AI tools to monitor adherence in real time while identifying vehicles requiring retrofitting or replacement with cleaner alternatives (XenonStack, 2025). Additionally, these systems evaluate the effectiveness of sustainability initiatives such as route optimization or engine upgrades by quantifying their impact on emissions levels over time.

AI-driven approaches enable shipping companies to significantly lower emissions while simultaneously reducing operational costs-a dual benefit that demonstrates the compatibility of environmental responsibility with economic performance. For example, a freight company reduced CO_2 emissions by 15% annually after implementing AI-powered route optimization tools that minimized idle times during peak traffic hours (Indmall Automation, 2024). Similarly, predictive maintenance practices targeting inefficient engine components contributed to an additional 10% reduction in NOx emissions across its fleet (ETA Transit, 2025).

Beyond compliance monitoring and operational adjustments, AI technologies support long-term sustainability planning through advanced forecasting models. These models predict future emissions levels based on anticipated changes in fleet composition or operating conditions-such as increased adoption of EVs or shifts toward urban delivery routes-and recommend strategies for achieving net-zero targets within specified timelines (LLumin, 2025). By aligning short-term actions with long-term goals through data-driven insights, organizations can position themselves as leaders in sustainable logistics practices.

AI-enabled emissions tracking also facilitates transparency in corporate reporting-a growing demand among stakeholders including investors and customers concerned about environmental impact. Detailed dashboards summarizing emissions data allow organizations to showcase their progress toward sustainability objectives while identifying areas requiring further improvement (Indmall Automation, 2024). This transparency fosters trust among stakeholders while reinforcing organizational commitment to environmental stewardship.

Environmental Lifecycle Assessment Beyond Emissions

While AI-driven fleet solutions contribute to emissions reduction, a more holistic perspective must also account for the environmental impacts across the entire lifecycle of supporting technologies. Electric vehicles (EVs), IoT sensors, and telematics platforms all introduce upstream and downstream ecological considerations that extend beyond operational efficiency.

Battery Production and Disposal. EV adoption relies heavily on lithium-ion batteries, which require rare earth elements such as cobalt and lithium. Mining these resources poses significant environmental and social challenges, including ecosystem disruption, water usage, and human rights concerns in supplier regions. At the end of their service life, batteries present disposal and recycling challenges, with improper handling contributing to hazardous waste.

IoT and Sensor E-Waste. AI-enabled fleet management depends on extensive IoT sensor networks, telematics gateways, and onboard computing devices. As fleets upgrade hardware frequently to match evolving AI standards, electronic waste (e-waste) becomes a growing concern. Without circular economy models, large volumes of outdated sensors and devices risk contributing to global e-waste problems.

Lifecycle Assessment (LCA) Tools. Environmental lifecycle assessment frameworks provide decision-makers with structured tools to evaluate these impacts comprehensively. By considering raw material sourcing, manufacturing energy use, operational efficiency, and end-of-life disposal, LCAs highlight sustainability trade-offs often overlooked in emissions-only analyses. For example, a European logistics firm used an LCA model to compare two EV adoption strategies and found that delayed replacement of existing vehicles resulted in lower lifetime carbon impact than rapid fleet electrification.

Circular Economy Approaches. To mitigate lifecycle impacts, organizations are exploring circular economy solutions such as second-life applications for EV batteries, closed-loop recycling of rare earth metals, and sustainable disposal policies for IoT hardware. These approaches ensure that the long-term sustainability benefits of AI adoption are not undermined by hidden environmental costs.

By extending sustainability analysis to cover the entire lifecycle of technologies, fleet operators and policymakers can make more informed decisions that balance environmental responsibility with operational gains.

Sustainability Beyond Emissions

AI's contribution to sustainable fleet ecosystems extends beyond emissions tracking and reduction efforts into broader resource optimization initiatives aimed at minimizing waste across operations. For example, predictive inventory management tools analyze delivery schedules alongside warehouse stocking patterns to reduce instances of overstocking or underutilization-a common source of inefficiency contributing indirectly to higher carbon footprints (ETA Transit, 2025). Similarly, packaging optimization algorithms recommend materials that balance durability with recyclability based on shipment characteristics such as weight or fragility.

While sustainability highlights the fleet-level benefits of AI, its true impact emerges when integrated across the broader logistics and urban mobility ecosystem. The next section explores how AI-enabled fleets interact with warehouses, supply chains, and smart city infrastructure.

Integration with Broader Supply Chain and Mobility Systems

Fleet management does not operate in isolation-it is one node in a larger logistics and urban mobility ecosystem. Artificial intelligence (AI) therefore delivers its greatest impact when integrated across supply chains, warehousing, and smart transportation systems.

Supply Chain Integration

AI-enabled fleets are increasingly linked with digital supply chain platforms that provide end-to-end visibility. For instance, predictive demand forecasting in warehouses can trigger dynamic adjustments in fleet routing, while IoT-enabled vehicles send real-time inventory data back to distribution centers. This closed feedback loop reduces stockouts, minimizes overstocking, and shortens fulfillment times.

Last-Mile Delivery

Last-mile logistics, often the most costly and complex segment, benefits significantly from AI integration. Dynamic routing combined with customer-facing platforms enables real-time delivery updates and improved accuracy. Companies such as Amazon and DHL are piloting AI-driven micro-fulfillment centers that optimize last-mile delivery routes in tandem with warehouse automation.

Urban Mobility and Smart Cities

AI-enabled fleets increasingly interface with smart city infrastructure such as adaptive traffic signals, connected road sensors, and digital tolling systems. This integration allows vehicles to adjust routes in response to real-time congestion data, reducing delays and emissions. In Mobility-as-a-Service (MaaS) models, public and private fleets are coordinated through shared AI platforms, enabling multimodal transport solutions that combine buses, EVs, and micromobility options.

Systemic Benefits.

By embedding AI in the broader logistics network, organizations can achieve systemic efficiency rather than isolated gains. For example, AI that synchronizes warehouse robotics with delivery fleets can reduce idle vehicle time by 20% and cut overall supply chain emissions by 15%. Similarly, city-level AI initiatives that link freight fleets to urban mobility platforms support congestion reduction and sustainability targets.

Incorporating a systemic perspective ensures that fleet AI adoption is not only operationally effective but also strategically aligned with the transformation of global supply chains and urban transport systems.

These broader integrations set the stage for understanding how AI creates tangible value in practice. The following case studies from industry leaders such as UPS, DHL, Amazon, La Poste, and Samsara illustrate how theoretical benefits translate into real-world outcomes.

Real-World Applications

Artificial intelligence (AI) has become a transformative force in logistics, enabling companies to optimize operations, improve customer experiences, and achieve sustainability goals. This section explores how leading organizations such as UPS, DHL, Amazon, and La Poste have integrated AI into their operations to address complex challenges and create value.

These real-world implementations can also be interpreted through established adoption frameworks. For example, UPS's ORION route optimization system illustrates relative advantage and observability from Rogers' Diffusion of Innovation theory, as the measurable fuel savings and reduced mileage make adoption benefits clear and visible. DHL's use of collaborative robots demonstrates organizational readiness under the TOE framework, as strong internal investment in automation enabled successful scaling. By analyzing case studies through these theoretical lenses, we can connect operational outcomes to broader patterns of innovation adoption.

UPS: AI-Driven Logistics Optimization

United Parcel Service (UPS) has been at the forefront of AI adoption, leveraging advanced technologies to enhance logistics management, customer service, and operational efficiency. One of the company's most notable AI implementations is the On-Road Integrated Optimization and Navigation (ORION) system. ORION uses AI algorithms to optimize delivery routes for UPS drivers, analyzing over 200,000 route alternatives per driver daily to determine the most efficient path (DigitalDefynd, 2025). By incorporating variables such as traffic patterns, package destinations, and delivery deadlines, ORION has reduced UPS drivers' total mileage by an estimated 100 million miles annually. This reduction translates into significant fuel savings and a decrease in greenhouse gas emissions (Wall Street Journal, 2024).

ORION's dynamic route optimization capabilities are particularly valuable during peak periods when delivery volumes surge. For example, during the holiday season, ORION adjusts routes in real-time based on traffic congestion and weather conditions, ensuring timely deliveries despite increased demand. This adaptability has enabled UPS to maintain high service levels while reducing operational costs (DigitalDefynd, 2025).

Beyond route optimization, UPS has integrated AI into its customer service operations through the Message Response Automation (MeRA) tool. MeRA uses large language models (LLMs) to automate responses to over 52,000 customer emails daily, cutting email resolution times by 50% (Supply Chain 24/7, 2024). This automation allows human agents to focus on complex inquiries while ensuring consistent and accurate responses for routine questions. The success of MeRA highlights how generative AI can enhance customer satisfaction while improving operational efficiency.

UPS has also addressed workforce management challenges through its Languages Across Logistics (LAL) platform. This AI-powered tool provides real-time translation capabilities for employees from diverse linguistic backgrounds, fostering seamless collaboration across global teams. By integrating AI into various facets of its operations-from logistics optimization to workforce management-UPS demonstrates how technology can drive efficiency while addressing both environmental and human resource challenges (Wall Street Journal, 2024).

DHL: AI-Powered Warehouse Automation

DHL Group has strategically incorporated AI into its operations to enhance warehouse automation, talent acquisition, and global trade services. A key component of this strategy is DHL's partnership with Robust.AI to deploy collaborative robots (cobots) such as the Carter robot in its warehouses. These cobots use machine vision and real-time data processing to adapt to changing warehouse conditions, optimizing picking workflows and reducing workplace injuries (Robotics 24/7, 2025). By automating repetitive tasks like cart picking and pallet transport, Carter cobots free human workers to focus on higher-value activities such as quality control and exception handling.

DHL's investment in AI extends beyond robotics to include its My Global Trade Services (MyGTS) platform. MyGTS simplifies international shipping by providing businesses with tools to navigate customs regulations and calculate landed costs accurately. The platform's AI capabilities enable users to compare trade lanes and identify cost-efficient procurement strategies, making it easier for companies to expand into new markets (DHL Press Release, 2024). This application underscores how AI can streamline complex processes like cross-border trade while supporting business growth.

Warehouse automation remains a cornerstone of DHL's AI strategy. The company's deployment of robotic arms for sorting parcels has increased sorting efficiency by 40%, enabling DHL to handle surging e-commerce volumes without additional labor costs (Copper Digital, 2025). Additionally, DHL's use of autonomous mobile robots for order picking has reduced order cycle times significantly while minimizing errors. These innovations highlight how AI-driven automation can enhance scalability and precision in logistics operations.

DHL has also embraced predictive analytics through its Resilience360 platform (now part of Everstream Analytics), which provides real-time insights into potential supply chain disruptions. For instance, if a natural disaster affects a supplier region, the platform alerts managers immediately so they can reroute shipments or adjust inventory levels proactively. This capability demonstrates how AI can enhance supply chain resilience by enabling organizations to anticipate and mitigate risks effectively (Copper Digital, 2025).

Amazon: Supply Chain Intelligence

Amazon has consistently leveraged AI to revolutionize its supply chain operations, driving improvements in delivery speed, inventory management, and sustainability practices. One of Amazon's most impactful AI tools is the Sequoia robotic inventory management system, which identifies and stores inventory 75% faster than traditional methods (Reuters, 2023). By combining mobile robots with advanced algorithms, Sequoia has reduced warehouse processing times by up to 25%, enabling Amazon to fulfill orders more quickly while minimizing labor requirements.

During peak shopping events like Cyber Monday in 2023, Amazon used AI systems to forecast daily demand for over 400 million products and predict order origins based on historical data (CDO Times, 2024). These predictive analytics allowed Amazon to allocate resources efficiently across its global network of fulfillment centers, ensuring timely deliveries even during periods of unprecedented demand.

Amazon's commitment to sustainability is evident in its use of the Packaging Decision Engine (PDE)-an AI model that optimizes packaging choices based on product characteristics and shipping requirements. Since its implementation in 2015, PDE has helped Amazon eliminate over two million tons of packaging material globally by recommending more efficient options such as padded mailers instead of cardboard boxes for certain items (Chain Store Age, 2024). This innovation demonstrates how AI can align operational efficiency with environmental responsibility.

Additionally, Amazon's dynamic route planning algorithms optimize last-mile deliveries by accounting for factors like traffic conditions and weather forecasts in real time. These systems not only reduce delivery times but also lower fuel consumption across Amazon's extensive fleet of delivery vehicles (Sifted Resources, 2024). By integrating AI into every stage of its supply chain-from inventory management to last-mile logistics-Amazon continues to set industry benchmarks for efficiency and sustainability.

La Poste: IoT-Powered Fleet Intelligence

La Poste Group has leveraged AI-powered solutions to transform its logistics operations through enhanced data utilization and real-time decision-making capabilities. In partnership with Pathway Technologies, La Poste implemented an IoT-based platform that processes geolocation data from postal containers to create actionable business insights (Pathway Success Stories, 2022). This system enables La Poste to monitor truck movements across its network of industrial platforms in real time while providing operators with accurate arrival times and route information.

One of the most significant outcomes of this implementation is the creation of an AI-powered digital twin that maps La Poste's transport processes dynamically. This digital twin allows managers to shift from an asset-centric perspective-focused on individual vehicles-to a process-centric approach that optimizes routes and platform-level operations holistically (Pathway Success Stories, 2022). By identifying inefficiencies such as underutilized assets or suboptimal routes, La Poste has achieved a 50% reduction in total cost of ownership for its IoT data platform and a 16% decrease in fleet capital expenditure (Pathway Newsroom, 2025).

La Poste's use of predictive analytics extends beyond route optimization to include anomaly detection within its logistics network. Machine learning models analyze sensor data continuously to identify deviations from expected patterns-such as delays caused by traffic congestion or equipment failures-and recommend corrective actions proactively (Pathway Newsroom, 2025). These capabilities have improved operational reliability while reducing costs associated with disruptions or delays.

In addition to operational benefits, La Poste's adoption of AI supports sustainability goals by minimizing fuel consumption through optimized routing strategies. For instance, the company reduced CO_2 emissions across its fleet by implementing predictive maintenance practices that ensure vehicles operate at peak efficiency (Pathway Newsroom, 2025). These initiatives highlight how AI can drive both financial performance and environmental stewardship simultaneously.

Samsara: Clover Dairy Optimizes Fleet Management

Clover Dairy provides an excellent example of Samsara's impact on fleet management through real-time tracking capabilities that enhance customer satisfaction and operational efficiency. After evaluating several fleet tracking solutions, Clover Dairy selected Samsara due to its ability to provide minute-by-minute updates-a feature critical for responding promptly to customer inquiries about delivery status (IoT One Case Study Database, 2025). By installing Samsara's vehicle gateways across its entire delivery fleet, Clover Dairy enabled its distribution manager, Paul Drake, to monitor truck locations remotely. This real-time visibility also simplified maintenance workflows through automated alerts for vehicle diagnostics and servicing needs.

Samsara's routing features further improved Clover Dairy's operations by enabling automatic notifications for customers regarding shipment status updates. This capability reduced the need for frequent customer calls requesting delivery updates and ensured better communication throughout the supply chain. Additionally, Samsara's door sensors provided valuable insights by monitoring trailer openings and unloadings, which helped protect against rejected load claims and ensured product quality during transit. These innovations saved Clover Dairy thousands of dollars annually while enhancing customer satisfaction and operational efficiency.

By leveraging Samsara's AI-driven tools, Clover Dairy achieved measurable improvements in ROI through streamlined workflows, reduced operational costs, and enhanced service reliability. This case demonstrates how advanced fleet management solutions can transform logistics operations and drive long-term strategic growth.

Table 2 below summarizes the key takeaways from these real-world applications, highlighting how AI technologies have delivered measurable improvements across various operational domains.

Table 2. Key Takeaways from Real-World Applications of AI in Fleet Management

Company	Key Takeaway
UPS	AI-driven route optimization via ORION reduced total mileage by 100 million miles annually, leading to significant fuel savings and emissions reduction.
DHL	Collaborative robots (cobots) optimized picking workflows, reducing workplace injuries and increasing efficiency by 40%.
Amazon	AI-powered inventory management reduced warehouse processing times by 25%, enabling faster order fulfillment and improved sustainability through packaging optimization.
La Poste	IoT-based platforms provided real-time insights, reducing total cost of ownership by 50% and fleet capital expenditure by 16%.
Samsara	Real-time tracking and automated maintenance alerts improved operational efficiency, reduced costs, and enhanced customer satisfaction for Clover Dairy.

Taken together, these cases highlight how Rogers' and TOE frameworks provide analytical depth to practical adoption stories. Amazon's predictive analytics embody Rogers' concept of trialability, where pilots during high-demand events like Cyber Monday validated the technology before broader rollout. Similarly, La Poste's deployment of digital twins reflects TOE's environmental context, responding to regulatory and sustainability pressures. Integrating theoretical perspectives with case evidence ensures that AI adoption is understood not only as a set of isolated success stories but as part of a structured process shaped by technology, organizational capacity, and environmental forces.

Challenges and Opportunities

Data Quality and Model Accuracy

The effectiveness of AI systems in fleet management hinges on the quality and integrity of data inputs. Fleet operations generate vast quantities of data from telematics, IoT sensors, and driver behavior monitoring systems. However, inconsistent data collection methods, sensor malfunctions, and transmission failures can compromise data accuracy, leading to flawed insights (TechTarget, 2025; SSRN, 2023). For example, incomplete GPS data or mislabeled maintenance records may skew predictive maintenance models, resulting in unnecessary repairs or unaddressed vehicle failures (DBB Software, 2025). Organizations must implement data governance frameworks to standardize data collection, validation, and storage processes. These frameworks should include automated anomaly detection tools and protocols for auditing data sources to ensure completeness and consistency (dbt Labs, 2024).

Model accuracy presents additional challenges, as predictive algorithms require extensive training on diverse datasets to account for variables such as vehicle types, driver habits, and regional traffic patterns. A study of European logistics firms found that AI models trained on limited or biased data produced route optimization errors of up to 18%, leading to increased fuel consumption (SSRN, 2023). Continuous model refinement is critical, particularly as operational environments evolve. For instance, seasonal weather changes or new regulatory requirements may render existing models obsolete. Techniques such as ensemble modeling-combining multiple algorithms to balance their strengths-have proven effective in improving prediction reliability. UPS, for example, reduced route planning errors by 22% after adopting ensemble models that integrated weather forecasts and real-time traffic updates (DBB Software, 2025).

Opportunities to enhance data quality and model performance are emerging through advancements in IoT and edge computing. High-resolution sensors now provide granular data on engine performance, tire pressure, and driver biometrics, enabling more precise predictive analytics (WalkingTree Tech, 2025). Edge computing further reduces latency by processing data locally on vehicles, ensuring real-time decision-making without reliance on centralized cloud systems. A North American trucking company improved fuel efficiency by 14% after deploying edge-based AI models that adjusted driving patterns instantaneously based on road conditions (SSRN, 2023). Additionally, synthetic data generation-using AI to simulate rare operational scenarios-helps address data scarcity issues, particularly for fleets transitioning to electric vehicles (EVs) with limited historical data (TechTarget, 2025).

Cybersecurity and Data Protection Risks

The integration of artificial intelligence (AI) with Internet of Things (IoT) systems in fleet management creates new cybersecurity vulnerabilities that can significantly disrupt operations if not properly addressed. Connected vehicles and telematics platforms generate vast amounts of sensitive data-such as GPS locations, driver biometrics, and engine diagnostics-which can become high-value targets for malicious actors.

Types of Cybersecurity Threats. Fleet operators face risks such as telematics manipulation, GPS spoofing, ransomware attacks on dispatch systems, and unauthorized access to in-vehicle control units. Adversarial attacks on AI models pose an additional concern, as malicious inputs can mislead predictive algorithms used for routing or risk scoring (NIST, 2021).

Industry Standards and Frameworks. To mitigate these risks, fleets must align with international standards such as ISO/SAE 21434 on road vehicle cybersecurity and the NIST Cybersecurity Framework. These provide structured guidelines for protecting vehicle communication systems, ensuring secure data transmission, and responding to breaches.

Risk Mitigation Strategies. Best practices include encryption of telematics data, implementation of secure application programming interfaces (APIs), deployment of intrusion detection systems, and use of edge computing to process sensitive data locally rather than transmitting it to the cloud. For example, a European logistics operator reduced cyber vulnerability by 30% by adopting edge-based AI models that limited exposure of sensitive GPS data (McKinsey & Company, 2022).

Data Privacy and Compliance. Beyond operational risks, cybersecurity is tightly linked to data protection regulations such as the General Data Protection Regulation (GDPR) and the California Consumer Privacy Act (CCPA). Ensuring anonymization of driver data and strict access controls is essential to maintain compliance and build trust among employees and customers.

Taken together, these cybersecurity concerns highlight the need for fleets to treat data security not merely as an IT function but as a core operational risk in AI-driven logistics. Establishing robust cyber resilience is essential for scaling AI adoption in complex, connected fleet ecosystems.

AI Ethics and Algorithmic Accountability

As AI systems become more embedded in fleet management, ethical considerations and algorithmic accountability are increasingly important. Beyond technical efficiency, organizations must address how AI impacts drivers, employees, and broader society.

Bias and Fairness. AI models can inadvertently reinforce bias if trained on incomplete or skewed datasets. For example, risk scoring systems may unfairly penalize certain driving styles or regional behaviors, while facial recognition tools in driver monitoring systems have been criticized for lower accuracy across demographic groups (Eubanks, 2018). Ensuring fairness requires diverse datasets, continuous auditing, and transparent reporting of AI decision criteria.

Transparency and Explainability. Many AI systems function as "black boxes," where decision rules are not visible to operators. In fleet contexts, this opacity can create trust issues-such as drivers questioning why a route was reassigned or why their safety score declined. To build confidence, organizations should prioritize explainable AI (XAI) approaches that provide clear, human-understandable reasons for decisions (AI Now Institute, 2023).

Worker Autonomy and Privacy. AI-enabled driver monitoring raises ethical concerns around constant surveillance and reduced autonomy. While monitoring improves safety, it may negatively affect morale if not balanced with respect for employee rights. Consent, anonymization, and policies limiting data use strictly to safety or compliance are essential for ethical deployment (European Commission, 2021).

Responsible AI Guidelines. Emerging frameworks such as the EU AI Act, IEEE's *Ethically Aligned Design*, and the OECD AI Principles provide benchmarks for responsible AI. Fleet operators can use these guidelines to establish governance mechanisms, conduct regular ethics reviews, and ensure that adoption aligns with organizational values as well as regulatory expectations.

By integrating fairness, transparency, and worker protections into fleet AI strategies, organizations can move beyond a narrow focus on efficiency to foster more sustainable and socially responsible adoption.

Regulatory Compliance

Fleet operators face escalating regulatory pressures, particularly regarding data privacy and environmental sustainability. The General Data Protection Regulation (GDPR) and California Consumer Privacy Act (CCPA) impose strict requirements for handling personal data, such as driver biometric information or customer delivery addresses (SupplyChainDive, 2024). Noncompliance can result in fines exceeding €20 million or 4% of annual revenue under GDPR, necessitating robust data anonymization and access control measures (SupplyChainDive, 2024). AI-powered compliance tools automate data masking and encryption, ensuring sensitive information remains protected. For example, DHL's AI systems anonymize driver behavior data in real-time, allowing managers to monitor safety metrics without accessing personally identifiable information (NetworkON, 2025).

Policy and Legal Complexity in AI-Enabled Fleets. The regulatory landscape surrounding AI in fleet management is rapidly evolving, and compliance extends well beyond GDPR and CCPA. Differences across jurisdictions introduce significant uncertainty for operators managing international or interstate fleets.

AI-Specific Liability Frameworks. The European Union has taken early steps toward regulating AI systems through the proposed EU AI Act, which categorizes

AI applications by risk level. Fleet-related applications such as driver monitoring and predictive safety analytics may fall into the "high-risk" category, requiring explainability, bias testing, and human oversight mechanisms. By contrast, the United States has yet to establish a unified AI law, relying instead on sectoral regulations from agencies such as the NHTSA for autonomous vehicle trials. This divergence complicates compliance for global fleets operating across regions.

Electric Vehicle (EV) Mandates and Standards. Legal complexity also arises from varying EV adoption requirements. The EU's *Fit for 55* package mandates a gradual phase-out of internal combustion engines by 2035, forcing fleets to invest in electric vehicles and charging infrastructure. California's Advanced Clean Fleets Regulation requires phased electrification by 2035, whereas other U.S. states lack equivalent mandates. India's FAME II program provides subsidies for EV purchases, but infrastructure rollout remains uneven. These differences shape how quickly and cost-effectively fleets can adopt AI systems designed for EV optimization.

Data Protection and Cross-Border Rules. Beyond GDPR/CCPA, countries such as India are introducing their own data protection frameworks (e.g., India's Digital Personal Data Protection Act, 2023), which include data localization requirements. For multinational fleets, this raises questions about where sensitive driver and vehicle data can be stored and processed, complicating AI deployment in global operations.

Uncertainty and Compliance Costs. Legal fragmentation increases compliance costs and creates uncertainty for long-term investment planning. Organizations must often maintain parallel compliance systems to satisfy overlapping or conflicting regulations. For example, a fleet operating between the EU and the U.S. may need to anonymize driver data under GDPR, while simultaneously meeting Federal Motor Carrier Safety Administration (FMCSA) reporting requirements in the U.S.

Strategic Implications. Instead of treating compliance purely as a constraint, fleet operators can use AI to simulate regulatory scenarios and test adoption strategies. "Regulatory digital twins" allow companies to model the financial and operational impact of potential laws-such as stricter emissions caps or liability rules for AI-driven decisions-before they come into force. This proactive approach turns compliance into a source of strategic advantage.

Environmental regulations further complicate compliance efforts. The European Union's Corporate Sustainability Reporting Directive (CSRD) mandates detailed emissions disclosures, requiring fleets to track CO_2 outputs at the vehicle level. AI systems simplify this process by integrating fuel consumption data, engine diagnostics, and route efficiency metrics into automated reports. A logistics firm in Germany achieved 98% compliance accuracy after deploying AI tools that correlated GPS data with emissions sensors, reducing manual reporting labor by 40 hours per month (NetworkON, 2025). However, regulatory variations across jurisdictions create implementation hurdles. For instance, California's Advanced Clean Fleets

Regulation requires phased EV adoption, while Texas has no equivalent mandate, complicating compliance for interstate carriers (SupplyChainDive, 2024).

AI transforms compliance from a cost center to a strategic advantage by identifying optimization opportunities aligned with regulatory goals. Predictive maintenance systems, for example, not only prevent costly breakdowns but also ensure adherence to emissions standards by maintaining engines at peak efficiency (WhipAround, 2025). Furthermore, AI-driven "compliance digital twins" simulate regulatory scenarios, allowing fleets to test strategies-such as EV charging schedules or route modifications-before implementation. La Poste used such models to reduce emissions fines by 30% while cutting fuel costs by 12% (Pathway, 2025).

Integration and Scalability

Integrating AI into legacy fleet management systems remains a significant barrier. Many organizations rely on outdated software for tasks like dispatching or maintenance tracking, which lack APIs for seamless data exchange with modern AI platforms (LinkedIn, 2024). This fragmentation forces managers to manually reconcile data across systems, increasing error risks. A mid-sized logistics company reported a 25% drop in operational efficiency during its initial AI integration phase due to incompatible legacy tools (WalkingTree Tech, 2025). Middleware solutions, such as cloud-based integration platforms, mitigate these issues by bridging data silos. For example, SAP's Cloud Integration Suite enables fleets to aggregate telematics, ERP, and CRM data into unified dashboards, improving decision-making speed by 35% (SSRN, 2023).

Scalability challenges emerge as fleets expand AI deployment beyond pilot projects. Computational demands increase exponentially with larger datasets, necessitating scalable cloud infrastructure. Amazon Web Services (AWS) offers AI-as-a-Service (AIaaS) solutions that allow fleets to dynamically allocate resources during peak periods, such as holiday delivery surges (Redwood Logistics, 2025). However, small and medium-sized enterprises (SMEs) often lack the capital for such investments. Modular AI tools, which allow incremental implementation, provide a cost-effective alternative. For instance, predictive maintenance modules can be added to existing telematics systems without overhauling entire IT architectures, reducing upfront costs by up to 60% (LinkedIn, 2024).

The shift to electric vehicles introduces unique scalability challenges. Charging infrastructure management requires AI systems to balance energy demand across fleets, a task complicated by varying battery capacities and charging station availability. AI platforms like ChargePoint's Power Management System optimize charging schedules based on real-time electricity prices and vehicle usage patterns, reducing energy costs by 20% for early adopters (ETA Transit, 2025). Similarly, AI-driven "smart grids" enable fleets to sell excess battery storage back to utilities during peak demand, creating new revenue streams (LLumin, 2025).

Despite these hurdles, the proliferation of 5G networks and IoT advancements offers unprecedented scalability opportunities. Real-time data transmission speeds allow fleets to manage thousands of vehicles simultaneously, while edge AI chips process complex algorithms onboard, reducing cloud dependency. A case study involving FedEx demonstrated a 30% improvement in delivery route scalability after deploying 5G-enabled AI systems across its North American fleet (SSRN, 2023).

Global and SME Adoption Context

The adoption of artificial intelligence (AI) in fleet management varies significantly across organizational size and regional context. While multinational corporations in technologically advanced economies are early adopters of AI solutions, small and medium enterprises (SMEs) and fleets in developing countries face unique constraints that influence their adoption pathways.

Adoption Challenges for SMEs. Smaller fleets often lack the financial resources and technical expertise to invest in comprehensive AI solutions. High upfront costs for telematics devices, cloud subscriptions, and training programs can be prohibitive. Additionally, SMEs typically operate with lean staff structures, where drivers and managers perform multiple roles, leaving limited capacity for managing advanced technologies.

Incremental and Modular Approaches. To overcome these challenges, SMEs frequently adopt modular AI tools that can be integrated incrementally without requiring a full system overhaul. For example, predictive maintenance modules can be layered onto existing telematics systems, or basic route optimization software can be deployed without full AI-driven fleet platforms. These incremental approaches reduce upfront costs while still delivering measurable efficiency gains.

Emerging Market Barriers. In developing regions, adoption is further constrained by limited digital infrastructure, unreliable internet connectivity, and fragmented logistics networks. For instance, fleets in South Asia and Sub-Saharan Africa often rely on basic GPS tracking rather than advanced IoT-enabled platforms. Financing models, such as government subsidies or vendor-based leasing, are essential to lower adoption barriers in these contexts.

Policy and Public Sector Role. Governments and public institutions can play a critical role in democratizing access to AI for smaller fleets. Examples include subsidized telematics programs in India and cooperative fleet-sharing models in Latin America that pool resources among SMEs. These interventions provide affordable entry points while promoting digital transformation across fragmented logistics sectors.

Global Asymmetries. Without targeted strategies, the AI revolution in fleet management risks widening the digital divide between large enterprises in advanced economies and SMEs in emerging markets. By tailoring AI tools to smaller operators and diverse regional contexts, stakeholders can ensure broader inclusivity and long-term sustainability in adoption.

While these challenges highlight the barriers fleets face in adopting AI, theoretical frameworks help explain how organizations navigate such complexities. The next section introduces Rogers' Diffusion of Innovation and the Technology–Organization–Environment (TOE) model to provide structured perspectives on adoption.

Theoretical Frameworks

The adoption of artificial intelligence (AI) in fleet management can be better understood through established theories of technology diffusion and organizational innovation. Two widely recognized frameworks-Rogers' Diffusion of Innovation (DOI) Theory and the Technology–Organization–Environment (TOE) Framework-offer structured perspectives on the drivers and barriers to adoption. Drawing on these models provides conceptual depth and positions fleet AI adoption within broader streams of research on digital transformation and information systems.

Rogers' Diffusion of Innovation Theory

Rogers' *Diffusion of Innovations* (2003) is one of the most influential models for analyzing how new technologies spread within social systems. The theory categorizes adopters into five groups-innovators, early adopters, early majority, late majority, and laggards-based on their willingness to embrace innovation. These categories help explain the varying pace of AI uptake across different fleet operators.

Rogers identifies five characteristics that influence adoption rates: relative advantage, compatibility, complexity, trialability, and observability. Each dimension is highly relevant to AI in fleet management:

- **Relative Advantage:** AI provides measurable benefits, such as predictive maintenance reducing downtime by up to 45% (XenonStack, 2025).
- **Compatibility:** Fleets with robust telematics systems integrate AI more smoothly than those relying on legacy software (Oliveira & Martins, 2011).
- **Complexity:** Smaller fleets often perceive AI as difficult to implement due to limited IT resources, which slows adoption.
- **Trialability:** Pilot programs (e.g., predictive maintenance trials at UPS) allow organizations to test AI effectiveness before scaling.

- **Observability:** Tangible outcomes, such as Amazon's 25% warehouse processing efficiency gains (Reuters, 2023), enhance adoption likelihood.

Together, these attributes illustrate why some fleets are early leaders in AI adoption, while others remain cautious. Recent studies extend Rogers' framework by linking it to IT adoption research, such as the Unified Theory of Acceptance and Use of Technology (UTAUT), which emphasizes performance expectancy and organizational readiness as additional drivers of adoption (Venkatesh et al., 2003).

Technology–Organization–Environment (TOE) Framework

The TOE Framework (Tornatzky & Fleischer, 1990) provides an organizational-level perspective by considering three contextual factors that influence technology adoption:

1. **Technological Context:** Refers to available infrastructure, IoT sensor networks, and interoperability with AI platforms. For example, fleets with advanced telematics integrate predictive analytics more readily (AlSheibani et al., 2018).
2. **Organizational Context:** Includes leadership commitment, financial resources, technical expertise, and change management capacity. Leadership advocacy is particularly critical in driving cultural acceptance of AI innovations.
3. **Environmental Context:** Encompasses competitive pressure, regulatory requirements, and industry standards. For instance, EU emissions regulations are pushing European fleets toward AI-enabled emissions monitoring and compliance systems.

The TOE framework highlights how adoption success depends not only on technological capability but also on organizational preparedness and regulatory or market environments. More recent work emphasizes how SMEs in emerging economies face barriers under the TOE model due to financial and infrastructure limitations, making modular or incremental AI adoption more practical (Oliveira & Martins, 2011).

Integrating Both Frameworks

While Rogers' DOI theory focuses on individual and group adopter behaviors, the TOE framework emphasizes organizational and environmental readiness. Integrating these perspectives provides a holistic view of fleet AI adoption. For example:

- UPS's ORION route optimization system demonstrates relative advantage (Rogers) while also reflecting technological readiness (TOE).
- Amazon's predictive maintenance illustrates observability (Rogers) and organizational preparedness (TOE).
- Smaller logistics providers in developing countries exemplify adoption challenges shaped by complexity (Rogers) and environmental constraints (TOE).

Together, these frameworks reveal both the micro-level decision-making and macro-level organizational dynamics that influence the diffusion of AI in fleet ecosystems.

Application in Fleet Management

Rogers' theory provides actionable insights for fleet managers navigating AI adoption challenges. Innovators and early adopters often lead the charge by experimenting with cutting-edge technologies like autonomous vehicles or advanced driver-assistance systems (ADAS).

Organizations leveraging Rogers' framework can design tailored strategies that address specific adopter profiles while emphasizing the benefits of AI integration. For example, providing detailed cost-benefit analyses and compatibility assessments can help convert skeptical adopters into advocates for technological innovation. This progressive diffusion approach ensures sustainable integration of AI capabilities throughout fleet operations.

Technology-Organization-Environment Framework. The Technology-Organization-Environment (TOE) Framework developed by Tornatzky and Fleischer (1990) offers a comprehensive model for analyzing technology adoption at the organizational level. Unlike individual-focused theories like Rogers' model, TOE examines higher-level attributes across three contexts: technological readiness, organizational preparedness, and environmental influences.

Technological Context. The technological context refers to an organization's infrastructure capabilities and readiness to adopt new technologies. Key factors include IoT sensor networks, data management systems, and interoperability between existing platforms and AI tools (AlSheibani et al., 2018). Organizations with robust technological foundations demonstrate higher adoption potential than those lacking these resources.

For example, fleets equipped with advanced telematics systems can seamlessly integrate predictive maintenance algorithms that analyze real-time sensor data to forecast component failures (Facility Executive, 2024). Conversely, fleets relying on manual data collection methods face significant barriers to adopting such technologies due to limited scalability and automation capabilities. Addressing these gaps through targeted investments in infrastructure is essential for fostering technological readiness.

Organizational Context. Organizational factors-including leadership support, financial resources, technical expertise, and change management capabilities-play a pivotal role in determining adoption success. Leadership commitment is particularly critical; executives who champion AI initiatives create a culture of innovation that encourages employees to embrace new technologies (AlSheibani et al., 2018).

Financial constraints often impede smaller fleets from adopting AI solutions despite their potential benefits. However, government subsidies or industry partnerships can alleviate these challenges by providing access to affordable implementation options (Facility Executive, 2024). Technical expertise also influences adoption rates; organizations with skilled IT teams are better equipped to deploy complex AI systems compared to those lacking specialized personnel. Training programs and collaborative partnerships with technology providers can bridge this expertise gap effectively.

Change management is another crucial consideration within the organizational context. Resistance from employees accustomed to traditional workflows can hinder successful integration of AI tools like automated compliance systems or driver monitoring platforms. Implementing gradual transitions-such as hybrid models combining manual processes with automated solutions-can ease employee concerns while demonstrating the value of technological innovation.

Environmental Context. The environmental context encompasses external factors such as competitive pressure, regulatory requirements, market dynamics, and supplier relationships that shape technology adoption decisions (AlSheibani et al., 2018). For instance:

- **Competitive Pressure:** Companies operating in highly competitive markets are more likely to adopt AI technologies as a means of gaining a strategic edge over rivals.
- **Regulatory Requirements:** Stricter emissions standards or safety regulations often compel fleets to invest in compliance-focused AI tools like emissions tracking platforms or ADAS systems.
- **Market Dynamics:** E-commerce growth has accelerated demand for efficient logistics solutions powered by AI-driven route optimization algorithms.
- **Supplier Relationships:** Collaborations with technology providers offering scalable solutions enable fleets to overcome resource limitations while accessing cutting-edge innovations.

The TOE framework suggests that successful implementation requires alignment across all three contexts-technological readiness, organizational preparedness, and environmental influences-with deficiencies in any area potentially impeding progress. Together, these frameworks highlight how adoption drivers and barriers operate at both individual and organizational levels. Building on these theoretical insights, the next section outlines practical implications for fleet managers, policymakers, and enterprise leaders, translating theory into actionable strategies for real-world implementation.

Implications for Practice

Successfully integrating artificial intelligence (AI) into fleet management hinges on strategic actions from key stakeholders-fleet managers, policymakers, and enterprise leaders-who must ensure AI is adopted effectively, responsibly, and sustainably.

Recommendations for Fleet Managers

As primary drivers of AI deployment, fleet managers should take a phased, strategic approach. Early efforts should target high-ROI use cases like route optimization and predictive maintenance, which can reduce unplanned downtime by up to 45% (XenonStack, 2025) and cut fuel consumption by up to 15% (Facility Executive, 2024).

Once initial implementations demonstrate value, managers can expand AI use to areas like driver behavior monitoring, emissions tracking, and compliance automation-scaling capabilities while managing risk.

Data Strategy Development. A robust data strategy is essential for effective AI adoption. Fleet managers should implement governance frameworks that ensure consistent data collection, high-quality inputs, secure and scalable storage, and clear usage policies aligned with privacy regulations like GDPR and CCPA (Indmall Automation, 2024).

Investments in IoT sensors and cloud platforms lay the groundwork for sustainable AI. Advanced telematics systems, for example, enable seamless integration of predictive analytics to improve performance and resource allocation (ETA Transit, 2025).

Financial Cost-Benefit and ROI Analysis. While the operational advantages of AI in fleet management are clear, decision-makers also require structured frameworks to evaluate the financial return on investment (ROI) of adoption. A cost-benefit perspective ensures that AI initiatives are not only technologically feasible but also economically sustainable.

Capital Investments. Initial implementation often requires significant capital expenditure in hardware, software, and training. This includes telematics devices, IoT sensors, cloud subscriptions, and staff training programs. For example, predictive maintenance systems may require upfront sensor installations across the fleet, coupled with training technicians in diagnostic interpretation.

Operational Costs. Beyond capital, ongoing expenses include system maintenance, software licensing, cloud storage, and periodic updates to AI models. These recurring costs must be factored into total cost of ownership (TCO) calculations to avoid underestimating long-term commitments.

ROI Models. ROI in AI-enabled fleet management can be assessed through both direct and indirect benefits:

- **Direct savings:** Reduced downtime, lower fuel consumption, and optimized labor allocation.
- **Indirect benefits:** Fewer accidents, reduced insurance premiums, compliance avoidance penalties, and improved customer retention.

Industry benchmarks suggest that predictive maintenance alone can deliver ROI within 12–18 months by reducing unplanned downtime by up to 45% and extending vehicle lifespans by several years.

Simulation and Scenario Tools. Some organizations use ROI calculators and digital twin simulations to test investment scenarios before committing. For example, simulation tools can compare outcomes of adding 500 IoT-enabled trucks versus maintaining a smaller AI-enabled pilot fleet. This helps managers quantify potential savings, risks, and payback periods under different adoption scales.

By incorporating structured financial modeling into AI adoption strategies, fleet operators can move beyond anecdotal success stories and build stronger business cases for investment. A balanced framework that weighs upfront costs against quantifiable and long-term gains enhances confidence among executives, policymakers, and investors.

Workforce Development. Workforce readiness is another critical factor in successful AI adoption. Fleet managers must provide comprehensive training programs to prepare employees for working effectively with AI systems. These programs should address:

- The technical skills required to operate and maintain AI tools.
- The organizational changes associated with AI-driven workflows.
- Concerns about job displacement by emphasizing how AI augments human capabilities rather than replacing them (LLumin, 2025).

For example, training programs that teach drivers how to interpret real-time feedback from driver monitoring systems can improve safety outcomes while fostering acceptance of new technologies. Similarly, maintenance technicians trained in predictive diagnostics can use AI-generated insights to address vehicle issues proactively, reducing repair times and costs.

Workforce Displacement and Labor Relations. Although AI adoption creates opportunities for workforce upskilling, it also introduces challenges related to job displacement and changing labor dynamics. Fleet operations traditionally employ large numbers of drivers, dispatchers, and mechanics, many of whose roles are being reshaped by automation and predictive analytics.

Job Displacement Risks. As AI systems take over tasks such as route optimization, compliance reporting, and predictive diagnostics, there is potential for reduced demand for certain administrative and operational roles. Autonomous vehicles, in particular, pose a long-term challenge to driver employment, with industry forecasts predicting significant reductions in long-haul driving jobs within the next two decades.

Labor Relations and Union Responses. Labor unions have raised concerns about surveillance, fairness, and the erosion of bargaining power. Case studies in logistics and manufacturing show that collective bargaining has increasingly included provisions for retraining, reskilling, or financial compensation when automation displaces workers. In some regions, unions have negotiated agreements that require companies to reinvest part of AI-driven productivity gains into worker development programs.

Policy and Legal Considerations. Governments are beginning to address labor impacts through workforce transition programs and retraining grants. For example, public sector initiatives in Europe and North America provide subsidies for drivers to transition into fleet technology or logistics management roles. However, fragmented labor policies across jurisdictions make it difficult to establish consistent protections for affected workers.

Human–AI Collaboration Models. Rather than focusing exclusively on automation, many experts advocate for hybrid models where AI augments rather than replaces human capabilities. For instance, predictive maintenance platforms can reduce repetitive diagnostic tasks for mechanics, allowing them to focus on higher-value problem solving. Similarly, driver coaching systems can enhance safety without fully displacing human judgment.

Addressing workforce displacement openly is critical for ensuring long-term adoption success. Companies that proactively engage employees, unions, and policymakers in developing reskilling pathways will not only mitigate social backlash but also strengthen trust in AI as a collaborative rather than adversarial force in fleet management.

Guidance for Policymakers

Policymakers play a vital role in shaping the regulatory and infrastructural environment necessary for successful AI deployment in fleet management. Their actions influence industry-wide adoption rates and ensure responsible technology use.

Regulatory Frameworks. Policymakers should develop regulatory frameworks that balance innovation support with appropriate safeguards. Clear guidelines for AI applications in fleet management-such as those governing data privacy, cybersecurity, and algorithmic transparency-are essential for fostering trust among stakeholders (AlSheibani et al., 2018). For example:

- Regulations requiring anonymization of driver behavior data can address privacy concerns while enabling effective monitoring systems.
- Standards for emissions tracking tools can ensure consistency across fleets while supporting environmental compliance efforts.

Overly restrictive regulations may stifle innovation by creating unnecessary barriers to entry for smaller fleets or new technology providers. Policymakers must strike a balance that encourages investment in AI technologies while protecting public interests.

Infrastructure Investment. Advanced AI applications require robust supporting infrastructure, including high-quality road networks, reliable communication systems, and data-sharing platforms (Indmall Automation, 2024). Public investment in these foundational elements creates an environment conducive to private-sector innovation and deployment.

For instance:

- Upgrading road infrastructure with smart traffic management systems can enhance the effectiveness of AI-powered route optimization tools by providing real-time traffic data.
- Expanding broadband access in rural areas ensures connectivity for IoT devices used in fleet monitoring systems.

Educational Initiatives. Policymakers should also invest in educational initiatives aimed at building AI literacy and technical expertise within the workforce. Partnerships between educational institutions, industry organizations, and government agencies can develop curriculum resources and training programs tailored to the needs of fleet operators (ETA Transit, 2025).

For example:

- Vocational training programs focused on IoT device installation and maintenance can prepare technicians for roles in predictive maintenance workflows.
- Certification courses on ethical AI use can equip fleet managers with the knowledge needed to navigate complex regulatory landscapes.

These initiatives address potential skills gaps while supporting industry transformation toward more technologically advanced operations.

Strategies for Enterprise Leaders

Enterprise leaders must approach AI implementation as a strategic transformation initiative rather than merely a technical project. This perspective emphasizes the organizational changes required alongside technology deployment.

Vision and Alignment. Leaders should articulate a clear vision for how AI will enhance fleet operations while ensuring alignment across functional domains such as logistics, IT, human resources, and sustainability (AlSheibani et al., 2018). For example:

- A logistics company aiming to reduce carbon emissions might prioritize investments in emissions tracking tools alongside route optimization algorithms.
- A retail delivery service focused on customer satisfaction might emphasize last-mile delivery enhancements powered by dynamic routing systems.

By aligning technological investments with organizational goals, leaders can maximize the strategic value of AI initiatives.

Collaborative Partnerships. Building collaborative partnerships with technology providers, industry peers, and research institutions supports effective AI implementation. These relationships provide access to specialized expertise, emerging technologies, and best practices (LLumin, 2025). Collaborative approaches also facilitate mutual learning while distributing development costs across multiple stakeholders.

For instance:

- Partnering with IoT device manufacturers ensures seamless integration between hardware sensors and software analytics platforms.
- Collaborating with academic researchers enables organizations to stay ahead of technological trends by exploring innovative applications like autonomous vehicles or blockchain-based logistics solutions.

Performance Measurement Frameworks. Enterprise leaders should establish performance measurement frameworks that capture both direct and indirect impacts of AI adoption (Facility Executive, 2024). These frameworks should assess metrics such as:

1. Cost reduction (e.g., savings from fuel optimization or predictive maintenance).
2. Efficiency improvement (e.g., increased asset utilization rates or reduced delivery times).
3. Environmental impact reduction (e.g., lower greenhouse gas emissions or waste minimization).
4. Safety enhancement (e.g., fewer accidents due to driver monitoring systems).
5. Customer satisfaction improvement (e.g., higher on-time delivery rates or reduced complaints).

Comprehensive measurement supports effective resource allocation while demonstrating the strategic value of AI initiatives to stakeholders.

While these strategic actions illustrate how organizations can maximize AI's benefits, it is equally important to acknowledge the limitations and risks associated with adoption. The next section provides a critical reflection on the unintended consequences and potential downsides of AI in fleet operations.

Limitations and Risks of AI Adoption

Although artificial intelligence (AI) presents significant opportunities for improving fleet operations, its adoption is not without risks and limitations. Overemphasizing the benefits without acknowledging potential drawbacks can create unrealistic expectations and undermine long-term success.

System Failures and Reliability Risks

AI systems are dependent on continuous data flow from IoT sensors and telematics. Hardware malfunctions, sensor errors, or data transmission failures can compromise model accuracy, resulting in flawed routing recommendations or missed maintenance alerts. Overreliance on AI without adequate human oversight may magnify the operational impact of such failures.

False Positives and Overfitting

Predictive algorithms, while powerful, are prone to generating false alerts or overfitting to historical datasets. For example, driver monitoring systems may incorrectly flag safe drivers as risky, leading to reduced morale and potential labor disputes. Similarly, predictive maintenance models may trigger unnecessary servicing if not carefully calibrated.

Cybersecurity Vulnerabilities

As discussed earlier, interconnected fleets present an attractive target for malicious actors. Attacks such as GPS spoofing or ransomware targeting dispatch systems can cause significant financial and reputational harm. Without robust cybersecurity frameworks, expanding AI adoption may inadvertently increase exposure to digital threats.

Ethical and Legal Ambiguities

AI-driven surveillance raises privacy and consent concerns, while the opacity of "black-box" decision systems challenges transparency. Legal frameworks regarding liability for AI-driven decisions (e.g., accidents caused by automated route assignments or autonomous vehicles) remain underdeveloped, creating uncertainty for fleet operators.

Workforce Resistance

Employees may resist AI adoption if they perceive it as a threat to job security or autonomy. Without proactive engagement and reskilling strategies, negative workforce sentiment can delay or derail implementation.

Contextual Limitations

Not all fleets or markets are equally positioned to benefit from AI. In regions with weak digital infrastructure, low-data environments, or limited financial capacity, AI adoption may generate minimal value or even inefficiencies compared to traditional practices.

Balanced Adoption Approach

To mitigate these risks, organizations must adopt a balanced strategy that combines technological innovation with risk management, ethical safeguards, and human oversight. Pilot testing, transparent communication with employees, and continuous model evaluation are critical steps to ensure that AI enhances-rather than undermines-fleet operations.

CONCLUSION

Artificial intelligence (AI) is not just a technological advancement in fleet management-it represents a paradigm shift in how logistics operations are conceptualized, executed, and optimized. As demonstrated throughout this chapter, AI technologies have proven their transformative potential across key operational areas such as route optimization, predictive maintenance, safety enhancement, and sustainability. The case studies of industry leaders like UPS, DHL, Amazon, La Poste, and Samsara illustrate how AI can deliver measurable improvements in efficiency, cost savings, and environmental performance when strategically implemented within supportive organizational frameworks.

The Transformative Power of AI in Fleet Management

The integration of AI into fleet management has redefined traditional operational boundaries. AI-driven route optimization improves delivery times while reducing fuel consumption and emissions, predictive maintenance shifts fleets from reactive to proactive servicing, and safety monitoring tools have reduced collisions and insurance costs. At the same time, sustainability-focused applications like emissions tracking and EV optimization help organizations meet regulatory and climate objectives. These advancements underscore the multidimensional impact of AI on fleet operations.

Challenges That Require Attention

Despite these successes, full-scale adoption is not without hurdles. Data quality remains a critical issue, as incomplete or biased datasets can reduce model accuracy. Regulatory frameworks around privacy, algorithmic accountability, and electrification continue to evolve, introducing uncertainty for global fleets. Workforce readiness is another pressing challenge, with concerns around both reskilling and job displacement. Integration with legacy systems also remains a major barrier to scaling adoption.

Future Directions: The Next Frontier of Fleet Management

Emerging trends such as autonomous vehicles, edge computing, digital twins, and prescriptive analytics represent the next wave of AI-driven transformation. These technologies promise even greater efficiency and safety gains but will require robust regulatory frameworks, new skillsets, and cross-sector collaboration. At the same time, sustainability will remain a key driver of innovation, with AI central to achieving net-zero emissions goals.

A Collaborative Ecosystem for Success

The path forward requires multi-stakeholder collaboration. Policymakers must provide balanced regulations that safeguard ethics and privacy without stifling innovation. Industry leaders must invest in modular, scalable AI systems that can work across both large enterprises and SMEs. Educational institutions must prepare the next generation of fleet professionals with technical and ethical AI skills.

Key Takeaways

- **Operational Impact:** AI consistently delivers measurable outcomes, such as 15–20% reductions in fuel consumption, up to 45% fewer breakdowns through predictive maintenance, and 40% fewer collisions from driver monitoring systems.
- **Strategic Value:** Adoption of AI transforms fleet management into a competitive differentiator by aligning operational efficiency with sustainability and compliance.
- **Barriers Remain:** Data quality, workforce displacement, cybersecurity risks, and fragmented regulatory environments remain key challenges.
- **Inclusive Adoption:** SMEs and fleets in developing markets require incremental, modular solutions to bridge the digital divide and democratize AI adoption.
- **Policy and Governance:** Clear global standards (e.g., EU AI Act, ISO/SAE 21434) are essential for responsible deployment, ensuring fairness, transparency, and security.
- **Future Outlook:** Next-generation technologies such as autonomous fleets, edge-based decision-making, and digital twins will push fleet management into new frontiers, requiring ongoing collaboration between industry, policymakers, and academia.

REFERENCES

3SAutomation. (2024, August 23). Revolutionizing logistics: The power of predictive maintenance in automation. https://www.3sautomation.eu/revolutionizing-logistics-the-power-of-predictive- maintenance-in-automation

Abduljabbar, R., Dia, H., Liyanage, S., & Bagloee, S. A. (2019). Applications of artificial intelligence in transport: An overview. As cited in World Journal of Advanced Research and Reviews, 2025.

AI Now Institute. (2023). *Algorithmic accountability in transportation*. New York University.

AlSheibani, S., Cheung, Y., & Messom, C. (2018). Artificial intelligence adoption: AI-readiness at firm- level. *Pacific Asia Conference on Information Systems Proceedings*.

Arena Softwares. (2025, February 25). Why schools need a smart attendance & bus tracking system in 2025. https://www.arenasoftwares.com/blog/why-schools-need-a-smart-attendance-and-bus-tracking-system-in-2025/

Bridgestone, E. M. E. A. (2024). Webfleet AI fleet study. https://press.bridgestone-emea.com/fleet-managers- expect-artificial-intelligence-and-electric-vehicles-to-have-biggest-impact-on-fleet-management- in-the-coming-years-global-webfleet-study-reveals/

Business Insider. (2025). How Uber Freight is leveraging AI to make truck routes more efficient. https://www.businessinsider.com/ai-trucking-logistics-uber-freight-tech-optimize-routes-2025-4

CiGen. (2025). AI-powered fleet management: Optimizing costs, routes, and vehicle utilization. https://www.cigen.io/insights/ai-powered-fleet-management-optimizing-costs-routes-and-vehicle- utilization

Codework. (2024). AI Technologies Powering DHL's Logistics Success. https://thecodework.com/explore/ai-technologies-powering-dhls-logistics-success/

dbt Labs. (2024, Nov 27). Data governance frameworks for AI model development. https://www.getdbt.com/blog/data-governance-frameworks-ai

DHL Press Release. (2024, June 24). DHL launches My Global Trade Services (MyGTS) platform for AI- powered cross-border logistics. https://www.dhl.com/th-en/home/press/press-archive/2024/dhl- express-introduces-ai-powered-online-platform-my-global-trade-services.html

DigitalDefynd. (2025). 5 Ways UPS is Using AI. https://digitaldefynd.com/IQ/ups-use-ai-case-study/

Eubanks, V. (2018). *Automating inequality: How high-tech tools profile, police, and punish the poor*. St. Martin's Press.

European Commission. (2021). *Ethics guidelines for trustworthy AI*. Publications Office of the European Union.

Facility Executive. (2024). AI and fleet adoption: Building readiness. https://facilityexecutive.com

Ghosh, S., Chatterjee, S., & Malhotra, R. (2023). AI in logistics: A meta-review. *Journal of Business Research, 160*, 113702.

GreenRoad. (2025). Top fleet safety trends to watch in 2025.

IEEE. (2019). *Ethically aligned design: A vision for prioritizing human well-being with autonomous and intelligent systems*. IEEE Standards Association.

Indmall Automation. (2024). Predictive maintenance in transport fleets. https://www.indmallautomation.com/faq/what-is-the-growth-rate-of-industrial-iot/

Intangles. (2024). Fleet savings from accident reduction. https://intangles.ai/

Intangles. (2025, May 7). Fleet cost leaks: Hidden expenses you can eliminate with predictive analytics. https://www.intangles.ai/fleet-cost-leaks-hidden-expenses-you-can-eliminate-with-predictive- analytics/

Iotinsider. (2025). La Poste partners with Pathway to create digital twin of fleet. https://www.iotinsider.com/news/la-poste-partners-with-pathway-to-create-digital-twin-of-fleet/

ISO/SAE. (2021). *Road vehicles-Cybersecurity engineering (ISO/SAE 21434:2021)*. International Organization for Standardization.

LinkedIn. (2024, February 21). AI integration challenges in legacy fleet systems. https://www.linkedin.com/pulse/integrating-ai-legacy-systems-challenges-strategies-josh-denton- pksqe/

LLumin. (2025). Predictive maintenance in fleet sustainability. https://llumin.com/blog/predictive-maintenance-fleet-management-llu/

Magazine, E. V. (2024). Top 10: 2024 trends. https://evmagazine.com/top10/top-10-2024-trends

Markets and Markets. (2024). Fleet management market by solution, connectivity type, fleet type, industry, and region – Global forecast to 2026. https://www.marketsandmarkets.com/Market-Reports/fleet-management-systems-market-1020.html

McKinsey & Company. (2022). *The future of AI in transport and logistics*. McKinsey Insights.

Network, O. N. (2024). Fleet management solutions for the modern era. https://networkon.io/resources/blog/fleet-management-software/

OECD. (2024). *AI principles for responsible innovation in transport*. OECD Publishing.

Oliveira, T., & Martins, M. F. (2011). Literature review of information technology adoption models at firm level. *Electronic Journal of Information Systems Evaluation*, *14*(1), 110–121.

Ontruck. (2024, August). Optimal fleet strategy with AI forecasting. https://www.ontruck.com/en/blog/calculate-optimal-fleet-capacity-ai

Pathway. (2025). IoT and AI success with La Poste. https://pathway.com/news/la-poste-optimizes- colissimo-flows-in-real-time/

Redwood Logistics. (2025, July 9). Scaling AI in transport and logistics operations. https://www.redwoodlogistics.com/insights/how-ai-and-iot-can-change-transportation- management

451. Research. (2025, October 6). How AI fleet management platforms are advancing vehicle safety. https://blog.451alliance.com/how-ai-fleet-management-platforms-are-advancing-vehicle-safety/

Reuters. (2023). Amazon's Sequoia system speeds up inventory processing. https://www.reuters.com/technology/amazon-rolls-out-robotic-system-houston-warehouse-speed- up-deliveries-2023-10-18/

Rogers, E. M. (2003). *Diffusion of innovations* (5th ed.). Free Press.

Safety & Health Magazine. (2025). The 2025 CEOs who 'get it'. https://www.safetyandhealthmagazine.com/articles/26308-the-2025-ceos-who-get-it

Samsara. (2025). Case study: Clover Dairy improves logistics with real-time tracking and AI. https://www.samsara.com/customers/clover-dairy/

Sifted Resources. (2024, July 15). Amazon expands AI route-planning algorithms to optimize last-mile delivery. https://sifted.com/resources/how-to-implement-artificial-intelligence-to-boost-supply- chain-ops/

SimplyFleet. (2025, March 27). Spreadsheets vs. software: Why fleets are automating in 2025. https://www.simplyfleet.app/blog/spreadsheets-vs-fleet-software-2025

Social Science Research Network (SSRN). (2023). AI-driven optimization in fleet management. https://papers.ssrn.com/sol3/papers.cfm?abstract_id=4927212

Software, D. B. B. (2025). AI in Fleet Management: Specifics, Challenges, Benefits, and Use Cases. https://dbbsoftware.com/insights/harnessing-the-power-of-ai-for-fleet-management

Supply Chain 24/7. (2024, October 5). How UPS uses generative AI to automate customer service responses. https://www.supplychain247.com/article/ups-mera-ai-automation

Supply Chain Strategy Media. (2025, Feb 19). AI-driven risk scoring helps fleets reduce collisions and boost safety. https://supplychainstrategy.media/blog/2025/02/19/driving-change-ai-is- transforming-fleet-safety-and-visibility-in-modern-supply-chains

SupplyChainNuggets. (2025, July 26). How UPS' ORION algorithm transformed its route optimization. https://www.supplychainnuggets.com/how-ups-orion-algorithm-transformed-its-route- optimization/

TechRadar. (2024, December 31). TechRadar's year in review 2024 – from tri-fold phones and super- smart. https://www.techradar.com/tech/techradars-year-in-review-2024

The Australian. (2023, May 30). Qantas backs AI in transformation push. https://www.itnews.com.au/news/qantas-backs-ai-in-transformation-push-596352

Times, C. D. O. (2024, August 23). Case study: Amazon's AI-driven supply chain: A blueprint for the future of global logistics. https://cdotimes.com/2024/08/23/case-study-amazons-ai-driven-supply-chain-a-blueprint-for-the-future-of-global-logistics/

Tornatzky, L. G., & Fleischer, M. (1990). *The processes of technological innovation*. Lexington Books.

Transit, E. T. A. (2024). Artificial intelligence is reshaping public transit as we know it. https://etatransit.com/podcast/ai-reshaping-transit/

Tribe, A. I. (2025, March 27). Inside the machine: How composable agents are re-wiring AI architecture in 2025. https://www.tribe.ai/applied-ai/inside-the-machine-how-composable-agents-are-rewiring-ai-architecture-in-2025

Venkatesh, V., Morris, M. G., Davis, G. B., & Davis, F. D. (2003). User acceptance of information technology: Toward a unified view. *Management Information Systems Quarterly*, *27*(3), 425–478.

WalkingTree Tech. (2025). Edge AI adoption in fleet operations. https://walkingtree.tech/developing-ai- powered-fleet-management-apps-challenges-opportunities-strategies-future-scope

WhipAround. (2025). Predictive maintenance and emissions compliance. https://whiparound.com/5- benefits-of-fleet-maintenance-software-in-2023/

XenonStack. (2024). Predictive Maintenance for Fleet Management Using AI and IoT. https://www.xenonstack.com/blog/predictive-maintenance-for-fleet-management

XenonStack. (2025). Predictive maintenance for EVs. https://www.xenonstack.com/blog/predictive-maintenance-to-prevent-downtime

Zendu, I. T. (2025, February). New product updates: February 2025. https://zenduit.com/new-product-updates-february-2025/

Chapter 7
Animal Regognition and Repellent System for Smart Farming Using AI and Deep Learning

S. Theetchenya
https://orcid.org/0000-0001-5205-3049
Sona College of Technology, Salem, India

Prasuna Kantamaneni
Vijaya Institute of Technology for Women, India

Lakshmi Chandrakanth Kasireddy
https://orcid.org/0009-0002-0392-739X
ThoughtSpot Inc., Franklin, USA

R. Gopi
Dhanalakshmi Srinivasan Engineering College, Perambalur, India

Prakash B. S.
Vivekanandha College of Engineering for Women, India

V. Sathiyamoorthi
https://orcid.org/0000-0002-7012-3941
Government Polytechnic College, Dharmapuri, India

ABSTRACT

The automation of horticulture has been progressing rapidly, with Deep Neural Networks (DNN) and the Internet of Things (IoT) being utilized for precise monitoring, control, and tracking across various applications. However, managing interactions with external factors in the agricultural ecosystem, particularly wildlife, remains a critical challenge. One of the major concerns for modern farmers is safeguarding crops from wild animal intrusions. Traditional solutions range from lethal methods (e.g., shooting) to non-lethal strategies (e.g., trapping, scarecrows, chemical deterrents, natural repellents, mesh barriers, or electric fences). However, some of these conventional approaches pose environmental hazards to both humans and wildlife,

DOI: 10.4018/979-8-3373-2497-5.ch007

while others are expensive, require extensive maintenance.This paper introduces a system that integrates AI-driven Computer Vision and Deep Convolutional Neural Networks (DCNN) to identify and detect different animal species. It also employs species-specific ultrasonic signals to deter detected animals efficiently.

INTRODUCTION

Artificial intelligence (AI) is a branch of computer science that enables machines to learn and improve from experience without explicit programming. Machine learning, a subset of AI, includes deep learning, which utilizes deep artificial neural networks to achieve ground-breaking accuracy in various fields, such as image and speech recognition. Among these, convolutional neural networks (CNNs) are a specialized type of deep neural network widely used in deep learning for analysing visual images (Prakash et al., 2019).

The study of wild animals in their natural habitats plays a crucial role in ecosystem research. However, rapid population growth and economic development have led to the overexploitation of natural resources, resulting in significant and often irreversible changes to the Earth's ecosystems (Mishra, 2024). Human activities have increasingly impacted wildlife populations, their habitats, and behaviours. Unfortunately, many species have gone extinct, while others have been introduced into new environments, sometimes leading to the depletion of both natural and human resources. CNNs, commonly employed for image analysis, have proven to be highly effective in this domain. These deep neural networks have outperformed traditional classification methods, offering higher accuracy with reduced setup time (Bharathi, Palanisamy, & Moses, 2024).

Accurate and up-to-date information about various species is essential for effective environmental management. However, manually identifying and classifying animals remains a labour-intensive and costly process. To address this challenge, we propose leveraging deep learning neural network techniques to achieve precise and efficient identification (Ramya & Ramesh, 2025). One of the key advantages of deep learning is its ability to automatically extract features from training images, allowing the model to learn and make highly accurate predictions on test data. This approach not only saves time and resources but also aids in wildlife conservation by minimizing human interference in natural habitats (Kruthi et al., 2021).

In an AI-based recognition system, images are analysed to extract relevant features, which are then used for training and classification. The knowledge gained during training enables the system to identify and predict test images based on their characteristics. Recognition systems can be used for both identification and verification purposes (Miao & Zhang, 2024). Identification involves comparing a given image against a database to generate a ranked list of matches, while verification determines whether an image belongs to a specific category by confirming or denying its identity (Liu et al., 2021).

The primary objective of this research is to develop a system that protects crops from wild animals by deterring them from human settlements without causing harm. The project aims to design, implement, and evaluate an animal detection system that uses deep learning to identify different species and generate ultrasonic signals tailored to each animal type, effectively guiding them away from agricultural areas.

RELATED WORK

Santhanam et al. (2021) developed a model designed to efficiently detect animals and alert drivers to their presence. This model utilizes machine learning, specifically a deep learning algorithm to classify animals. Convolutional neural networks (CNNs) analyse each image frame captured by a live camera, predicting objects in real time. If an object is identified as an animal, the system triggers a three-second alert to warn the driver of potential danger. Since the dataset is publicly available, the model continues to evolve, improving its accuracy as more animal species are added for identification (Chen et al., 2014).

Qi et al. (2021) investigated the application of deep learning-based image recognition in the livestock industry. Their research provides a novel solution to challenges such as disease prevention, accurate identification, and biosafety management in animal farming (Kasthuri et al., 2025). The study employs CNNs for feature extraction, combined with pre-processing techniques like super pixel-based image segmentation and Scale-Invariant Feature Transform (SIFT) algorithms. By integrating CNNs with support vector machines (SVMs), the system achieves high classification accuracy, facilitating intelligent livestock management and supporting the industry's shift toward modernization.

Shanthakumari et al. (2022) emphasized the increasing importance of habitat conservation and the need to monitor wildlife populations to track the presence of endangered species. To address this, they proposed using the YOLOv5 model for animal detection in forest environments. YOLOv5 can recognize various animal species, including horses, sheep, cows, elephants, bears, zebras, giraffes, and birds, by analyzing photographs, real-time camera feeds, and recorded videos. Its lightweight architecture minimizes deployment costs, making it a practical tool for applications such as livestock management, wildlife monitoring, pest control, and security (Gupta, Sharma, & Mangal, 2025).

Singh et al. (2020) explored deep learning techniques to address challenges in object detection, segmentation, tracking, and edge detection within computer vision.

Their study highlights the difficulty of adapting object detection models trained on natural habitat images to artificial environments. To overcome this limitation, the researchers propose using semi-automated synthetic data generation for domain-specific training. They have also made the code and datasets from their experiments publicly available to encourage further research in this field (Vaish & Sharma, 2024).

El Abbadi et al. (2020) evaluated the accuracy of animal detection algorithms in computer vision under uncontrolled environmental conditions. While significant progress has been made in object detection, classification, and recognition, real-time tracking of animals remains a challenging research area. This study suggests leveraging deep convolutional neural networks (CNNs) for the detection and classification of vertebrate species in digital images, addressing existing gaps in dynamic object recognition methods.

Munian et al. (2020) introduced a novel approach for detecting wild animals at night using thermal image processing with a vehicle-mounted camera system. Their model processes radiometric images and applies intelligent feature extraction to detect hotspots and moving objects. By employing the Histogram of Oriented Gradients (HOG) transformation, the system normalizes radiometric images to identify and track animals, such as deer. These extracted features are then processed by a one-dimensional convolutional neural network (1D-CNN), utilizing binary cross-entropy to confirm the presence of an object.

PROPOSED METHODOLOGY

This chapter proposes an AI-driven deep convolutional neural network (DCNN) based on computer vision for identifying animals. It comprises designing, configuring, and evaluating an intelligent agriculture monitoring and repelling system. It aims to recognize different animals and emit customized ultrasonic signals for each animal. It assists farmers and agronomists in decision-making and management processes under crises management conditions. The following subsections provide the activities of each component in the proposed system.

DCNN

The Convolutional Neural Networks (CNN) is a type of neural network widely used for tasks such as image recognition and pattern analysis. It is based on Deep Neural Networks (DNN).It is function as multi-layer feed-forward networks with learnable weights, biases, and layers of interconnected neurons. It consists of multiple components such as filters. It takes input vector which performs convolution operations, and employ non-linear transformations. The CNN includes key layers such as convolutional, pooling, Rectified Linear Unit (ReLU), and fully connected layers (LeCun, Bottou, Bengio, & Haffner, 1998). A typical CNN structure is given in figure 1.

Figure 1. CNN

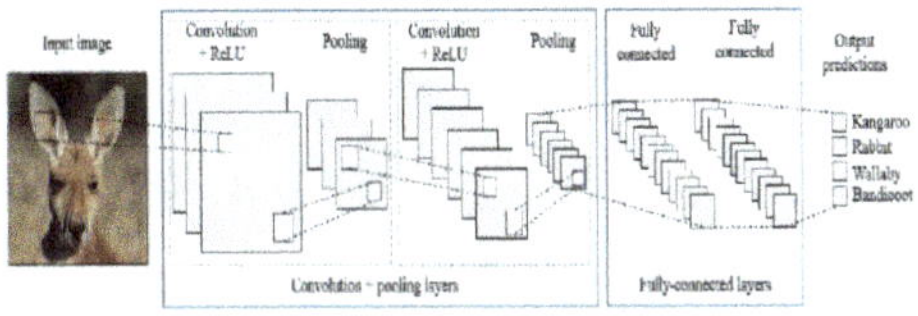

Convolution Layer

The convolution layer is the main building block of the convolutional neural network (CNN). It is responsible for computational processing and feature vector generation. The main function is to extract essential features from image data. In the proposed system, the convolution layer processes input images, detecting patterns and key attributes. The extracted features are passed to the next layer for further processing.

Pooling Layer

The pooling layer reduces the complexity of input features and preserves crucial information. It divides the input images into multiple non-overlapping regions. It applies average pooling or max pooling to extract significant features. It enhances generalization, convergence speed, improves spatial interpretation, and provides resistance to distortion.

ReLU Layer

The ReLU (Rectified Linear Unit) layer presents non-linearity through an activation function. It eplaces all negative values in the features into zero. It operates on a per-pixel basis. Given an input neuron with a value x, the ReLU function is defined as:

$$f(x)=\max(0,x)$$

It enhances model performance by allowing faster training and mitigating the vanishing gradient problem.

Figure 2. Proposed system

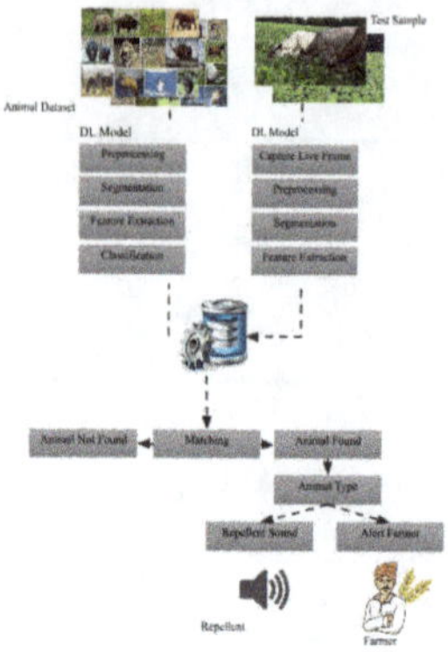

Fully Connected Layer

The Fully Connected Layer (FCL) links every neuron from the previous layer to each neuron in the subsequent layer. It integrates information extracted from convolutional, pooling, and ReLU layers to classify images into predefined classes. The final pooling layer sends extracted features to the FCL. It serves as an input for the classifier which uses SoftMax activation function (Bishop, 2006). It converts raw scores into probability distributions for facilitating accurate classification. The proposed system is shown in figure 2.

Animal Detection

The Region Proposal Network (RPN) generates Regions of Interest (RoIs) by sliding a window over features with different sizes and aspect ratios. It is designed for detecting and segmenting animals by consistently preserving spatial relationships within RoIs. It provides a set of predefined bounding boxes to predict object locations.

Region Proposal Network (RPN)

An RPN is a fully convolutional network that predicts object boundaries and confidence scores at each location. It generates image region by analyzing features produced by a CNN (Ren, He, Girshick, & Sun, 2015). Each feature is known as an anchor point and assigned to multiple anchor boxes with different aspect ratios. It enables effective object localization and recognition in various environments.

Feature Extraction

The Gray Level Co-occurrence Matrix (GLCM) is used for texture analysis in image processing. It calculates second-order statistics to extract five key features from each GLCM. It extracts 20 features per image (Haralick, Shanmugam, & Dinstein, 1973). Before classification, all extracted features should be normalized within a range of 0 to 1 to ensure consistency.

Animal Identification

Once an image is captured by the farm camera, it is sent to the animal detection module. This module identifies potential regions where animals may be present using an RPN. The detected animal image is then processed by the feature extraction module. It analyzes distinguishing characteristics of an animal for classification.

Prediction

In this phase, the extracted features from the input image are compared with a pre-existing dataset using a Deep Convolutional Neural Network (DCNN). The hamming distance metric is used to measure similarity and ensures accurate classification (Hamming, 1950). The identified animal is then assigned to the input image. Then if the presence of an animal is confirmed, the repelling module is activated.

Generation of Repelling Ultrasound

Upon detecting an animal, the system instructs the repeller module to emit ultrasonic waves to deter it. Ultrasound has been proven to be an effective method for protecting crops from wildlife. Animals have a significantly higher auditory sensitivity range compared to humans. While humans can perceive frequencies between **64 Hz and 23 kHz**, other animals have wider auditory ranges (Heffner & Heffner, 2007):

- **Goats & Sheep**: 78 Hz – 37 kHz
- **Pigs**: 10 Hz – 30 kHz
- **Dogs**: 67 Hz – 45 kHz
- **Cats**: 45 Hz – 64 kHz

By emitting species-specific ultrasonic signals, the system effectively repels animals without causing harm.

Monitoring and Visualization

The system provides real-time monitoring of the pasture, allowing farmers to remotely observe their fields. The animal detection module transmits data to a cloud-based server via Wi-Fi. A private cloud instance operates on a computer to store and analyze behavioral patterns of wild animals. This enables farmers to detect irregularities, take corrective actions, and enhance overall farm management.

Notification System

Upon detecting animal activity, the system sends alerts to the user via email and instant messaging. A captured image of the detected animal is included in the notification. The alerts are sent to the registered email address and the user's **Telegram account** linked to the registered phone number, ensuring timely awareness and response.

RESULTS AND DISCUSSION

This section presents empirical analysis of proposed system with datasets. It measures the accuracy and loss metrics found during training and validation phase for each epoch. It provides quantitative measure of model performance at that stage for each epoch. In addition, the plotted trend in figure 3 represents the loss computed on a subset of the entire dataset.

Figure 3. Training and Validation accuracy and loss graph

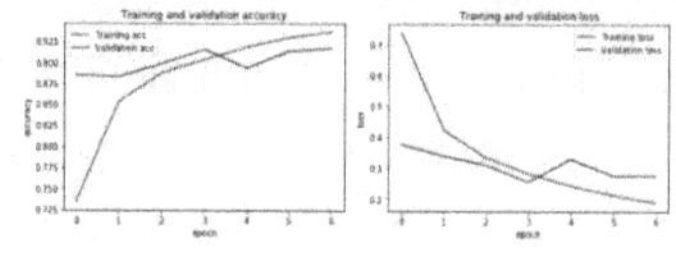

From the results it is understood that experiments using E2 dataset demonstrate higher accuracy compared to E1 dataset. It achieves 80.6% Top-1 accuracy and 94.1% Top-5 accuracy as shown in figure 3. The training and testing accuracy of the combined CNN is depicted in figure 4.

Figure 4. Training and Testing Accuracy of the joint CNN (Top-5).

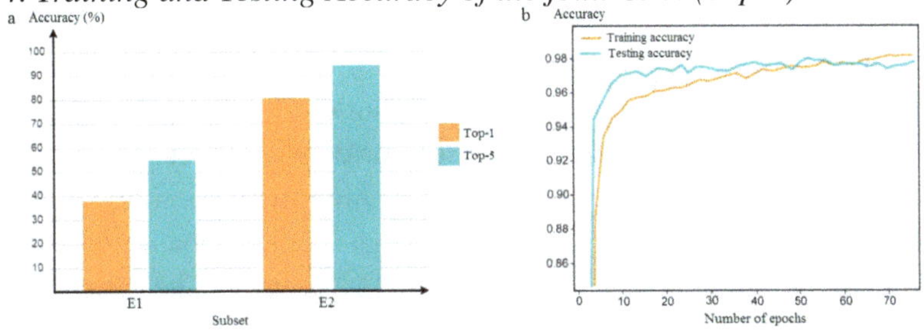

The first analysis is conducted using a single-branch SVM without accounting for gags. In the second analysis, the proposed joint CNN was implemented with selection-checking criteria. Table 1 shows the summary for the E2 dataset, including Average Precision (AP), Miss Rate (MR), and False Positives (FP).

Table 1. Animal recognition results using the joint CNN

Animals	AP,%	MR,%	FP, %	Animals	AP, %	MR,%	FP, %
Goat	83.37	10.7	9.7	Goat	81.93	6.9	14.4
Cow	84.29	9.1	13.2	Cow	85.69	7.1	10.8
Elephant	79.13	12.4	16.3	Elephant	79.14	12.3	14.7
Deer	80.21	11.8	16.5	Deer	75.35	18.6	19.8
Horse	84.9	7.9	12.9	Horse	69.52	21.6	24.8
Pig	83.07	8	15.6	Pig	81.23	14.9	17.2

CONCLUSION

A network of learnable neurons is used to process image data and forming feature vectors. It is transmitted to subsequent convolutional layers for further. The final output represents the extracted features from the input image. The pooling layer is used to reduce dimensionality and improves generalization of outputs. It also helps in preparing the input features for the Fully Connected Layer (FCL). Segmentation module divides the input image into non-overlapping regions. It applies average and max pooling to extract each region. It lies between convolutional layers and ReLU. The ReLU Layer introduces non-linearity using rectifier. It applies an element-wise operation that replaces negative values in the feature vector with zero. In ReLU, activation function is used to introduce non-linearity and enhance training efficiency.

FCL is used for final classification. It uses SoftMax function to provide output probability for identifying animal. Thus, convolutional, pooling, and ReLU layers are used to extract features and FCL is used for classification. The final pooling layer sends extracted features to classifier. It employs activation function to transform scores into output probability. It ensures that output probabilities sum to one, enabling accurate prediction. For detection, RPN is used. The proposed system enhances the object detection by identifying potential regions containing animals. It also ensures accurate classification and localization.

Challenges and Issues

- Manual Processes are Labour-Intensive and Costly
- Overexploitation of natural resources affect eco system
- Human activity on wildlife affects their populations, habitats, and animal behaviours
- It is harder to adapt models trained on natural images to artificial environments
- Real-time tracking of animal is still challenging tasks nowadays

REFERENCES

Bharathi, D., Palanisamy, R., Moses, L., Shanmugam, K., & Rangasamy, N. (2024). Smart detection and repulsive system for animal intrusion. *AIP Conference Proceedings, 3112*(1), 020003. DOI: 10.1063/5.0214577

Bishop, C. M. (2006). *Pattern recognition and machine learning*. Springer.

Chen, G., Han, T. X., He, Z., Kays, R., & Forrester, T. (2014). Deep convolutional neural network based species recognition for wild animal monitoring. In *2014 IEEE International Conference on Image Processing (ICIP)* (pp. 858–862). IEEE. https://doi.org/DOI: 10.1109/ICIP.2014.7025172

El Abbadi, N. K., & Alsaadi, E. M. T. A. (2020, April). *An automated vertebrate animals classification using deep convolution neural networks*. In *2020 International Conference on Computer Science and Software Engineering (CSASE)*. IEEE. https://doi.org/DOI: 10.1109/CSASE48920.2020.9142070

Gupta, A., Sharma, S., & Mangal, M. (2025). Animal repellent smart system using AI-based edge computing. *African Journal of Biological Sciences*. https://www.researchgate.net/publication/370281687_Animal_Repellent_Smart_System_using_AI_based_Edge_Computing

Hamming, R. W. (1950). Error detecting and error correcting codes. *The Bell System Technical Journal, 29*(2), 147–160. DOI: 10.1002/j.1538-7305.1950.tb00463.x

Haralick, R. M., Shanmugam, K., & Dinstein, I. (1973). Textural features for image classification. *IEEE Transactions on Systems, Man, and Cybernetics, SMC-3*(6), 610–621. DOI: 10.1109/TSMC.1973.4309314

Heffner, H. E., & Heffner, R. S. (2007). Hearing ranges of laboratory animals. *Journal of the American Association for Laboratory Animal Science; JAALAS, 46*(1), 20–22. PMID: 17203911

Kasthuri, U., Priyadharshini, P., Dhanush, R., Kumar, P. S., Madhu, N. G., & Riyaz, M. D. (2025). Enhancing animal repellent system using AI and deep learning. *Atlantis Press*. https://www.atlantis-press.com/article/126011278.pdf

Kruthi, H., Nisarga, A. C., Supriya, D. K., Sanjay, C. R., & Mohan Kumar, K. S. (2021). Animal detection using deep learning algorithm. *International Journal of Advanced Research in Computer and Communication Engineering, 10*(6).

LeCun, Y., Bottou, L., Bengio, Y., & Haffner, P. (1998). Gradient-based learning applied to document recognition. *Proceedings of the IEEE, 86*(11), 2278–2324. DOI: 10.1109/5.726791

Liu, Y., Ma, X., Shu, L., Hancke, G. P., & Abu-Mahfouz, A. M. (2021). From industry 4.0 to agriculture 4.0: Status, enabling technologies, and research challenges. *IEEE Transactions on Industrial Informatics, 17*(6), 4324–4334. DOI: 10.1109/TII.2020.3003910

Miao, J., & Zhang, X. (2024). A microservice-based smart agriculture system to detect and prevent animal intrusion. *Future Internet, 16*(8), 296. DOI: 10.3390/fi16080296

Mishra, A. (2024). Smart animal repelling device: Utilizing IoT and AI for effective anti-adaptive harmful animal deterrence. *BIO Web of Conferences, 82*, 05014. DOI: 10.1051/bioconf/20248205014

Munian, Y., Martinez-Molina, A., & Alamaniotis, M. (2020). Intelligent system for detection of wild animals using HOG and CNN in automobile applications. In *2020 11th International Conference on Information, Intelligence, Systems and Applications (IISA)* (pp. 1–8). IEEE. DOI: 10.1109/IISA50023.2020.9284365

Prakash, B., Jayakumar, R., Swaminathan, R., & Harikumar, S. (2019, September). *Animal detection using deep learning algorithm* [Preprint]. ResearchGate. https://www.researchgate.net/

Qi, Y., Baiyang, C., & Lan, L. (2021). Deep learning-based image recognition in animal husbandry. In *2021 18th International Computer Conference on Wavelet Active Media Technology and Information Processing (ICCWAMTIP)* (pp. 318–321). IEEE. DOI: 10.1109/ICCWAMTIP53232.2021.9674177

Ramya, G., & Ramesh, S. (2025). Animal detection for crop protection using deep learning. *Journal of Emerging Technologies and Innovative Research, 12*(8), 2150–2156. https://eprints.intimal.edu.my/2150/1/jods2025_08.pdf

Ren, S., He, K., Girshick, R., & Sun, J. (2015). Advances in Neural Information Processing Systems: Vol. 28. *Faster R-CNN: Towards real-time object detection with region proposal networks.*, https://arxiv.org/abs/1506.01497

Santhanam, S., S. S. B., Panigrahi, S. S., Kashyap, S. K., & Duriseti, B. K. (2021). Animal detection for road safety using deep learning. In *2021 International Conference on Computational Intelligence and Computing Applications (ICCICA)* (pp. 1–5). IEEE. DOI: 10.1109/ICCICA52458.2021.9697287

Shanthakumari, R., Nalini, C., Vinothkumar, S., Govindaraj, B., Dharani, S., & Chindhana, S. (2022). Image detection and recognition of different species of animals using deep learning. In *2022 International Mobile and Embedded Technology Conference (MECON)* (pp. 236–241). IEEE. DOI: 10.1109/MECON53876.2022.9752203

Singh, A., Pietrasik, M., Natha, G., Ghouaiel, N., Brizel, K., & Ray, N. (2020). Animal detection in man-made environments. In *2020 IEEE Winter Conference on Applications of Computer Vision (WACV)* (pp. 1427–1438). IEEE. DOI: 10.1109/WACV45572.2020.9093504

Vaish, R., & Sharma, S. (2024). Automated smart crop protection utilizing IoT: A comprehensive review. *E3S Web of Conferences, 540*, 13012. https://doi.org/DOI: 10.1051/e3sconf/202454013012

KEY TERMS AND DEFINITIONS

Activation Functions: It is used by the classifier in the FCL for classification.

Artificial Intelligence (AI): A machine that can learn from experience without any explicit programming.

Convolutional Neural Networks (CNNs): A multiple neural networks used in deep neural networks for analysing images.

Deep Convolutional Neural Network (DCNN): An AI-driven model used for predicting animals in the system.

Deep learning (DL): A field of machine learning comprises of neural networks. It is used in image and speech recognition.

Fully Connected Layer (FCL): Links every neuron from the previous layer to each neuron in the next layer. It is used final image classification.

Gray Level Co-Occurrence Matrix (GLCM): It is used to extract key features from image.

Hamming Distance Metric: It is used to measure similarity between input features with existing feature.

Identification: The process of comparing the given image and generate matches.

Machine Learning (ML): A field of AI used for decision making. It learn from dataset

Rectified Linear Unit (ReLU): It presents non-linearity through an activation function.

Region Proposal Network (RPN): A CNN generates Regions of Interest (RoIs) for detecting image segments.

Verification: Determining whether the given image belongs to sample or not

Chapter 8

Innovative Supply Chain Effect on Value Creation by Mediation of AI Technology in the Horn of Africa

Zenebe Elemo Ermias
https://orcid.org/0009-0002-7361-8728
Bule Hora University, Ethiopia

Shashank Mittal
https://orcid.org/0009-0007-8643-4350
O.P. Jindal Global University, India

Shashi Kant
https://orcid.org/0000-0003-4722-5736
Lovely Professional University, India

Mohit Verma
https://orcid.org/0009-0005-3036-3894
O.P. Jindal Global University, India

Abdulakim Erbo Gobena
https://orcid.org/0000-0002-5016-2476
Bule Hora University, Ethiopia

Bhumika Ray
https://orcid.org/0009-0002-6518-7227
O.P. Jindal Global University, India

Rakesh Kumar Gautam
https://orcid.org/0009-0001-4381-2338
Lovely Professional University, India

ABSTRACT

This chapter explores the relationship between value creation and innovative practices within supply chain management. Drawing on data from 390 supply chain professionals across diverse industries, the study employs a quantitative research design using structural equation modeling to analyze the interconnections. The findings reveal that innovative supply chain practices significantly enhance value

DOI: 10.4018/979-8-3373-2497-5.ch008

creation, with artificial intelligence (AI) technologies serving as a key mediating factor. The results suggest that organizations integrating AI into their supply chain operations can achieve higher productivity levels and greater customer satisfaction. The chapter concludes by recommending future research directions, including the long-term effects of technological integration, industry-specific variations, and the human factors influencing innovation adoption. These insights contribute to a deeper understanding of the evolving dynamics of supply chain management in the digital era.

INTRODUCTION

The Eastern Africa, which is characterized by a unique geopolitical climate and financial challenges (Ashuro et al., 2025), has begun to understand how a potentially groundbreaking solution to utilising artificial intelligence (AI) technology in its supply chains can be (Belhadi et al., 2024). Besides making various industries, such as commerce, logistics, and agriculture, highly efficient, this assimilation will deliver significant value to many industries (El Jaouhari and Hamidi, 2024). Global supply networks are so complex that they require new innovative solutions, which exploit new technology. This chapter focuses on the connection of supply chain innovation, artificial intelligence, and value creation with an accent on its local and global impact (Ali et al., 2024). The need to reduce costs and simplify processes led to the emergence of the notion of supply chain innovation that has evolved over several years (Kant et al., 2025). Given that old models are slow in embracing new technology, AI has become a key force in changing how supply chains work (Al-Shboul, 2024). According to an empirical study, artificial intelligence (AI) could enhance decision-making, forecast market trends, alongside optimise distribution, hence strengthening the supply chain. Furthermore, the adoption of these technologies has proven constrained in Eastern Africa due to a shortage of competent labour, legislative deficiencies, and insufficient resources (Khan et al., 2025). When it comes to politics, economics, and technology, there are several problems that make it hard to use AI-related supply chain solutions in the Eastern African market. These include limited access to data, stakeholders' unwillingness to change, and weak digital infrastructure (Ashiwaju et al., 2024).

Secondly, significant barriers to the investment in modern technology are also caused by the political and economic instability of the region (Jabo et al., 2026). The current research tends to ignore these contextual issues, which form a knowledge gap on how inference can incorporate AI into the supply chains in this specific environment (Oriekhoe et al., 2024). Today, in state of supply chain operations in the Eastern Africa, paying attention to the role artificial intelligence performs in value creation and to seal these gaps of investigation (Okoduwa et al., 2024). The review of the previous empirical studies and case study investigations in the region made this chapter useful to future scholars and policymakers. To support stakeholders, make superior choices, it plans to provide a framework to understand AI in supply chains (Okoye et al., 2024).

The advent of AI technology presents an opportunity to address all these problems (Ololade, 2024). Moreover, some problems are also linked to the application of AI in this context. An example of the case study on Kenya using AI in agriculture shows that data collection and interpretation is challenging. Artificial intelligence systems require quality and real-time data to be productive despite their ability to provide valuable information (Jabo et al., 2026). Implementation of AI in Kenya is complicated due to the fact that farmers do not always have access to reliable data bases and the necessary technology infrastructure is inefficient (Al-Shboul, 2024). In addition, AI is far more challenging to deploy due to political unpredictability. An example is that the Somali government has been struggling to establish a steady climate to invest in technology in the country because of its violence and challenges in governance (Olutimehin et al., 2024). Although AI improve logistics and distribution within the country where instability often poses a hindrance to product delivery, the development has been hindered by the absence of a favorable government system and the funding of digital infrastructure. This case can be regarded as an example of the regional tendency, according to which political and economic turmoil creates an environment that does not favor technical augment (Dza, 2024).

The other major challenge is the capability to build in human resources. The Eastern Africa is often characterized by the lack of qualified experts that can create, implement, and manage AI systems (Ashiwaju et al., 2024). A case in point is Djibouti, which has embarked on several digital transformation projects, but it has been failing to find qualified leaders to lead the projects. Besides the deceleration of the process of AI adoption, a shortage of local knowledge also casts doubts on issues of sustainability and long-term viability of such programs (Ali et al., 2024). With regards to inference, it cannot be denied that, in Africa, AI totally alters the work of SCM, however, there are also significant barriers to implementation (Rambe, 2024). Case studies of Ethiopia, Kenya, Somalia, and Djibouti show that there are numerous challenges to the adoption of AI (Ololade, 2024). These are shortage of skilled human resources, issues of data collection, political instability and infrastructural shortages. To contextualize the discussion of AI in the field and develop specific plans that can help the assimilation of its influence into supply chains, it is essential to understand these challenges. This investigation is aimed at shedding some light on how these issues can be addressed to be able to leverage AI technology to a comprehensive extent to enhance value creation (Oriekhoe et al., 2024).

PROBLEM STATEMENT

The integration of AI into the management of SC in the Eastern Africa demonstrates an exciting chance to improve the efficiency, cut the expenses, and generate value (Kant et al., 2026). An AI implementation in sustainability should, hopefully, result in enhanced demand analysis, efficient inventory control, and enhanced logistics all of which would transform the economic environment in the region (Amankwah, 2024). Even the present situation of AI adoption in the Eastern Africa shows an extreme contrast to this perfect situation. Even though the potential of AI technologies has been identified, the region suffers a plethora of challenges, which hamper influence implementation and use (Al-Shboul, 2024). There are many empirical studies that indicate the potential of AI and significant challenges to implementing AI offer conflicting results. As an illustration, even though some studies indicate that artificial intelligence (AI) can play a significant role in simplifying supply chain performance, other research studies present the fact that the implementation rates in the Eastern Africa are horrifying (Okoduwa et al., 2024). Such an inconsistency implies that certain aspects that facilitate or hinder the implementation of AI in this environment remain open to debate (Ashiwaju et al., 2024). The ambiguous results of the inference of AI applications also pose a challenge to the discussion since numerous projects have not yet provided quantifiable results, and the stakeholders do not know whether these investments are worthwhile or not (Ali et al., 2024).

Even the theoretical gaps, such as the theories that justify AI assimilation and supply chain innovation, are still numerous. Most of the existing concepts are grounded in the circumstances that do not represent the unique sociopolitical and economic setting of the Eastern Africa (Olutimehin et al., 2024). Theoretical models considerations of the complexity of the region in terms of its political instability, infrastructure challenges, and cultural peculiarities are sorely needed. The exact ways in which AI could be made sustainable to the supply chains in the areas remain unanswered, particularly in sectors that have a high potential of informational impact such as the logistics sector and agriculture (Dza, 2024). Contextual gaps also exacerbate the problem since most of the information on AI adoption is generated by developed countries and may not apply to the Eastern Africa setting (Rambe, 2024). The lack of context-specific investigation affects policymakers and practitioners less in their capacity to develop tailor-made AI assimilation plans that address the needs of the regions. Other real-life challenges such as inadequate infrastructure, access to limited data and qualification of personnel also prevent progress. These hurdles do not fulfill the promise of AI due to their stagnating cycle (Al-Shboul, 2024).

This chapter seeks to fill these gaps by offering a detailed review of the present state of the AI implementation in the Eastern Africa and pointing out the specific opportunities and issues within the supply chains of the region (Amankwah, 2024).

RELATED THEORIES

Technology Acceptance Model: It is a well-known paradigm to explain the way in which individuals adopt and utilize new technologies. The ease of use, which is the said determinant, plays the biggest role in influencing the adoption of a technology by a person (Ashiwaju et al., 2024). TAM will allow gaining an understanding of the attitude of politicians, farmers, and logistics managers towards the use of AI. These perceptions are important to understand how to improve user acceptance, as well as to facilitate more smooth deployment. Stakeholders can also establish an environment that fosters the use of technologies by addressing the complexity-related issues and proving the real benefits of AI (Ali et al., 2024).

Diffusion of Innovations Theory: It describes the way, the reason, and the speed at which new ideas and technology diffuse in an environment. (Okoduwa et al., 2024; Al-Shboul, 2024).

DEFINITION AND ORIGIN OF TERMS

Artificial Intelligence (AI)

AI may be divided into two categories: general AI, which has the capacity to comprehend, learn, and apply intelligence across a wide variety of activities, and narrow AI, which is made for certain tasks (such as language translation or facial recognition) (Dza, 2024). Investigations interested in how machines could be able to carry out activities that normally need human intellect came together for the meeting (Rambe, 2024). Investigations' hope that robots could replicate human cognitive processes propelled the early advancements in artificial intelligence (Ololade, 2024). Over the years, artificial intelligence has undergone several stages, including intense investigation and funding times (commonly called "AI summers") and periods of stagnation (often called "AI winters"), which were caused by the time's technological constraints and irrational expectations (Ali et al., 2024).

Management of Supply Chain (SCM)

The planning and administration of all sourcing, procurement, conversion, and logistics management tasks are included in management of supply chain, or SCM. It entails working with and coordinating with channel partners, which may include customers, suppliers, middlemen, and third-party service providers. Achieving a sustained competitive advantage and increasing customer value are the ultimate goals of management of supply chain (Belhadi et al., 2024). In the 1980s, the idea of management of supply chain came into being as companies realized how imperative it was to look at operations holistically rather than separately. The majority of early supply chain operations were centered on inventory control and logistics, but as globalization grew, it became clear that more integrated strategies were required (Olutimehin et al., 2024). As businesses looked to streamline their supply networks in order to increase productivity and cut expenses, the phrase "management of supply chain" gained use. By the 1989s, management of supply chain (SCM) had emerged as a crucial element of corporate strategic planning, sparking the creation of several frameworks and theories targeted at supply chain process optimization (Oriekhoe et al., 2024).

Creation of Value

Creation of value is the process by which businesses raise the value of their goods or services by making them more useful to consumers. Innovation, increased productivity, enhanced customer satisfaction, and distinctiveness from rivals may all help achieve this. Since creation of value has a direct influence on profitability and market position, it is a key idea for firms (Oriekhoe et al., 2024). Economic theory, namely the frameworks of value theory and utility theory, is where the idea of creation of value first emerged (Ashiwaju et al., 2024). The consequence of creation of value as a strategic goal was further highlighted by the emergence of ideas like stakeholder theory and customer-centric methods. Creation of value in practice has developed into a multifaceted framework that takes into account social and environmental influences in addition to financial indicators (Ololade, 2024).

Political Instability

Political instability can be characterized by civil unrest, political violence, or the breakdown of governmental institutions. It also alludes to the possibility of regime transition or disruption in governance. It frequently causes political and economic contexts to become unclear, which has an influence on augment and investment (Okoduwa et al., 2024). In sociology and political science, the phrase has been used to characterize the circumstances that lead to conflict or instability in political institutions (Ashiwaju et al., 2024). Economic inequality, ethnic conflicts, corruption, and a lack of democratic administration are some of the causes of political instability. Political instability has historically been a recurrent subject in many locations, especially in those that are dealing with governance and socioeconomic difficulties (Rambe, 2024).

EMPIRICAL LITERATURE REVIEW

Supply Chain Innovative and Creation of Value

Value generation for businesses and their stakeholders is greatly increased by using supply chain innovative methods (Dza, 2024). Businesses may improve many facets of their supply chains and boost operational responsiveness and efficiency by utilizing cutting-edge technology like AI and IoT (Ashiwaju et al., 2024). AI-driven analytics, for example, let companies predict demand more precisely, which minimizes stock outs and surplus inventory. This enhances the entire value offer by reducing inventory holding costs and increasing customer satisfaction through prompt product delivery (Belhadi et al., 2024). Also, innovative supply chains augment improved cooperation among manufacturers, distributors, and suppliers.

Using online environments for data sharing and real-time cooperation can help enterprises develop a more connected supply chain ecosystem (Amankwah, 2024). This cooperative methodology makes it easier to align goals and expectations, which is important for meeting changing market conditions and consumer needs. This lets firms respond to problems more quickly, regardless of whether they are triggered by unexpected events like natural disasters or changes in what customers want. This adaptation helps keep the creation of value going in the long run while rendering the system more resilient (Oriekhoe et al., 2024).

Integrating sustainable practices into new supply chains makes it even easier to create value. Businesses can reduce waste, lower their ecological footprints, and improve ethical sourcing by taking sustainability considerations into account when making supply chain planning (Okoduwa et al., 2024). This makes customers more loyal and the company looks better (Rambe, 2024). Companies that consider sustainability foremost in their supply chains often do better in the market and attract both investors and customers who care about the environment (Ololade, 2024). Innovative supply chains may also be able to find new ways to make money by offering a wider range of products and services. For example, businesses that employ cutting-edge tracking along with transparency technologies may let customers see more and let them keep track of their orders in real time. (Ashiwaju et al., 2024; Oriekhoe et al., 2024).

Supply Chain Innovative and AI Technology

Innovative approaches to the supply chain can provide a groundbreaking approach to the use of AI to enhance operational efficiency and resilience as the sector grapples with challenges such as political instability, poor infrastructures, and limited resources access (Oriekhoe et al., 2024). The AI-driven solutions that optimize the logistics of a business, improve the demand forecasting, and simplify the inventory management process will help the businesses to solve some of the most dire supply chain problems in the region (Dza, 2024). Among the most noticeable impacts of supply chain innovative on AI technology in the Eastern Africa, there is facilitating data-driven decision-making (Rambe, 2024). AI algorithms can enable businesses to gain a lot of insight into customer behavior, market trends and bottlenecks in their operations by analyzing the vast amounts of data collected at various touch-points of the supply chain. With the help of this data-centric approach, stakeholders can also make informed choices to enhance the performance of the supply chain (Olutimehin et al., 2024). In particular, logistics companies can make their routes more fuel-efficient by optimizing transportation costs and delivery times, whereas farmers can predict crop yields with the help of AI and control the time of planting (Belhadi et al., 2024).

Moreover, the emphasis of collaboration within innovative supply chains generates a conducive condition that is positive towards the implementation of AI (Amankwah, 2024). The region can build a robust ecosystem that will support production and consumption of AI solutions through encouraging partnerships between companies, technology vendors, and the government within the region. To address the challenges to the use of AI, knowledge sharing, capacity building, and access to finance can be facilitated through collaborative platforms. Moreover, such a collaborative mindset could potentially reduce the reliance on external consultants because the local knowledge base can be fostered, which would allow sustainable development (Khan et al., 2025). Moreover, sustainable practices integrated in new supply chains can be used to hasten adoption of AI systems to enhance environmental stewardship. This can include AI that can be utilized to enhance supply chain transparency, waste reduction, and resource utilization (Ashiwaju et al., 2024). Predictive analytics can enable an organization to avoid overproduction and surplus inventory, which is a significant issue in most industries, particularly agricultural ones, by accurately predicting demand. Besides ensuring environmental concerns, the need to transform the technology related to the sustainability of products also satisfies the growing demand of the consumers towards the sustainable products, which enhances competitiveness in the market (El Jaouhari and Hamidi, 2024).

AI Technology and Creation of Value

The integration of AI technology in different business operations significantly contributes to the creation of value and changes the way businesses operate radically in terms of offering goods and services. One of the most urgent implications of AI is the potential of the latter to enhance operational efficacy (Olutimehin et al., 2024).

AI assists companies to reduce costs, minimize errors, and improve manufacturing through repeating tasks and facilitating complex processes. Predictive maintenance, such as AIs, can be used to predict equipment failures before they occur during production, reducing costs of maintaining equipment and downtime. Besides allowing immediate cash flow benefits, this efficiency also allows the businesses to manage more resources strategically, which increases the total generation of value further (Oriekhoe et al., 2024). Another urgency of AI technology on value creation is the capacity of the technology to drive innovation. AI can help companies to analyze vast amounts of data quickly and draw valuable conclusions (Ololade, 2024; Rambe, 2024. Belhadi et al., 2024; Olutimehin et al., 2024).

In addition, the AI technology encourages greater client engagement and personalization (Khan et al., 2025). By analyzing consumer data with the help of AI algorithms, businesses can create personalized experiences that signal each customer with his/her individual interests and habits (Amankwah, 2024). Besides enhancing the pleasure of a client, such level of customization leads to trusts and brand loyalty. Artificial intelligence, such as on e-commerce websites, is used to suggest products to their users based on their browsing habits, which increases the retention of customers and sells (Olutimehin et al., 2024). It could be assumed that organizations should achieve a significant value creation, as a result of better customer relations and increased revenue in case they prioritize AI-driven customer-centric projects (El Jaouhari and Hamidi, 2024).

Supply Chain Innovative, Creation of Value Mediated by AI Technology

The innovative supply chains apply cutting-edge technology to enhance the responsiveness to the market needs, improve collaboration, and speed up processes (Amankwah, 2024). When introduced to these supply chains, AI is a driving force that enhances the possibility of value creation in many ways. An example of AI-based analytics can provide real-time observation of the supply chain performance and allow a business to identify inefficiency and optimize operations (Oriekhoe et al., 2024). This optimization is immediately optimistic to customers and other stakeholders because it reduces costs and increases the quality of services (Khan et al., 2025). Innovative supply chains are also easier to make better decisions with the help of the AI technology. AI allows enterprises make highly smart decisions quickly and correctly because it looks at a lot of data and makes predictions. This flexibility is crucial in today's fast-paced economy, where being on time might be the difference between winning and losing (Ashiwaju et al., 2024). AI, through particular, may enquire into market trends and how people behave as consumers. This lets enterprises change their supply chain plans ahead of time. Having this versatility not only improves operational inference, but it also leads to the creation of novel services and products that meet consumer wants as well as add value (El Jaouhari and Hamidi, 2024).

It's also crucial to say that AI helps people work together in new supply chains. Businesses may employ AI technology to make it easier for vendors in the supply chain to share data and talk to each other. A more coherent supply chain ecosystem is the consequence of better collaboration, where all the people involved cooperate in order to reach a set of common goals (Okoduwa et al., 2024). A prime instance of these kinds of activities is AI used in collaborative forecasting, which helps partners coordinate their inventory levels and cuts down on stock outs and overstocking. These partnerships lead to greater alignment of resources and capabilities, which in the end gives clients more value (Belhadi et al., 2024). Also, using AI in creative supply chains makes them more sustainable, which is becoming more and more crucial for creating value. AI technology can improve the management as well as logistics about resources, which will cut down on garbage and its negative effects on the surroundings (Olutimehin et al., 2024). AI can help plan transport routes better so that they use less fuel as well as produce fewer pollutants. Companies that use sustainable methods not only satisfy the needs of their clientele and the law, but they also make their brand look better. This dedication to environmentalism could also be strengthened by continuing to enhance the production of wealth, recruit socially responsible investors, alongside cultivate a base of satisfied customers (Oriekhoe et al., 2024).

CONCEPTUAL FRAMEWORK

Figure 1. Conceptual Framework

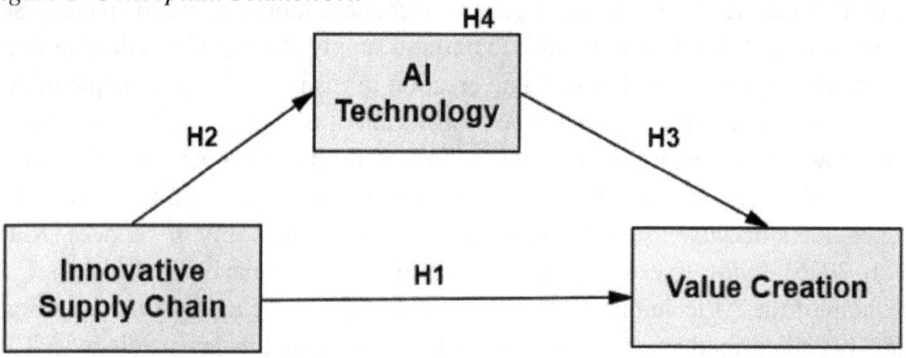

INVESTIGATION METHODOLOGY

To make sure the collection of data was viable for analysis, 389 people were chosen as a representative quantity. The participants were chosen using a random stratified method of selection to make sure that a wide range of supply chain-related business sectors were included. The approach of collecting data employed was an organised assessment with proven indicators to measure the parts of creating value, using AI technology, and coming up with new ways to do things in the chain of custody. The research employed a comprehensive scale creation technique to guarantee both the accuracy and dependability of the scales. The prior research was initially reviewed in order to find pertinent constructs alongside portions.

The sample size was deemed enough for the next analyses when the KMO value was greater than 0.70. EFA was then used to determine the constructions' underlying structures. EFA assisted in ensuring that each item loaded heavily into its corresponding factor, lowering the number of items, and verifying the dimensionality of the scales. The scale was further validated by the investigation, which produced distinct components that manifested creation of value, AI technology, and innovative supply chain techniques Following the CFA, and SEM. Through the use of AI technology, SEM offering mediation insights into how innovative supply chain activities influence value generation.

Imperative concepts and aspects pertinent to the investigation's goals were found in this preliminary literature evaluation. The literature focused on aspects like technological assimilation, agility, and teamwork for supply chain innovations. In order to ensure cultural relevance and clarity, elements from scales used in earlier investigation were modified to meet the unique setting of the Eastern Africa. Conferring to the Technology Acceptance Model (TAM), the evaluation emphasized adoption, perceived utility, and simplicity of use as crucial aspects of the AI technology architecture. The items were taken from and adjusted from pre-existing measures that assessed people' opinions of AI's usefulness and influence on decision-making. This made sure that the scale that was produced took into account the subtleties of how supply chain operations use and interpret AI technology.

The investigation identified a number of determinants, including competitive advantage, customer happiness, and operational efficiency that contribute to value generation. After assessing existing scales, pertinent components were chosen and adjusted to fit the unique context of supply chains influenced by AI technology. The goal was to capture the whole influence on stakeholders by making sure the items manifested both the concrete and intangible components of creation of value. To further confirm the scale's applicability and clarity, the investigations consulted experts after determining and improving the items for each component. The final changes to the goods' phrasing and structure were influenced by input from management of supply chain and artificial intelligence specialists, guaranteeing that they were clear and simple. Also, a limited number of responders participated in a pilot test, which allowed for additional improvement based on their input. Each construct had several items on the final scale, which was rated on a Likert scale from "strongly disagree" to "strongly agree." This method made quantitative analysis easier and guaranteed a complete scale that captured the key elements of value generation, AI technology, and innovative supply chains. The investigations sought to produce a trustworthy instrument that faithfully manifested the constructs being examined, eventually enhancing the validity of the investigation outcomes, by grounding the scale creation process in well-established literature and iterative feedback.

DATA ANALYSIS

Table 1. Reliability Statistics

Cronbach's Alpha	Cronbach's Alpha Based on Standardized Items	N of Items
.845	.852	18

Source: Authors

Its reliability statistics as shown in Table 1 demonstrate the internal consistency of the scale applied in the research. The value of Cronbachs Alpha at 0.845 indicates that the instrument has a high degree of reliability, indicating that the items incorporated in it are strongly correlated, and they have a common underlying construct that is highly consistent. The Cronbach Alpha increases slightly when the analysis is done on the basis of the standardized items and is equal to 0.852 which once again justifies the consistency and reliability of the measurement scale. Using generally established scales, Cronbachs Alpha value above 0.7 is assumed to be acceptable, a value above 0.8 is assumed to be good, and above 0.9 is assumed to be excellent. Thus, the received values (0.845 and 0.852) suggest that the questionnaire or measurement tool applied to this study has a good internal consistency and can be statistically reliable to be further analyzed. The number of items that are taken in the reliability test is 18, which is quite large and, hence, indicates a sufficient number of variables that are added to the construct. The high score on reliability suggests that the items are consistent and can be reliably used to make valid conclusions regarding the constructs it is measuring. Therefore, the findings justify the validity and consistency of the information gathered using this tool in the future statistical applications.

Table 2. Item-Total Statistics

	Scale Mean if Item Deleted	Scale Variance if Item Deleted	Corrected Item-Total Correlation	Squared Multiple Correlation	Cronbach's Alpha if Item Deleted
Innovative Supply Chain	62.65	59.179	.437	.284	.838
AI Technology	62.68	58.544	.405	.328	.841
Value Creation	62.56	59.212	.454	.314	.837

The Item-Total Statistics table informs about the contribution of each separate item to the upper level of reliability and internal consistency of the scale. It is observed that the values of item-total correlation of the three items used in the analysis, that is, In innovative supply chain (0.437), AI Technology (0.405) and value creation (0.454) are all above the acceptable level of 0.3. This implies that all the items are moderately to strongly positively correlated with the total scale, that is, these items are highly consistent with the underlying construct that is measured. All items are not weakly correlated and this indicates that each one of them is relevant and they add value to the overall reliability of the instrument. The values of the Cronbachs Alpha if deleted item are between 0.837 and 0.841 that are quite close to the value of the Cronbachs Alpha that was earlier mentioned, that is 0.845. This would mean that the deletion of either of these items would not have a great impact on improving or lowering the internal consistency of the scale. This is to say that all the three items are properly constructed and can be maintained because they enhance the overall measurement consistency. Also, Scale Mean if Item Deleted and Scale Variance if Item Deleted values have slight differences in the values of items and indicate that each item makes the same contribution to the total score. Thus, the results prove that the factors Instrumental Supply Chain, AI Technology, and Value Creation can be used as valid elements of the measurement tool, and their presence increases the solidity and internal consistency of the scale as a whole.

Table 3. Hotelling's T-Squared Test

Hotelling's T-Squared	F	df1	df2	Sig
160.610	9.064	17	378	.000

The findings on the T-Squared Test of the Hoteling displayed in Table 3 reveal the total significance of the multivariate difference of mean of the items in the scale. The T-Squared value of the Hotelling is 160.610, or an F-value of 9.064 with degrees of freedom df1 = 17 and df2 = 378. The value of significance (Sig = 0.000) does not exceed the standard value of 0.05, therefore, this means that the outcome is statistically significant. It implies that the average scores of the variables put in the analysis are significantly different among one another, and it is possible that the respondents rated the items in equal levels. The large value of T-Squared of Hotelling indicates the support that the set of items are measuring a different and significant construct and not the random or irrelevant response. The items in other words show the discriminant power which verifies that the items provide unique information to the general scale. The construct validity of the instrument is also substantiated by the strong level of statistical significance ($p < 0.001$). It means that the items are not redundant and the scale is able to measure various dimensions of the underlying concept. In general, the findings of Hotelling T-Squared Test prove the consistency of the findings of the reliability test, which means that the measurement tool is both statistically sound and conceptually strong to be analyzed further.

Table 4. Model Summary[b]

Model	R	R Square	Adjusted R Square	Std. Error of the Estimate	Durbin-Watson
1	.578[a]	.334	.333	.615	1.708

Table 3 results on the T-Squared Test of the Hoteling show that the overall significance of the multivariate difference of the mean of the items in the scale is significant. The T-Squared value of the Hotelling of 160.610 or a F-value of 9.064 at a degrees of freedom of df1 = 17 and df2 = 378. The significance (Sig = 0.000) is not greater than the standard value (0.05), hence, this implies that the result is statistically significant. It means that mean scores of the variables included in the analysis are greatly dissimilar to each other, and there is a possibility that the respondents estimate the items equally. The high T-Squared of the Hotelling shows that the collection of items is measuring some other and important construct and not the chance or random response. The discriminant power is indicated in the items in other words and this is what validates that the items contain unique information to the general scale. The high degree of the statistical significance ($p < 0.001$) also supports the construct validity of the tool. It implies that the items are not redundant and the scale can cover the different dimensions of the underlying concept. Overall, the results of Hotelling T- Squared Test confirm the consistency of the results of the reliability test that is, that the measurement instrument is statistically sound and conceptually strong to continue the analysis.

Table 5. ANOVA[a]

Model		Sum of Squares	df	Mean Square	F	Sig.
1	Regression	74.733	1	74.733	197.418	.000[b]
	Residual	148.771	393	.379		
	Total	223.504	394			

a. Dependent Variable: value creation
b. Predictors: (Constant), Innovative supply chain, AI technology

Table 5 is the analysis of variance (ANOVA) result which is a test of the overall significance of the regression model. As the table indicates, regression sum of squares = 74.733, and the residual sum of squares = 148.771 and the sum of squares = 223.504. These values return the extent of a total variation in the dependent variable, Value Creation, which is caused by the independent variables (Innovative Supply Chain and AI Technology) compared to the unknown part (residual error). The F-value of 197.418 with the corresponding level of significance(Sig.) of 0.000 shows that the regression model is very significant. The p-value is far less than the traditional level of 0.05, which proves the hypothesis that the independent variables in combination with each other play a significant statistical role on the dependent variable. To put it in simpler words, the hybrid of Innovative Supply Chain and AI Technology makes a huge contribution to the explanation of differences in Value Creation. The regression mean square (74.733) is also far greater than the residual mean square (0.379), which also supports the strong model. Overall, the ANOVA findings indicate that the regression equation is largely appropriate, and both Innovative Supply Chain and AI Technology have significant predictive power of Value Creation. The meaning of the F-statistic is very significant indicating that the model can be effectively applied to the further interpretation and making decisions in the framework of the study.

Figure 2. Structure Equation Model

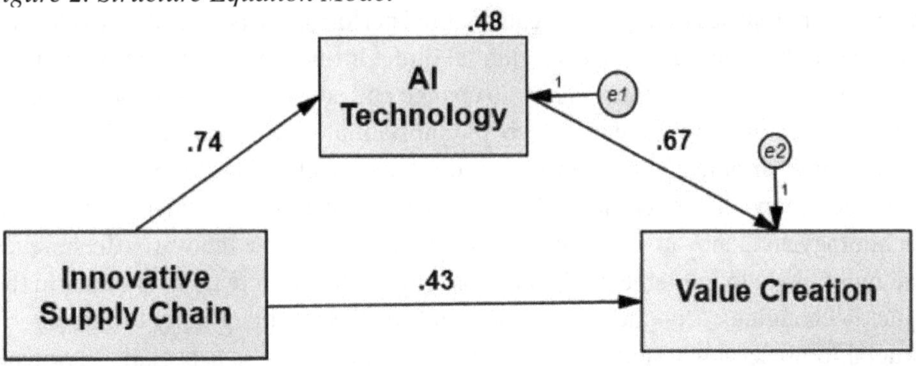

Table 6. Mediation

	worth
Supply chain innovative → Creation of value	.44
Supply chain innovative → AI Technology → Creation of value	.74*.67=.49
	.92

Source: Authors

Table 6 manifests the direct influence of Supply chain innovative on Creation of value is quantified at 0.43, indicating a strong and substantial influence. This investigation looks at the mediating role of AI technology in the associations among Supply chain innovative and Creation of value. Apart from the direct influence, the table also manifests an indirect influence through AI technology, which is 0.48 (the indirect influence of AI technology on creation of value) multiplied by 0.74 (the influence of Supply chain innovative on AI technology). A scenario of partial mediation is suggested by the outcomes, which show that although AI Technology improves the association among Supply chain innovative and Creation of value, the direct influence is still substantial and substantial. The total, comes to 0.91, demonstrating a substantial overall influence of Supply chain innovative on Creation of value when taking into account both pathways. All things considered, Table 7's outcomes highlight the two ways that supply chain innovative techniques may improve creation of value, both directly and indirectly using AI technology. It is to incorporate technology augmentations into supply chain plans in order to efficiently optimize creation of value.

DISCUSSION

Chapter inferences shed imperative light on the associations among creation of value, artificial intelligence, and supply chain innovative techniques. Adopting innovative approaches to improve organizational performance is crucial, as evidenced by the supply chain innovative substantial direct influence on creation of value. It manifests the need for supply chains to change and adjust to shifting market conditions using innovative strategies. Also, the substantial influence of AI technology as a mediating variable emphasizes how revolutionary technical augmentations might be in the context of supply chains. Conferring to the favorable association among AI technology and innovative supply chains, businesses that use innovative techniques are more likely to implement AI solutions, which enhance creation of value. In the quickly changing corporate environment of today, when integrating technology is crucial to preserving competitive advantage, this outcome is especially pertinent. A partial mediation scenario is also shown by the investigation, suggesting that although AI technology strengthens the link among creation of value and supply chain innovations, the direct channel is still robust and imperative. This implies that businesses should give equal weight to the creation of innovative supply chain strategies that naturally create value as well as the application of AI technology. All things considered, the investigation supports the idea that firms looking to optimize value generation must strategically link innovative processes with technology adoption. Future investigations might look more closely at the precise ways that AI technology influences creation of value as well as the contextual elements that may have an influence on these associations.

CONCLUSION

This investigation concludes by highlighting the crucial interactions among creation of value, AI technology, and supply chain innovative strategies. The outcomes highlight how sustainability supply chain innovative methods greatly increase creation of value, highlighting the consequence of innovation in the cutthroat business environment of today. Also, the mediating function of AI technology manifests how revolutionary it is for management of supply chain. AI technology becomes a crucial tool for businesses looking to maximize their performance by establishing the link among innovative activities and creation of value. A dual focus should be adopted by organizations: investing in both supply chain innovative methodologies and the assimilation of advanced technologies. The evidence of partial mediation manifests that while AI Technology amplifies the influences of Supply chain innovative practices on Creation of value, the direct influence of these practices is still substantial. In the end, the investigation offers insightful information to both practitioners and academics, promoting more investigation into the ways in which supply chains might benefit from technology breakthroughs. Organizations may improve their overall efficacy and sustainability while better navigating the complexity of the modern market by proactively coordinating the adoption of innovative practices with technology.

Implications

To begin with, managers must also know the urgency of the need to develop a supply chain innovative culture. By emphasizing innovative technology literacy, businesses can raise the level of operational efficiency and place them in a better position to respond swiftly to the market and client demands. This involves investing in employee training and addition in a bid to instill an innovative and continuous improvement culture. The ability of organizations to develop and sustainability is one of the ways in which organizations can use AI technologies: by breaking down organizational silos and encouraging collaboration. This inference suggests that future investigation might examine different types of technology and their particular influences on supply chain dynamics, encouraging more investigation into the association among distinct technical breakthroughs and organizational practices. The chapter also introduces the idea of partial mediation, which calls for a reconsideration of current ideas about mediation and interaction influences in supply chain settings. This detailed knowledge leads investigations to think about more intricate models that take into account several paths influencing value generation, even though technology can improve associations among variables.

Recommendations

To generate new ideas and techniques, leadership ought to vigorously expand programs that aid in the innovation, including cross-functional seminars and brainstorming. Companies ought to consider conducting profound studies of their visible processes to identify some areas, such as demand prediction, inventory management, and optimization of logistics, in which AI has the greatest potential to have a significant impact. Moreover, it is essential that the companies train their employees continuously and enlarge it. It will help the staff to adapt to the evolving demands and maximize the benefits of new methods. Group projects, online courses, and workshops that promote technical skills and creativity in thought might be categorized in this category. Finally, but not least, the businesses are supposed to find strategic partnerships with technology vendors and industry experts. Collaborating with external addicts is good to allow companies to transmit information and have access to new solutions that may not be readily available within the company. Through the creation of good network of partners, businesses will be able to enhance their ability to innovate and sustainability incorporate new technologies and eventually the resultant effect will be the creation of more value in their supply markets.

Future Directions

It is also possible to incorporate AI in supply chains and businesses and policymakers can consider exploring the contextual factors that guide the relationship between the adoption of AI technology and supply chain innovative practices. The scenario could change a lot based on things like the sort of business, the scope of the company, and the state of the local economy. A retrospective examination across several industries can assist organisations in acquiring useful insights and standard operating procedures. The interplay of different technological innovations within the supply chain framework is a significant subject for investigation. It is possible that a combination of the many technologies currently being used could better show how they all add value as organisations adopt more digital tools. Second, an ongoing investigation could help us figure out how new behaviours and technological advances affect supply chain performance over time. By monitoring alterations as time passes, examinations may be more equipped to assess the long term viability of such techniques and their capacity to react to market fluctuations. Lastly, we need qualitative studies on the human factors that determine how people in the supply chain adopt new technologies and ideas. Examining the roles of corporate culture, executive management, alongside staff involvement may yield essential insights into how organisations might foster environmental responsibility as a means of initiating innovations alongside cultivating a creative attitude.

REFERENCES

Al-Shboul, M. D. A. (2024). Do artificial intelligence system adoptions foster production management supply chain performance in pharmaceutical manufacturing firms? An empirical exploring investigation from the MENA region. *Business Process Management Journal, 30*(7), 2427–2455. DOI: 10.1108/BPMJ-02-2024-0089

Ali, A., Sharabati, A., Alqurashi, D., Shkeer, A., & Allahha, M. (2024). The influence of artificial intelligence and supply chain collaboration on supply chain resilience: Mediating the influences of information sharing. *Uncertain Management of supply chain, 12*(3), 1801-1812.

Amankwah-Amoah, J., & Lu, Y. (2024). Harnessing AI for business augment: A review of drivers and challenges in Africa. *Production Planning and Control, 35*(13), 1551–1560. DOI: 10.1080/09537287.2022.2069049

Ashiwaju, B. I., Agho, M. O., Okogwu, C., Orikpete, O. F., & Daraojimba, C. (2024). Digital transformation in pharmaceutical supply chain: An African case. *Matrix Science Pharma, 7*(3), 95–102. DOI: 10.4103/mtsp.mtsp_16_23

Ashuro, T., Kant, S., & Adula, M. (2025). Multi-Stakeholder Collaboration Effect on Sustainable Supply Chain Optimization by Mediation of Vendor Managed Inventory in the Horn of Africa. In *Multi-Stakeholder Collaboration for Sustainable Supply Chain* (pp. 203–224). IGI Global Scientific Publishing. DOI: 10.4018/979-8-3693-8925-6.ch009

Belhadi, A., Mani, V., Kamble, S. S., Khan, S. A. R., & Verma, S. (2024). Artificial intelligence-driven innovation for enhancing supply chain resilience and performance under the influence of supply chain dynamism: An empirical investigation. *Annals of Operations Research, 333*(2), 627–652. DOI: 10.1007/s10479-021-03956-x

Dza, M. (2024). Agribusiness Supply Chain Collaboration: Role of Innovation Capacity and Business Process Agility as Antecedents of Supply Chain Performance. *Journal of Operations and Strategic Planning*, 2516600X241249235.

El Jaouhari, A., & Hamidi, L. S. (2024). Assessing the influence of artificial intelligence on agri-food supply chain performance: The mediating influence of distribution network efficiency. *Technological Forecasting and Social Change, 200*, 123149. DOI: 10.1016/j.techfore.2023.123149

Jabo, D., Kant, S., Adula, M., Niguse, T., Nimbrain, N., & Chauhan, B. (2026). Mediating Function of Supply Chain Integration Among Supply Chain Strategy and Logistic Sustainability in the Coffee Industry of Gedeo Zone, Ethiopia. In *Enhancing Sustainable Performance With Low-Carbon Supply Chains* (pp. 253–280). IGI Global Scientific Publishing.

Kant, S., Ashuro, T., Adula, M., & Alemu, Z. K. (2026). Generative AI Effect on Circular Economy Sustainability by Mediation of Food Supply Chain Agility. In Impact of Generative AI on Food Supply Chain Management (pp. 67-90). IGI Global Scientific Publishing.

Kant, S., Niguse, T., Terefe, A., & Adula, M. (2025). Emerging Trends and Innovations: Effect on Social Sustainability in Manufacturing Supply Chains by Shifts in Consumer Behavior in the Horn of Africa. *Enhancing Social Sustainability in Manufacturing Supply Chains*, 135-162.

Khan, S. A. R., Sheikh, A. A., Shamsi, I. R. A., & Yu, Z. (2025). The Implications of Artificial Intelligence for Small and Medium-Sized Enterprises' Sustainable Augment in the Areas of Blockchain Technology, Supply Chain Resilience, and Closed-Loop Supply Chains. *Sustainability (Basel)*, *17*(1), 334. DOI: 10.3390/su17010334

Okoduwa, I. O., Ashiwaju, B. I., Asuzu, O. F., Arowoogun, J. O., Awonuga, K. F., & Ndubuisi, N. L. (2024). Supply chain assimilation in manufacturing: A comparative review of USA and African industries. *International Journal of Management & Entrepreneurship Investigation*, *6*(2), 254–266.

Okoye, C. C., Addy, W. A., Adeoye, O. B., Oyewole, A. T., Ofodile, O. C., Odeyemi, O., & Ololade, Y. J. (2024). Sustainable supply chain practices: A review of innovations in the USA and Africa. *International Journal of Applied Investigation in Social Sciences*, *6*(3), 292–302.

Olutimehin, D. O., Ofodile, O. C., Ejibe, I., Odunaiya, O. G., & Soyombo, O. T. (2024). THE ROLE OF TECHNOLOGY IN SUPPLY CHAIN RISK MANAGEMENT: INNOVATIONS AND CHALLENGES IN LOGISTICS. *International Journal of Management & Entrepreneurship Investigation*, *6*(3), 878–889.

Oriekhoe, O. I., Ashiwaju, B. I., Ihemereze, K. C., Ikwue, U., & Udeh, C. A. (2024). Review of technological advancements in food management of supply chain: A comparative investigation among the US and Africa. *International Journal of Management & Entrepreneurship Investigation*, *6*(1), 132–149.

Rambe, P. (2024). Digitalisation and Digital Innovation for Sustainable Business Model Augment and Creation of value: Implications for Policy and Practice for African SMMEs. In *The Future of Entrepreneurship in Southern Africa: Technological and Managerial Perspectives* (pp. 97–133). Springer Nature Switzerland. DOI: 10.1007/978-3-031-55935-8_4

KEY TERMS AND DEFINITIONS

Agility: the capacity of a business to quickly adjust to shifting consumer needs while keeping command of its supply chain and operational procedures.

AI Technology: sophisticated computer systems that automate procedures, improve decision-making, and optimize supply chain operations via the use of AI.

Continuous Improvement: a continual endeavor to improve processes, goods, or services using both small-scale and large-scale advancements in order to boost inference and quality.

Creation of Value: the method by which businesses raise the value of their goods or services, which improves financial performance, competitive advantage, and customer pleasure.

Cross-Functional Collaboration: a collaborative strategy that augments creativity and boosts overall performance by bringing together people from various departments or functional areas within a company to work toward a shared objective.

Lean Methodology: A methodical technique to outcome and removing process waste in order to maximize customer value while using the least amount of time, money, and effort.

Mediation: A statistical notion that helps explain how or why an influence arises is the influence of a third variable (the mediator) on the direction or intensity of the link among two other variables.

Organizational Culture: attitudes OF how workers collaborate and interact inside a company, which in turn influences creativity and flexibility.

Predictive Analytics: methods that support proactive decision-making in supply chains by analyzing previous data and projecting future outcomes using statistical algorithms and machine learning.

Supply Chain Innovative Practices: Organizations use innovative and forward-thinking strategies and processes to increase the inference, responsiveness, and flexibility of their supply chains.

Chapter 9
Revolutionizing Marketing Strategies:
The Role of AI in Value Creation and Consumer Engagement

Parihar Suresh Dahake
https://orcid.org/0000-0002-2286-4120
Ramdeobaba University, Nagpur, India

Sanjiv Kumar
https://orcid.org/0000-0002-8401-6346
G.H. Raisoni College of Engineering, Nagpur, India

Nihar Suresh Dahake
https://orcid.org/0009-0007-8971-9247
G.H. Raisoni College of Engineering, Nagpur, India

ABSTRACT

This paper discusses how AI is enabling companies to mainstream innovations for beat-your-competitor strategies in value creation and enhancing consumer engagement in the context of India. It illustrates the use of AI in playbooks for both segmentation and targeting in value theme creation. Interpretability is also discussed to rekindle the heterogeneity mass-market buyer-seller mismatch in product personalization. The paper provides insights for India-specific behavioral consumer engagement application challenges. Predicting behavior, unbiased features for prescient customization, telecom chatbots, identifying social media influencers, branding biases in foods and groceries, and curing e-commerce affordably can be value-generated ideas by companies to beat competitors that are being mainstreamed.

DOI: 10.4018/979-8-3373-2497-5.ch009

1) INTRODUCTION

Recently, in the digital age, Artificial Intelligence (AI) has rapidly emerged as an essential value creation tool and has found its vast application in almost every field of life(P. S. Dahake, Jain, et al., 2024). It has changed the dynamics of value co-creation activities of organizations worldwide. High social presence communication fosters parasocial interactions and dialogues, significantly impacting user satisfaction, engagement, and attitudes toward brands(Tsai et al., 2021), Exploring AI in holistic and expanded form, as a set of electronic and cutting-edge tools and techniques, has narrowed the traditional gaps in interaction with end users (i.e., retailers, clinics, customers, etc.). Building these Premises Social media marketing elements, interaction, electronic word-of-mouth and trendiness as critical drivers of consumer brand engagement, these elements effectively enhance brand awareness and brand knowledge, facilitating strong brand-building outcomes(Cheung, Pires, & Rosenberger, 2020)

Thus an ample array of opportunities have evolved for co-creating value throughout wide domains, where stakeholders can now participate in a range of novel and out-of-the-box engagement activities with service providers(Hermann, 2022a). India possesses a unique market environment paved with a set of traditions, norms, languages, cultures, and digital divide across its states and is looked upon as the shining future economy(P. S. Dahake & Dahake, 2024). In such a backdrop, the role of AI is both challenging and engaging where it has to enhance customer engagement, design products and services to add to value roaming across the state and central governments, domestic industries and foreign investments, foreign corporations, non-government organizations (NGOs), and institutions such as colleges and customer care sections, along with rural developments, at the cross-section(Sun et al., 2022). With its various roles ranging from fully or partially intelligent systems in collaborative and/or enhanced value-creation activities, AI has burgeoned in shaping new kinds of intelligent value propositions, creating and presenting value to customer behavior, and catapulting customer engagement to higher realms of experience, knowledge, satisfaction, and value customers long for.AI can enhance marketing research, strategy, and actions by automating repetitive functions, processing data, and analyzing interactions and emotions(Huang & Rust, 2021a).This period of time also marks an era of technological revolution, where artificial intelligence, big data and analytics, augmented reality and technology intervention, all of which have started to completely and totally redefine the definition of the millennium customer as we know it. Artificial intelligence will significantly change marketing strategies and customer behaviors(Davenport et al., 2020). AI represents an enabling and potentially path-breaking technology that is attracting huge investment interest from across the globe. AI has been gradually permeating through different aspects of firms, with marketing standing out as one of the potentially biggest applications of AI. Currently, the primary focus of AI applications in marketing is on the fine-grained and data-driven personalization and customization of products, services, and the marketing mix variables along the entire customer journey and service process to engage about the customers and optimize the experiential value derived from the usage about about products and services. Here is the proposed multi-layered AI marketing strategic planning framework tailored to insights from the frontier science and productive practices in this emerging area(P. S. Dahake, Chandak, et al., 2023). At the core of the multimodal framework are ramp-up tasks consisting of three generic actions: executive leadership training, the creation of enterprise-wide AI teams, and the alignment of AI projects with business strategy. the AI & AR features significantly influence utilitarian, hedonic, and experiential values, resulting in improved attitudes, decision-making, and behavioral intentions(H. Kumar, 2022),

This aids in the creation of superior customer value and enhanced customer experience, both of which contribute conspicuously to a business's long-term performance. As Brand engagement strengthens brand trust, which subsequently drives brand loyalty too(Samarah et al., 2022), That is also Recognizing the importance of AI in this regard, a few firms, albeit a handful globally, are already using AI, which is allowing them to improve their understanding of customer preferences and deliver an enhanced value proposition faster, cost-effectively and conveniently. In this research study, the primary theoretical frame is proposed to analyze and establish the advantages and disadvantages of AI Stack and Customer AI, which, in the present scenario, are primarily used as customer relationship management tools and in the creation of consumer engagement in India. This study deploys a qualitative method to derive the results. Data for this research originate from interviews, focused group discussions and some user experiences. The use of multiple data collection helps in the cross-validation of findings, thereby making the results reliable(P. S. Dahake, Chandak, et al., 2024). A thematic approach is adopted to synthesize the results of the study.

2) BACKGROUND AND RATIONALE

The AI revolution will significantly impact society and life, leading to interconnected organizations, increased global competition, and entrepreneurial opportunities(Makridakis, 2017). Currently, over 500 million people in India are on the internet with only about half of them able to read English. This has opened up a wide gap, as the internet is content-rich, but on the flip side, huge social and economic opportunities are also waiting to be explored, in this case, by another half-billion who happen to be language challenged. At the same time, the last five years have seen the blooming of AI-powered systems specialized in NLP and traditional sectors; surveys have shown that only 13% of AI implementation was in traditional sectors, but 2020 onwards, the implementation in traditional sectors like marketing, healthcare, education has surged due to the open-source community, and hence, the need was sensed to execute text-based data analysis projects. With the advent of social media and economic growth in India, customer experience is the key factor to be focused on by all firms to retain and grow its customer base, more easy, 72% of several thousand articles about Indian customer satisfaction and customer experience that have appeared in the last few years are focused directions to Indian customers(Sun et al., 2022). Indian brands have also understood the customer treaty importance of customer experience (CE). Digital content marketing fosters consumer engagement, trust, and value by creating and distributing relevant, valuable content on digital platforms, ultimately leading to increased brand equity(Hollebeek & Macky, 2019) and Modern AI and its subsets have the ability to create quantum leaps in customer experiences, and Indian businesses and marketers are to be educated about it in view of having a better customer base in upcoming years (Hermann, 2022a). These things will Improving consumer benefits through strategic strategies can create value by increasing consumer payments to an entire value system, clarifying the distinction between value creation and value capture(Priem, 2007).

3) THEORETICAL FRAMEWORK

Value is an elusive term. Value is subjective, it is not a physical property of elements themselves but of the perception of people. It varies in context. Among frameworks explaining value, the widest are the theories of value creation during business interactions that can involve the exchange of goods or services between two or more parties where Competitive Advantage is the focus of value creation and the development or exploration of business opportunities where there are no explicit physical good or services exchanged between business parties but that may involve the exchange of knowledge, access, or relationship. In between there is a multifaceted area of business relationships with deep ties between partners that include the development of joint projects alongside commercial transactions of goods and services(P. S. Dahake & Bansod, 2019). Marketing must create perceived value for customers and manage customer lifetime value to drive satisfaction, loyalty, and profitability(V. Kumar & Reinartz, 2016).In all of these frameworks, where the scope can evolve from the dyadic relationship to the intersection of multiple interactions among multiple parties, there is an acknowledge of value created through the actions of value propositions. As customers engage passively across the internet, a vast reservoir of data is generated on platforms like PCs, smartphones and smart devices, from clicking to call data. This vast expanse of data is stored in cloud databases of third parties, where data quality is complex to ensure since it is a combination of first- and third-party cookies abstracted through machine learning models, the latter being cookies of conglomerates. Even though these ad platforms are pieced together by way of auction each time served as an ad, there is value to a comprehensive marketplace in terms of negotiations off-platform. When visiting the advertiser's webpage, the agent collects the information needed to make a bid, like bid direction and valid auction regions, requests are then forwarded to the Censored Action Value model. The CAV predicts the estimated number of wins, given the historical exploring bids, and by reversing this model it is possible to infer the bid to be accepted on Real Time Bidding auctions. Prospective bids are normalized and sent to the advertiser with calibration instructions. The marketer reconciles target exposure, budget, and time with curiously placed prefetch instructions to boost the winning chances in the eyes of other marketers. These New AI-powered technologies significantly transform the customer experience, impacting each stage of the shopping journey and creating experiential value (Hoyer et al., 2020).

4) CURRENT STATUS OF AI IN INDIA

Artificial Intelligence (AI) is already here and will affect everyone and everything in the near future. One of the pillars of the third Industrial Revolution is the availability of cheap and accessible processing power. By that revolution computing is being integrated into everyday objects to communicate and act locally, with social, economic, and political effects. AI systems are advancing towards general intelligence, and there are fears that super intelligence cascades will create a runaway intelligence explosion, as machines outsmart humans and hasten the end of humanity. On the other hand, there is great hope AI can solve all issues looming on humanity. Many of those claims have also been projected on marketing and accounted for a yet greater perception of threat but also of promise.

Marketing technology became radically accessible, amassing digital inventories capable of being stalked by machines(P. S. Dahake, Bagaregari, et al., 2024). AI has entered the marketing function to boost productivity and profitability in the short run, or better, could another intelligence change the game. AI-based giant models have proven to be capable of massively scaling workflows across categories. AI services with low or no coding efforts can allow non-technical people to handle data privacy, lacing legally admissible agreements around data with zero administrative efforts. AI could allow for massive social good creation.

AI bestowed machines with feelings an empathy processing standard 20% effective in spotting the context of human feelings and brands now engage with consumers as with another human being. Brands delivering the question manually push engagement up to 37% through similarity versus dissimilarity answered cues(Hermann, 2022b).

5) GROWTH OF AI IN INDIA

Despite concerns about containing the pandemic, populations across the globe are increasingly returning to pre-COVID behaviors. It's a return to the globe's densest urban centers, bustling public transport, and all the crowded local experiences consumers have been missing. Just as the pandemic was detrimental to many industries, increased online and ad engagement was fruitful for others. Smart marketers pivoted to meet evolving economic and personal concerns, adapting their strategies to offer consumers relevant value. The rise of the omnichannel consumer is fundamentally changing the landscape of value creation, communication, and delivery. The value that brands create today is broader than individual monetary value or a single brand-consumer relationship. With the new context emerging, the focus on brand level action is inadequate, and what is required is a new creation of value across a complex network of consumers, brands, and the environment (Bajpai et al., 2018).

AI is fast becoming essential to every brand and business. As industries evolve, organizations need to be equipped for immersion in this marketplace.(N. S. Dahake, Suresh Dahake, et al., 2024) Organizations must recognize the value of AI solutions in shaping their companies for success in a digital ecosystem. The pandemic has initiated this new era, where online is the marketing strategy of the future. Current engagement is radically, quickly altering, and budget post analysis for what worked is no longer sustainable. Marketers, content creators, digital experts, and communities must be led into this arena. Teams need to be connected to the top and part of a journey to understand how AI can work from the margins of the business inwards.

AI works as a techno-social behavior to allow organizations to leverage access to analysts and data, which means emerging technologies such as natural language processing, machine learning, image recognition, and big data can radically improve processes, engagement and conversion. So what does this need from organizations? It calls for a new mindset led by dedicated business leaders who understand how consumer behaviors will change and where the opportunity lies. Leaders need to question everything; the endorsement of traditional knowledge and all recommendations should be put under scrutiny. AI works best with chaos, not certainties. Think of how the first app stores changed everything.

6) TREND OF AI IS IN INDIA

AI has been drastically transforming the way of living of people throughout the globe. In India, people are using artificial intelligence-enabled applications like Google Assistant, Siri, Alexa, etc., for better interactions. AI-enabled customer experience like Netflix and YouTube recommendations, customer chats in e-commerce applications, targeted ads on social networking sites, revolutionized bookkeeping assistance, bots for scheduling topics, etc., are expected to grow rapidly. Six AI-enabled customer engagement trends are predicted, out of which the first two will replace some of the social communications. Many applications may touch base with customers invisibly. AI assistants are expected to remain responsive and may be accessible into people's daily tasks and interactions deeply(Varghese et al., 2022a). AI refers to machines, computers, and systems that act intelligently; perform logical and numerical computations based on mathematical models created on inputs; analyze big data by recognizing the patterns and relations in order to improve their performance and to create a positive impact on the stakeholders. AI industries include AI-based solutions for financial inclusion, health, smart cities, security, sales & marketing, etc.(N. S. Dahake, Gajghate, et al., 2024), and AI-based prediction solutions for proactive behavior to address social needs like education, skill development, livelihood intervention, etc. AI-based solutions in health patterns of predicting diseases, its treatment, health follow-up, and preventive healthcare are available. The collection of relevant data from insurance and payment history, medication history, and health patterns using ML and neural network enables consideration of financial, family, and social needs of a patient(Hermann, 2022b). Literature review were conducted with thesaurus-based query formulation to search the journals reviewed and indexed in Scopus and Web of Science with the following keywords: Trend's Adoption of artificial intelligence, Challenges in acceptance of artificial intelligence, Barriers to AI Adoption in marketplaces, Trend's behaviour of artificial intelligence, AI-Related jobs, Frameworks for adoption and implementation of AI technologies, AI and marketing in general, and since 2020 Pandemic's output. Some journals provide enormous and in-depth knowledge but have too much publishing volume. Journals like AI & Society, Journal of Business Research, International Journal of Information Management.

7) UNDERSTANDING ARTIFICIAL INTELLIGENCE IN MARKETING

Artificial intelligence (AI) has revolutionized marketing strategies by enabling companies to increase the value they offer to customers (James Keegan et al., 2022).

AI enables the dynamic analysis of customer big data, which leads to improved consumer understanding and contributes to customer relationship management. AI can enhance customer engagement by standardizing routine tasks, personalizing data-rich services, and fostering relationships(Huang & Rust, 2021b). Companies use AI for online and offline marketing activities because AI has the potential to revolutionize industries like finance, healthcare, manufacturing, and retail, with its impact ranging from finance to healthcare to manufacturing to retail(Dwivedi et al., 2021). The main goal of marketing organizations is to acquire, engage, retain, and foster customers. Because these are complex processes, marketing theory divides them into four steps: attracting customers, acquiring customers, keeping customers, and promoting customers (Hermann, 2022a).: Authenticity and pre-existing attitudes toward sponsors play pivotal roles in how activations drive engagement(Schönberner & Woratschek, 2023), Significantly: Successful brand anthropomorphism on Twitter depends on emotionally resonant content and interactive strategies. Aligning message types with appropriate dialogic principles enhances consumer-brand relationships(Wu et al., 2023).Also Strategically timing and emotionally tuning live comments alongside thoughtful ad integration can optimize engagement in short-form videos. Brands and creators should leverage dynamic interactions to enhance audience response(Zhang et al., 2024). Hence there is No Doubt that, Tailoring engagement strategies to individual and team-level dynamics fosters sustained value co-creation(Liu et al., 2023)

Figure 1. Artificial Intelligence in Marketing

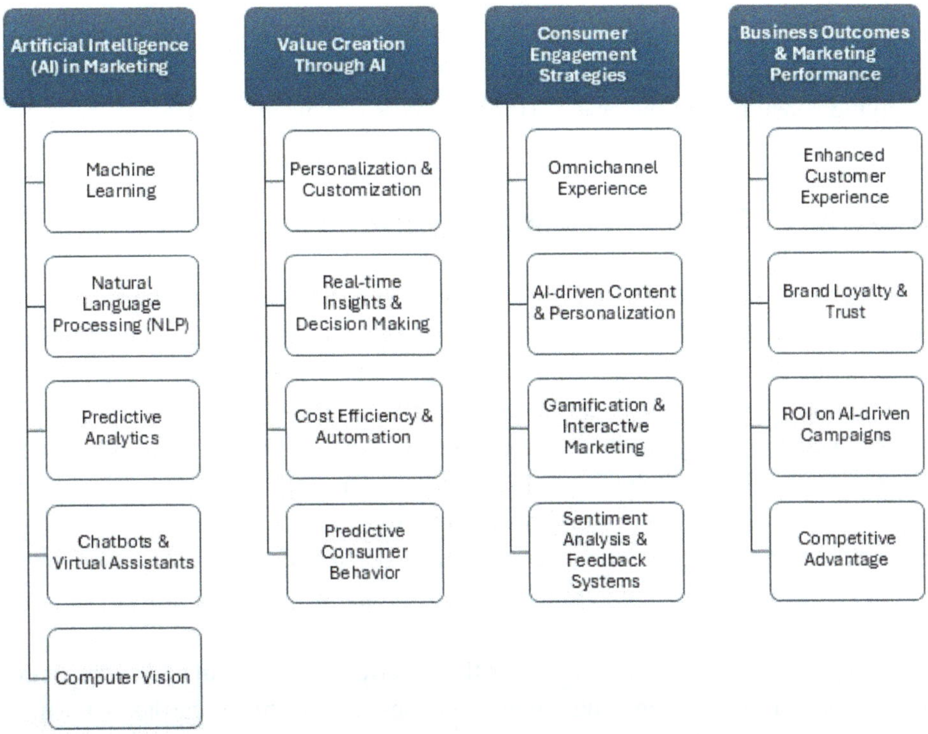

AI is revolutionizing the energy industry by increasing operational performance and efficiency, while also enhancing cybersecurity and reducing costs (Ahmad et al., 2021). India is on its way to becoming a digitally empowered country, with constant efforts towards implementing technology in various sectors. Indian marketing managers obtain insights into AI marketing, with a focus on whether AI marketing application generates change; if so, then how and what kind of changes emerge. The common use of new technology-induced AI marketing applications is criticized. Especially in the late majority and laggards stages, the disappointing marketing performance results of AI marketing application users are suggested as the main reasons preventing potential adopters from adopting such applications because Personalized consumer experiences are shifting value creation from product- and firm-centric to co-creation between consumers and firms, promoting dialogue, access, transparency, and risk-benefits(Prahalad & Ramaswamy, 2004b). These suggested reasons of contingent difficulties are further explained by a sociocultural coding scheme. Marketing activity theory is used as a theoretical framework. The framework extends existing uses and gratifications research, supporting the use and value of marketing in academia and AI marketing applications to managers and market decision-maker because Successful innovation relies on understanding consumer resistance and developing a marketing strategy to attack its causes, rather than ignoring them(Ram & Sheth, 1989). Hence Companies must shift from company-centric value creation to personalized co-creation experiences to create unique value for each individual, involving consumers in the process(Prahalad & Ramaswamy, 2004a).

8) BASICS OF ARTIFICIAL INTELLIGENCE

Artificial Intelligence (AI) is rapidly gaining momentum across different verticals, including marketing (Kose & Sert, 2017). The implications of artificial intelligence in marketing are radically changing the way marketing activities are performed. In recent years, AI has enabled data-driven marketing, allowing companies to provide improved customer experiences with the help of personalized content, offers, and advertisements. Some of the AI-enabled use cases in marketing are customer segmentation, predictive lead scoring, optimization of bids for customer acquisition, churn prediction, preference prediction, customized search results, chatbots, personalized product recommendations, and scoring customer engagement indicators to identify potential brand advocates.

AI and its subset machine learning (ML) are effective in making data-driven insights, producing predictions, and driving decisions based on historical data. Consumers' expectations for virtual co-creation vary based on their motivations and personal characteristics, with monetary reward, recognition, challenge, intrinsic interest, and curiosity being key factors(Füller, 2010). This contrasts with classical marketing statistics and econometrics, which typically estimate, given a set of assumptions, a transfer function from independent to dependent variables. AI's contribution to marketing is about value creation beyond the transfer function, by the automation of tasks, the gaining of a comprehensive understanding of data and relevant patterns beyond what human observers can notice, and the optimization of processes and campaigns (Hermann, 2022). When data, learning algorithms, computational power, and analysts are combined, this can lead to actionable outcomes, insights, and recommendations from data that are unobservable or not imaginable a priori.

AI is serving as a catalyst for wider data sharing within organizations and is fostering a convergence of mainstream marketing data and rich customer behavioral data, creating a holistic view of the customer and, in turn, enabling sophisticated marketing and service personalization. Interfaces are being developed that marry, often in real-time, data-driven analytics outputs and graphical displays, providing marketeers with advanced analytical functionalities that are more intuitive and accessible than technical programming languages. A recurring theme in the scholarly approach to leveraging AI in marketing is focusing on client-side customizable insights, underlining the relevance of providing actionable recommendations and detailed customizable analytics.

9) REVIEW OF LITERATURE

Conceptual understanding from 227 journals was taken for visualization which was conducted on VOS Viewer software. Network map was made on VOS Viewer in terms of keywords. There were 860 islands and 160 links were present in this network map. The minimum number of occurrences for a keyword to be considered was 4. With that many keyword occurrences, 12/162 detected keywords were selected as the main keyword. Nine new keywords found in this study were "artificial intelligence", "marketing", "consumers", "value", "creation", "engagement", "India", "strategy", and "culture". Main keywords with the strongest occurrences in the network map are as follows: "artificial intelligence", "marketing", "brands", "consumer engagement", "strategy", "business", "social media", "media", "culture", "industries", "technology", and "India" (Mayahi & Vidrih, 2022).

Figure 2. All Keywords Analysis by VOS Viewer

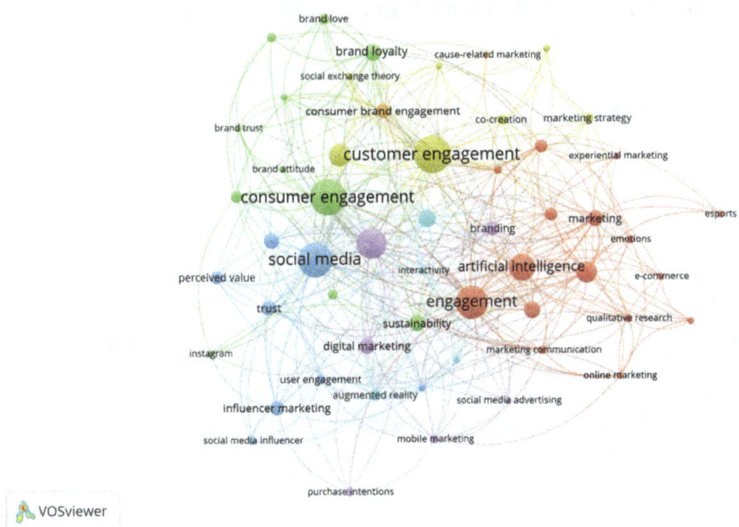

Figure 3. Author Keywords Analysis by VOS Viewer

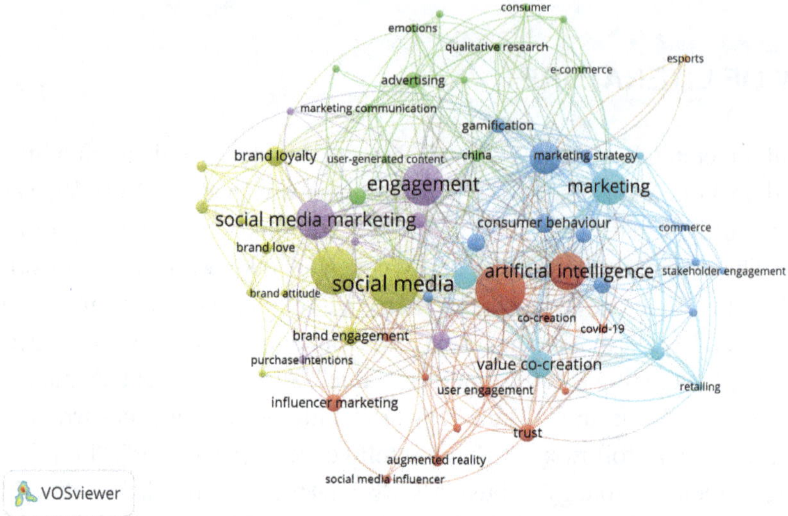

Figure 4. Index Keywords Analysis by VOS Viewer

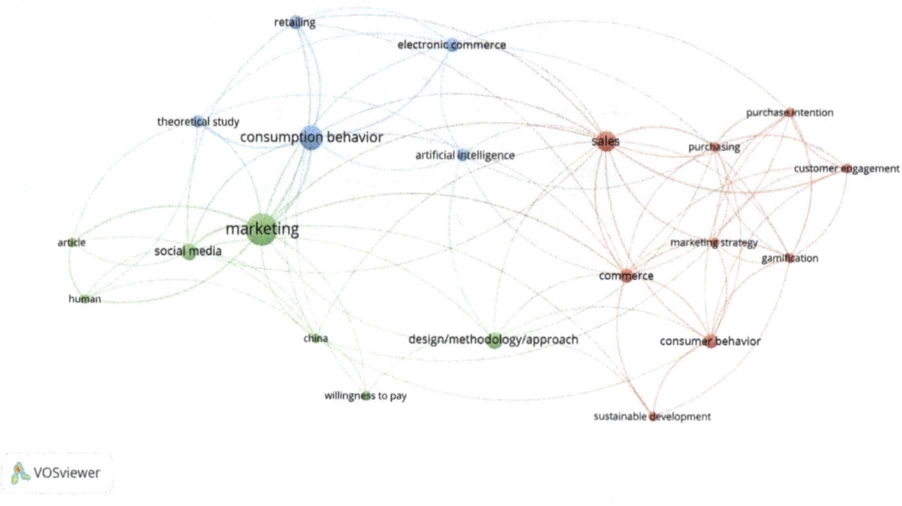

Artificial intelligence (AI) is the science and engineering of intelligent computer programs that can learn, understand, think, act, and feel like human beings. (J. Park et al., 2021)Investigated that perceived quality significantly influences functional and social value, while personal and functional value strongly drive social media WOM. Moreover, demographic factors and perceived social status act as critical moderators, affecting luxury purchase decisions. In Conjuction with (Onofrei et al., 2022) revealed that source credibility, homophily, and content quality significantly mediate the relationship between these interactions and consumer behaviors. High-quality content shared by trusted and relatable sources enhances consumer engagement, highlighting the importance of both source and message factors. Whereas, (Manser Payne et al., 2021) highlights the need to analyze AI-consumer interactions and their effects on engagement at varying levels. In addition to this (Gupta et al., 2020) Identifies external forces that influence firm capabilities, leading to data-driven and analytics-driven decision-making. Key findings emphasize the creation of value-based outcomes for firms and customers, moderated by external and internal factors. In the same way (Vander Schee et al., 2020) highlight the role of affective, cognitive, and behavioral engagement in shaping branding outcomes, including brand attitude, affirmation, and loyalty. By the same token (AlFarraj et al., 2021) evaluates the credibility of social media influencers attractiveness, trustworthiness, and expertise and their impact on purchase intention in the aesthetic dermatology industry, However (Mariani et al., 2023) reviews conversational AI adoption in marketing and consumer behavior, identifying key drivers like trust, engagement, and personalization as motivators for user interaction and oin his study he identified that the role of advanced Natural Language Processing (NLP) in designing effective conversational agents (CAs). Conversely (Muda & Hamzah, 2021) revealed that consumers' attitudes toward UGC mediate the relationship between source credibility and behavioral outcomes. Additionally, source homophily plays a crucial role, positively impacting attitudes and credibility perceptions. Subsequently (Smith & Colgate, 2007) presents a new framework for marketers to create customer value in developing new products and services, enhancing marketing strategy, and recognizing new product opportunities. In fact,(Gursoy et al., 2019) noticed that customer undergo a three-step acceptance generation process, with social influence, hedonic motivation, and anthropomorphism positively influencing performance expectancy and effort expectancy, ultimately influencing their acceptance of AI device use in service encounters. Moreover (Mostafa & Kasamani, 2022) stated that, the antecedents and consequences of initial trust in artificial intelligence (AI) chatbots, focusing on factors like compatibility, perceived ease of use, and social influence and though study it is revealed that these factors significantly enhance initial trust, which boosts chatbot usage intention and customer engagement. The AI applications in marketing have revolutionized the creation of value along the customer journey. Forging a strategic alliance between AI applications and marketing strategy, this investigation targets the evolution of marketing strategies and goes beyond the current state of the art to examine the future. It should be noted (Cheung, Pires, Rosenberger, et al., 2020) that elements like entertainment interactivity, cognitive information-transfer interaction, and up-to-date information interactivity significantly enhance consumer–brand engagement. Interestingly, customization interactivity and ease of use showed non-significant impacts. It offers a thorough understanding of how AI-enabled marketing strategies can be designed and implemented as a roadmap for practitioners. (Rabbanee et al., 2020) reveal that self-congruity, specifically social and ideal self-congruity, significantly enhances brand attachment, which mediates behaviors like liking, sharing, and commenting. Additionally, self-extension tendency (SET) moderates the link between self-congruity and brand attachment, strengthening this relationship when SET is high. To conceptualize the intricate relationship between AI and classic marketing, a comprehensive research framework is presented. The emergence of AI technologies has set the course for the paradigm shift of business and delivery, including profound implications for marketing strategies. These are relying on a logical foundation essential for all informed management decisions. AI applications in marketing rely on an extensive level of deeply created and statistically reliable marketing intelligence. Such intelligence collection and analysis systematically enhance the differentiating marketing skills which result in a superior customer advantage in creating, providing, and communicating customer value to put it differently (Bag et al., 2022) revealed a positive relationship between AI deployment and increased user engagement, leading to higher conversion rates and satisfying online shopping experiences.AI is integrated with marketing for the automation of activities carried out with the use of algorithms so that the tasks are completed faster and with higher efficiency. The AI marketing activities considered here encompass marketing research, marketing environmental scanning, marketing reporting, marketing analysis, marketing strategic planning, marketing goal setting, marketing budgeting, marketing implementation, and marketing controlling. In doing so, emphasize increased coverage, customization, and reduced skepticism, along with the potential to trigger positive word-of-mouth behaviors(Christofi et al., 2020) these marketing activities are related, first, to the content utilized for decision-making impact and, second, to the different marketing mix variables impacted. The application of AI technologies in managing the marketing mix, understanding customer behaviors, creating customer experiences, and better using marketing resources is subsequently covered(Hermann, 2022a).

Value Creation Through AI in Marketing, But Conversely (M. Park et al., 2020) suggests that maintaining psychological distance is crucial for protecting the exclusivity and core values of luxury brands in social media marketing. This offers practical insights for luxury brand managers to balance engagement and exclusivity effectively. Marketing is a crucial function as it determines the success of a business by creating value and consumer engagement. Marketing is the practice of communicating the value of a product or service to consumers for the purpose of selling the service, including market research and advertising. In business, value adds to the company's product and services and creates loyalty among consumers, leading to potential revenue growth. AI in modern times has made rapid strides with the help of machines, text, and voice in an automated manner. This support has made it possible to predict product sales well and plan operations in such a way that resources can be used effectively and efficiently. Consumers engage in marketing activities according to their knowledge of the market and brand, and they experience good or bad feelings depending on the actions of marketers. Marketers have multiple methods defined in the initial stages of the product life cycle to attract and retain consumers. However, in the era of big data, manual methods like sampling are largely ignoring important data and brands that make profit differences yet successful; AI can handle a large amount of data and find a method to make predictions. AI adoption would also improve sales forecasting, customer interaction, data analysis, and product suggestion making, highlighting the new strategies to be formulated in the marketing sector. According to these strategies, a more tailored and attractive consumer's purchasing desire is generated. As cognitive algorithms drive effective mobile commerce adoption by revealing decision-making processes underpinning technology acceptance(Andronie et al., 2021), That is why Consumer engagement is difficult to achieve, as consumer desires change frequently due to improvements in taste, technological advancements, and various other factors. One of the most important forms of business growth is revenue growth is customer activation and engagement, an essential aspect of profitability. It is a herculean task to initiate and sustain the involvement of the consumer, since the needs and wishes of consumers are different and change with time based on technological advances and taste improvement. In contrast, AI has the ability to learn from past experiences and pattern recognition engagement prediction levels, which suggests multiple business strategies should be created with the help of AI tools as it relates to both marketing and consumer engagement simultaneously.

10) PERSONALIZATION AND CUSTOMIZATION

An AI capability in a firm leads to increased organizational creativity and performance(Mikalef & Gupta, 2021). The development of artificial intelligence (AI), particularly AI-based decision support systems and chatbots, has the potential to revolutionize marketing strategies. It is suggested that AI-based decision support systems will capitalize this potential by assisting marketing decision makers in taking optimal decisions on the four components of the marketing mix, customer segments to target, and customer value management strategies. The proposed AI-based decision support system's incentive structures for the outperformance of marketing strategies are elaborated. Consumer engagement in online brand communities is complex and dynamic, with different engagement states and varying levels of intensity over time, leading to enhanced loyalty, satisfaction, empowerment, connection, emotional bonding, trust, and commitment(Brodie et al., 2013). The potential of AI-based chatbots to support tailoring-based persuasive communication strategies is discussed as well. Both types of AI-based marketing tools are expected to increase the effectiveness of marketing strategies in fueling consumption while reducing environmental or social harm. In turn, the utilization of AI in marketing can drive the need for the regulation of marketing activities and anchor sustainable marketing activities around free-market values(Hermann, 2022a).The development and broad application of AI have created the opportunity to use vast amounts of structured data and texts to predict the outcomes of future events with unprecedented accuracy. AI-enabled Marketing 4.0 framework elevates marketing by enhancing personalization, engagement, automation with dynamic capabilities(Mukhopadhyay et al., 2024). In the field of marketing, such data can be used to increase the effectiveness of marketing mix measures in the four areas of product, place, price, and promotion. Customer relationship management activities can also benefit from AI-based tools as vast amounts of information about customer needs, attitudes, and behaviors become more accessible. Hence, in the traditional areas of marketing, the utilization of AI has the potential to revolutionize marketing strategies.

11) PREDICTIVE ANALYTICS

Artificial intelligence (AI) is proving to be a crucial strategy for several businesses and helps in procuring more customer intelligence. In addition to predictive analytics on customer conversion propensity and lifetime value, several other AI models are being leveraged, such as the churning models, demand forecasting algorithms, and the models for optimized marketing mix (Bayoude et al., 2018). Like any technology, the widespread use of AI in marketing is exposing customers to numerous positives and negatives. The latter comprise, amongst others, counter-productive marketing and potential exploitation in everyday lives. From an ethical viewpoint, for fostering and ensuring fair behavior in companies, it is important to curb such negatives sooner rather than later.AI features heighten digital satisfaction(Bhatnagr & Rajesh, 2024) and AI is revolutionizing current digital marketing practices and reshaping the ways of attaining, retaining, and engaging customers. Particularly for this domain, service providers' predictive analytics on customer travel through the website, app, and social media and product conversion propensity are main fertilizers and determinants of its ever-rising soil (Hermann, 2022). An exploration of how different brands employ this powerful insight for taking immediate and medium-term marketing actions and counteracting preventive attack strategies is presented. This study goes further by detailing an ethical assessment of the discovered practices.

12) ENHANCING CONSUMER ENGAGEMENT WITH AI

With recent advancements in artificial intelligence, consumers' interests and preferences can be obtained from a company's website, customer relationship management, mobile applications, social media, and numerous other channels. Accordingly, a product and service mix can be personalized for such consumers.

Figure 5. Role of AI in Enhancing Consumer Engagement

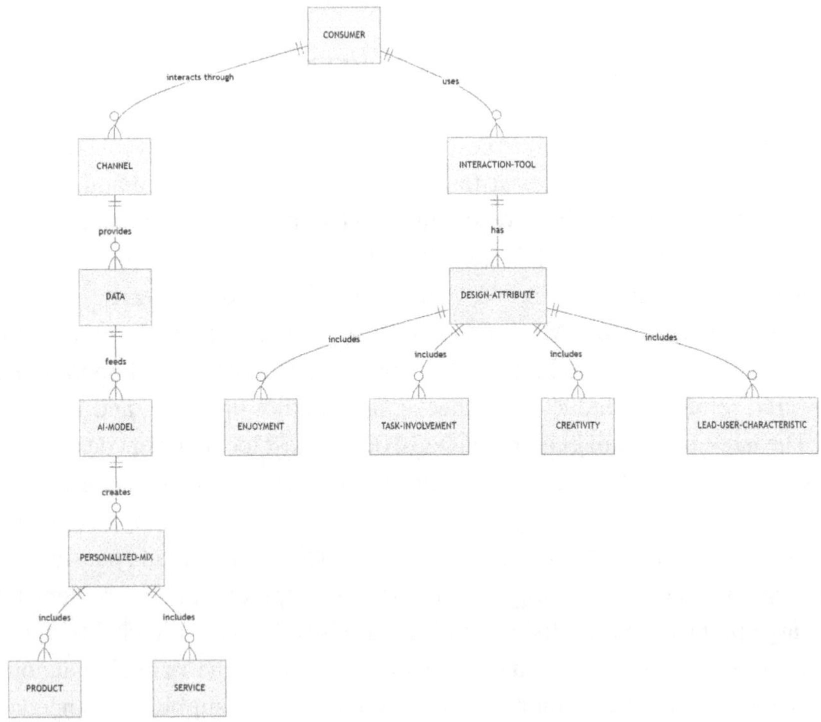

Consumer empowerment through virtual co-creation depends on the design of the interaction tool, enjoyment, task involvement, creativity, and lead-user characteristics, which in turn influence their willingness to participate in future projects(Füller et al., 2009). Thus, the artificial intelligence algorithms in marketing must be developed to understand the latent hidden preferences or interests of individual consumers.

These models might also predict a customer's clicking rate toward online campaigns or the possible websites a customer will visit. Consumers can be shown advertisements in real-time based upon their prior interests. (Sun et al., 2022) Thus far, it is widely accepted that 80% of consumer decisions are driven by emotions, which are also crucial for brand adoption. A deep learning model is integrated for analyzing unstructured content due to social media data and a consumer's interest prediction can be identified. The concept of working consumers highlights the importance of consumers' immaterial labor in increasing the value of market offerings, challenging service-dominant logic in marketing(Cova & Dalli, 2009). Knowledge is transferred across different utilizations under product categories. It is not only a time-insensitive approach but also demonstrates itself the most accurate benchmark comparison. Ultimately, a direct understanding of the connection between the machine learning and surrounding world is offered.

13) CHATBOTS AND VIRTUAL ASSISTANTS

AI is revolutionizing the business world with a broad array of applications including chatbots and virtual assistants. Businesses in developed and developing nations are making substantial investments in AI to improve and expand operations. Business volumes in excess of 1-1.5 billion USD were obtained from automation through AI-led exchanges after 5-6 years. Several technology startups specialize in offering bespoke AI and ML models to businesses that have developed growth forecast plans aimed at introducing AI scripts to drive commercial operations, run AI-powered remarks, conduct A/B checks, and predict upselling and intersecting alerts. The late-entry retail giant manages to outdo most local players despite having fully owned stores. Intelligence generation, involving four distinct modes, is essential for organizations to continuously create superior customer value by understanding and satisfying customer needs(Slater & Narver, 2000). This is made possible in part by the implementation of AI algorithms for store depreciation and replenishment and in large part by the establishment of hundreds of leases with local transporters ensuring timely restocking. As a consequence, last year, the firm also announced cut-price deals with telecommunication networks to align supply chain needs with demand stockouts in assortment screens becoming a relic of the past. AI remains a multibillion-dollar sector with revenue outperforming India's service industry for the third year in a row. Burning the midnight oil and relying on hardback town guides, hotels and taxi companies anxiously grapple with individual portions of business opportunities. AI-enhanced CSR communication, with consumer trust emerging(Hua et al., 2024) and At the same time, digital contact tracing and crowd density are entrusted to AI geospatial analysts(Varghese et al., 2022b).Consumer engagement in India is experiencing a major transformation. Live streaming services like Facebook Live can increase customer engagement and trust in small online sellers, with symbolic value directly and indirectly affecting engagement through trust in sellers and product trust(Moran et al., 2019)(Wongkitrungrueng & Assarut, 2020). India has the world's second largest internet market, driven largely by an inbuilt demographic tied to social, beauty, and e-commerce. Businesses generally take a mismatched approach in the region when planning consumer engagement options, often replicating models applied in China, which almost never succeeds. On the southern edge, a huge firm elects to create a meta-social platform. The decision pays off, when, impressed by the platform's possibilities to engage and communicate with users in a targeted way, more than 60 Indian firms adopt DSPs as their primary consumer marketing strategy, radically rethinking the role of current meta with their comprehensive consumer information advantage. In conversation, meta DSPs communicate at least 20% higher ROI and consumer LTV increases by an average of 30%. With a progressive lower-down plan agreed, companies are significantly expanding their marketing budgets in the form of ROAS triggers, making 75% of the current assets ranging from decor and milk prints to Excel ads and consumption agreements, and focused on building a more integrated shopping and entertainment ecosystem. Large consumer markets commonly use coupon offers as a key component of their consumer engagement platforms. In one giant market, thousands of companies open in e-commerce, vista, social, or streaming cylindrical screens with metaplasm is, user gratifies with a draw to receive a coupon, but only if the measure is completed, referring products and leads to viewing within a certain time frame (Perez Garcia, 2018).

14) RECOMMENDATION SYSTEMS

Nowadays, more and more companies are leveraging the profits of implementing recommender systems for customers. The rapid growth of electronic commerce and the enormous amount of data available in the digital world are facilitating the acquisition of information about the implicit preferences of users for a broad range of products or services, so that implementing recommender systems has been the cornerstone of a new wave of strategies for attracting and retaining customers. E-commerce websites have been using recommendation systems for cross-selling purposes to match customers that bought complementary items or to identify customers that are likely to buy or receptive to a given product. And combining interactive and visually rich content leads to higher consumer responses, providing actionable insights for brands seeking to optimize their content strategies for social media engagement(Moran et al., 2019). Also Digital self-efficacy and relational quality promote shared decision-making, fueling AI co-creation and adoption(Swan et al., 2024), Furthermore, with the rapid increase in the number of available items, customers find difficulties finding the ones which better suit their needs. In this line, recommendation systems have demonstrated to be an effective strategy for smoothing the search process of customers or for unveiling products to customers of which they were unaware. AI drives impulse buys in Indian fashion outlets: duration, recommendations, and interaction essential(Jain & Gandhi, 2021), Therefore, recommendation systems can be also implemented as a pull-based channel for sending individuals' advertisements recommending the most suitable products. On the other hand, it is common to find newsletter sent by web stores in which the products are chosen randomly, which often leads to unsatisfied responses. Therefore, instead of adopting a batch approach, it is more profitable to dynamically send ads that can be adjusted to a user's preferences. By profiling the customers' behavior, companies can know their preferences better and thus increase the impact of their campaigns. Newsletter sent as a recommendation system can be profitably implemented as a push-based strategy for promoting products as well (M. Gardete & D. Santos, 2020).

15) APPLICATIONS OF AI IN MARKETING

Artificial intelligence (AI) is ubiquitously deployed in marketing and has a profound impact on customer-brand interactions. The interplay between human agency and technology capability in marketing actions to analyze the value generated by AI marketing strategies (James Keegan et al., 2022). It is necessary to do a SUSTAINED EMPIRICAL STUDY that applied AI to daily news coverage. This will analyze how AI marketing actions with given activities generate realized and perceived value and how market actors navigate the use of AI. Data is generated through interviews with media professionals in charge of AI marketing actions and in-depth understanding of AI solutions.Brands can optimize influencer partnerships by aligning emotional tone and network characteristics with engagement goals(Holiday et al., 2023).

Industrial marketing, also known as business-to-business (B2B) marketing, is enjoying a boom with the commercialization and widespread adoption of AI and machine learning. In this respect, the large technology firms provide a multitude of excellent AI and machine learning applications that are effective in harnessing the vast and diverse data from customers and business stakeholders of a firm to generate actionable insights for strategic decision-making. However, most of the early academic explorations overlook the field. For firms, AI lies at the essence to contemporary industrial marketing, with AI-employed algorithms being deployed to forecast buyer behavior, analyze purchasing patterns, engage in price discrimination, prioritize worth of individual customers, and automate the sales follow-up process.

Most of these operations replaced high-powered managerial actions, predicting prices for example, performed by AI, rather than human staffs. With upwards of 73% of AI algorithmic processing in Europe and nearly 48% of the US mediated by computers, dependent AI algorithms foresee a host of variables, skewing the marketing activities in a manner unknowable by human actors. Like other disciplinary, these shifts have precipitated a slow and inconclusive conversation about the implications in the context. There is a need to outline the impacts of AI marketing actions, how participants, consisting of the activities as augmented intelligence solutions, perceive the yielded value, and how they engage in the AI-navigate activities and associated adaptations.

16) ADOPTION TRENDS IN INDIA

The Indian economy has grown rapidly in recent years, thereby resulting in increased disposable incomes and, consequently, increasing consumer expenditures, creating a ripe environment for marketing value creation by large corporations, small and medium enterprises (SMEs), and startups. The marketing discipline in India is fast catching up with the ongoing global trends and developments. COVID-19 has forced Indian firms to accelerate their initiatives to adopt AI for myriad activities and adopt alternative contactless channels, especially online sales and social media and Indian youth online retail engagement driven by economic, functional, and emotional values, boosting brand equity(Bhattacharya & Anand, 2021). Marketing in the network economy will shift from being a seller's agent to a customer consultant and manager of consumption assets, reshaping markets through technology convergence and electronic commerce(Achrol & Kotler, 1999) and AI applications in marketing in India aim at the fine-grained and data-driven personalization and customization of products, services, and the marketing mix variables along the entire customer journey and service process to engage customers and optimize experiential value, a keyword in India, while creating the consumer-centred focus.: Livestreaming services enhance customer engagement by creating interactive, value-driven experiences. Building trust through perceived value is essential for converting short-term interactions into long-term loyalty(Ye et al., 2023). The fulfillment of opportune value leads to satisfaction and, eventually, to loyalty, word of mouth, and other positive outcomes. The marketing mix encompasses the core attributes of the products (goods or services), the packaging, the labeling, engraving, the appearance (including aesthetics conveyed via scents and sounds), the messaging via advertisements and labeling, signage, etc., and the store atmosphere. It comprises a bouquet of customer-centric marketing mix activities: household (energy consumption, water use and leaks, air quality) and beauty (hair and skin) applications, wearable device usage (VR and AR) for virtual browsing, shopping, and interacting with products, online engagement and e-commerce via social media, messaging, and live Q&A sessions regarding new arrivals, products. In turn, businesses obtain detailed comments and valid data on customer wants, perceptions, preferences, and concerns (Sun et al., 2022), Thus Big data can revolutionize management by capturing business value through strategic and operational applications(Fosso Wamba et al., 2015).

17) CHALLENGES AND ETHICAL CONSIDERATIONS

The remarkable ability of AI systems to process, evaluate, and interpret vast volumes of data significantly outstrips human capability. The Internet offers a powerful platform for customer engagement in product innovation, enabling co-creation of value with customers at various stages of the New Product Development process(Sawhney et al., 2005) and with AI allows companies to analyze consumer data, execute real-time voice and image recognition, and personalize customer interactions while achieving operational efficiencies at scale. Consequently, marketing professionals are able to deliver highly personalized promotions, content, and product offers across a range of distribution platforms. While traditional empirical research on marketing-to-customer dynamics assumes marketers and consumers as two main agents, AI—in conjunction with the IoT—gives rise to "smart marketing" that includes algorithms, devices, and physical objects among these agents. AI can function in tandem with marketing objects such as products, prices, QR codes, and promotions for product recommendations, while such objects are also capable of influencing AI parameters and operations. Therefore, the role of marketers and consumers might become less involved in the design, development, and monitoring of synergies and smart interactions between AI and IoT devices. In this regard, smart marketing offers (a) personalized and localized IoT-AI product recommendations, (b) sustainable AI-IIoT price adaptation strategies, and (c) AI-manipulation-proof generic product-object promotional compatibility guidelines, each of which has several implications for academics and practitioners (Hermann, 2022).With the advancement of Artificial Intelligence (AI) and its application in marketing, a boundless treasure trove of new opportunities has opened for understanding consumer preferences and their thinking and behavior. AI in marketing captures the minds of marketing practitioners, but there are concerns regarding the potential side effects of AI in marketing and the ethical use of AI in this area (Hermann, 2022). AI in marketing has aggressively invaded so many marketing activities in terms of AI-enhanced collaboration and partnerships, infrastructure, and applications, which evoke many new and profound theoretical, conceptual, and methodological questions for marketing researchers. The advent of AI has already challenged marketer-centric concepts in terms of time and space for customer activities, multi-channel customer journeys, and relationship-building processes, and paved the way for the redefinition of brand equity, positioning, engagement, attachment, loyalty, and abandonment.

There are several ethical challenges and considerations particularly raised in AI marketing. From a broad brush point of view, these ethical challenges can be unpacked into four categories: explainability, privacy, funding and accessibility, and culture and society. AI in marketing not only helps detect and analyze related patterns but also predicts impactful unseen patterns that help optimize marketing decisions, marketing programs, and market changes. Uncovering the mechanistic processes and causal relations of AI in marketing is paramount to give rise to interpretable models that can be used for identification of control variables, enhancing decision-making reliability, robustness, and validity, and avoiding erroneous conclusions for practical action.

Privacy and boundary regulation have emerged to be core sides of the concern regarding AI use. AI systems may invade privacy by constantly monitoring, profiling, and predicting private behavior. Undercover information requests and consent or participation efforts may be seen as a new form of advertisement. AI marketing may also bring about inequalities in funding and accessibility. The development of AI systems requires massive data and better-trained algorithms. Adverse behavioral targeting may raise concerns regarding social justice and fairness. If greater advertising budgets are not allowed, there is concern that only large companies are able to achieve algorithmic targeting advantages.

18) BIAS AND FAIRNESS IN AI ALGORITHMS

In drawing on the extensive literature on ethics of AI and data privacy, the article has explored potential risks of the use of AI in marketing strategies. It has suggested two types of unintended consequences relating to bias and fairness in AI algorithms that are relevant to the design, distribution or application of AI tools in commercial marketing. The intended scope of this article has focused on AI tools to the extent that companies may be using AI to predict customer behaviours, to develop targeted messaging or content, to tailor marketing strategies, or to develop new products. Possible responses for the regulator of potential implications of AI for value creation and consumer engagement are then considered. Given the current environment where the usage of AI in marketing strategies is growing fast, potential unintended consequences of the widespread use of AI in value creation bear significant economic implications. Consumer-facing AI tools in target setting, content curation, and advertising, when not regulated properly, can perpetuate disinformation and extremist content, hide unethical corporate behaviour, marginalize smaller brands, and deepen the time of market power in the hands of big-tech monopolies. Subsequently the Frequent updates and incentives for participation are crucial for consumer engagement in branded social media content, while experiential, image, and exclusivity messages enhance customer engagement(Ashley & Tuten, 2015) this broad understanding of algorithmic fairness is that it is an ethical ideal for AI algorithms that seeks to preclude discrimination. AI fairness has become a flourishing area of research within Machine Learning. Despite the exponential growth of fairness in AI research, much of the debate continues to be centred on the concerns and histories of the West. Since fairness metrics require the delineation of protected attributes, and hence a construction of those groups in terms of pre-existing institutional delimiters, conventional measurements of algorithmic fairness make several surrounding assumptions based on the institutions and infrastructure of the West. Moreover, while there have been genuine concerns that algorithmic fairness is still too often used as a form of whitewash, an excuse to hoard proprietary models that accustom high-stakes decisions. There is some growing evidence that AI fairness serves its intended purpose, to a certain extent, by keeping AI deployments within the ethical and legal boundaries of Western societies. In contrast, there are compelling concerns that the naive generalisation of fairness will fail to keep AI deployments in check on much else of the world. At its worst, without the engagement with the conditions, values, politics, and histories of the non-West, a normativised fairness can be a tokenistic, even pernicious gesture for communities of the unseeable. If algorithmic fairness is to serve as the ethical compass of AI, it is imperative that the field of ethics of machine learning recognize its defaults, biases, and blindspots. Prejudices in machine learning arise unintentionally when mathematical artefacts are trained on imperfect training data. AI "Black Box" technologies can misinterpret subtle correlations contained in incomplete training datasets not intended for interpretation to infer biases that were not even previously reflected by the data. When it comes to images, for instance, gender bias shows up in how facial recognition programmes distinguish professional people from domestic helpers by ethnicity. For AD/HD diagnostics, it appears in an absence of sufficient clinical data on pre-manifest/adult subjects, which could incorrectly map a similar pattern of fidgety marks as inattentiveness, leading to unnecessary pharmacopeia for hyperactivity.

ML can also be maliciously exploited and intervened to gain an unfair advantage. Too low a bid for a tender can be filled with probabilistic noise. Placing offers in online-learning auctions unlikely to be attained can clog the market channel and make future auctions unprofitable. Beyond data interference or algorithmic manipulation, AI-supported marketing can face a question of ethical content. To systematically code for fairness, explainability, or transparency, affordable transparency must be aligned with the nature of proprietary algorithms nowadays dominated by digital platforms (Hermann, 2022).

Should a marketing team only detect and prevent incendiary content, or monitor it throughout the chain to caution the same fear-mongering narrative about a particular ethnic group being employed internationally while adjusting to interference patterns of a different locality? Given all this, AI-supported Marketing must innovate beyond tools and techniques to integrate ethics into the mission and practices of marketing departments and agencies alike. The aim is to go beyond purely strategic and tactical roles to address the social worthiness of marketing for the data-enabled future.

19) REAL-LIFE CASE STUDIES

Clearly, consumer behavior in India has changed, which is one of the reasons why brands are trying new tools to stay relevant. The need to reach maximum people with the right content has made businesses switch to AI. Indian brands are seeing the change and preparing to adopt AI marketing strategies(Keegan et al., 2024). AI-powered data analytics aids brands in identifying target audiences and serving customized advertisements to them, as well as dynamically fetching and adjusting ads on platforms that need quick turnaround times.

An example of AI-powered marketing is Tata Play's OTT Ads, which allows advertisers to broadcast ads on specific genres to targeted audience segments across Indian households by engaging with viewing habits. This also allows targeting audiences by demographics, such as household size, members, adult entertainment viewers, etc. As a result, the organization can curate campaigns in a more cohesive and engaging manner.

Additionally, one of the fastest-growing fashion retail brands in India, Zivame, has been localized through in-store experts and a local style tool to recommend products based on preferences, which was made possible by the trained model. The recommendations dramatically increased conversions compared to other channels. In terms of hyperlocal marketing, brands like Domino's target geolocations targeted for marketing. By using predictive algorithms, a recommendation to the user's immediate area to order from a nearby location is possible.

AI marketing is the future of marketing for brands that depend heavily on digitally generated leads, as it allows for precise targeting of the right audience. This has broad applications when delving deeper into industries with higher lead generation competitiveness, like real estate. With AI marketing, while users are searching for something related on the internet, the product and service will follow them online, creating a sense of necessity that will lead them to action.

20) FURTHER DIRECTIONS AND INNOVATIONS

As the role of marketing in bringing the growth and success of a firm into the limelight, globalization and the advent of the digital era have made marketers conscious about their strategies. Earlier, marketers solely focused on the 'product' and its properties to satisfy customer needs. The digital era, however, has flipped this concept upside down. In today's advanced world, customer-centric marketing has been receiving an enormous amount of attention from firms, marketers, and researchers alike. Artificial Intelligence (AI) encompasses a set of tools, technologies, algorithms, and software programs that facilitate machines to perform intellectual tasks that require human cognition abilities . AI acts as a marketing brain to help marketer take strategic decisions to target and engage prospective consumers effectively. While Asia-Pacific alone is disseminating its wings in digital marketing with extensive research on AI, there is an absence of empirical research on the role of AI in the value creation and consumer engagement of Indian marketers. In the wake of this, there is a need to discern the ways in which AI-driven marketing techniques have revolutionized the strategy of Indian marketers. A mediating force, across these dimensions, perceived by the marketing executives and leading them to follow a profitable path of digital and AI marketing strategies, is value creation and consumer engagement. This chapter aims to demonstrate how AI-driven marketing, when strategically approached, leads to significant value creation and consumer engagement.India has remarkably evolved its strategies. Incorporating the metaheuristic algorithm to traditional marketing has proven to be so popular and effective. The Wheel of Consumer Analysis, which combines consumer affect, cognition, behavior, environment, and marketing strategy, helps guide successful marketing activities(*Consumer Behavior*, n.d.). The intelligence produced by AI aids in targeting initial advertisements, creating creative content and maintaining customer engagement throughout; thereby fulfilling the marketer–customer gap. Contemporary marketing is exceedingly competitive and in order to survive in the market, just understanding customer behaviour is not enough. With an increase in the exploration of digital gadgets, including smart devices, the data acquisition capacity of the marketer has raised to a noteworthy level(Gillpatrick et al., 2019). Marketers are able to gather an extensive amount of data regarding customer preferences, dealing it with the existing database, and targeting customer cohorts through digital mediums. Digitization is driving innovation and change in all sectors of the economy, with platform-based cooperation and a dual innovation strategy being key instruments for enhanced value creation in the Age of Industry 4.0(Kagermann, 2015). In such pertinent circumstances, Indian marketers have begun to twig the enormous advantages of Artificial Intelligence (AI) in setting their footprints and are implementing such marketing strategies diligently to accomplish their destinations.

21) AI-DRIVEN MARKETING TRENDS

The artificial intelligence models of today are still highly dependent on the input of humans. Creativity and imagination are defining features of our species, and we believe it is essential for artists to continue investigating technology tools such as artificial intelligence. If we want to automate creativity, expressivity, and imagination, we need to exercise extra caution and have a conversation that includes both the sciences and the humanities.

22) POTENTIAL DISRUPTIONS AND OPPORTUNITIES

The rise of AI can be seen as a radical transition over the conventional Marketing Resource-based View (RBV), driven by a blend of customer-generated Big Data, query algorithms, 'smart' business media, and automated consumer analytics. For the firms, Data Analytics Reservoirs (DARs) are conceptualized as a network of knowledge-steered value chains whose very geometry promises distinctive sources of competitive advantage. For the scholars, instead of continuing the service of latent knowledge discovery, the new research landscape shifts the focus to the emerging operational, technical, and ethical challenges of consumer AI-powered engagement. A centralized Big Data hub, utterly independent, catches and sanitizes two types of customer-generated data, viz. explicit and implicit (Bashir Dar et al., 2021). A straightforward API query is released over this data, yielding the prediction of the likelihood the user will continue the price recognition process. Provided a subset of customers with a letter could contain the winning coupon, a 'smart' search in business media occurs, namely, an integration with machines curl data from a score of actively publicized commercial channels(P. S. Dahake & Somani, 2024). Finally, an algorithm assembles an automated playlist of recipes, whose supposed effects on customer habits range from increased click-through rates, through revitalizing attention susception, to a galvanizing movement dissecting.

23) RESULT & DISCUSSION BASED ON THE LITERATURE

The increasing digitalization of economies worldwide drives the proliferation and use of AI technologies including the digital marketing space, a subfield by which the advent is termed the next transformation in marketing. As AI is seen pervading numerous aspects of business, industry blogs and magazines talk how technologies will reshape commerce, empowering brands to better understand their target audience, urging the need to embed systems before competitors do so.

Simultaneously, academic consortia offer a deep understanding of how to practically harness novel technologies, getting prepared to guide clients and cultivate an innovative image. A transformation of the sales routine is proposed, envisaging how AI technologies will improve most B2B marketing activities, from pre-sale product development to post-sale customer service, bolstering the firm's competitive advantage. Spying on B2B sellers using AI in parallel shows how these firms struggle to properly implement such technologies but also how some consumer organizations harness novel tools to challenge the buyer superior position, foreshadowing novel buyer/supplier dynamics. The discussion about technology implementation evolves around Activity Theory to frame tensions, conflicts, and development scenarios while prompting both buyers and sellers to commit to smarter decisions.

Not surprisingly, industrial marketing is undergoing a boom in AI and machine learning . In North America, B2B firms are by now the most engaged in AI projects(P. S. Dahake, Parchake, et al., 2024). Large tech corporations provide software applications that take advantage of both the immense raw data these companies can harness from final consumers as well as industrial stakeholders, often overlooked by these technological giants. The aim is to enhance decision-making strategies, offering insights and analyses that would otherwise go largely unnoticed for business managers. Unlike other business sectors where AI projects happen; the industrial sector is quite unique in that AI technologies are mostly unfit to substitute core technical knowledge and activities, but can still play a pivotal role on other more traditional marketing aspects.

24) CONCLUSION AND FUTURE DIRECTIONS

In the digitally intertwined, tech-driven era where advertisement maintains a vital part in selecting products, services are produced and delivered to an individual, exploring buy based content has since become a complicated cyclist (Sun et al., 2022). It is necessary to assure proportional, insightful, and relatable goods and services, which safeguard along customer amendments. In the context of advertisement, value generation cites sales, clicks, retention, conversions, or similarly applied significances. Assuring value then requires developed content, target, planning, evaluation, strategies, and semi-automatic driving—using a method that supports created content education and its spontaneous expansion, in particular for the developing investment markets of nations such as India (Hermann, 2022). The approach investigated in this chapter explores strategies that can sustain a comprehensive, automatic customer interest by enabling the contextual promotion of deep video content(Selvakumar et al., 2025). Here the inferred content is divided into tokens that are semantically aligned across content components. Reciprocal learning from the simultaneously consumed video and text deducts the required target embeddings whilst estimating the contextual promotional probability of a given piece of viewed content. Further, the obtained embeddings of visible content after being consumed then fuel strategies to promote content interested users might pursue next. Empirical results on a diverse set of combative benchmarks gathered focusing on YouTube suggests significant improvements of the proposed methods over state-of-the-art strategies.

Advancements in the technological realm have brought innovative concepts and ideas to the larger purview(P. S. Dahake, Mohare, et al., 2023). Significantly, organizations changed their mode of operation by rapidly transitioning from conventional marketing to e-marketing. The advent of online marketing transformed the foundational principles of marketing used hitherto. Very much like the internet, artificial intelligence and machine learning technologies are increasingly changing the methods used in online marketing. Companies in the US and worldwide have taken the lead in adopting AI technologies in marketing. The efficiency of these efforts is borne out by the experience of companies like Google, Facebook, and others, which have shown that investments in this direction increase the ROI and efficiency of marketing strategies. In the Indian context, it is also essential to consider the dynamic transition that has happened. After the Digital India campaign was launched, companies have started showing more interest in online marketing and implementing AI technologies in the advertising investments. Therefore, it is important to probe how the use of artificial intelligence technology will interrupt the operation of online marketing. There will be a comprehensive analysis of the work behavior and attitude toward advertisements of consumers in the younger age category, how the use of AI technologies in online marketing changes the perception of these consumers, and how these changes contribute to better understanding the consumer pattern of engagement (Sun et al., 2022). Broadly, since artificial intelligence has a deeper effect on the psychological and cognitive process on group advertising, changes in the behavior and intention of consumer advertising for consumer engagement are very important. The clever use of natural language processing AI technologies can help generate significant insights that can be used by marketing decision-makers (Hermann, 2022).

REFERENCES

Achrol, R. S., & Kotler, P. (1999). Marketing in the Network Economy. *Journal of Marketing*, *63*(4, suppl1), 146–163. DOI: 10.1177/00222429990634s114

AlFarraj, O., Alalwan, A. A., Obeidat, Z. M., Baabdullah, A., Aldmour, R., & Al-Haddad, S. (2021). Examining the impact of influencers' credibility dimensions: Attractiveness, trustworthiness and expertise on the purchase intention in the aesthetic dermatology industry. *Review of International Business and Strategy*, *31*(3), 355–374. DOI: 10.1108/RIBS-07-2020-0089

Andronie, M., Lăzăroiu, G., tefănescu, R., Ionescu, L., & Coco atu, M. (2021). Neuromanagement decision-making and cognitive algorithmic processes in the technological adoption of mobile commerce apps. *Oeconomia Copernicana*, *12*(4), 1033–1062. DOI: 10.24136/oc.2021.034

Ashley, C., & Tuten, T. (2015). Creative Strategies in Social Media Marketing: An Exploratory Study of Branded Social Content and Consumer Engagement. *Psychology and Marketing*, *32*(1), 15–27. DOI: 10.1002/mar.20761

Bag, S., Srivastava, G., Bashir, M. M. A., Kumari, S., Giannakis, M., & Chowdhury, A. H. (2022). Journey of customers in this digital era: Understanding the role of artificial intelligence technologies in user engagement and conversion. *Benchmarking*, *29*(7), 2074–2098. DOI: 10.1108/BIJ-07-2021-0415

) Bajpai, N., Biberman, J., & Ye, Y. (2018). *National ICT-Driven Development Policy: Comparing Approaches in India and China*.

Bhatnagr, P., & Rajesh, A. (2024). Artificial intelligence features and expectation confirmation theory in digital banking apps: Gen Y and Z perspective. *Management Decision*. Advance online publication. DOI: 10.1108/MD-07-2023-1145

Bhattacharya, S., & Anand, V. (2021). What Makes the Indian Youths to Engage with Online Retail Brands: An Empirical Study. *Global Business Review*, *22*(6), 1507–1529. DOI: 10.1177/0972150918822106

Brodie, R. J., Ilic, A., Juric, B., & Hollebeek, L. (2013). Consumer engagement in a virtual brand community: An exploratory analysis. *Journal of Business Research*, *66*(1), 105–114. DOI: 10.1016/j.jbusres.2011.07.029

Cheung, M. L., Pires, G., & Rosenberger, P. J. (2020). The influence of perceived social media marketing elements on consumer–brand engagement and brand knowledge. *Asia Pacific Journal of Marketing and Logistics*, *32*(3), 695–720. DOI: 10.1108/APJML-04-2019-0262

Cheung, M. L., Pires, G. D., Rosenberger, P. J., & De Oliveira, M. J. (2020). Driving consumer–brand engagement and co-creation by brand interactivity. *Marketing Intelligence & Planning*, *38*(4), 523–541. DOI: 10.1108/MIP-12-2018-0587

Christofi, M., Vrontis, D., Leonidou, E., & Thrassou, A. (2020). Customer engagement through choice in cause-related marketing: A potential for global competitiveness. *International Marketing Review*, *37*(4), 621–650. DOI: 10.1108/IMR-04-2018-0133

Cova, B., & Dalli, D. (2009). Working consumers: The next step in marketing theory? *Marketing Theory*, *9*(3), 315–339. DOI: 10.1177/1470593109338144

Dahake, N. S., Gajghate, A., Dahake, P. S., & Bansod, S. (2024). A Transformative Impact of IoT and AI by Predictive Analytics on Modern Marketing Strategies: A Study of its Significance & Accuracy. *2024 2nd International Conference on Advances in Computation, Communication and Information Technology (ICAICCIT)*, 1150–1158. DOI: 10.1109/ICAICCIT64383.2024.10912388

Dahake, N. S., Suresh Dahake, P., & Gajghate, A. (2024). Beyond the Hype: A Critical Evaluation of Predictive Analytics Accuracy in High-Stakes Business Decisions. *2024 2nd DMIHER International Conference on Artificial Intelligence in Healthcare, Education and Industry (IDICAIEI)*, 1–6. DOI: 10.1109/IDICAIEI61867.2024.10842857

Dahake, P. S., Bagaregari, P., & Dahake, N. S. (2024). Shaping the Future of Retail: A Comprehensive Review of Predictive Analytics Models for Consumer Behavior. In Inder, S., Min, B., & Sharma, S. (Eds.), (pp. 143–160). Advances in Business Strategy and Competitive Advantage. IGI Global., DOI: 10.4018/979-8-3693-1734-1.ch011

Dahake, P. S., & Bansod, S. N. (2019). The role of Chinese electronics products to sway middle-class buyers. *International Journal of Public Sector Performance Management*, *5*(3/4), 337. DOI: 10.1504/IJPSPM.2019.10022488

Dahake, P. S., Chandak, S., & Dahake, N. S. (2024). Predictive Analytics in Performance Appraisal Systems: Enhancing Objectivity and Fairness. *2024 2nd DMIHER International Conference on Artificial Intelligence in Healthcare, Education and Industry (IDICAIEI)*, 1–5. DOI: 10.1109/IDICAIEI61867.2024.10842916

Dahake, P. S., Chandak, S., Mohare, R. V., Wadhwani, K., & Bhadade, P. (2023). The Crystal Ball of Marketing: How Predictive Analytics is Reshaping the Industry? *2023 Second International Conference On Smart Technologies For Smart Nation (SmartTechCon)*, 304–311. DOI: 10.1109/SmartTechCon57526.2023.10391334

Dahake, P. S., & Dahake, N. S. (2024). The Role of Big Data in Predictive Analytics for E-Commerce: Examine How Big Data Contributes to Better Predictions in Online Shopping. In Tarnanidis, T., Papathanasiou, J., Ismyrlis, V., & Kittu Manda, V. (Eds.), (pp. 403–426). Advances in Marketing, Customer Relationship Management, and E-Services. IGI Global., DOI: 10.4018/979-8-3693-9122-8.ch018

Dahake, P. S., Jain, M., Anusha, B., Poojitha, S., Singh, N., & Sharma, A. (2024). Integrating Organisational Theory, Resource-Based View, and Big Data Culture to Improve Manufacturing Performance. In D. Jelonek, N. Kumar, M. Chahar, R. Kinkladze, & L. Knop, *Recent Trends In Engineering and Science for Resource Optimization and Sustainable Development* (1st ed., pp. 156–159). CRC Press. DOI: 10.1201/9781003596721-36

Dahake, P. S., Mohare, R. V., & Somani, N. (2023). Exploring Machine Learning's Potential in Predicting Consumer Behavior for Captivating Marketing. *2023 Second International Conference On Smart Technologies For Smart Nation (SmartTechCon)*, 1347–1352. DOI: 10.1109/SmartTechCon57526.2023.10391558

Dahake, P. S., Parchake, S., Somani, N., & Ingale, A. R. (2024). Predictive Analytics in Automotive Consumer Behaviour: An Insight into Personal use 4-Wheeler Purchase Decisions. *2024 2nd International Conference on Advances in Computation, Communication and Information Technology (ICAICCIT)*, 1143–1149. DOI: 10.1109/ICAICCIT64383.2024.10912242

Dahake, P. S., & Somani, N. (2024). Harnessing Predictive Analytics for Accurate Consumer Behaviour Forecasting: A Comprehensive Review. *2024 2nd DMIHER International Conference on Artificial Intelligence in Healthcare, Education and Industry (IDICAIEI)*, 1–6. DOI: 10.1109/IDICAIEI61867.2024.10842743

Davenport, T., Guha, A., Grewal, D., & Bressgott, T. (2020). How artificial intelligence will change the future of marketing. *Journal of the Academy of Marketing Science*, *48*(1), 24–42. DOI: 10.1007/s11747-019-00696-0

Dwivedi, Y. K., Hughes, L., Ismagilova, E., Aarts, G., Coombs, C., Crick, T., Duan, Y., Dwivedi, R., Edwards, J., Eirug, A., Galanos, V., Ilavarasan, P. V., Janssen, M., Jones, P., Kar, A. K., Kizgin, H., Kronemann, B., Lal, B., Lucini, B., & Williams, M. D. (2021). Artificial Intelligence (AI): Multidisciplinary perspectives on emerging challenges, opportunities, and agenda for research, practice and policy. *International Journal of Information Management*, *57*, 101994. DOI: 10.1016/j.ijinfomgt.2019.08.002

Fosso Wamba, S., Akter, S., Edwards, A., Chopin, G., & Gnanzou, D. (2015). How 'big data' can make big impact: Findings from a systematic review and a longitudinal case study. *International Journal of Production Economics*, *165*, 234–246. DOI: 10.1016/j.ijpe.2014.12.031

Füller, J. (2010). Refining Virtual Co-Creation from a Consumer Perspective. *California Management Review*, *52*(2), 98–122. DOI: 10.1525/cmr.2010.52.2.98

Füller, J., Mühlbacher, H., Matzler, K., & Jawecki, G. (2009). Consumer Empowerment Through Internet-Based Co-creation. *Journal of Management Information Systems*, *26*(3), 71–102. DOI: 10.2753/MIS0742-1222260303

Gillpatrick, T., Blunck, E., & Boğa, S. (2019). UNDERSTANDING THE ROLE OF CONSUMER BEHAVIOR IN FORECASTING THE IMPACT OF INDUSTRY 4.0 AND THE WAVE OF DIGITAL DISRUPTION DRIVING INNOVATION IN RETAILING. *DIEM : Dubrovnik International Economic Meeting*, *4*(1), 165–176.

Gupta, S., Leszkiewicz, A., Kumar, V., Bijmolt, T., & Potapov, D. (2020). Digital Analytics: Modeling for Insights and New Methods. *Journal of Interactive Marketing*, *51*(1), 26–43. DOI: 10.1016/j.intmar.2020.04.003

Gursoy, D., Chi, O. H., Lu, L., & Nunkoo, R. (2019). Consumers acceptance of artificially intelligent (AI) device use in service delivery. *International Journal of Information Management*, *49*, 157–169. DOI: 10.1016/j.ijinfomgt.2019.03.008

Hermann, E. (2022a). Leveraging Artificial Intelligence in Marketing for Social Good—An Ethical Perspective. *Journal of Business Ethics*, *179*(1), 43–61. DOI: 10.1007/s10551-021-04843-y PMID: 34054170

Hermann, E. (2022b). Leveraging Artificial Intelligence in Marketing for Social Good—An Ethical Perspective. *Journal of Business Ethics*, *179*(1), 43–61. DOI: 10.1007/s10551-021-04843-y PMID: 34054170

Holiday, S., Hayes, J. L., Park, H., Lyu, Y., & Zhou, Y. (2023). A Multimodal Emotion Perspective on Social Media Influencer Marketing: The Effectiveness of Influencer Emotions, Network Size, and Branding on Consumer Brand Engagement Using Facial Expression and Linguistic Analysis. *Journal of Interactive Marketing*, *58*(4), 414–439. DOI: 10.1177/10949968231171104

Hollebeek, L. D., & Macky, K. (2019). Digital Content Marketing's Role in Fostering Consumer Engagement, Trust, and Value: Framework, Fundamental Propositions, and Implications. *Journal of Interactive Marketing*, *45*(1), 27–41. DOI: 10.1016/j.intmar.2018.07.003

Hoyer, W. D., Kroschke, M., Schmitt, B., Kraume, K., & Shankar, V. (2020). Transforming the Customer Experience through New Technologies. *Journal of Interactive Marketing*, *51*(1), 57–71. DOI: 10.1016/j.intmar.2020.04.001

Hua, X., Hasan, N. A. M., Costa, F. D., & Qiao, W. (2024). Opportunities or Challenges? The Interplay between Artificial Intelligence and Corporate Social Responsibility Communication. *Business Systems Research Journal*, *15*(1), 131–157. DOI: 10.2478/bsrj-2024-0007

Huang, M.-H., & Rust, R. T. (2021a). A strategic framework for artificial intelligence in marketing. *Journal of the Academy of Marketing Science*, *49*(1), 30–50. DOI: 10.1007/s11747-020-00749-9

Huang, M.-H., & Rust, R. T. (2021b). Engaged to a Robot? The Role of AI in Service. *Journal of Service Research*, *24*(1), 30–41. DOI: 10.1177/1094670520902266

Jain, S., & Gandhi, A. V. (2021). Impact of artificial intelligence on impulse buying behaviour of Indian shoppers in fashion retail outlets. *International Journal of Innovation Science*, *13*(2), 193–204. DOI: 10.1108/IJIS-10-2020-0181

Kagermann, H. (2015). Change Through Digitization—Value Creation in the Age of Industry 4.0. In Albach, H., Meffert, H., Pinkwart, A., & Reichwald, R. (Eds.), *Management of Permanent Change* (pp. 23–45). Springer Fachmedien Wiesbaden., DOI: 10.1007/978-3-658-05014-6_2

Keegan, B. J., Dennehy, D., & Naudé, P. (2024). Implementing Artificial Intelligence in Traditional B2B Marketing Practices: An Activity Theory Perspective. *Information Systems Frontiers*, *26*(3), 1025–1039. DOI: 10.1007/s10796-022-10294-1 PMID: 35637917

Kumar, H. (2022). Augmented reality in online retailing: A systematic review and research agenda. *International Journal of Retail & Distribution Management*, *50*(4), 537–559. DOI: 10.1108/IJRDM-06-2021-0287

Kumar, V., & Reinartz, W. (2016). Creating Enduring Customer Value. *Journal of Marketing*, *80*(6), 36–68. DOI: 10.1509/jm.15.0414

Liu, H., Perera, S. C., Wang, J.-J., & Leonhardt, J. M. (2023). Physician engagement in online medical teams: A multilevel investigation. *Journal of Business Research*, *157*, 113588. DOI: 10.1016/j.jbusres.2022.113588

Makridakis, S. (2017). The forthcoming Artificial Intelligence (AI) revolution: Its impact on society and firms. *Futures*, *90*, 46–60. DOI: 10.1016/j.futures.2017.03.006

Manser Payne, E. H., Dahl, A. J., & Peltier, J. (2021). Digital servitization value co-creation framework for AI services: A research agenda for digital transformation in financial service ecosystems. *Journal of Research in Interactive Marketing, 15*(2), 200–222. DOI: 10.1108/JRIM-12-2020-0252

Mariani, M. M., Hashemi, N., & Wirtz, J. (2023). Artificial intelligence empowered conversational agents: A systematic literature review and research agenda. *Journal of Business Research, 161*, 113838. DOI: 10.1016/j.jbusres.2023.113838

Mayahi, S., & Vidrih, M. (2022). *The Impact of Generative AI on the Future of Visual Content Marketing* (Version 1). arXiv. DOI: 10.48550/ARXIV.2211.12660

Mikalef, P., & Gupta, M. (2021). Artificial intelligence capability: Conceptualization, measurement calibration, and empirical study on its impact on organizational creativity and firm performance. *Information & Management, 58*(3), 103434. DOI: 10.1016/j.im.2021.103434

Moran, G., Muzellec, L., & Johnson, D. (2019). Message content features and social media engagement: Evidence from the media industry. *Journal of Product and Brand Management, 29*(5), 533–545. DOI: 10.1108/JPBM-09-2018-2014

Mostafa, R. B., & Kasamani, T. (2022). Antecedents and consequences of chatbot initial trust. *European Journal of Marketing, 56*(6), 1748–1771. DOI: 10.1108/EJM-02-2020-0084

Muda, M., & Hamzah, M. I. (2021). Should I suggest this YouTube clip? The impact of UGC source credibility on eWOM and purchase intention. *Journal of Research in Interactive Marketing, 15*(3), 441–459. DOI: 10.1108/JRIM-04-2020-0072

Mukhopadhyay, S., Singh, R. K., & Jain, T. (2024). Developing artificial intelligence enabled Marketing 4.0 framework: An Industry 4.0 perspective. *Qualitative Market Research, 27*(5), 841–865. DOI: 10.1108/QMR-06-2023-0086

Onofrei, G., Filieri, R., & Kennedy, L. (2022). Social media interactions, purchase intention, and behavioural engagement: The mediating role of source and content factors. *Journal of Business Research, 142*, 100–112. DOI: 10.1016/j.jbusres.2021.12.031

Park, J., Hyun, H., & Thavisay, T. (2021). A study of antecedents and outcomes of social media WOM towards luxury brand purchase intention. *Journal of Retailing and Consumer Services, 58*, 102272. DOI: 10.1016/j.jretconser.2020.102272

Park, M., Im, H., & Kim, H.-Y. (2020). "You are too friendly!" The negative effects of social media marketing on value perceptions of luxury fashion brands. *Journal of Business Research, 117*, 529–542. DOI: 10.1016/j.jbusres.2018.07.026

Prahalad, C. K., & Ramaswamy, V. (2004a). Co-creating unique value with customers. *Strategy and Leadership*, *32*(3), 4–9. DOI: 10.1108/10878570410699249

Prahalad, C. K., & Ramaswamy, V. (2004b). Co-creation experiences: The next practice in value creation. *Journal of Interactive Marketing*, *18*(3), 5–14. DOI: 10.1002/dir.20015

Priem, R. L. (2007). A Consumer Perspective on Value Creation. *Academy of Management Review*, *32*(1), 219–235. DOI: 10.5465/amr.2007.23464055

Rabbanee, F. K., Roy, R., & Spence, M. T. (2020). Factors affecting consumer engagement on online social networks: Self-congruity, brand attachment, and self-extension tendency. *European Journal of Marketing*, *54*(6), 1407–1431. DOI: 10.1108/EJM-03-2018-0221

Ram, S., & Sheth, J. N. (1989). Consumer Resistance to Innovations: The Marketing Problem and its solutions. *Journal of Consumer Marketing*, *6*(2), 5–14. DOI: 10.1108/EUM0000000002542

Samarah, T., Bayram, P., Aljuhmani, H. Y., & Elrehail, H. (2022). The role of brand interactivity and involvement in driving social media consumer brand engagement and brand loyalty: The mediating effect of brand trust. *Journal of Research in Interactive Marketing*, *16*(4), 648–664. DOI: 10.1108/JRIM-03-2021-0072

Sawhney, M., Verona, G., & Prandelli, E. (2005). Collaborating to create: The Internet as a platform for customer engagement in product innovation. *Journal of Interactive Marketing*, *19*(4), 4–17. DOI: 10.1002/dir.20046

Schönberner, J., & Woratschek, H. (2023). Sport sponsorship as a booster for customer engagement: The role of activation, authenticity and attitude. *International Journal of Sports Marketing & Sponsorship*, *24*(2), 259–277. DOI: 10.1108/IJSMS-05-2022-0098

) Selvakumar, P., Shanthi, M., Pitchiah, R., Sharma, M., Dahake, P. S., & T. C., M. (2025). The Role of Artificial Intelligence in Business Model Innovation: Overview of AI Technologies. In M. Khokhar (Ed.), *Advances in Business Strategy and Competitive Advantage* (pp. 219–246). IGI Global. DOI: 10.4018/979-8-3693-9571-4.ch009

Slater, S. F., & Narver, J. C. (2000). Intelligence Generation and Superior Customer Value. *Journal of the Academy of Marketing Science*, *28*(1), 120–127. DOI: 10.1177/0092070300281011

Smith, J. B., & Colgate, M. (2007). Customer Value Creation: A Practical Framework. *Journal of Marketing Theory and Practice*, *15*(1), 7–23. DOI: 10.2753/MTP1069-6679150101

Sun, H., Zafar, M. Z., & Hasan, N. (2022). Employing Natural Language Processing as Artificial Intelligence for Analyzing Consumer Opinion Toward Advertisement. *Frontiers in Psychology, 13*, 856663. DOI: 10.3389/fpsyg.2022.856663 PMID: 35769737

Swan, E. L., Peltier, J. W., & Dahl, A. J. (2024). Artificial intelligence in healthcare: The value co-creation process and influence of other digital health transformations. *Journal of Research in Interactive Marketing*, *18*(1), 109–126. DOI: 10.1108/JRIM-09-2022-0293

Tsai, W.-H. S., Liu, Y., & Chuan, C.-H. (2021). How chatbots' social presence communication enhances consumer engagement: The mediating role of parasocial interaction and dialogue. *Journal of Research in Interactive Marketing*, *15*(3), 460–482. DOI: 10.1108/JRIM-12-2019-0200

Vander Schee, B. A., Peltier, J., & Dahl, A. J. (2020). Antecedent consumer factors, consequential branding outcomes and measures of online consumer engagement: Current research and future directions. *Journal of Research in Interactive Marketing*, *14*(2), 239–268. DOI: 10.1108/JRIM-01-2020-0010

Varghese, M., Raj, S., & Venkatesh, V. (2022a). *Influence of AI in human lives* (Version 1). arXiv. DOI: 10.48550/ARXIV.2212.12305

Varghese, M., Raj, S., & Venkatesh, V. (2022b). *Influence of AI in human lives* (Version 1). arXiv. DOI: 10.48550/ARXIV.2212.12305

Wongkitrungrueng, A., & Assarut, N. (2020). The role of live streaming in building consumer trust and engagement with social commerce sellers. *Journal of Business Research*, *117*, 543–556. DOI: 10.1016/j.jbusres.2018.08.032

Wu, L., Dodoo, N. A., & Choi, C.-W. (2023). Brand anthropomorphism on Twitter: Communication strategies and consumer engagement. *Journal of Product and Brand Management*, *32*(6), 799–811. DOI: 10.1108/JPBM-12-2021-3787

Ye, X., Batool, H., & Huang, S.-Z. (2023). The effect of e-commerce livestreaming services on customer loyalty: A test of the chain mediation model. *Journal of Innovation and Entrepreneurship*, *12*(1), 41. DOI: 10.1186/s13731-023-00310-2

Zhang, X., Zhao, Z., & Wang, K. (2024). The effects of live comments and advertisements on social media engagement: Application to short-form online video. *Journal of Research in Interactive Marketing*, *18*(3), 485–505. DOI: 10.1108/JRIM-02-2023-0069

Compilation of References

Abduljabbar, R., Dia, H., Liyanage, S., & Bagloee, S. A. (2019). Applications of artificial intelligence in transport: An overview. As cited in World Journal of Advanced Research and Reviews, 2025.

Abutabenjeh, S., Nukpezah, J. A., & Azhar, A. (2022). Do Smart Cities Technologies Contribute to Local Economic Development? *Economic Development Quarterly*, *36*(1), 3–16. Advance online publication. DOI: 10.1177/08912424211053599

Achrol, R. S., & Kotler, P. (1999). Marketing in the Network Economy. *Journal of Marketing*, *63*(4, suppl1), 146–163. DOI: 10.1177/00222429990634s114

Ahn, T., Ryu, S., & Han, I. (2004). The impact of the online and offline features on the user acceptance of internet shopping malls. *Electronic Commerce Research and Applications*, *3*(4), 405–420.

AI Now Institute. (2023). *Algorithmic accountability in transportation*. New York University.

Alaziz, S. N., Alshowiman, A. A., Albayati, B., & El-Bagoury, A. (2023). Clustering of COVID-19 Multi-Time Series-Based K-Means and PCA With Forecasting. *International Journal of Data Warehousing and Mining*, *19*(3), 1–25. Advance online publication. DOI: 10.4018/IJDWM.317374

AlFarraj, O., Alalwan, A. A., Obeidat, Z. M., Baabdullah, A., Aldmour, R., & Al-Haddad, S. (2021). Examining the impact of influencers' credibility dimensions: Attractiveness, trustworthiness and expertise on the purchase intention in the aesthetic dermatology industry. *Review of International Business and Strategy*, *31*(3), 355–374. DOI: 10.1108/RIBS-07-2020-0089

Ali, A., Sharabati, A., Alqurashi, D., Shkeer, A., & Allahha, M. (2024). The influence of artificial intelligence and supply chain collaboration on supply chain resilience: Mediating the influences of information sharing. *Uncertain Management of supply chain, 12*(3), 1801-1812.

Aljunaid, S. K., Almheiri, S. J., Dawood, H., & Khan, M. A. (2025). Secure and Transparent Banking: Explainable AI-Driven Federated Learning Model for Financial Fraud Detection. *Journal of Risk and Financial Management, 18*(4), 179. DOI: 10.3390/jrfm18040179

Alkhoori, A. A., AL-shami, S. A., & Sedik, S. (2021). The Relationship between Leadership Factors and Successful Technopreneur through the Mediator Role of Digital Enabler. *Webology, 18*(SpecialIssue 2), 344–356. DOI: 10.14704/WEB/V18SI02/WEB18100

Alkhudhayr, H. (2025). Internet of things based parking slot detection and occupancy classification for smart city traffic management. *Engineering Applications of Artificial Intelligence, 152*, 110802. Advance online publication. DOI: 10.1016/j.engappai.2025.110802

Alnssyan, B., Ahmad, Z., Malela-Majika, J. C., Seong, J. T., & Shafik, W. (2023). On the identifiability and statistical features of a new distributional approach with reliability applications. *AIP Advances, 13*(12), 125211. Advance online publication. DOI: 10.1063/5.0178555

Al-Shboul, M. D. A. (2024). Do artificial intelligence system adoptions foster production management supply chain performance in pharmaceutical manufacturing firms? An empirical exploring investigation from the MENA region. *Business Process Management Journal, 30*(7), 2427–2455. DOI: 10.1108/BPMJ-02-2024-0089

AlSheibani, S., Cheung, Y., & Messom, C. (2018). Artificial intelligence adoption: AI-readiness at firm- level. *Pacific Asia Conference on Information Systems Proceedings*.

Alt, R., & Puschmann, T. (2012). The rise of customer-oriented banking-electronic markets are paving the way for change in the financial industry. *Electronic Markets, 22*(4), 203–215. DOI: 10.1007/s12525-012-0106-2

Amankwah-Amoah, J., & Lu, Y. (2024). Harnessing AI for business augment: A review of drivers and challenges in Africa. *Production Planning and Control, 35*(13), 1551–1560. DOI: 10.1080/09537287.2022.2069049

Amarasinghe, T., Aponso, A., & Krishnarajah, N. (2018). Critical analysis of machine learning based approaches for fraud detection in financial transactions. In *Proceedings of the 2018 International Conference on Machine Learning Technologies* (pp. 12-17). DOI: 10.1145/3231884.3231894

Amoroso, D. L., & Magnier-Watanabe, R. (2012). Building a Research Model for Mobile Wallet Consumer Adoption: The Case of Mobile Suica in Japan. *Journal of Theoretical and Applied Electronic Commerce Research*, *7*(1), 94–110.

Andreadis, I. I., Gioumouxouzis, C. I., Eleftheriadis, G. K., & Fatouros, D. G. (2022). The Advent of a New Era in Digital Healthcare: A Role for 3D Printing Technologies in Drug Manufacturing? In *Pharmaceutics* (Vol. 14, Issue 3). DOI: 10.3390/pharmaceutics14030609

Andronie, M., Lăzăroiu, G., tefănescu, R., Ionescu, L., & Coco atu, M. (2021). Neuromanagement decision-making and cognitive algorithmic processes in the technological adoption of mobile commerce apps. *Oeconomia Copernicana*, *12*(4), 1033–1062. DOI: 10.24136/oc.2021.034

Anwar, N., Widodo, A. M., Sekti, B. A., Ulum, M. B., Rahaman, M., & Ariessanti, H. D. (2024). Comparative Analysis of NIJ and NIST Methods for MicroSD Investigations: A Technopreneur Approach. *APTISI Transactions on Technopreneurship*, *6*(2), 169–181. DOI: 10.34306/att.v6i2.407

Apasrawirote, D., Yawised, K., & Muneesawang, P. (2022). Digital marketing capability: the mystery of business capabilities. In *Marketing Intelligence and Planning* (Vol. 40, Issue 4). DOI: 10.1108/MIP-11-2021-0399

Araújo, M. R. P., Sa-Barreto, L. L., Gratieri, T., Gelfuso, G. M., & Cunha-Filho, M. (2019). The digital pharmacies era: How 3D printing technology using fused deposition modeling can become a reality. In *Pharmaceutics* (Vol. 11, Issue 3). DOI: 10.3390/pharmaceutics11030128

Arena Softwares. (2025, February 25). Why schools need a smart attendance & bus tracking system in 2025. https://www.arenasoftwares.com/blog/why-schools-need-a-smart-attendance-and-bus-tracking-system-in-2025/

Arifin, Z., & Frmanzah, . (2015). The Effect of Dynamic Capability to Technology Adoption and its Determinant Factors for Improving Firm's Performance; Toward a Conceptual Model. *Procedia: Social and Behavioral Sciences*, *207*, 786–796. DOI: 10.1016/j.sbspro.2015.10.168

Ashiwaju, B. I., Agho, M. O., Okogwu, C., Orikpete, O. F., & Daraojimba, C. (2024). Digital transformation in pharmaceutical supply chain: An African case. *Matrix Science Pharma*, *7*(3), 95–102. DOI: 10.4103/mtsp.mtsp_16_23

Ashley, C., & Tuten, T. (2015). Creative Strategies in Social Media Marketing: An Exploratory Study of Branded Social Content and Consumer Engagement. *Psychology and Marketing*, *32*(1), 15–27. DOI: 10.1002/mar.20761

Ashuro, T., Kant, S., & Adula, M. (2025). Multi-Stakeholder Collaboration Effect on Sustainable Supply Chain Optimization by Mediation of Vendor Managed Inventory in the Horn of Africa. In *Multi-Stakeholder Collaboration for Sustainable Supply Chain* (pp. 203–224). IGI Global Scientific Publishing. DOI: 10.4018/979-8-3693-8925-6.ch009

Åström, J., Reim, W., & Parida, V. (2022). Value creation and value capture for AI business model innovation: A three-phase process framework. *Review of Managerial Science*, *16*(7), 2111–2133. DOI: 10.1007/s11846-022-00521-z

Atzei, N., Bartoletti, M., & Cimoli, T. (2017). A survey of attacks on Ethereum smart contracts (SoK). In *Principles of Security and Trust* (pp. 164–186). Springer., DOI: 10.1007/978-3-662-54455-6_8

Bag, S., Srivastava, G., Al Bashir, M. M., Kumari, S., Giannakis, M., & Chowdhury, A. H. (2022). Journey of customers in this digital era: Understanding the role of artificial intelligence technologies in user engagement and conversion. *Benchmarking*, *29*(7), 2074–2098. Advance online publication. DOI: 10.1108/BIJ-07-2021-0415

Bakare, Y. B. (2023). Machine Learning-Based Smart Irrigation System and Soil Nutrients analysis to Increase Productivity in Agriculture Field. *AIP Conference Proceedings*, *2523*, 020030. Advance online publication. DOI: 10.1063/5.0116007

Barney, J. (1991). Firm Resources and Sustained Competitive Advantage. *Journal of Management*, *17*(1), 99–120. DOI: 10.1177/014920639101700108

Bartosik-Purgat, M., & Filimon, N. (2022). European consumers in the digital era: Implications of technology, media and culture on consumer behavior. In *European Consumers in the Digital Era: Implications of Technology*. Media and Culture on Consumer Behavior., DOI: 10.4324/9781003263685

BBC News. (2019). Millions using 123456 as password, security study finds, 21-Apr-2019. [Accessed: 23-Jul-2019].

Belhadi, A., Mani, V., Kamble, S. S., Khan, S. A. R., & Verma, S. (2024). Artificial intelligence-driven innovation for enhancing supply chain resilience and performance under the influence of supply chain dynamism: An empirical investigation. *Annals of Operations Research*, *333*(2), 627–652. DOI: 10.1007/s10479-021-03956-x

Bernot, G., Claude Gaudel, M., & Marre, B. (1991). Software testing based on formal specifications: A theory and a tool. *Software Engineering Journal*, *6*(6), 387–405. DOI: 10.1049/sej.1991.0040

Bharathi, D., Palanisamy, R., Moses, L., Shanmugam, K., & Rangasamy, N. (2024). Smart detection and repulsive system for animal intrusion. *AIP Conference Proceedings, 3112*(1), 020003. DOI: 10.1063/5.0214577

Bhatnagr, P., & Rajesh, A. (2024). Artificial intelligence features and expectation confirmation theory in digital banking apps: Gen Y and Z perspective. *Management Decision*. Advance online publication. DOI: 10.1108/MD-07-2023-1145

Bhattacharya, S., & Anand, V. (2021). What Makes the Indian Youths to Engage with Online Retail Brands: An Empirical Study. *Global Business Review*, *22*(6), 1507–1529. DOI: 10.1177/0972150918822106

Bishop, C. M. (2006). *Pattern recognition and machine learning*. Springer.

Bliznets, I. A., Kartskhiya, A. A., & Smirnov, M. G. (2018). Technology Transfer in Digital Era: Legal Environment. *Tarih Kültür ve Sanat Arastirmalari Dergisi*, *7*(1), 354. Advance online publication. DOI: 10.7596/taksad.v7i1.1466

Boonmoh, A., Jumpakate, T., & Karpklon, S. (2021). Teachers' perceptions and experience in using technology for the classroom. *CALL-EJ, 22*(1).

Bourbon, B., & Murimi, R. (2024). Decentralization, Blockchains, and the Development of Smart Communities in Economically Challenging Environments. *Ledger*, *9*, 30–50. DOI: 10.5195/ledger.2024.302

Bridgestone, E. M. E. A. (2024). Webfleet AI fleet study. https://press.bridgestone-emea.com/fleet-managers- expect-artificial-intelligence-and-electric-vehicles-to-have-biggest-impact-on-fleet-management- in-the-coming-years-global-webfleet-study-reveals/

Brock, J. K.-U., & Von Wangenheim, F. (2019). Demystifying AI: What digital transformation leaders can teach you about realistic artificial intelligence. *California Management Review*, *61*(4), 110–134. DOI: 10.1177/1536504219865226

Brodie, R. J., Ilic, A., Juric, B., & Hollebeek, L. (2013). Consumer engagement in a virtual brand community: An exploratory analysis. *Journal of Business Research*, *66*(1), 105–114. DOI: 10.1016/j.jbusres.2011.07.029

Brynjolfsson, E., & Mcafee, A. (2017) The Business of Artificial Intelligence. Harvard Business Review, 7, 3-11. Retrieved August 7, 2025, from https://www.scirp.org/reference/referencespapers?referenceid=3524395

Budiarti, I., Hibatulloh, F., & Salman, M. (2021). Financial Technology as Payment Methods in the Digital Era. *International Journal of Research and Applied Technology*, *1*(1), 9–16. Advance online publication. DOI: 10.34010/injuratech.v1i1.5454

Business Insider. (2025). How Uber Freight is leveraging AI to make truck routes more efficient. https://www.businessinsider.com/ai-trucking-logistics-uber-freight-tech-optimize-routes-2025-4

Byrne, B. M. (1998). *Structural Equation Modeling with LISREL, PRELIS, and SIMPLIS: Basic Concepts, Applications, and Programming*. Lawrence Erlbaum Associates.

Carter, L., & Liu, D. (2025). How was my performance? Exploring the role of anchoring bias in AI-assisted decision making. *International Journal of Information Management*, *82*, 102875. Advance online publication. DOI: 10.1016/j.ijinfomgt.2025.102875

Chang, K. W. (2022). Interdisciplinary treatment in the digital era. *APOS Trends in Orthodontics*, *12*(2), 71–76. Advance online publication. DOI: 10.25259/APOS_126_2022

Chatterjee, P., Das, D., & Rawat, D. B. (2024). "A Generative AI Approach for Ensuring Data Integrity Security Resilience in Fintech Systems," 2024 IEEE 24th International Symposium on Cluster, Cloud and Internet Computing Workshops (CCGridW), Philadelphia, PA, USA, pp. 168-173, DOI: 10.1109/CCGridW63211.2024.00027

Chatterjee, S., Rana, N. P., Tamilmani, K., & Sharma, A. (2021) The Role of Artificial Intelligence in Reshaping Digital Marketing A Review and Research Agenda. Journal of Business Research, 124, 202-217. - Retrieved August 7, 2025, from https://www.scirp.org/reference/referencespapers?referenceid=4040078

Chatterjee, S., Rana, N. P., Tamilmani, K., & Sharma, A. (2021). The effect of AI-based CRM on organization performance and competitive advantage: An empirical analysis in the B2B context. *Industrial Marketing Management*, *97*, 205–219. DOI: 10.1016/j.indmarman.2021.07.013

Cheah, C. M., Oon, K. M., Teo, A. C., Tan, B. I., & Sim, J. J. (2011). Factors Affecting Malaysian Mobile Banking Adoption: An Empirical Analysis. *International Journal of Network and Mobile Technologies*, *2*(3), 149–160.

Chen, D. M., & Lai, P. C. (2023). *Exploration on Teaching Innovation and Reform of "Computer Application Fundamentals" Course in Higher Vocational Colleges: Taking Guangzhou City Construction College as an Example. echnology Management and Its Social Impact on Education.* IGI Global.

Chen, G., Han, T. X., He, Z., Kays, R., & Forrester, T. (2014). Deep convolutional neural network based species recognition for wild animal monitoring. In *2014 IEEE International Conference on Image Processing (ICIP)* (pp. 858–862). IEEE. https://doi.org/DOI: 10.1109/ICIP.2014.7025172

Chen, X. S., & Lai, P. C. (2023). The novel thinking exploration model for Blockchain Technology Financial Sharing Services. *Journal of Information Systems and Technology Management*. Advance online publication. DOI: 10.4301/S1807-1775202320005

Chen, Y., Wang, Y., Nevo, S., Jin, J., Wang, L., & Chow, W. S. (2014). IT capability and organizational performance: The roles of business process agility and environmental factors. *European Journal of Information Systems*, *23*(3), 326–342. DOI: 10.1057/ejis.2013.4

Cheung, M. L., Pires, G. D., Rosenberger, P. J., & De Oliveira, M. J. (2020). Driving consumer–brand engagement and co-creation by brand interactivity. *Marketing Intelligence & Planning*, *38*(4), 523–541. DOI: 10.1108/MIP-12-2018-0587

Cheung, M. L., Pires, G., & Rosenberger, P. J. (2020). The influence of perceived social media marketing elements on consumer–brand engagement and brand knowledge. *Asia Pacific Journal of Marketing and Logistics*, *32*(3), 695–720. DOI: 10.1108/APJML-04-2019-0262

Chiasson, S. and Biddle, R. (2007). "Issues in User Authentication," Semantic Scholar, 08-Mar-2007.

Chiba, Z., Abghour, N., Moussaid, K., El Omri, A., & Rida, M. (2019). Intelligent and improved self-adaptive anomaly based intrusion detection system for networks. *International Journal of Communication Networks and Information Security*, *11*(2), 312–330.

Choi, T. M., Wallace, S. W., & Wang, Y. (2018). Big data analytics in operations management. *Production and Operations Management*, *27*(10), 1868–1883.

Christofi, M., Vrontis, D., Leonidou, E., & Thrassou, A. (2020). Customer engagement through choice in cause-related marketing: A potential for global competitiveness. *International Marketing Review*, *37*(4), 621–650. DOI: 10.1108/IMR-04-2018-0133

Ciancarini, P., Iorio, A. D., Nuzzolese, A. G., Peroni, S., & Vitali, F. (2013). Semantic Annotation of Scholarly Documents and Citations. AI*IA. "CAPTCHA: Telling Humans and Computers Apart Automatically," The OÔ¨Écial CAPTCHA Site. [Online]. Available: http://www.captcha.net/. [Accessed: 27-Jul-2019].

CiGen. (2025). AI-powered fleet management: Optimizing costs, routes, and vehicle utilization. https://www.cigen.io/insights/ai-powered-fleet-management-optimizing-costs-routes-and-vehicle- utilization

Codework. (2024). AI Technologies Powering DHL's Logistics Success. https://thecodework.com/explore/ai-technologies-powering-dhls-logistics-success/

Commission work programme 2023—European Commission. (n.d.). Retrieved August 6, 2025, from https://commission.europa.eu/strategy-and-policy/strategy-documents/commission-work-programme/commission-work-programme-2023_en

Cooper, D. R., & Schindler, P. S. (2008). *Business research methods* (10th ed.). McGraw-Hill.

Cova, B., & Dalli, D. (2009). Working consumers: The next step in marketing theory? *Marketing Theory*, *9*(3), 315–339. DOI: 10.1177/1470593109338144

Cyber Risk for the Financial Sector: A Framework for Quantitative Assessment, WP/18/143, July 2018. (n.d.). Retrieved August 7, 2025, from https://download
.ssrn.com/18/06/26/ssrn_id3203026_code524055.pdf?response-content-disposition
=inline&X-Amz-Security-Token=IQoJb3JpZ2luX2VjEFAaCXVzLWVhc3Q
tMSJHMEUCIFSFYmXX7prbvGt3C6XGppwzr5Dk9bBd5P0jhjMntAblAiEA7gC
xrssH3wnwtuuIKfJozu9%2FTarxMUuMYqS26xGDKREqxwUIif%2F%2F%2F
%2F%2F%2F%2F%2F%2F%2F%2FARAEGgwzMDg0NzUzMDEyNTciDNjx2rp3N
FLIsgAoAyqbBYLaiTIGyFwRyV7wxmf%2FK1VS9mHlnq%2F5e6AWUg6u6hC
VGGnHKBgBaGbseWccu6iDrX3ZAlhc96sriEy08hm%2FenPMEVAfIF4N
5FH6FA0wSHvDfZrM0jrAcg2yDgGiYdWUtl71WxfW6YZWN740e8
CYClzTsqo8iB37HSiB7HvkHwR3cCFNS8Q4YC7xfizLNTTexcfT%2F4rGpo
QqEsIGQAIt5bjIPRx1gk%2FkbSMKpoz%2Btq615YJXYBBxfYiiOib367lgsJ88
Bvpxg25URJ%2FHEgt6UT58Mc%2ByuTQWbmjoR88N5vp6J3DCUfODU
mBAfVbTTd3Lz50YNmqGc9m7kJRVqIetOKzHezHngSrMMvaKDrf
%2FEmIHpojog28tRzbTfa5XDzmWxPLewj7OcDUEUKuu9zxcm7y1BRV7R8n6
Gza5Tmz7xVyVurwQf8ii%2BMnO3eynDhu%2BpPlL1Blc6qwJEMydGZ
ZfO1V8pMyslUUU8GwdBUWA1n1zH8k6%2BjYZy9vRFb%2BOvKZoJKE
%2FKD%2FVOwbAHmpnpU8DWeZ0784LEMl%2FzDLA%2BTVPhzopwJg
jSbNItF5o7bzQsJHMBuOsS2bXDKwu8%2FfTr%2BmT1rr90Y9IIu7K1wu%2B
nCHP6xvsD0YQSjvuQ50v%2FUo9HW7%2BZWQHjWrNt44fZYSLqINW
UkjurJX5SY%2B%2FFG3VGI8aFoFIwXxUmQGmK2dzictIq6W7rDR
%2FA64cy1Uh4ssURYhD8Oprkd7jwq%2FMklXpqEyVMFBFh39yAXy
EdJGUjtUNM%2B09pj9Wvb2RwOsoY1JpS%2FdC13UEqUgxH7N9qQ
%2B4tQJMr4jE1C9ARYxM91EIhYQo5KB8iJ9mU%2FdKnUMefD3oQfIk
oAkGkc5NgL%2BUPKbJfZOVkzA78MCCathBhHnd9qAwqLPRxAY6sQF
4jLmwBuixRlcDvgs8edYxkjHdWH5Rj%2BN6R3XvVCjxe4U9B5NVW6tOi4T
ery38Fm485ssVNaTGMpQpY3n7hzEgevqvDbK3Elx%2BvDvM2%2FA
%2BMlpkpGjLE4sOOmcbVm3Nx5%2Fzqlo9wHS92LPsPx%2BVxsRqnNno
oeJqSAQDLYBoj4vjGZLy%2BeAJrHeOb0j4l03g59aZCK%2FuCge3GdNNf
xaQPEZNAfoXm3Aimt5QIXNYlnqDbHw%3D&X-Amz-Algorithm=AWS4-
HMAC-SHA256&X-Amz-Date=20250807T081537Z&X-Amz-SignedHeaders=
host&X-Amz-Expires=300&X-Amz-Credential=ASIAUPUUPRWEZF4XKSEK
%2F20250807%2Fus-east-1%2Fs3%2Faws4_request&X-Amz-Signature=
a7fa28c3112acc2c146d1a7ed7829707d1ef9824fb45e1ce9cc9236095966f36&
abstractId=3203026

Dahake, N. S., Gajghate, A., Dahake, P. S., & Bansod, S. (2024). A Transformative Impact of IoT and AI by Predictive Analytics on Modern Marketing Strategies: A Study of its Significance & Accuracy. *2024 2nd International Conference on Advances in Computation, Communication and Information Technology (ICAICCIT)*, 1150–1158. DOI: 10.1109/ICAICCIT64383.2024.10912388

Dahake, N. S., Suresh Dahake, P., & Gajghate, A. (2024). Beyond the Hype: A Critical Evaluation of Predictive Analytics Accuracy in High-Stakes Business Decisions. *2024 2nd DMIHER International Conference on Artificial Intelligence in Healthcare, Education and Industry (IDICAIEI)*, 1–6. DOI: 10.1109/IDICAIEI61867.2024.10842857

Dahake, P. S., & Somani, N. (2024). Harnessing Predictive Analytics for Accurate Consumer Behaviour Forecasting: A Comprehensive Review. *2024 2nd DMIHER International Conference on Artificial Intelligence in Healthcare, Education and Industry (IDICAIEI)*, 1–6. DOI: 10.1109/IDICAIEI61867.2024.10842743

Dahake, P. S., Chandak, S., & Dahake, N. S. (2024). Predictive Analytics in Performance Appraisal Systems: Enhancing Objectivity and Fairness. *2024 2nd DMIHER International Conference on Artificial Intelligence in Healthcare, Education and Industry (IDICAIEI)*, 1–5. DOI: 10.1109/IDICAIEI61867.2024.10842916

Dahake, P. S., Jain, M., Anusha, B., Poojitha, S., Singh, N., & Sharma, A. (2024). Integrating Organisational Theory, Resource-Based View, and Big Data Culture to Improve Manufacturing Performance. In D. Jelonek, N. Kumar, M. Chahar, R. Kinkladze, & L. Knop, *Recent Trends In Engineering and Science for Resource Optimization and Sustainable Development* (1st ed., pp. 156–159). CRC Press. DOI: 10.1201/9781003596721-36

Dahake, P. S., Parchake, S., Somani, N., & Ingale, A. R. (2024). Predictive Analytics in Automotive Consumer Behaviour: An Insight into Personal use 4-Wheeler Purchase Decisions. *2024 2nd International Conference on Advances in Computation, Communication and Information Technology (ICAICCIT)*, 1143–1149. DOI: 10.1109/ICAICCIT64383.2024.10912242

Dahake, P. S., Bagaregari, P., & Dahake, N. S. (2024). Shaping the Future of Retail: A Comprehensive Review of Predictive Analytics Models for Consumer Behavior. In Inder, S., Min, B., & Sharma, S. (Eds.), (pp. 143–160). Advances in Business Strategy and Competitive Advantage. IGI Global., DOI: 10.4018/979-8-3693-1734-1.ch011

Dahake, P. S., & Bansod, S. N. (2019). The role of Chinese electronics products to sway middle-class buyers. *International Journal of Public Sector Performance Management*, *5*(3/4), 337. DOI: 10.1504/IJPSPM.2019.10022488

Dahake, P. S., Chandak, S., Mohare, R. V., Wadhwani, K., & Bhadade, P. (2023). The Crystal Ball of Marketing: How Predictive Analytics is Reshaping the Industry? *2023 Second International Conference On Smart Technologies For Smart Nation (SmartTechCon)*, 304–311. DOI: 10.1109/SmartTechCon57526.2023.10391334

Dahake, P. S., & Dahake, N. S. (2024). The Role of Big Data in Predictive Analytics for E-Commerce: Examine How Big Data Contributes to Better Predictions in Online Shopping. In Tarnanidis, T., Papathanasiou, J., Ismyrlis, V., & Kittu Manda, V. (Eds.), (pp. 403–426). Advances in Marketing, Customer Relationship Management, and E-Services. IGI Global., DOI: 10.4018/979-8-3693-9122-8.ch018

Dahake, P. S., Mohare, R. V., & Somani, N. (2023). Exploring Machine Learning's Potential in Predicting Consumer Behavior for Captivating Marketing. *2023 Second International Conference On Smart Technologies For Smart Nation (SmartTechCon)*, 1347–1352. DOI: 10.1109/SmartTechCon57526.2023.10391558

Dalam, P. M., Kinerja, P., Melalui, U., Keuangan, L., Digital, D., Desa, M. Di, Kecamatan, K., Kabupaten, P., Sriyono1, P., Sugiarto2, H., Dearelsa3, G. B., Anisyah4, D., Nur, F., & Islakhudin5, A. (2022). The Role of Mbkm in Improving MSME Performance Through Financial Literacy and Digital Marketing in Ketanireng Village, Prigen District, Pasuruan Regency. *Pssh.Umsida.Ac.Id.*

Davenport, T. H., & Mittal, N. (2023b). Stop Tinkering with AI. *Harvard Business Review, 2023-Janua*. Retrieved from https://www.scopus.com/inward/record.uri?eid=2-s2.0-85158877740&partnerID=40&md5=0f3e957470856651b8c3a4737d340160a

Davenport, T. H., & Ronanki, R. (2018). Artificial Intelligence for the Real World. Harvard Business Review (HBR). - Retrieved August 7, 2025, from https://www.scirp.org/reference/referencespapers?referenceid=3166319

Davenport, T. H., & Mittal, N. (2023a). How companies can prepare for the coming "AI-first" world. *Strategy and Leadership*, *51*(1), 26–30. DOI: 10.1108/SL-11-2022-0107

Davenport, T., Guha, A., Grewal, D., & Bressgott, T. (2020). How artificial intelligence will change the future of marketing. *Journal of the Academy of Marketing Science*, *48*(1), 24–42. DOI: 10.1007/s11747-019-00696-0

Davis, F. D. (1989). Perceived usefulness, perceived ease of use, and user acceptance of information technology. *Management Information Systems Quarterly*, *13*(3), 319–340.

Davis, F. D., & Venkatesh, V. (1996). "A critical assessment of potential measurement biases in the technology acceptance model: Three experiments," Internet J. Human-Comput. *Stud*, *45*, 19–45.

dbt Labs. (2024, Nov 27). Data governance frameworks for AI model development. https://www.getdbt.com/blog/data-governance-frameworks-ai

Dellermann, D., Lipusch, N., Ebel, P., & Leimeister, J. M. (2019). Design principles for a hybrid intelligence decision support system for business model validation. *Electronic Markets*, *29*(3), 423–441. DOI: 10.1007/s12525-018-0309-2

Demirkiran, Y., & Öztürko lu, Ö. (2022). Key Performance Measures and Digital-Era Technologies in Warehouses. *Operations and Supply Chain Management*, *15*(2). Advance online publication. DOI: 10.31387/oscm0490340

Dewan and Chen. (2005). Mobile payment adoption in the US: A cross-industry, cross platform solution. *Journal of Information Privacy and Security*, *1*(2), 4–25.

DHL Press Release. (2024, June 24). DHL launches My Global Trade Services (MyGTS) platform for AI- powered cross-border logistics. https://www.dhl.com/th-en/home/press/press-archive/2024/dhl- express-introduces-ai-powered-online-platform-my-global-trade-services.html

Digital Economy Report 2021 I UN Trade and Development (UNCTAD). (n.d.). Retrieved August 1, 2025, from https://unctad.org/page/digital-economy-report-2021

DigitalDefynd. (2025). 5 Ways UPS is Using AI. https://digitaldefynd.com/IQ/ups-use-ai-case-study/

DiMaggio, P. J., & Powell, W. W. (1983). The Iron Cage Revisited: Institutional Isomorphism and Collective Rationality in Organizational Fields. *American Sociological Review*, *48*(2), 147. DOI: 10.2307/2095101

Dong, F., Yin, J., Xiang, J., Chang, Z., Gu, T., & Han, F. (2023). EWM-FCE-ODM-Based Evaluation of Smart Community Construction: From the Perspective of Residents' Sense of Gain. *Sustainability (Basel)*, *15*(8), 6587. Advance online publication. DOI: 10.3390/su15086587

Dorathy, M. B. C. (2017). Green Shipping - A plethora of business opportunities for ecopreneurs. *International Journal of Civil Engineering and Technology*, *8*(5), 189–198. https://www.scopus.com/inward/record.uri?eid=2-s2.0-85020138162&partnerID=40&md5=9cfc1ceec0a8793a631e78190514dc8d

Dubey, R., Gunasekaran, A., Childe, S. J., Bryde, D. J., Giannakis, M., Foropon, C., Roubaud, D., & Hazen, B. T. (2020). Big data analytics and artificial intelligence pathway to operational performance under the effects of entrepreneurial orientation and environmental dynamism: A study of manufacturing organisations. *International Journal of Production Economics*, *226*, 107599. Advance online publication. DOI: 10.1016/j.ijpe.2019.107599

Dwivedi, Y. K. Kshetri, N., Hughes, L., Slade, E. L., Jeyaraj, A., Kar, A. K., … Wright, R. (2023). Opinion Paper: "So what if ChatGPT wrote it?" Multidisciplinary perspectives on opportunities, challenges and implications of generative conversational AI for research, practice and policy. *International Journal of Information Management, 71*, 102642. https://doi.org/https://doi.org/10.1016/j.ijinfomgt.2023.102642

Dwivedi, Y. K., Hughes, L., Ismagilova, E., Aarts, G., Coombs, C., Crick, T., Duan, Y., Dwivedi, R., Edwards, J., Eirug, A., Galanos, V., Ilavarasan, P. V., Janssen, M., Jones, P., Kar, A. K., Kizgin, H., Kronemann, B., Lal, B., Lucini, B., & Williams, M. D. (2021). Artificial Intelligence (AI): Multidisciplinary perspectives on emerging challenges, opportunities, and agenda for research, practice and policy. *International Journal of Information Management*, *57*, 101994. Advance online publication. DOI: 10.1016/j.ijinfomgt.2019.08.002

Dza, M. (2024). Agribusiness Supply Chain Collaboration: Role of Innovation Capacity and Business Process Agility as Antecedents of Supply Chain Performance. *Journal of Operations and Strategic Planning*, 2516600X241249235.

El Abbadi, N. K., & Alsaadi, E. M. T. A. (2020, April). *An automated vertebrate animals classification using deep convolution neural networks*. In *2020 International Conference on Computer Science and Software Engineering (CSASE)*. IEEE. https://doi.org/DOI: 10.1109/CSASE48920.2020.9142070

El Jaouhari, A., & Hamidi, L. S. (2024). Assessing the influence of artificial intelligence on agri-food supply chain performance: The mediating influence of distribution network efficiency. *Technological Forecasting and Social Change*, *200*, 123149. DOI: 10.1016/j.techfore.2023.123149

Elwaked, D. K., Kassim, N. M., & Thurasamy, R. (n.d.). Enhancing Internal Integration Through Ai: A Resource-Based View With Data-Driven Culture As Moderator.

Elyta, M., Martoyo, , & Herlan, . (2021). Formulation Model of Power Based Technopreneurship in the Digital Technology Era. *International Journal on Advanced Science, Engineering and Information Technology*, *11*(6), 2344. Advance online publication. DOI: 10.18517/ijaseit.11.6.10968

Eubanks, V. (2018). *Automating inequality: How high-tech tools profile, police, and punish the poor*. St. Martin's Press.

European approach to artificial intelligence | Shaping Europe's digital future. (n.d.). Retrieved August 7, 2025, from https://digital-strategy.ec.europa.eu/en/policies/european-approach-artificial-intelligence

European Commission. (2021). *Ethics guidelines for trustworthy AI*. Publications Office of the European Union.

Executive Program in Social Innovation Design. (n.d.). The Center for Social Impact Strategy. Retrieved August 7, 2025, from https://csis.upenn.edu/executive-program/xsd/

Experiment: https://github.com/nazgulseralina/IGI-Global_experiment

Facility Executive. (2024). AI and fleet adoption: Building readiness. https://facilityexecutive.com

Floridi, L., & Cowls, J. (2022). A unified framework of five principles for AI in society. *Machine Learning and the City: Applications in Architecture and Urban Design*, 535–545.

Fortuna, K. L., Myers, A. L., Walsh, D., Walker, R., Mois, G., & Brooks, J. M. (2020). Strategies to increase peer support specialists' capacity to use digital technology in the era of COVID-19: Pre-post study. *JMIR Mental Health*, *7*(7), e20429. Advance online publication. DOI: 10.2196/20429 PMID: 32629424

Fosso Wamba, S., Akter, S., Edwards, A., Chopin, G., & Gnanzou, D. (2015). How 'big data' can make big impact: Findings from a systematic review and a longitudinal case study. *International Journal of Production Economics*, *165*, 234–246. DOI: 10.1016/j.ijpe.2014.12.031

Fu, JL, Lai, P. C., (2023) Construction of Occupational Competence Model for Higher Vocational Teachers. Technology Management and Its Social Impact on Education, 165-184

Füller, J. (2010). Refining Virtual Co-Creation from a Consumer Perspective. *California Management Review*, *52*(2), 98–122. DOI: 10.1525/cmr.2010.52.2.98

Füller, J., Mühlbacher, H., Matzler, K., & Jawecki, G. (2009). Consumer Empowerment Through Internet-Based Co-creation. *Journal of Management Information Systems*, *26*(3), 71–102. DOI: 10.2753/MIS0742-1222260303

Ganguly, A. K., Bhattacharya, S., & Chattopadhyay, S. (2024). "AI-Enabled Customer Authentication for Efficient and Secure AI-Driven Model for Banking Fintech Transaction," 2024 4th International Conference on Advance Computing and Innovative Technologies in Engineering (ICACITE), Greater Noida, India, pp. 482-486, DOI: 10.1109/ICACITE60783.2024.10616904

Ghasemaghaei, M., & Kordzadeh, N. (2024). Understanding how algorithmic injustice leads to making discriminatory decisions: An obedience to authority perspective. *Information & Management, 61*(2), 103921. Advance online publication. DOI: 10.1016/j.im.2024.103921

Gheibi, O., Weyns, D., & Quin, F. (2021). Applying machine learning in self-adaptive systems: A systematic literature review. [TAAS]. *ACM Transactions on Autonomous and Adaptive Systems, 15*(3), 1–37. DOI: 10.1145/3469440

Ghimire, P., Kim, K., & Acharya, M. (2024). Opportunities and Challenges of Generative AI in Construction Industry: Focusing on Adoption of Text-Based Models. *Buildings (Basel, Switzerland), 14*(1), 1. Advance online publication. DOI: 10.3390/buildings14010220

Ghosh, S., Chatterjee, S., & Malhotra, R. (2023). AI in logistics: A meta-review. *Journal of Business Research, 160*, 113702.

Gillpatrick, T., Blunck, E., & Boğa, S. (2019). UNDERSTANDING THE ROLE OF CONSUMER BEHAVIOR IN FORECASTING THE IMPACT OF INDUSTRY 4.0 AND THE WAVE OF DIGITAL DISRUPTION DRIVING INNOVATION IN RETAILING. *DIEM : Dubrovnik International Economic Meeting, 4*(1), 165–176.

Goodyear, P. (2021). Navigating difficult waters in a digital era: Technology, uncertainty and the objects of informal lifelong learning. *British Journal of Educational Technology, 52*(4), 1594–1611. Advance online publication. DOI: 10.1111/bjet.13107

Gopal, S., Gupta, P., & Minocha, A. "Advancements in Fin-Tech and Security Challenges of Banking Industry," 2023 4th International Conference on Intelligent Engineering and Management (ICIEM), London, United Kingdom, 2023, pp. 1-6, doi: DOI: 10.1109/ICIEM59379.2023.10165876

GreenRoad. (2025). Top fleet safety trends to watch in 2025.

Gupta, A., Sharma, S., & Mangal, M. (2025). Animal repellent smart system using AI-based edge computing. *African Journal of Biological Sciences*. https://www.researchgate.net/publication/370281687_Animal_Repellent_Smart_System_using_AI_based_Edge_Computing

Gupta, S., Leszkiewicz, A., Kumar, V., Bijmolt, T., & Potapov, D. (2020). Digital Analytics: Modeling for Insights and New Methods. *Journal of Interactive Marketing, 51*(1), 26–43. DOI: 10.1016/j.intmar.2020.04.003

Gursoy, D., Chi, O. H., Lu, L., & Nunkoo, R. (2019). Consumers acceptance of artificially intelligent (AI) device use in service delivery. *International Journal of Information Management, 49*, 157–169. DOI: 10.1016/j.ijinfomgt.2019.03.008

Hamming, R. W. (1950). Error detecting and error correcting codes. *The Bell System Technical Journal*, *29*(2), 147–160. DOI: 10.1002/j.1538-7305.1950.tb00463.x

Haralick, R. M., Shanmugam, K., & Dinstein, I. (1973). Textural features for image classification. *IEEE Transactions on Systems, Man, and Cybernetics*, *SMC-3*(6), 610–621. DOI: 10.1109/TSMC.1973.4309314

Harbani, M., Muna, N., & Judiarni, J. A. (2021). Digital Leadership in Facing Challenges in the Era Industrial Revolution 4.0. *Webology*, *18*(Special Issue), 975–990. Advance online publication. DOI: 10.14704/WEB/V18SI05/WEB18275

Harrison, R., Scheela, W., Lai, P. C., & Vivekarajah, S. (2017). Beyond institutional voids and the middle income trap? The emerging business angel market in Malaysia. *Asia Pacific Journal of Management*, •••, 1–27.

Hashim, H. (2018). Application of Technology in the Digital Era Education. *International Journal of Research in Counseling and Education*, *1*(2), 1. Advance online publication. DOI: 10.24036/002za0002

Hasin, H., Johari, Y. C., & Jamil, A. (2022). Accountant's Digital Technologies Competencies in The Digitalisation Era. *International Journal of Academic Research in Business & Social Sciences*, *12*(10). Advance online publication. DOI: 10.6007/IJARBSS/v12-i10/14894

Hazzan, M. K. (2022). Deception in the era of digital technologies and the distortion of reality and facts: An X-Ray of Nigerian peculiarities. *E-Learning and Digital Media*. Advance online publication. DOI: 10.1177/20427530221124002

Heffner, H. E., & Heffner, R. S. (2007). Hearing ranges of laboratory animals. *Journal of the American Association for Laboratory Animal Science; JAALAS*, *46*(1), 20–22. PMID: 17203911

Henderson, R., & Divett, M. J. (2003). Perceived usefulness, ease of use and electronic supermarket use. *International Journal of Human-Computer Studies*, *59*(3), 383–395.

Herman, H., Sherly, S., Sinaga, Y. K., Sinurat, B., Sihombing, P. S. R., Panjaitan, M. B., Purba, L., Sinaga, J. A. Br., Marpaung, T. I., & Tannuary, A. (2022). Socialization of The Implementation of Digital Literacy for Educators and Students in The Digital Era in Pematangsiantar City. *JURNAL KREATIVITAS PENGABDIAN KEPADA MASYARAKAT (PKM)*, *5*(6). DOI: 10.33024/jkpm.v5i6.5864

Hermann, E. (2022a). Leveraging Artificial Intelligence in Marketing for Social Good—An Ethical Perspective. *Journal of Business Ethics*, *179*(1), 43–61. DOI: 10.1007/s10551-021-04843-y PMID: 34054170

Hidayat, A. S., & Pok, W. C. (2025). Empowering SMEs innovation through intangible factors. *Journal of Innovation and Entrepreneurship, 14*(1), 1. Advance online publication. DOI: 10.1186/s13731-024-00437-w

Holiday, S., Hayes, J. L., Park, H., Lyu, Y., & Zhou, Y. (2023). A Multimodal Emotion Perspective on Social Media Influencer Marketing: The Effectiveness of Influencer Emotions, Network Size, and Branding on Consumer Brand Engagement Using Facial Expression and Linguistic Analysis. *Journal of Interactive Marketing, 58*(4), 414–439. DOI: 10.1177/10949968231171104

Hollebeek, L. D., & Macky, K. (2019). Digital Content Marketing's Role in Fostering Consumer Engagement, Trust, and Value: Framework, Fundamental Propositions, and Implications. *Journal of Interactive Marketing, 45*(1), 27–41. DOI: 10.1016/j.intmar.2018.07.003

Hoyer, W. D., Kroschke, M., Schmitt, B., Kraume, K., & Shankar, V. (2020). Transforming the Customer Experience through New Technologies. *Journal of Interactive Marketing, 51*(1), 57–71. DOI: 10.1016/j.intmar.2020.04.001

Huang, M. H., & Rust, R. T. (2018). Artificial intelligence in service. *Journal of Service Research, 21*(2), 155–172.

Huang, M.-H., & Rust, R. T. (2021a). A strategic framework for artificial intelligence in marketing. *Journal of the Academy of Marketing Science, 49*(1), 30–50. DOI: 10.1007/s11747-020-00749-9

Huang, M.-H., & Rust, R. T. (2021b). Engaged to a Robot? The Role of AI in Service. *Journal of Service Research, 24*(1), 30–41. DOI: 10.1177/1094670520902266

Hua, X., Hasan, N. A. M., Costa, F. D., & Qiao, W. (2024). Opportunities or Challenges? The Interplay between Artificial Intelligence and Corporate Social Responsibility Communication. *Business Systems Research Journal, 15*(1), 131–157. DOI: 10.2478/bsrj-2024-0007

Hu, L., & Bentler, P. M. (1999). Cutoff criteria for fit indexes in covariance structure analysis: Conventional criteria versus new alternatives. *Structural Equation Modeling, 6*(1), 1–55.

Humphrey, D. B., & Aris, K., & Grete √ò. (2004). The future of cash: Falling legal use and implications for government policy. *Journal of International Financial Markets, Institutions and Money, 14*(3), 221–223.

Husain, A. P. (2021). Pendidikan Karakter pada Anak Usia Dasar dalam Pembelajaran Daring di Era Digital. *Nusantara: Jurnal Pendidikan Indonesia, 1*(3), 439–456. Advance online publication. DOI: 10.14421/njpi.2021.v1i3-1

Ibrahim, S. M., Alshraideh, M. A., Leiner, M., Aldajani, I. M., & Ouarda, B. (2024). Artificial intelligence ethics: Ethical consideration and regulations from theory to practice. *IAES International Journal of Artificial Intelligence*, *13*(3), 3703–3714. DOI: 10.11591/ijai.v13.i3.pp3703-3714

IEEE. (2019). *Ethically aligned design: A vision for prioritizing human well-being with autonomous and intelligent systems*. IEEE Standards Association.

India banking and finance report 2024. (2024). Academic Foundation in association with National Institute of Bank Management (NIBM), Pune.

Indmall Automation. (2024). Predictive maintenance in transport fleets. https://www.indmallautomation.com/faq/what-is-the-growth-rate-of-industrial-iot/

Intangles. (2024). Fleet savings from accident reduction. https://intangles.ai/

Intangles. (2025, May 7). Fleet cost leaks: Hidden expenses you can eliminate with predictive analytics. https://www.intangles.ai/fleet-cost-leaks-hidden-expenses-you-can-eliminate-with-predictive- analytics/

Iotinsider. (2025). La Poste partners with Pathway to create digital twin of fleet. https://www.iotinsider.com/news/la-poste-partners-with-pathway-to-create-digital-twin-of-fleet/

Ismandianto, I., Suyanto, S., Latifah, K., & Muchid, M. (2022). Transformation of Radio Technology in The Digital Age. *Nyimak: Journal of Communication*, *6*(1), 115. Advance online publication. DOI: 10.31000/nyimak.v6i1.5547

ISO/SAE. (2021). *Road vehicles-Cybersecurity engineering (ISO/SAE 21434:2021)*. International Organization for Standardization.

Istenič, A., Rosanda, V., Volk, M., & Gačnik, M. (2023). Parental Perceptions of Child's Play in the Post-Digital Era: Parents' Dilemma with Digital Formats Informing the Kindergarten Curriculum. *Children (Basel, Switzerland)*, *10*(1), 101. Advance online publication. DOI: 10.3390/children10010101 PMID: 36670651

Jaafar, M., Jalali, A., Suffarruddin, S. H., & Ramasamy, N. (2023). The Determinants of Becoming Sustainable Agropreneurs: Evidence from the Bottom 40 Groups in Malaysia. *Sustainability (Basel)*, *15*(10), 8283. Advance online publication. DOI: 10.3390/su15108283

Jabo, D., Kant, S., Adula, M., Niguse, T., Nimbrain, N., & Chauhan, B. (2026). Mediating Function of Supply Chain Integration Among Supply Chain Strategy and Logistic Sustainability in the Coffee Industry of Gedeo Zone, Ethiopia. In *Enhancing Sustainable Performance With Low-Carbon Supply Chains* (pp. 253–280). IGI Global Scientific Publishing.

Jain, S., & Gandhi, A. V. (2021). Impact of artificial intelligence on impulse buying behaviour of Indian shoppers in fashion retail outlets. *International Journal of Innovation Science*, *13*(2), 193–204. DOI: 10.1108/IJIS-10-2020-0181

Jarrahi, M. H., Newlands, G., Butler, B., Savage, S., Lutz, C., Dunn, M., & Sawyer, S. (2021). Flexible work and personal digital infrastructures. *Communications of the ACM*, *64*(7), 72–79. DOI: 10.1145/3419405

Jun, Y., Craig, A., Shafik, W., & Sharif, L. (2021). Artificial Intelligence Application in Cybersecurity and Cyberdefense. In *Wireless Communications and Mobile Computing* (Vol. 2021). DOI: 10.1155/2021/3329581

Kagermann, H. (2015). Change Through Digitization—Value Creation in the Age of Industry 4.0. In Albach, H., Meffert, H., Pinkwart, A., & Reichwald, R. (Eds.), *Management of Permanent Change* (pp. 23–45). Springer Fachmedien Wiesbaden., DOI: 10.1007/978-3-658-05014-6_2

Kant, S., Ashuro, T., Adula, M., & Alemu, Z. K. (2026). Generative AI Effect on Circular Economy Sustainability by Mediation of Food Supply Chain Agility. In Impact of Generative AI on Food Supply Chain Management (pp. 67-90). IGI Global Scientific Publishing.

Kant, S., Niguse, T., Terefe, A., & Adula, M. (2025). Emerging Trends and Innovations: Effect on Social Sustainability in Manufacturing Supply Chains by Shifts in Consumer Behavior in the Horn of Africa. *Enhancing Social Sustainability in Manufacturing Supply Chains*, 135-162.

Kapoor, N., Kapoor, T., Sisodiya, D. R., & Sushma, J. (2024). "Impact of Fintech: Revolution in Banking and Financial Industry," 2024 IEEE 4th International Conference on ICT in Business Industry & Government (ICTBIG), Indore, India, pp. 1-6, DOI: 10.1109/ICTBIG64922.2024.10911635

Kasthuri, U., Priyadharshini, P., Dhanush, R., Kumar, P. S., Madhu, N. G., & Riyaz, M. D. (2025). Enhancing animal repellent system using AI and deep learning. *Atlantis Press*. https://www.atlantis-press.com/article/126011278.pdf

Keegan, B. J., Dennehy, D., & Naudé, P. (2024). Implementing Artificial Intelligence in Traditional B2B Marketing Practices: An Activity Theory Perspective. *Information Systems Frontiers*, *26*(3), 1025–1039. DOI: 10.1007/s10796-022-10294-1 PMID: 35637917

Khan, S. A. R., Sheikh, A. A., Shamsi, I. R. A., & Yu, Z. (2025). The Implications of Artificial Intelligence for Small and Medium-Sized Enterprises' Sustainable Augment in the Areas of Blockchain Technology, Supply Chain Resilience, and Closed-Loop Supply Chains. *Sustainability (Basel)*, *17*(1), 334. DOI: 10.3390/su17010334

Kitsios, F., & Kamariotou, M. (2021). Artificial Intelligence and Business Strategy towards Digital Transformation: A Research Agenda. *Sustainability (Basel)*, *13*(4), 4. Advance online publication. DOI: 10.3390/su13042025

Kollmann, T., Kleine-Stegemann, L., de Cruppe, K., & Then-Bergh, C. (2022). Eras of Digital Entrepreneurship: Connecting the Past, Present, and Future. *Business & Information Systems Engineering*, *64*(1), 15–31. Advance online publication. DOI: 10.1007/s12599-021-00728-6

Kontaxis, G., Polychronakis, M., & Markatos, E. P. (2012). Minimizing information disclosure to third parties in social login platforms. *International Journal of Information Security*, *11*(5), 321–332.

Krejcie, R., & Morgan, D. W. (1970). Determining Sample size for Research Activities. *Educational and Psychological Measurement*, *30*, 607–610.

Kruthi, H., Nisarga, A. C., Supriya, D. K., Sanjay, C. R., & Mohan Kumar, K. S. (2021). Animal detection using deep learning algorithm. *International Journal of Advanced Research in Computer and Communication Engineering*, *10*(6).

Kuang, B. W., & Lai, P. C. (2023) Factors Influencing Behavioural Intention to Use e-CNY Among College Students in Guangzhou City, China. Technology Management and Its Social Impact on Education, 185-201, IGI Global

Kumar, A., Jindal, K., Sharma, H., & Chaudhary, A. (2024). "Enhancing Syndicate Lending Through AI-Powered Fine-Tuning: Leveraging LLAMA2 for Dynamic Decision Support," 2024 International Conference on Communication, Computer Sciences and Engineering (IC3SE), Gautam Buddha Nagar, India, pp. 342-347, DOI: 10.1109/IC3SE62002.2024.10593463

Kumar, H. (2022). Augmented reality in online retailing: A systematic review and research agenda. *International Journal of Retail & Distribution Management*, *50*(4), 537–559. DOI: 10.1108/IJRDM-06-2021-0287

Kumar, R. (2021). Managing Business in the Digital Era–The use of IT and Analytics for Process Transformation. *Journal of Decision Systems, 30*(4), 410–413. Advance online publication. DOI: 10.1080/12460125.2021.1925397

Kumar, S., Arya, R. K., Singh, N., & Singh, S. (2024). Productivity of rainfed maize as influenced by hydrogel and mulching under conventional and zero tillage in maize–wheat cropping system. *Cereal Research Communications*, *52*(2), 885–898.

Kumar, V., & Reinartz, W. (2016). Creating Enduring Customer Value. *Journal of Marketing*, *80*(6), 36–68. DOI: 10.1509/jm.15.0414

Kurniawan, A., Suwarno, , Komara, B. D., Rajiani, I., & Prasetya, A. (2019). Small and medium enterprises (SMES) in the era digital marketing technology. *International Journal of Recent Technology and Engineering*, *8*(3), 8532–8535. Advance online publication. DOI: 10.35940/ijrte.B3774.098319

Lai, P. C. (2024). Image Security App (ISA): A cognitive approach to secure authentication. Internal White Paper.

Lai, P. C. (2018). Research, Innovation and Development Strategic Planning for Intellectual Property Management. *Economic Alternatives.*, *12*(3), 303–310.

Lai, P. C. (2023). Intention to use the innovative Covid-19 technology "TheSafeCheck" Solution. 19 (1-19). *Journal of Information Systems and Technology Management*. Advance online publication. DOI: 10.4301/S1807-1775202219016

Lai, P. C., & Lim, C. S. (2019).. . *The Effects of Efficiency, Design and Enjoyment on Single Platform E-payment Research in Business and Management*, *6*(2), 19–34.

Lai, P. C., & Tong, D. L. (2022). *An Artificial Intelligence-Based Approach to Model User Behavior on the Adoption of E-Payment. Handbook of Research on Social Impacts of E-Payment and Blockchain*. IGI Global.

Lamine, W., Mian, S., Fayolle, A., & Linton, J. D. (2021). Educating scientists and engineers for technology entrepreneurship in the emerging digital era. In *Technological Forecasting and Social Change* (Vol. 164). DOI: 10.1016/j.techfore.2020.120552

Latour, B. (2005). *Reassembling the social: An introduction to actor-network-theory*. Oxford university press.

LeCun, Y., Bottou, L., Bengio, Y., & Haffner, P. (1998). Gradient-based learning applied to document recognition. *Proceedings of the IEEE*, *86*(11), 2278–2324. DOI: 10.1109/5.726791

Lee, K. F. (2018). AI Superpowers China, Silicon Valley, and the New World Order. Houghton Mifflin Harcourt. - Retrieved August 1, 2025, from https://www.scirp.org/reference/referencespapers?referenceid=3933846

Lee, I., Ali, S., Zhang, H., DiPaola, D., & Breazeal, C. (2021). Developing middle school students' AI literacy. In *Proceedings of the 52nd ACM technical symposium on computer science education* (pp. 191–197). DOI: 10.1145/3408877.3432513

Lee, T. M., & Jun, J. K. (2007). The role of contextual marketing offer in Mobile commerce acceptance: Comparison between Mobile Commerce users and nonusers. *International Journal of Mobile Communications*, *5*(3), 339–356.

Lee, Y., Kozar, K. A., & Larsen, K. R. T. (2003). The technology acceptance model; past, present and future. *Communication of AIS*, *12*(50), 752–780.

Liebig, L., Güttel, L., Jobin, A., & Katzenbach, C. (2024). Subnational AI policy: Shaping AI in a multi-level governance system. *AI & Society*, *39*(3), 1477–1490. DOI: 10.1007/s00146-022-01561-5

Li, K., Cai, Y., Pei, Y., & Yuan, C. (2025). The impact of artificial intelligence adoption on firms' innovation performance in the digital era: Based on dynamic capabilities theory. *International Theory and Practice in Humanities and Social Sciences*, *2*(3), 3. Advance online publication. DOI: 10.70693/itphss.v2i3.343

Li, N., & Huang, F. (2024). Evaluating the Financial Returns on Investment in Sustainable Enterprise Digitalization Initiatives Using AI Information System. *Journal of Internet Services and Information Security*, *14*(4), 21–44. DOI: 10.58346/JISIS.2024.I4.002

LinkedIn. (2024, February 21). AI integration challenges in legacy fleet systems. https://www.linkedin.com/pulse/integrating-ai-legacy-systems-challenges-strategies-josh-denton- pksqe/

Lin, Y., Ahmad, Z., Shafik, W., Khosa, S. K., Almaspoor, Z., Alsuhabi, H., & Abbas, F. (2021). Impact of Facebook and Newspaper Advertising on Sales: A Comparative Study of Online and Print Media. *Computational Intelligence and Neuroscience*, *2021*(1), 5995008. Advance online publication. DOI: 10.1155/2021/5995008 PMID: 34475947

Liu, H., Perera, S. C., Wang, J.-J., & Leonhardt, J. M. (2023). Physician engagement in online medical teams: A multilevel investigation. *Journal of Business Research*, *157*, 113588. DOI: 10.1016/j.jbusres.2022.113588

Liu, Y., & Du, Y. (2025). The Effect of Generative AI Ethics on Users' Continuous Usage Intentions: A PLS-SEM and fsQCA Approach. *International Journal of Human-Computer Interaction, 41*(20), 12831–12842. Advance online publication. DOI: 10.1080/10447318.2025.2465861

Liu, Y., Ma, X., Shu, L., Hancke, G. P., & Abu-Mahfouz, A. M. (2021). From industry 4.0 to agriculture 4.0: Status, enabling technologies, and research challenges. *IEEE Transactions on Industrial Informatics, 17*(6), 4324–4334. DOI: 10.1109/TII.2020.3003910

Li, Y., Dai, J., & Cui, L. (2020). The impact of digital technologies on economic and environmental performance in the context of industry 4.0: A moderated mediation model. *International Journal of Production Economics, 229*, 107777. Advance online publication. DOI: 10.1016/j.ijpe.2020.107777

LLumin. (2025). Predictive maintenance in fleet sustainability. https://llumin.com/blog/predictive-maintenance-fleet-management-llu/

Lorente-Martínez, J., Navío-Marco, J., & Rodrigo-Moya, B. (2022). Are retailers leveraging in-store analytics? An exploratory study. *International Journal of Retail & Distribution Management, 50*(5), 599–618. DOI: 10.1108/IJRDM-04-2020-0151

Lovelock, C. (2001). *Services Marketing, People, Technology, Strategy*. Prentice Hall.

Luarn, P., & Lin, H. H. (2005). Toward an understanding of the behavioral intention to use mobile banking. *Computers in Human Behavior, 21*, 873–891.

Lu, Y., Liu, S., & Bai, Y. (2022). Analysis of Digital Photography Technology in the Era of Big Data. *Mobile Information Systems, 2022*, 1–8. Advance online publication. DOI: 10.1155/2022/3880755

Magazine, E. V. (2024). Top 10: 2024 trends. https://evmagazine.com/top10/top-10-2024-trends

Makridakis, S. (2017). The forthcoming Artificial Intelligence (AI) revolution: Its impact on society and firms. *Futures, 90*, 46–60. DOI: 10.1016/j.futures.2017.03.006

Mallam, S. C., Nazir, S., & Renganayagalu, S. K. (2019). Rethinking maritime education, training, and operations in the digital era: Applications for emerging immersive technologies. In *Journal of Marine Science and Engineering* (Vol. 7, Issue 12). DOI: 10.3390/jmse7120428

Manser Payne, E. H., Dahl, A. J., & Peltier, J. (2021). Digital servitization value co-creation framework for AI services: A research agenda for digital transformation in financial service ecosystems. *Journal of Research in Interactive Marketing*, *15*(2), 200–222. DOI: 10.1108/JRIM-12-2020-0252

Mariani, M. M., Hashemi, N., & Wirtz, J. (2023). Artificial intelligence empowered conversational agents: A systematic literature review and research agenda. *Journal of Business Research*, *161*, 113838. DOI: 10.1016/j.jbusres.2023.113838

Marimuthu, M., Arokiasamy, L., Samad, M., Moorthy, M. K., & Kok, N. K. (2011). CASHLESS SOCIETY AND THE DETERMINANTS: AN EMPIRICAL INVESTIGATION. *International Journal of Academic Research*, *3*(3).

Markets and Markets. (2024). Fleet management market by solution, connectivity type, fleet type, industry, and region – Global forecast to 2026. https://www.marketsandmarkets.com/Market-Reports/fleet-management-systems-market-1020.html

Marr, B. (2017). Data Strategy How to Profit from a World of Big Data, Analytics and the Internet of Things. London Kogan Page Ltd. - Retrieved August 7, 2025, from https://www.scirp.org/reference/referencespapers?referenceid=2760459

Martin, M., & Vacca, F. (2018). Heritage narratives in the digital era: How digital technologies have improved approaches and tools for fashion know-how, traditions, and memories. *Research Journal of Textile and Apparel*, *22*(4), 335–351. Advance online publication. DOI: 10.1108/RJTA-02-2018-0015

Massood, A. (2025, May 14). Measuring the Effectiveness of AI Adoption: Definitions, Frameworks, and Evolving Benchmarks. Medium. https://medium.com/@adnanmasood/measuring-the-effectiveness-of-ai-adoption-definitions-frameworks-and-evolving-benchmarks-63b8b2c7d194

Mathieson, K. (1999). Predicting user intentions: Comparing the technology acceptance model with the theory of planned behavior. *Information Systems Research*, *2*(3), 173–191.

Mayahi, S., & Vidrih, M. (2022). *The Impact of Generative AI on the Future of Visual Content Marketing* (Version 1). arXiv. DOI: 10.48550/ARXIV.2211.12660

McKinsey & Company. (2022). *The future of AI in transport and logistics*. McKinsey Insights.

Mckinsey. (2023). https://www.mckinsey.de/~/media/mckinsey/locations/europe%20and%20middle%20east/deutschland/news/presse/2023/2023-06-14%20mgi%20genai%20report%2023/the-economic-potential-of-generative-ai-the-next-productivity-frontier-vf.pdf

Meng, K., Dong, Z. Y., Wang, D. H., & Wong, K. P. (2010, August). A Self-Adaptive RBF Neural Network Classifier for Transformer Fault Analysis. *IEEE Transactions on Power Systems*, *25*(3), 1350–1360. DOI: 10.1109/TPWRS.2010.2040491

Mgi-notes-from-the-ai-frontier-modeling-the-impact-of-ai-on-the-world-economy-september-2018.ashx. (n.d.). Retrieved August 7, 2025, from https://www.mckinsey.com/~/media/mckinsey/featured%20insights/artificial%20intelligence/notes%20from%20the%20frontier%20modeling%20the%20impact%20of%20ai%20on%20the%20world%20economy/mgi-notes-from-the-ai-frontier-modeling-the-impact-of-ai-on-the-world-economy-september-2018.ashx MODGIL 2022 Artificial intelligence for supply chain (AAM).pdf

Miao, J., & Zhang, X. (2024). A microservice-based smart agriculture system to detect and prevent animal intrusion. *Future Internet*, *16*(8), 296. DOI: 10.3390/fi16080296

Mikalef, P., & Gupta, M. (2021). Artificial intelligence capability: Conceptualization, measurement calibration, and empirical study on its impact on organizational creativity and firm performance. *Information & Management*, *58*(3), 103434. DOI: 10.1016/j.im.2021.103434

Mishra, A. (2024). Smart animal repelling device: Utilizing IoT and AI for effective anti-adaptive harmful animal deterrence. *BIO Web of Conferences*, *82*, 05014. DOI: 10.1051/bioconf/20248205014

Mittelstadt, B. D., Allo, P., Taddeo, M., Wachter, S., & Floridi, L. (2016). The ethics of algorithms: Mapping the debate. *Big Data & Society*, *3*(2), 2053951716679679.

Mohammed, M., & Shahda, M. (2018). Vision and Methodology to Support Sustainable Architecture through Building Technology in the Digital Era. *The International Journal of Environmental Science & Sustainable Development*, *2*(1). Advance online publication. DOI: 10.21625/essd.v2i1.169.g71

Moran, G., Muzellec, L., & Johnson, D. (2019). Message content features and social media engagement: Evidence from the media industry. *Journal of Product and Brand Management*, *29*(5), 533–545. DOI: 10.1108/JPBM-09-2018-2014

Mostafa, R. B., & Kasamani, T. (2022). Antecedents and consequences of chatbot initial trust. *European Journal of Marketing*, *56*(6), 1748–1771. DOI: 10.1108/EJM-02-2020-0084

Moura, L., Barcaui, A., & Payer, R. (2025). AI and Financial Fraud Prevention: Mapping the Trends and Challenges Through a Bibliometric Lens. *Journal of Risk and Financial Management*, *18*(6), 323. DOI: 10.3390/jrfm18060323

Muda, M., & Hamzah, M. I. (2021). Should I suggest this YouTube clip? The impact of UGC source credibility on eWOM and purchase intention. *Journal of Research in Interactive Marketing*, *15*(3), 441–459. DOI: 10.1108/JRIM-04-2020-0072

Mukhopadhyay, S., Singh, R. K., & Jain, T. (2024). Developing artificial intelligence enabled Marketing 4.0 framework: An Industry 4.0 perspective. *Qualitative Market Research*, *27*(5), 841–865. DOI: 10.1108/QMR-06-2023-0086

Mulliner, C., Borgaonkar, R., Stewin, P., & Seifert, J. P. (2013, July). SMS-Based One-Time Passwords: Attacks and Defense: (Short Paper). In International Conference on Detection of Intrusions and Malware, and Vulnerability Assessment (pp. 150-159). Berlin, Heidelberg: Springer Berlin Heidelberg.

Munian, Y., Martinez-Molina, A., & Alamaniotis, M. (2020). Intelligent system for detection of wild animals using HOG and CNN in automobile applications. In *2020 11th International Conference on Information, Intelligence, Systems and Applications (IISA)* (pp. 1–8). IEEE. DOI: 10.1109/IISA50023.2020.9284365

Musleh Al-Sartawi, A. M. A., Al-Qudah, A. A., & Shihadeh, F. (Eds.). (2024). *Artificial Intelligence-Augmented Digital Twins: Transforming Industrial Operations for Innovation and Sustainability* (Vol. 503). Springer Nature Switzerland., DOI: 10.1007/978-3-031-43490-7

Ndou, A. T., Madonsela, N. S., & Twala, B. (2020). The era of digital technology: Analysis of factors contributing to economic growth and sustainability. *Proceedings of the International Conference on Industrial Engineering and Operations Management,* 59.

Network, O. N. (2024). Fleet management solutions for the modern era. https://networkon.io/resources/blog/fleet-management-software/

OECD. (2024). *AI principles for responsible innovation in transport.* OECD Publishing.

Okoduwa, I. O., Ashiwaju, B. I., Asuzu, O. F., Arowoogun, J. O., Awonuga, K. F., & Ndubuisi, N. L. (2024). Supply chain assimilation in manufacturing: A comparative review of USA and African industries. *International Journal of Management & Entrepreneurship Investigation*, *6*(2), 254–266.

Okoye, C. C., Addy, W. A., Adeoye, O. B., Oyewole, A. T., Ofodile, O. C., Odeyemi, O., & Ololade, Y. J. (2024). Sustainable supply chain practices: A review of innovations in the USA and Africa. *International Journal of Applied Investigation in Social Sciences*, *6*(3), 292–302.

Oliveira, T., & Martins, M. F. (2011). Literature review of information technology adoption models at firm level. *Electronic Journal of Information Systems Evaluation*, *14*(1), 110–121.

Olutimehin, D. O., Ofodile, O. C., Ejibe, I., Odunaiya, O. G., & Soyombo, O. T. (2024). THE ROLE OF TECHNOLOGY IN SUPPLY CHAIN RISK MANAGEMENT: INNOVATIONS AND CHALLENGES IN LOGISTICS. *International Journal of Management & Entrepreneurship Investigation*, *6*(3), 878–889.

Onofrei, G., Filieri, R., & Kennedy, L. (2022). Social media interactions, purchase intention, and behavioural engagement: The mediating role of source and content factors. *Journal of Business Research*, *142*, 100–112. DOI: 10.1016/j.jbusres.2021.12.031

Ontruck. (2024, August). Optimal fleet strategy with AI forecasting. https://www.ontruck.com/en/blog/calculate-optimal-fleet-capacity-ai

Oppenheim, A. N. (1992). *Questionnaire design, interviewing and attitude measurement* (2nd ed.). Continuum International Publishing.

Oriekhoe, O. I., Ashiwaju, B. I., Ihemereze, K. C., Ikwue, U., & Udeh, C. A. (2024). Review of technological advancements in food management of supply chain: A comparative investigation among the US and Africa. *International Journal of Management & Entrepreneurship Investigation*, *6*(1), 132–149.

Ortiz De Guinea, A., & Raymond, L. (2020). Enabling innovation in the face of uncertainty through IT ambidexterity: A fuzzy set qualitative comparative analysis of industrial service SMEs. *International Journal of Information Management*, *50*, 244–260. DOI: 10.1016/j.ijinfomgt.2019.05.007

Pan, W. X., & Lai, P. C. (2023). (2023) A Study of College Students' Use of Live Streaming Platforms as Anchors. Technology Management and Its Social Impact on Education, 243-267

Pan, W. X., & Lai, P. C. (2023). Research on college students' purchasing using webcast platform. In *Strategies and Opportunities for Technology in the Metaverse World* (pp. 166–185). IGI Global.

Park, J., Hyun, H., & Thavisay, T. (2021). A study of antecedents and outcomes of social media WOM towards luxury brand purchase intention. *Journal of Retailing and Consumer Services, 58*, 102272. DOI: 10.1016/j.jretconser.2020.102272

Park, M., Im, H., & Kim, H.-Y. (2020). "You are too friendly!" The negative effects of social media marketing on value perceptions of luxury fashion brands. *Journal of Business Research, 117*, 529–542. DOI: 10.1016/j.jbusres.2018.07.026

Patel, K. (2023). Credit card analytics: A review of fraud detection and risk assessment techniques. *International Journal of Computer Trends and Technology, 71*(10), 69–79. DOI: 10.14445/22312803/IJCTT-V71I10P109

Pathway. (2025). IoT and AI success with La Poste. https://pathway.com/news/la-poste-optimizes- colissimo-flows-in-real-time/

Peng, B. (2022). Digital leadership: State governance in the era of digital technology. *Cultura e Scuola, 5*(4), 210–225. Advance online publication. DOI: 10.1177/2096608321989835

Prahalad, C. K., & Ramaswamy, V. (2004a). Co-creating unique value with customers. *Strategy and Leadership, 32*(3), 4–9. DOI: 10.1108/10878570410699249

Prahalad, C. K., & Ramaswamy, V. (2004b). Co-creation experiences: The next practice in value creation. *Journal of Interactive Marketing, 18*(3), 5–14. DOI: 10.1002/dir.20015

Prakash, B., Jayakumar, R., Swaminathan, R., & Harikumar, S. (2019, September). *Animal detection using deep learning algorithm* [Preprint]. ResearchGate. https://www.researchgate.net/

PricewaterhouseCoopers. (n.d.). 2025 AI Business Predictions. PwC. Retrieved August 7, 2025, from https://www.pwc.com/us/en/tech-effect/ai-analytics/ai-predictions.html

Priem, R. L. (2007). A Consumer Perspective on Value Creation. *Academy of Management Review, 32*(1), 219–235. DOI: 10.5465/amr.2007.23464055

Qi, Y., Baiyang, C., & Lan, L. (2021). Deep learning-based image recognition in animal husbandry. In *2021 18th International Computer Conference on Wavelet Active Media Technology and Information Processing (ICCWAMTIP)* (pp. 318–321). IEEE. DOI: 10.1109/ICCWAMTIP53232.2021.9674177

Rabbanee, F. K., Roy, R., & Spence, M. T. (2020). Factors affecting consumer engagement on online social networks: Self-congruity, brand attachment, and self-extension tendency. *European Journal of Marketing*, *54*(6), 1407–1431. DOI: 10.1108/EJM-03-2018-0221

Radanliev, P. (2024). Artificial intelligence and quantum cryptography. *Journal of Analytical Science and Technology*, *15*(1), 4. Advance online publication. DOI: 10.1186/s40543-024-00416-6

Radanliev, P., De Roure, D., Maple, C., Nurse, J. R. C., Nicolescu, R., & Ani, U. (2024). AI security and cyber risk in IoT systems. *Frontiers in Big Data*, *7*, 1402745. Advance online publication. DOI: 10.3389/fdata.2024.1402745 PMID: 39449740

Rahman, A., Kundu, D., Debnath, T., Rahman, M., & Islam, M. J. (2024). Blockchain-based AI Methods for Managing Industrial IoT: Recent Developments, Integration Challenges and Opportunities. https://doi.org//arXiv.2405.12550DOI: 10.48550

Rambe, P. (2024). Digitalisation and Digital Innovation for Sustainable Business Model Augment and Creation of value: Implications for Policy and Practice for African SMMEs. In *The Future of Entrepreneurship in Southern Africa: Technological and Managerial Perspectives* (pp. 97–133). Springer Nature Switzerland. DOI: 10.1007/978-3-031-55935-8_4

Rampton, V., Böhmer, M., & Winkler, A. (2022). Medical Technologies Past and Present: How History Helps to Understand the Digital Era. *The Journal of Medical Humanities*, *43*(2), 343–364. Advance online publication. DOI: 10.1007/s10912-021-09699-x PMID: 34232480

Ram, S., & Sheth, J. N. (1989). Consumer Resistance to Innovations: The Marketing Problem and its solutions. *Journal of Consumer Marketing*, *6*(2), 5–14. DOI: 10.1108/EUM0000000002542

Ramya, G., & Ramesh, S. (2025). Animal detection for crop protection using deep learning. *Journal of Emerging Technologies and Innovative Research*, *12*(8), 2150–2156. https://eprints.intimal.edu.my/2150/1/jods2025_08.pdf

Rao, C. L., Sontakke, K. A., Shah, J. A., Sontakke, A. A., Shah, S. J., & Dhole, M. (2024, November). AI for Enhanced Customer Experience in Banking. In 2024 Second International Conference Computational and Characterization Techniques in Engineering & Sciences (IC3TES) (pp. 1-5). IEEE.

Redwood Logistics. (2025, July 9). Scaling AI in transport and logistics operations. https://www.redwoodlogistics.com/insights/how-ai-and-iot-can-change-transportation- management

Ren, S., He, K., Girshick, R., & Sun, J. (2015). Advances in Neural Information Processing Systems: Vol. 28. *Faster R-CNN: Towards real-time object detection with region proposal networks.*, https://arxiv.org/abs/1506.01497

Reuters. (2023). Amazon's Sequoia system speeds up inventory processing. https://www.reuters.com/technology/amazon-rolls-out-robotic-system-houston-warehouse-speed- up-deliveries-2023-10-18/

Rinaldi, L. (2001). Payment Cards and Money Demand in Belgium. Center for Economic Studies, Leuven Universities' Discussion Paper Series 01.16.

Robles, P., & Mallinson, D. (2023). West Darrel M and Allen John R (2020) Turning Point: Policymaking in the Era of Artificial Intelligence. *Science & Technology Studies*, *36*(3), 3. Advance online publication. DOI: 10.23987/sts.125194

Rogers, E. M. (2003). *Diffusion of innovations* (5th ed.). Free Press.

Safety & Health Magazine. (2025). The 2025 CEOs who 'get it'. https://www.safetyandhealthmagazine.com/articles/26308-the-2025-ceos-who-get-it

Sahut, J.-M., Schweizer, D., & Peris-Ortiz, M. (2022). Technological forecasting and social change introduction to the VSI technological innovations to ensure confidence in the digital world. *Technological Forecasting and Social Change*, *179*, 121680. DOI: 10.1016/j.techfore.2022.121680

Salava, A., & Kluger, N. (2022). Teaching dermatology in the era of digital technology. In *Annales de Dermatologie et de Venereologie* (Vol. 149, Issue 4). DOI: 10.1016/j.annder.2022.04.002

Samarah, T., Bayram, P., Aljuhmani, H. Y., & Elrehail, H. (2022). The role of brand interactivity and involvement in driving social media consumer brand engagement and brand loyalty: The mediating effect of brand trust. *Journal of Research in Interactive Marketing*, *16*(4), 648–664. DOI: 10.1108/JRIM-03-2021-0072

Sam, S., & Pearson, A. (2019). Community Legal Centres in the Digital Era: The Use of Digital Technologies in Queensland Community Legal Centres. *Law. Technology and Humans*, *1*(1), 64–79. Advance online publication. DOI: 10.5204/lthj.v1i0.1305

Samsara. (2025). Case study: Clover Dairy improves logistics with real-time tracking and AI. https://www.samsara.com/customers/clover-dairy/

Samuel, O., Javaid, N., Almogren, A., Javed, M. U., Qasim, U., & Radwan, A. (2022). A secure energy trading system for electric vehicles in smart communities using blockchain. *Sustainable Cities and Society*, *79*, 103678. Advance online publication. DOI: 10.1016/j.scs.2022.103678

Santhanam, S., S. S. B., Panigrahi, S. S., Kashyap, S. K., & Duriseti, B. K. (2021). Animal detection for road safety using deep learning. In *2021 International Conference on Computational Intelligence and Computing Applications (ICCICA)* (pp. 1–5). IEEE. DOI: 10.1109/ICCICA52458.2021.9697287

Saura, J. R., Ribeiro-Soriano, D., & Zegarra Saldaña, P. (2022). Exploring the challenges of remote work on Twitter users' sentiments: From digital technology development to a post-pandemic era. *Journal of Business Research*, *142*, 242–254. Advance online publication. DOI: 10.1016/j.jbusres.2021.12.052

Sawhney, M., Verona, G., & Prandelli, E. (2005). Collaborating to create: The Internet as a platform for customer engagement in product innovation. *Journal of Interactive Marketing*, *19*(4), 4–17. DOI: 10.1002/dir.20046

Schönberner, J., & Woratschek, H. (2023). Sport sponsorship as a booster for customer engagement: The role of activation, authenticity and attitude. *International Journal of Sports Marketing & Sponsorship*, *24*(2), 259–277. DOI: 10.1108/IJSMS-05-2022-0098

Sekaran, U. (2003). *Research Methods for Business: A Skill-Building Approach* (4th ed.). John Wiley and Sons, Inc.

Seralina, N. (2021). Information systems for machine intelligence to automated software testing. In: Herald of the Kazakh-British Technical University, Volume 18, Issue 1, pp.157-161, Almaty DOI: 10.55452/1998-6688-2021-18-1-157-161

Seralina, N., & Akzhalova, A. (2023). Anomaly Detection Framework. In: Abraham, A., etc. (eds) Innovations in Bio-Inspired Computing and Applications. IBICA 2022. Lecture Notes in Networks and Systems, vol 649. Springer, Cham. DOI: 10.1007/978-3-031-27499-2_7

Shafik, W. (2024d). Energy policies and infrastructure requirements for efficient green buildings. *Sustainable Technologies for Energy Efficient Buildings*, 212.

Shafik, W. (2024e). Exploring the Potential of Internet of Things (IoT) and Challenges in Enabling Circular Economy Practices in Smart Cities. In *Smart Cities and Circular Economy* (pp. 125–138). Emerald Publishing Limited. DOI: 10.1108/978-1-83797-957-820241012

Shafik, W. (2024f). Factors Affecting Green Purchase Behaviors for Small and Medium Enterprises (SMEs) in Uganda. In *Entrepreneurial Strategies for the Internationalization and Digitalization of SMEs* (pp. 198–224). IGI Global. DOI: 10.4018/979-8-3693-3518-5.ch009

Shafik, W. (2024g). Generative AI for Social Good and Sustainable Development. In *Generative AI: Current Trends and Applications* (pp. 185–217). Springer. DOI: 10.1007/978-981-97-8460-8_10

Shafik, W. (2025). Quantum Computing and Generative Adversarial Networks (GANs): Ethics, Privacy, and Security. In *Quantum AI and its Applications in Blockchain Technology* (pp. 111–156). IGI Global Scientific Publishing.

Shafik, W. (2024a). Artificial Intelligence and Internet of Things Roles in Sustainable Next-Generation Manufacturing. In *Sustainable Innovation for Industry 6.0* (pp. 207–239). IGI Global., DOI: 10.4018/979-8-3693-3140-8.ch012

Shafik, W. (2024b). Data Privacy and Security Safeguarding Customer Information in ChatGPT Systems. In *Revolutionizing the Service Industry Wth OpenAI Models* (pp. 52–86). IGI Global., DOI: 10.4018/979-8-3693-1239-1.ch003

Shafik, W. (2024c). Deep Learning Impacts in the Field of Artificial Intelligence. In *Deep Learning Concepts in Operations Research* (pp. 9–26). Auerbach Publications., DOI: 10.1201/9781003433309-2

Shanthakumari, R., Nalini, C., Vinothkumar, S., Govindaraj, B., Dharani, S., & Chindhana, S. (2022). Image detection and recognition of different species of animals using deep learning. In *2022 International Mobile and Embedded Technology Conference (MECON)* (pp. 236–241). IEEE. DOI: 10.1109/MECON53876.2022.9752203

Sharma, A., Rana, N. P., & Nunkoo, R. (n.d.). Fifty years of information management research: A conceptual structure analysis using structural topic modeling. Elsevier, Volume 58(June 2021), 102316.

Shi, Y., Song, H., & Xu, J. (2023). "Responsible and Effective Federated Learning in Financial Services: A Comprehensive Survey," 2023 62nd IEEE Conference on Decision and Control (CDC), Singapore, Singapore, pp. 4229-4236, DOI: 10.1109/CDC49753.2023.10384119

Shrestha, Y. R., Krishna, V., & von Krogh, G. (2021). Augmenting organizational decision-making with deep learning algorithms: Principles, promises, and challenges. *Journal of Business Research, 123*, 588–603. https://doi.org/https://doi.org/10.1016/j.jbusres.2020.09.068. DOI: 10.1016/j.jbusres.2020.09.068

Sifted Resources. (2024, July 15). Amazon expands AI route-planning algorithms to optimize last-mile delivery. https://sifted.com/resources/how-to-implement-artificial-intelligence-to-boost-supply- chain-ops/

SimplyFleet. (2025, March 27). Spreadsheets vs. software: Why fleets are automating in 2025. https://www.simplyfleet.app/blog/spreadsheets-vs-fleet-software-2025

Singh, D. P. D. (2024). Generative AI through the Lens of Institutional Theory (SSRN Scholarly Paper No. 4953180). Social Science Research Network. DOI: 10.2139/ssrn.4953180

Singh, J., Sajid, M., Gupta, S. K., & Haidri, R. A. (2022). Artificial intelligence and blockchain technologies for smart city. In *Intelligent Green Technologies for Sustainable Smart Cities* (pp. 317–330). DOI: 10.1002/9781119816096.ch15

Singh, A., Pietrasik, M., Natha, G., Ghouaiel, N., Brizel, K., & Ray, N. (2020). Animal detection in man-made environments. In *2020 IEEE Winter Conference on Applications of Computer Vision (WACV)* (pp. 1427–1438). IEEE. DOI: 10.1109/WACV45572.2020.9093504

Sivakorn, S., Polakis, I., & Keromytis, A. D. (2016, March). I am robot:(deep) learning to break semantic image captchas. In 2016 IEEE European Symposium on Security and Privacy (EuroS&P) (pp. 388-403). IEEE.

Slater, S. F., & Narver, J. C. (2000). Intelligence Generation and Superior Customer Value. *Journal of the Academy of Marketing Science*, *28*(1), 120–127. DOI: 10.1177/0092070300281011

SmartDev—AI Powered Software Development. (n.d.). SmartDev. Retrieved August 7, 2025, from https://smartdev.com/

Smith, J. B., & Colgate, M. (2007). Customer Value Creation: A Practical Framework. *Journal of Marketing Theory and Practice*, *15*(1), 7–23. DOI: 10.2753/MTP1069-6679150101

Social Science Research Network (SSRN). (2023). AI-driven optimization in fleet management. https://papers.ssrn.com/sol3/papers.cfm?abstract_id=4927212

Software, D. B. B. (2025). AI in Fleet Management: Specifics, Challenges, Benefits, and Use Cases. https://dbbsoftware.com/insights/harnessing-the-power-of-ai-for-fleet-management

Stormpath. (2016). S. S. O. Vs. Centralized Authentication," Stormpath User Identity API, 31-Oct-2016. [Online]. Available: https://stormpath.com/blog/sso-vs-centralized-auth. [Accessed: 25-Jul-2019].

Su, C. W., Xie, Y., Shahab, S., Faisal, C. M. N., Hafeez, M., & Qamri, G. M. (2021). Towards achieving sustainable development: Role of technology innovation, technology adoption and co2 emission for brics. *International Journal of Environmental Research and Public Health*, *18*(1), 277. Advance online publication. DOI: 10.3390/ijerph18010277 PMID: 33401479

Sudrajat, D. (2019). Effective English Learning Through Scientific Approach In The Era Of Digital Technology. In *International Journal of Global Community: Vol. II* (Issue 3).

Sun, H., Zafar, M. Z., & Hasan, N. (2022). Employing Natural Language Processing as Artificial Intelligence for Analyzing Consumer Opinion Toward Advertisement. *Frontiers in Psychology*, *13*, 856663. DOI: 10.3389/fpsyg.2022.856663 PMID: 35769737

Sun, H., & Zhang, P. (2006). Causal Relationships between Perceived Enjoyment and Perceived Ease of Use: An Alternative Approach 1. *Journal of the Association for Information Systems*, *7*(9), 618–645.

Sunu, I. G. K. A. (2022). The Impact of Digital Leadership on Teachers' Acceptance and Use of Digital Technologies. *Mimbar Ilmu*, *27*(2), 311–320. Advance online publication. DOI: 10.23887/mi.v27i2.52832

Supply Chain 24/7. (2024, October 5). How UPS uses generative AI to automate customer service responses. https://www.supplychain247.com/article/ups-mera-ai-automation

Supply Chain Strategy Media. (2025, Feb 19). AI-driven risk scoring helps fleets reduce collisions and boost safety. https://supplychainstrategy.media/blog/2025/02/19/driving-change-ai-is- transforming-fleet-safety-and-visibility-in-modern-supply-chains

SupplyChainNuggets. (2025, July 26). How UPS' ORION algorithm transformed its route optimization. https://www.supplychainnuggets.com/how-ups-orion-algorithm-transformed-its-route- optimization/

Surekha, M., Umesh, U., & Dhinakaran, D. P. (2022). A study on utilization and convenient of credit card. *Journal of Positive School Psychology*, •••, 5635–5645.

Sutopo, W. (2019). The Roles of Industrial Engineering Education for Promoting Innovations and Technology Commercialization in the Digital Era. *IOP Conference Series. Materials Science and Engineering*, *495*(1), 012001. Advance online publication. DOI: 10.1088/1757-899X/495/1/012001

Swan, E. L., Peltier, J. W., & Dahl, A. J. (2024). Artificial intelligence in healthcare: The value co-creation process and influence of other digital health transformations. *Journal of Research in Interactive Marketing*, *18*(1), 109–126. DOI: 10.1108/JRIM-09-2022-0293

Tabachnick, B. G., & Fidell, L. S. (2007). *Using Multivariate Statistics*. Pearson Education Inc.

Tan, L., Yu, K., Yang, C., & Bashir, A. K. (2021). A blockchain-based Shamir's threshold cryptography for data protection in industrial internet of things of smart city. In *Proceedings of the 1st Workshop on Artificial Intelligence and Blockchain Technologies for Smart Cities with 6G* (pp. 13–18). New York, NY, USA: Association for Computing Machinery. DOI: 10.1145/3477084.3484951

TechRadar. (2024, December 31). TechRadar's year in review 2024 – from tri-fold phones and super- smart. https://www.techradar.com/tech/techradars-year-in-review-2024

Teece, D. J. (2007). Explicating dynamic capabilities: The nature and microfoundations of (sustainable) enterprise performance. *Strategic Management Journal, 28*(13), 1319–1350. DOI: 10.1002/smj.640

The Australian. (2023, May 30). Qantas backs AI in transformation push. https://www.itnews.com.au/news/qantas-backs-ai-in-transformation-push-596352

The Business of Artificial Intelligence. (n.d.). Retrieved August 1, 2025, from https://hbr.org/2017/07/the-business-of-artificial-intelligence

The Digital Transformation of SMEs. (2021, February 3). OECD. https://www.oecd.org/en/publications/the-digital-transformation-of-smes_bdb9256a-en.html

Times, C. D. O. (2024, August 23). Case study: Amazon's AI-driven supply chain: A blueprint for the future of global logistics. https://cdotimes.com/2024/08/23/case-study-amazons-ai-driven-supply-chain-a-blueprint-for-the-future-of-global-logistics/

Tong, D. L., Lai, P. C., & Liew, E. J. Y. (2024). Exploring intention to use cryptocurrencies payment across age groups and gender: A multi-stage machine learning application on the extended UTAUT model. *International Journal of Applied Decision Sciences, 17*(5), 571–594.

Tornatzky, L. G., & Fleischer, M. (1990) The Processes of Technological Innovation. Lexington Books, Lexington. - Retrieved August 6, 2025, from https://www.scirp.org/reference/referencespapers?referenceid=1771512

Tornatzky, L. G., & Fleischer, M. (1990). *The processes of technological innovation.* Lexington Books.

Transit, E. T. A. (2024). Artificial intelligence is reshaping public transit as we know it. https://etatransit.com/podcast/ai-reshaping-transit/

Tribe, A. I. (2025, March 27). Inside the machine: How composable agents are rewiring AI architecture in 2025. https://www.tribe.ai/applied-ai/inside-the-machine-how-composable-agents-are-rewiring-ai-architecture-in-2025

Trisiana, A. (2019). Innovation design development of citizenship education model on characters of indonesian communities in digital media era and technology revolution. *International Journal of Recent Technology and Engineering, 8*(2 Special Issue 9). DOI: 10.35940/ijrte.B1074.0982S919

Trovato, S. (2025, May 19). From hype to real business impact: How to lead AI transformation in 2025. Monday.Com Blog. https://monday.com/blog/project-management/ai-transformation/

Tsai, W.-H. S., Liu, Y., & Chuan, C.-H. (2021). How chatbots' social presence communication enhances consumer engagement: The mediating role of parasocial interaction and dialogue. *Journal of Research in Interactive Marketing*, *15*(3), 460–482. DOI: 10.1108/JRIM-12-2019-0200

Vaish, R., & Sharma, S. (2024). Automated smart crop protection utilizing IoT: A comprehensive review. *E3S Web of Conferences, 540*, 13012. https://doi.org/DOI: 10.1051/e3sconf/202454013012

van Dijk, A., & van Grieken, H. (2017). Digital era Technology Operating Models. *Deloitte, October*.

Van Quaquebeke, N., Tonidandel, S., & Banks, G. C. (2025). Beyond efficiency: How artificial intelligence (AI) will reshape scientific inquiry and the publication process. *The Leadership Quarterly*, *36*(4), 101895. DOI: 10.1016/j.leaqua.2025.101895

Vander Schee, B. A., Peltier, J., & Dahl, A. J. (2020). Antecedent consumer factors, consequential branding outcomes and measures of online consumer engagement: Current research and future directions. *Journal of Research in Interactive Marketing*, *14*(2), 239–268. DOI: 10.1108/JRIM-01-2020-0010

Varatharajoo, P. M., Zakaria, N. H., Bakar, J. A., & Mahmuddin, M. (2024). "Explainable Artificial Intelligence (XAI) Model for Online Fraud Detection: A Critical Review in Malaysia's Digital Economy," 2024 7th International Conference on Internet Applications, Protocols, and Services (NETAPPS), Kuala Lumpur, Malaysia, pp. 1-8, DOI: 10.1109/NETAPPS63333.2024.10823585

Varghese, M., Raj, S., & Venkatesh, V. (2022a). *Influence of AI in human lives* (Version 1). arXiv. DOI: 10.48550/ARXIV.2212.12305

Venkatesh, V., Morris, M. G., Davis, G. B., & Davis, F. D. (2003). User acceptance of information technology: Toward a unified view. *Management Information Systems Quarterly*, *27*(3), 425–478.

Venkatesh, V., Speier, C., & Morris, M. (2002). User acceptance enablers in individual decision making about technology: Toward an integrated model. *Decision Sciences*, *33*(2), 297–316.

Verhoef, P. C., Kooge, E., Walk, N., & Wieringa, J. E. (2021). *Creating value with data analytics in marketing: Mastering data science. Creating Value with Data Analytics in Marketing: Mastering Data Science*. DOI: 10.4324/9781003011163

Vial, G. (2019). Understanding digital transformation: A review and a research agenda. *The Journal of Strategic Information Systems*, *28*(2), 118–144. DOI: 10.1016/j.jsis.2019.01.003

WalkingTree Tech. (2025). Edge AI adoption in fleet operations. https://walkingtree.tech/developing-ai- powered-fleet-management-apps-challenges-opportunities-strategies-future-scope

Wamba, S. F., & Queiroz, M. M. (2022). A Framework Based on Blockchain, Artificial Intelligence, and Big Data Analytics to Leverage Supply Chain Resilience considering the COVID-19. *IFAC-PapersOnLine*, *55*(10), 2396–2401. DOI: 10.1016/j.ifacol.2022.10.067 PMID: 38620980

Wamba-Taguimdje, S.-L., Fosso Wamba, S., Kala Kamdjoug, J. R., & Tchatchouang Wanko, C. E. (2020). Influence of artificial intelligence (AI) on firm performance: The business value of AI-based transformation projects. *Business Process Management Journal*, *26*(7), 1893–1924. DOI: 10.1108/BPMJ-10-2019-0411

Wang, Q., Li, Y., & Li, R. (2024). Ecological footprints, carbon emissions, and energy transitions: The impact of artificial intelligence (AI). *Humanities & Social Sciences Communications*, *11*(1), 1043. DOI: 10.1057/s41599-024-03520-5

Wang, Y. S., Wang, Y. M., Lin, H. H., & Tang, T. I. (2003). Determinants of user acceptance of internet banking: An empirical study. *International Journal of Service Industry Management*, *14*(5), 501–519.

Weforum: https://www3.weforum.org/docs/WEF_Generative_AI_Governance_2024.pdf

Westerman, G., Bonnet, D., & McAfee, A. (2014). Leading Digital Turning Technology into Business Transformation. Harvard Business Press. - Retrieved August 1, 2025, from https://www.scirp.org/reference/referencespapers?referenceid=3404468

WhipAround. (2025). Predictive maintenance and emissions compliance. https://whiparound.com/5- benefits-of-fleet-maintenance-software-in-2023/

Widodo, A. M., Pappachan, P., Sekti, B. A., Anwar, N., Widayanti, R., Rahaman, M., & Bansal, R. (2024). Quantum-resistant cryptography. In *Innovations in Modern Cryptography* (pp. 100–130). DOI: 10.4018/979-8-3693-5330-1.ch005

Wongkitrungrueng, A., & Assarut, N. (2020). The role of live streaming in building consumer trust and engagement with social commerce sellers. *Journal of Business Research, 117*, 543–556. DOI: 10.1016/j.jbusres.2018.08.032

Wu, L., Dodoo, N. A., & Choi, C.-W. (2023). Brand anthropomorphism on Twitter: Communication strategies and consumer engagement. *Journal of Product and Brand Management, 32*(6), 799–811. DOI: 10.1108/JPBM-12-2021-3787

XenonStack. (2024). Predictive Maintenance for Fleet Management Using AI and IoT. https://www.xenonstack.com/blog/predictive-maintenance-for-fleet-management

XenonStack. (2025). Predictive maintenance for EVs. https://www.xenonstack.com/blog/predictive-maintenance-to-prevent-downtime

Xiao, H. (2022). Innovation of Digital Multimedia VR Technology in Music Education Curriculum in Colleges and Universities. *Scientific Programming, 2022*, 1–9. Advance online publication. DOI: 10.1155/2022/6566144

Yang, Z., Jianjun, L., Faqiri, H., Shafik, W., Talal Abdulrahman, A., Yusuf, M., & Sharawy, A. M. (2021). Green Internet of Things and Big Data Application in Smart Cities Development. *Complexity, 2021*(1), 4922697. Advance online publication. DOI: 10.1155/2021/4922697

Ye, X., Batool, H., & Huang, S.-Z. (2023). The effect of e-commerce livestreaming services on customer loyalty: A test of the chain mediation model. *Journal of Innovation and Entrepreneurship, 12*(1), 41. DOI: 10.1186/s13731-023-00310-2

Yujie, Z., Al Imran Yasin, M., Alsagoff, S. A. B. S., & Hoon, A. L. (2022). The Mediating Role of New Media Engagement in This Digital Age. *Frontiers in Public Health, 10*, 879530. Advance online publication. DOI: 10.3389/fpubh.2022.879530 PMID: 35586011

Yusup, M., Suhaepi, M. I., & Ramadhan, R. (2022). Blockchain Technology for Cashless Investments and Transactions in Digital Era With SWOT Approach. *Blockchain Frontier Technology, 2*(1), 17–23. Advance online publication. DOI: 10.34306/bfront.v2i1.91

Yu, X., Washida, Y., & Sasaki, M. (2022). Impact of qualified gatekeepers on team absorptive capacity: The mediating role of knowledge combination capability. *Journal of Knowledge Management*, *26*(11), 259–292. DOI: 10.1108/JKM-04-2022-0331

Zendu, I. T. (2025, February). New product updates: February 2025. https://zenduit.com/new-product-updates-february-2025/

Zhang, X., Zhao, Z., & Wang, K. (2024). The effects of live comments and advertisements on social media engagement: Application to short-form online video. *Journal of Research in Interactive Marketing*, *18*(3), 485–505. DOI: 10.1108/JRIM-02-2023-0069

Zhao, L., Zhu, D., Shafik, W., Matinkhah, S. M., Ahmad, Z., Sharif, L., & Craig, A. (2022). Artificial intelligence analysis in cyber domain: A review. In *International Journal of Distributed Sensor Networks* (Vol. 18, Issue 4). DOI: 10.1177/15501329221084882

Zurdo, R. P., Dopacio, C. I., & Paredes, V. R. (2022). Social sustainability and employment as a challenge of digital transformation: The new sixth digital sector of the economy. *REVESCO Revista de Estudios Cooperativos*, *142*. Advance online publication. DOI: 10.5209/reve.83719

About the Contributors

PC Lai was the Scholarship holder for both her doctorates (DBA and Ph.D. with Distinction), a Chartered Marketer by profession, and the Head of Innovation with UM Centre for Innovation and commercialization as well as a Research Fellow with UM Deputy Vice-Chancellor (Research & Innovation). She received a fellowship twice from the Asia Pacific Regional Internet Conference on Operational Technology (APRICOT) and the Asia Pacific Networking Group (APNG) as well as being selected to be part of the MIT Global Innovation & Entrepreneurship Bootcamp. She has more than two decades of experience in the Asia Pacific region in various industries, mainly in telecommunications and Finance. Her works also involved corporate strategy, e-business, marketing, and transforming business processes between the PEOPLE (employees), PRODUCTS, PARTNERS, and CUSTOMERS by enhancing customer satisfaction levels and ultimately resulting in enhanced Business Relationships, reduced costs, processes, and increased revenue. She has won numerous Asia Pacific ICT Awards (incl the prestigious ICT Oscar award) and the only ASIAN who voted 1 of the Top 3 favorites at Next Bank Asia. She is the 1st Malaysian to receive the Asia Pacific Next Generation Leadership Award from Japan and made it to the Top 15 of the world's most promising young science and technology by Global Innovation through Science Technology led by the U.S. Department of State and the American Association for the Advancement of Science. Her last two champion projects are in the field of HealthCare. Her hobbies include sports, the outdoors, traveling, and photography. She has won travel essay and photography contests and was a national sportswoman and received the Gold Award for the National Physical Fitness program. She was a trained instructor for the Air Taser (Star War-style non-lethal weapon) technology that catered for the Armed Forces. Alongside her industrial capability, she has been imparting her knowledge while facilitating matured MBA & doctorate students as well as corporate training to organizations. She also spoke and judged at local and international conferences, competitions, and events. Her publications in research methodology, her analytics skill, and her novel innovation of Artificial Intelligent Decision making (AIDM™) that can be an alternative to SPSS, AMOS or SMART PLS is useful for university. She also conducts analyses for clinical medical research and others.

***

Prakash B.S. is an Assistant Professor in the Department of Computer Science and Engineering at Vivekanandha College of Engineering for Women. He received his Master's degree in Computer science and Engineering from Anna University in 2008, 17 years of teaching experience, where his research focused on Deep learning. His recent book, "Data Science using Python," was published by Notion Press in 2022. He has published many research papers in international journals and presented articles in national and international conferences. In addition to his academic and research work, he is committed to mentoring students and fostering innovation in the field of engineering.

Nihar Suresh Dahake is working as an Assistant Professor at G H Raisoni College of Engineering, Nagpur in the Department of MBA. He received his B.Com, M.Com, MBA, from the Rashtrasant Tukdoji Maharaj Nagpur University and and Ph.D. from Sant gadge baba Amravati University, Amravati. Dr.Nihar Dahake has Qualified SET(Commerce) and SET (Management). He has 14 Years of Teaching Experience and 8 years of Research Experience. His areas of expertise are Financial Accounting, Consumer behavior, Marketing Management and Financial Management

Parihar Suresh Dahake is working as an Assistant Professor at Ramdeobaba University in the School of Management. He received his BTech, MBA, and Ph.D. from the Rashtrasant Tukdoji Maharaj Nagpur University and PGDIBO, M.Com from Indira Gandhi National Open University (IGNOU). Dr.Parihar dahake has Qualified SET(Commerce) and SET (Management). He has 15 Years of Teaching Experience and 14 years of Research Experience. His areas of expertise are Consumer behavior, Organizational Behaviour, Marketing management, and IMC.

Abdulakim Erbo is a PhD Candidate in Management.

Zenebe Ermias is a Lecturer with the Department of Logistics and Management of supply chain, College of Business and Economics, Bule Hora University - (Ethiopia).

Rakesh Gautam is an Associate Professor with the Department of Marketing, Mittal School of Business, Lovely Professional University, India.

PrasunaK. is working as an Associate Professor in dept. of Electronics and Communication Engineering in Vijaya Institute of Technology for women. Her areas of interest are Image and Signal Processing, Wireless Communication, Deep Learning, Artificial Intelligence.

Shashi Kant is an Associate Professor with the Mittal School of Business, Lovely Professional University, India

Lakshmi Chandrakanth Kasireddy is an experienced professional with a strong background in computer science. They hold a Master of Computer Applications (MCA) degree from Jawaharlal Nehru Technological University, Kakinada, and a Bachelor of Science (B.Sc.) degree from Andhra University. Currently based in the United States, they work as a Cloud Architect, where they leverage their expertise in Cloud Architecture to design and implement robust cloud solutions. With over 14 years of experience in the computer science industry, they have developed a deep specialization in cloud technologies. They are also currently pursuing a Ph.D. with a focus on AI-Driven Cybersecurity, contributing to cutting-edge research at the intersection of artificial intelligence and cybersecurity. They have published several research papers in prestigious journals and conferences, particularly in the fields of Cybersecurity, Artificial Intelligence, and Machine Learning. Their work has been featured on platforms such as Web of Science, Scopus-indexed journals, and IEEE conferences, reflecting their ongoing contributions to both industry and academia.

Suryakant Kaushik is a seasoned technology and operations leader known for his collaborative style and innovative mindset. With over 15 years in IoT, enterprise software, and utilities, he solves complex challenges with scalable, data-driven solutions. At Samsara Inc., as a Program Management and Business Operations Leader, he enhances fleet safety, regulatory compliance, and operational efficiency for large vehicle fleets in North America. His AI-driven insights and automation help optimize performance, reduce risks, and improve service reliability. At VMware, he drove partner ecosystem growth and led digital transformation initiatives, boosting program scalability and business impact. Previously, as an Operations Manager in electricity distribution, he managed power reliability, outage resolution, and network performance under high-stakes conditions. Suryakant holds an MBA from MAYS Business School, Texas A&M University, is a Certified COPC CX Leader, and an active member of the Sigma Xi Texas A&M Chapter, underscoring his commitment to scientific excellence and research-driven innovation.

Ajay Kumar is a Professor at Chanakya National Law University. He also serves as the Dean, Academic Affairs & Law; and Head, Centre for Post-Graduate Legal Studies at Chanakya National Law University, Patna.

Sanjiv Kumar is an accomplished academic and industry professional with a Ph.D. and UGC-NET qualification in Management. With over 14 years of academic experience complemented by 13 years in corporate leadership roles within the sales and marketing domain of the financial sector at Delhi and NCR, he bridges the gap between theoretical knowledge and practical expertise. His research interests span consumer behavior, brand management, retail management, organizational behavior, with several publications in Scopus-indexed International journals and a case study featured in ET Cases.Dr. Kumar is an active member of the Vidarbha Management Association (VMA) and has delivered numerous sessions at esteemed forums, showcasing his commitment to knowledge dissemination and professional development.

Shashank Mittal is an Assistant Professor with Jindal Global Business School, O.P. Jindal Global University, Sonipat, Haryana.

GopiR. is a Professor in the Department of Computer Science and Engineering at Dhanalakshmi Srinivasan Engineering College, Perambalur. He received his Ph.D. degree in the year 2019 from St.Peter's Institute of Higher Education and Research. He received his Master of Technology (M.Tech) degree in 2012 from Veltech University Chennai. He received his Bachelor Degree (B.E) in 2006 at Sona College of Technology. He had published more than 25- SCI journal, 5 patent and one patent granted in the year 2023 His research area are AI Techniques, Cloud Computing, Machine Learning, Big Data, Vehicular Adhoc Networks (VANET).

Bhumika Ray is an Assistant Professor with JGBS, O.P. Jindal Global University, Sonipat, Haryana.

Theetchenya S is currently doing Ph.d and working as an Assistant Professor in the Department of Computer Science and Engineering at Sona College of Technology, Salem, Tamil Nadu, India. Her research interests include data mining, machine learning, deep learning, and distributed systems. She has published over 20 research articles in reputed international journals and conferences, covering areas such as brain tumor analysis, IoT-driven analytics, and image retrieval. She has also been involved in collaborative projects applying artificial intelligence to healthcare and smart city applications.

Inastya Anggara Sekti has been a Lecturer at the faculty of Computer Science, at Esa Unggul University, Jakarta since 2016 and is active in the Artificial Intelligence and Information Security Study Group. He is a graduate of Informatics Engineering from the Bandung Institute of Technology and achieved a Master's Degree from Trisakti University, Jakarta. Before as a Lecture, he was an IT practitioner at several companies in Jakarta for more than 25 years. Some of the projects that have been completed are building Data Centers at Internet Service Providers. He also finished many IT projects.

Wasswa Shafik (Member, IEEE) received a Bachelor of Science degree in information technology from Ndejje University, Uganda, a Master of Engineering degree in Information Technology (Computer and Communication Networks) from Yazd University, Iran, and a PhD in Computer Science with the School of Digital Science, Universiti Brunei Darussalam, Brunei Darussalam. He is also the Founder and Research Director of the Dig Connectivity Research Laboratory (DCRLab) after serving as a Research Associate at the Network Interconnectivity Research Laboratory at Yazd University. Prior to this, he worked as a Community Data Analyst at Population Services International (PSI-Uganda), a Community Data Officer at the Programme for Accessible Health Communication (PACE-Uganda), a Research Assistant at the Socio-Economic Data Centre (SEDC-Uganda), Uganda, an Assistant Data Officer at TechnoServe, Kampala, Uganda, and Asmaah Charity Organization as Cheif Executive Officer. He has hundreds of publications with renowned publishers. His research interests include Artificial Intelligence, Neural Networks, Computer Vision, Smart Agriculture, Digital Health, and Green Computing.

Dong Ling Tong is a researcher in artificial neural networks and machine learning for healthcare. She is an Assistant Professor at Universiti Tunku Abdul Rahman (UTAR), Malaysia, and a member of the Malaysia Board of Technology (MBOT). Her work includes disease prediction, financial distress modelling, and blockchain adoption studies. She has led multiple research projects on big data and AI applications in healthcare and security. Previously, she was a research associate at the John van Geest Cancer Research Centre, UK.

SathiyamoorthiV. is currently working as Lecturer in Computer Engineering Department at Government polytechnic college, Dharmapuri,Tamil Nadu, India. He was born on June 21, 1983, at Omalur in Salem District, Tamil Nadu, India. He received his Bachelor of Engineering degree in Information Technology from Periyar University, Salem with First Class. He obtained his Master of Engineering degree in Computer Science and Engineering from Anna University, Chennai with Distinction and secured 30th University Rank.He received his Ph.D degree from Anna University, Chennai in Web Mining. His areas of specialization include Web Usage Mining, Data Structures, Design and Analysis of Algorithm and Operating System. He has published many papers in International Journals and conferences. He has published many books and book chapters in various renowned international publishers. He has also participated in various National level Workshops and Seminars conducted by various reputed institutions.

Mohit Verma is an Assistant Professor with Jindal Global Law School, O.P. Jindal Global University, Sonipat, Haryana, India.

Index

A

B

C

D

E

T

U

V

X

www.ingramcontent.com/pod-product-compliance
Lightning Source LLC
LaVergne TN
LVHW080900300926
849162LV00003B/495